CRITICAL RAVES FOR DANNY PEARY'S
Cult Movies

"Wild bunches of film freaks would brave the badlands of a forbidden planet for a compendium like this . . . anyone who has vamped to a midnight showing of *The Rocky Horror Picture Show* will love this survey . . . almost as much as doing the Time Warp. . . . Here's a performance that will help you trash a hard day's night or two."
—*Playboy*

"Virtually impossible to put down, crammed with all sorts of obscure information, off-beat interpretations and criticism. Peary not only makes us want to catch and enjoy obscure, underrated gems . . . but also offers new insight into old favorites . . . a book for both the fan and the serious student."
—*Publishers Weekly*

"With a fine sensitivity to plot and character, and a true movie maniac's attention to detail, Peary romps happily through film history. . . . Peary is a very smooth writer; he's full of unexpected insights and fascinating tidbits . . . irresistible late-night reading."
—*Cineaste*

"[Peary] rescues from undeserved oblivion a number of real gems, adds to the celebration of several acknowledged masterpieces, comments enticingly on some seldom shown oddities, and debunks the inflated reputations of a few others . . . reading [his] book is like spending a couple of hours with some good old friends."
—*Film Quarterly*

"An excellent collection . . . so interesting that even if you have not seen many of the films covered . . . you are almost compelled to catch up . . . with any you may have missed. . . . A valuable reference source . . . an enjoyable work that can be read straight through or at a slow savor." —*Films in Review*

Books by Danny Peary

CLOSE-UPS: THE MOVIE STAR BOOK (Editor)
THE AMERICAN ANIMATED CARTOON (Co-editor)
CULT MOVIES

Cult Movies 2

*50 More
of the Classics, the Sleepers,
the Weird, and the Wonderful*

Danny Peary

A DELL TRADE PAPERBACK

To Suzanne and Zoë
and Laura, Joe, and Bea

A DELL TRADE PAPERBACK

Published by
Dell Publishing Co., Inc.
1 Dag Hammarskjold Plaza
New York, New York 10017

First Dell Trade Paperback printing—October 1983

Designed by Bob Fitzpatrick and MaryJane DiMassi
Research assistants: Henry Blinder and Beth Robinson

Library of Congress Cataloging in Publication Data
Peary, Danny, 1949–
   Cult movies 2.
   Includes index.
   1. Moving-pictures—Plots, themes, etc. I. Title.
II. Title: Cult movies 2.
PN1997.8.P368 1983   791.43′75   83-7668
ISBN 0-440-51632-3

Acknowledgments

Many people generously gave their time and energy to help me assemble this book. I would like to express my gratitude to these old friends and new friends: Henry Blinder, my researcher and lone guest-contributor; Beth Robinson, for research beyond the call of duty; Bob Fitzpatrick, who I hope will design all of my books; my wife, Suzanne Rafer, who read the manuscript with a straight face and supported me in other ways as well; my daughter, Zoë, who allowed me to win our movie arguments until I finished this book; my agent Chris Tomasino, who's surprised someone else didn't decide to write the sequel to volume one; Gerald Peary; Bob Nowacki; Doug Marshall; Paula Klaw; Ira Kramer; Reid Rosefelt; Carol Summers; Marc Ricci; Cory Gann; Norine Gann; Helen Gasparian; Bruce Trinz; Mary Lugo; Suzanne Fedak; Charles Bennett; Virginia Mayo; Blair Brown; Edgar Ievins; Paul Jarrico; Tamar Macher; Abel Ferrara; Kathryn Galan; Janis Rothbard-Chaskin; Bill Lange; Saul Shiffrin; David Chaskin; Zoë Tamerlis; Ann DeHavilland; Joel McCrea; Bill Banning; Terry Gilliam; Tracy Condon; Lorette Haven; Susan Reu; Johanna Tani; Frances Dominguez; Jack Ennis; Michael Carney; Allan Gale; Jeri Cummins; Peter Weissman; Mindy McAdams; and Dell's art director, MaryJane DiMassi. Also, I would like to thank the numerous individuals who sent in suggestions for titles to include in the book.

Photo credits go to the following: Warner Bros., New Yorker Films, Paramount, Analysis Releasing, United Artists, United Artists Classics, 20th Century-Fox, Columbia, Box Office Spectaculars, LQJaf, Impéria, Universal, Pathé Consortium, Gemini, Rumson Films, World Northal, New World Pictures, Metro-Goldwyn-Mayer, Brian Distributing, Atlantic Releasing, Svensk Filmindustri, Abraxas, British Lion, New Line Cinema, Cinema 5, Movie Star News, Eddy Brandt's Saturday Matinee, and the Memory Shop.

Finally, I would like to express great appreciation to my editors, Cynthia Vartan and Gary Luke.

Contents

Foreword

Not so long ago "cult movies" were considered to be only those obscure pictures that were admired by a small, sad coterie of film "experts" and other social outcasts. (It's still mighty hard to get a middle-of-the-week date to an Edgar G. Ulmer double feature.) The phenomenal success of Midnight Movies, particularly *The Rocky Horror Picture Show,* resulted in "cult movies" becoming those pictures that are seen countless times by large, somewhat fanatical communal groups who turn every screening into an audience-participation party. I choose to define "cult movies" quite broadly. I consider them those special films that elicit a fiery passion in moviegoers long after their initial releases; that have been taken to heart as if they were abandoned orphans in a hostile world, cherished, protected, and enthusiastically championed by segments of the movie audience; that are integral parts of people's lives. These are pictures that people will not miss whether they are playing on the *Late Late Late Show,* at a grindhouse in the most dangerous part of town, or at a drive-in in the next county; pictures that people will brave blizzards, skip their weddings, ignore their most solemn religious holidays, and even date their least-appealing cousins to see for what may be their tenth, twentieth, or one hundredth time.

I wrote in the Foreword to *Cult Movies:* "When you speak of cult movies, you speak in extremes. Hard-core cultists, ranging from polite to lunatic, insist that their favorite films are the most intriguing, unusual, outrageous, mysterious, absurd, daring, entertaining, erotic, exotic, and/or best films of all time. Also they point out that cult movies differ radically from standard Hollywood films in that they characteristically feature atypical heroes and heroines; offbeat dialogue; surprising plot resolutions; highly original story lines; brave themes, often of a sexual or political nature; 'definitive' performances by stars who have cult status; the novel handling of popular but stale genres. Outstanding special effects, spectacular camerawork, and a willingness by the filmmakers to experiment distinguish many cult movies. . . .

"The typical Hollywood product has little potential for becoming a cult favorite because it is perceived by *everyone* in basically the same way. Almost everyone agrees on the quality of these films, on what the directors are trying to say, and on the correct way to interpret the films' messages. On the other hand, cult films are born in controversy, in arguments over quality, themes, talent, and other matters. Cultists believe they are among the blessed few who have discovered something in particular films that the average moviegoer and critic have missed—the something that makes the pictures extraordinary. They grasp the elusive points of their favorite films, the filmmakers' most personal visions, the cult stars' real selves coming through; and they find glory that they are among the few on the same wavelength as the people involved in making these films. While word of mouth certainly plays a large part in the growth of cults for individual films, what is fascinating is that *in the beginning* pockets of people will embrace a film they have heard nothing about while clear across the country others independently will react identically to the same picture. There is nothing more exciting than discovering you are not the only person obsessed with a picture critics hate, the public stays away from en masse, and film texts ignore."

When writing *Cult Movies,* I regretted that space requirements dictated that I omit several films which fit my definition for "cult movies." As I expected, readers also felt that some obvious choices were missing; as I hoped, many readers sent in suggestions for titles that demanded inclusion if I were to do a sequel. *Cult Movies 2* contains chapters on fifty films that appeared repeatedly on lists submitted to me, as well as a few personal selections. Once again, I have attempted to present a strong cross section of cult films, ranging from those adored only by critics to those that fans have rallied around because critics unduly attacked them; from those that never have emerged from obscurity to those that were initially successful, faded away, and re-emerged as objects of cult adoration; from classics to fiascos. As before, I have limited the number of horror and science fiction films because I realize every one ever made has at least a minor cult. I have been more selective on the inclusion of Midnight Movies, since it's apparent that all movies that play midnight screenings have not achieved cult status. Although the three *Star Wars* movies, *Raiders of the Lost Ark, Gone With the Wind,* and *E.T.* have fanatical followings, I have not included them because they are still distributed with the intention of attracting mass audiences. Only when they are released primarily for their hardcore fans and play in repertory houses and/or on the Midnight Movie circuit, will they be classified as legitimate cult movies.

Altered States

1980 Warner Bros.
Director: Ken Russell
Producer: Howard Gottfried
Screenplay: Sidney Aaron
(Paddy Chayefsky)
From a novel by Paddy
Chayefsky

Cinematography: Jordan
Cronenweth
Special Visual Effects: Bran
Ferren
Special Makeup: Dick Smith
Music: John Corigliano
Editor: Eric Jenkins
Running time: 102 minutes

Cast: William Hurt (Eddie Jessup), Blair Brown (Emily Jessup), Bob Balaban (Arthur Rosenberg), Charles Haid (Mason Parrish), Thaao Penghlis (Eccheverria), Miguel Godreau (Primal Man), Dori Brenner (Sylvia Rosenberg), Peter Brandon (Hobart), Charles White Eagle (The Brujo), Drew Barrymore (Margaret Jessup), Megan Jeffers (Grace Jessup).

Synopsis: In 1967, in New York, psychophysiologist Edward Jessup spends time floating in an isolation tank, researching sensory deprivation. He hallucinates religious allegories and cries while re-experiencing his father's painful death. His friend Arthur Rosenberg, a pharmacologist, records his EEG tracings. Jessup admits he doesn't know what he's searching for.

At a party Jessup meets Emily, a doctoral candidate in physical anthropology. After they make passionate love, he reveals that as a child he believed in God and had visions—until his father died. Emily realizes that he is someone willing to sell his soul for Truth. She tries to convince him that "Life doesn't have truths." And that in his fanatical search for Truth, all he has done is replace God with the Original Self.

When both get teaching positions at Harvard, Emily suggests that they get married. He agrees, although he cannot reciprocate her great love for him.

In 1974, Arthur and his wife Sylvia move to Boston. They learn that Jessup and Emily, who have two daughters, are separating. Jessup has no time for a family and sentimental feelings when he must find his Original Self. Emily goes to Nairobi to study baboons. Jessup goes to South America to participate in a mushroom ceremony held by a backward tribe of Mayan descendants. All who partake are supposed to have a common experience. When Jessup drinks the ceremonial liquid, he hallucinates he is propelled into a crack in the Nothing, from which, the chief explains, comes one's unborn soul.

Back in Boston, Jessup resumes isolation tank experimentation while Arthur and his friend Mason Parrish record his words. He injects himself with the mushroom solution and has amazing hallucinations and blackouts while in the tank. At one point he tells his assistants that he has become an apeman and is killing a sheep. He emerges from the tank with blood on his mouth; X rays reveal that his skull has temporarily taken on the shape of a gorilla skull. At night he briefly experiences genetic change, and hair grows on his body. Emily returns to Boston, still in love with Jessup and worried that he is cracking up. He goes into the tank alone and emerges as an apeman. He brutally beats a guard before escaping to the zoo. He kills and eats a sheep. Jessup is discovered by the police—in his human form. Jessup insists that he go back into the tank with Emily, Arthur, and Mason present to witness that he really can turn into an apeman. There is an explosion that knocks out Arthur and Mason. A whirlpool forms in the lab, and Jessup, in an embryonic state, is sucked toward the moment of creation. Emily pulls him out.

Jessup tells Emily he now knows that all that is important is human life, not the terrible moment of creation. Only her love is keeping him from being pulled back to that time. Suddenly he changes into his embryonic form. Emily tells him to fight it if he loves her. They touch and she becomes an energy form. Jessup slams his arm into the wall, over and over. Suddenly, human again, he hugs Emily, who also reverts to her human form.

In 1980 any science fiction or horror film that boasted expensive special effects was a good bet to do blockbuster business. Warner Bros. was optimistic about *Altered States* when it opened strongly in urban areas, even breaking box office records at some theaters. But it lost its momentum once it hit Middle America, dropped off dramatically in attendance in cities once critics had their say, and proved to be a major commercial disappointment. That it has become a regular on revival theater schedules (playing in four New York theaters in one recent month) and often turns up as a Midnight Movie is not unexpected, considering the cult for director Ken Russell, the increasing popularity of star William Hurt, and the fanaticism some moviegoers have for pyrotechnics; but why it initially fizzled is unclear. Perhaps SF fans didn't think the trip through Eddie Jessup's unconscious world was as visually thrilling or mentally challenging as most movie trips through outer space. Perhaps horror fans, who were weaned on films in which Lon Chaney, Jr., turned into a werewolf under a full moon, didn't think the transformation of the tall, blond Jessup into a short, brown-haired apeman should have been done offscreen. Or perhaps they did not feel there were enough gruesome special effects to warrant an ad campaign that promised plentiful horror elements. Probably some moviegoers decided to boycott Ken Russell movies after wasting good money on such inexcusable exercises in self-indulgence as *Lisztomania* (1976) and *Valentino* (1976). (When I saw *Lisztomania*, the projector broke down in the middle of the film, but no one complained.) It's likely

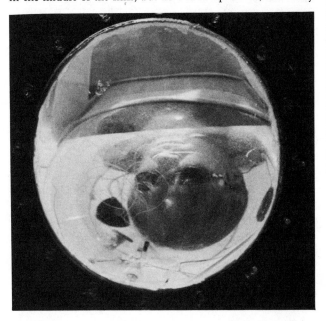

Jessup lies in a sensory deprivation tank. Prior to filming, as Blair Brown told me, she, William Hurt, and Ken Russell spent time in tanks from the sixties. "I was very relaxed, Bill hallucinated like crazy, and Ken was convinced bad spirits had been left over in his tank. Therein lie our three personalities."

that the staunch admirers of the late screenwriter Paddy Chayefsky—*Marty* (1955), *The Goddess* (1958), *The Hospital* (1971), *Network* (1976)—considered themselves too sophisticated to rush to a film in the fantastic vein. Or perhaps audiences couldn't buy the premise that someone who cared as little about mankind as Jessup would be so obsessed with finding man's origins.

Still, there's an easier guess as to why *Altered States* didn't generate enough positive word of mouth to make it successful. For about ninety-five uneven but "acceptable" minutes, the film takes viewers on an ambitious exploration of man's origins and simultaneously advances the intriguing theory that there can be genetic change if one's consciousness is manipulated. Then, suddenly, the picture drops several intellectual planes, disregards Arthur's and the viewer's desire to make further discoveries with Jessup, and settles safely on Jessup expounding a simplistic philosophy about the importance of love and life that could be sold to manufacturers of religious Mother's Day cards. Sure, it's grand that the long-suffering Emily finally gets the affection she deserves. Emily is a great character: brilliant, funny, loyal, concerned, brave. Unfortunately, once Jessup tells her that the Ultimate Truth is that there is no Ultimate Truth (some revelation!), that what's really meaningful is what's happening in our present everyday world (i.e., their love for each other), and that his journey to the point of creation to find his Original Self was painful and unsatisfying, then, for us, his seven-year search automatically becomes irrelevant. Much sound and fury signifying nothing. We can't enjoy putting puzzle pieces together and figuring out all those religious symbols Jessup hallucinated if Jessup himself believes it's of no consequence. He should know. It's as if Jessup returned from Mars to report it's sandy and cold there, and he, Chayefsky, and Russell concluded that there should be no further exploration or discussion of the planet. We know from countless horror films that man shouldn't tamper in some areas he doesn't comprehend; but we still agree with Stanley Kubrick in his belief, expressed in *2001: A Space Odyssey* (1968), that man's noblest characteristic is an insatiable desire to make discoveries even if they will lead to culture shock.

All that we're left to discuss at the end of *Altered States* are its blasting soundtrack; Bran Ferren's special effects, which utilized computer animation, rotoscoping, and scores of opticals; and the special effects makeup work ("the mole" and "the bladder" effects where it looks like there's movement beneath the skin, the use of specially designed body suits, the sculpturing of figures used in Jessup's metamorphosis back to an embryonic state) by the legendary Dick Smith (1973's *The Exorcist*, 1981's *Scanners*). That's apparently been enough for the film's cultists, but not for anyone else. As awful as is Disney's *The Black Hole* (1980), at least there was an ambitious attempt to visualize the inconceivable at the picture's end—a trip into a black hole. I want to see what Jessup experiences when he's in his ghastly embryonic form and is screaming. And it shouldn't look as if paint is splattering under a microscope, as does Ferren's inadequate ninety-second light show.

If only Jessup had died like most movie scientists who venture in no man's land (rather than having Emily's love redeem him); or if he had pulled Emily into the whirlpool with him; or if he and his beloved had not reappeared after momentarily vanishing (becoming an energy force?) in the hall sequence. Then at the fadeout, Arthur, with a cup of coffee in his hand, and Mason, shouting as usual, could look at each other with confusion, and ask such questions as "What did Jessup experience?"; "What did he see that made him scream?"; "Where did they go?"; "What will they find?"; "What have they become?" And viewers could answer these questions and formulate opinions about the meanings of various images and occurrences. Granted, these endings would have been as trite as the present one, and would not have improved the film at all, but they just might have sparked the controversy necessary to have made the film a hit. Except for a few southern fundamentalists who protested the theory of evolution espoused, no one bothered to debate the film's content. Everything's too spelled out. How popular would *2001* have been if everyone understood the meanings of the black monolith and the star child?

Probably inspired by John Lilly's mind expansion experiments of the midsixties, Chayefsky wrote his only novel—in which he sprinkled scientific data like other people drop names—with the intention of its becoming a film. Columbia was originally set to produce the adaptation for an estimated $12.2 million. To direct, Chayefsky hand-picked Arthur Penn, whom he had known since they'd been driving forces in live television in the fifties. After six months of preproduction, during which the two men supposedly planned different pictures, Penn quit. Six weeks and $1.5 million later, Chayefsky and producer Howard Gottfried happily announced they had signed Ken Russell to direct his first American film. The flamboyant British director's outrageously excessive style certainly seemed suitable for this, if any,

Classic horror films had the same actor play the scientist and the creature he becomes after weird experiments. But in Altered States *Hurt's Primal Man is played by tiny Mexican dancer Miguel Godreau.*

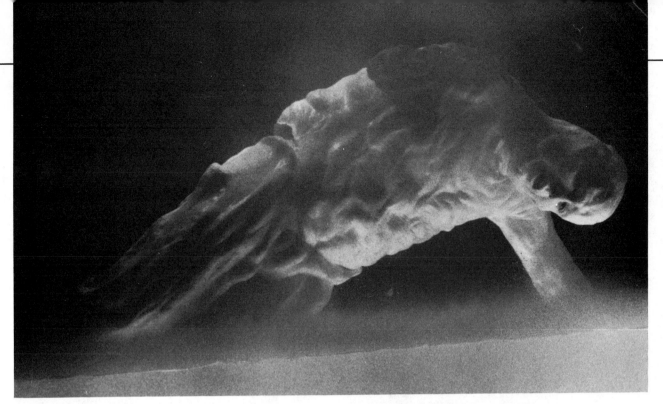

Jessup regresses to an embryonic state. Dick Smith created this single-piece head-to-toe foam latex suit.

picture, because it depends on mind-blowing visuals. Yet he was an odd choice. Foremost, he was not the partner or puppet Chayefsky desired, but someone who would insist that *his* personal vision make it to the screen. His refusal to control his outlandish artistic notions already had resulted in cinematic chaos. Only *Women in Love* (1970), *The Devils* (1971), where Russell's delirious style truly worked, and cult hit *Tommy* (1975) had done well financially. *The Boy Friend* (1971), an original tribute to Hollywood musicals starring Twiggy, the one Russell film I *enjoy,* at least had scattered critical recognition. But his other works—which, like *Altered States,* are about eccentrics striving for some form of immortality—had flopped with critics and ticket buyers: *The Music Lovers* (1971), *Savage Messiah* (1972), *Mahler* (1974), *Lisztomania,* and *Valentino.* His aim was to shock viewers; instead they were repelled. When Columbia lost interest in financing *Altered States* soon after Russell took the helm, it seemed like good business sense.

Warners took over the film, which wound up costing $14.9 million. It would have cost another $4 million if Russell had gotten along with the Penn-hired John Dykstra, the special effects wiz of *Star Wars* (1977), and not replaced him with the much less expensive Ferren, then only twenty-seven. Not surprisingly, Russell and Chayefsky didn't get along either. A week after filming began, Chayefsky walked out. He still collected all monies, but insisted titles credit go to his alias Sidney (his real name) Aaron. Chayefsky claimed that Russell was ruining his novel, but I can think of no other movie adaptation that is so close to its source. It's more than likely that he came out publicly against Russell because he realized early on that no faithful adaptation of his book could result in a good film. He needed a scapegoat in order to keep his own reputation intact. But if you don't like *Altered States,* blame Chayefsky.

I find no director as infuriating as Ken Russell, but I admit some admiration for his work on *Altered States.* Consider that if he had changed one word of Chayefsky's unwieldy dialogue he would have been sued. The proposal scene, in which Emily tells Jessup exactly how peculiar he is (he's a weird lover, a Faust freak, etc.), is an example of what Russell had to contend with: Emily's monologue goes on and on without fluidity. Russell solved much of this overwritten-dialogue problem by having his actors talk so quickly that

Emily rescues Jessup from the whirlpool. "I loved Emily for her grand passion for Eddie," Brown told me. "She was extremely intelligent and lived a rational existence except for him. If she hadn't met him, she'd have had everything organized and lifeless. Her passion turned everything upside down. I'm envious of those women with a calm center who are fixed on a man in such a real, powerful way."

In the finale hall sequence Eddie and then Emily move into a quantum state where there is no matter. It is their great love for each other that saves them from oblivion.

lines that would make no sense to the average viewer anyway are lost; when Jessup must spout a lot of intellectual mumbo jumbo upon meeting Emily, Russell has him talk with a mouth full of food. Russell realized that words were less important than impressing viewers that the characters are loquacious about erudite subjects. William Hurt, Blair Brown, Bob Balaban, and Charles Haid—the fine cast assembled by Arthur Penn—also must be credited for figuring out ways to circumvent the much too literate dialogue. They all are believable, and smooth, as they deliver intellectual diatribes.

The film actually improves on the novel in several ways. By eliminating the book's sequence in which Emily unsuccessfully tries to live without Jessup (before giving up and marrying him although he doesn't love her), she retains her strength throughout the film—and is not the least bit pathetic in her devotion. Such a sequence also would have implied that Emily would never be able to go without Jessup to Nairobi. (Her excited rap to Jessup about her baboon studies upon her return is handled especially well by Russell. It not only establishes her expertise in a scholarly field in which Jessup, a genius, isn't expert, and reveals the importance of her work in her life, but also illustrates the difference between a passion {hers} and a mania {his} for scientific discovery. Furthermore, it reaffirms the thrill of exploration to viewers turned off by Jessup's mad Jekyll-Hyde experiments.) Two changes serve to make Jessup a more palatable character. In the book Jessup vomits at the beginning of every experiment, indicating his masochistic, self-destructive nature. We are thankful such scenes were done away with, particularly because Russell is known for gross-out sequences (like having

his characters swimming in "filth" in *Tommy* and *Valentino*). The most important deletion was the dialogue in which Jessup cruelly confesses to Arthur that he has no love, not even warm feelings, for his children. Onscreen we see Jessup, in the same sequence minus the dialogue, kiss his sleeping kids on their brows. From this tenderness we suspect that he does have subliminal feelings of love toward them—and we get to like him better than he likes himself. That this alienating character who thinks of God, Christ, and crucifixes when he makes love—in *Play It Again, Sam* Woody Allen thinks of Willie Mays during lovemaking—is played by the talented, charismatic William Hurt also makes some of his more insensitive actions easier to take. And because it is Hurt in the role, we can feel sympathy for Jessup and also understand why Emily loves him so much.

At times Russell's symbolism is heavy-handed—for instance, he repeatedly places Jessup in doorways, on the threshold of discovery and displaced in time and space—but surprisingly he keeps things under control. Especially impressive are his realistic apartment and lab sets, with their seedy designs; the successful presentation of highly competitive academic types without making them obnoxious; a fairly tense atmosphere and a particularly spooky scene in which the apeman runs loose in the lab basement; and some lengthy, one-shot scenes that reveal the theatrical background of the performers. What I like best of all are his closeups of Blair Brown when Emily reacts, as if dazed and amazed, to her husband's strange thought processes.

Two years in production—six months of work for the actors—*Altered States* is famous in film circles because those involved were under so much stress. Blair Brown told me about filming the climactic scene in the hall:

> We didn't start working in the hallucination suits until the end, which was wise because Ken wouldn't have had any actors left. It was hard on Dick Smith, who is a genuinely nice man. You'd come in with tears rolling down your cheeks and he'd have to put you back in the suit. It would take three hours for makeup. It was horrible and it went on for weeks and weeks. You couldn't sit, you couldn't eat, you couldn't go to the bathroom. They glued things to our palms and the soles of our feet. And they covered our ears too. I wanted to scream. It's as if you were in a death trance, or a coma. When we weren't filming they'd put us on slant boards, at an angle. And people would come by and tell me jokes and their intimate secrets as if I were a priest or mummy. The worst: Ken didn't like the action, so he put a harness under my suit so he could drag me down the hall. I already had lenses that covered my eyes and someone got the idea to put seed light bulbs on my eyelids and then cover them with rubber eyes. And they covered my nose all black and gave me a mouthpiece that made it look as if my teeth were gone. I'd get dragged down the hall backward until my head would crash into the wall. We did that all day, every day. One day, Bill had just done the hand slamming bit and his arm was black and blue from the wall. I was brought on as the next course. And I was crawling down the wall with my arms spread, saying, "Aaaghhh." And Ken was screaming "More despair! More despair!" And my body said, "I'm leaving," and I fell over and got a big bump on my head. I have pictures from an *Altered States* party. Everyone is so white and swollen. We should have been put away for several months. Instead we got T-shirts that said "I survived *Altered States*."

1977 West Germany–France Filmverlag der Autoren–Les Films Moli release of a Road Movie Filmproduktion–Les Films du Losange–Wim Wenders Produktion–Westdeutschen Rundfunk co-production (released in the United States by New Yorker Films)

Director: Wim Wenders
Screenplay: Wim Wenders
From the novel *Ripley's Game* by Patricia Highsmith
Cinematography: Robby Muller
Music: Jürgen Kneiper
Editor: Peter Przygodda
Running time: 123 minutes

Cast: Bruno Ganz (Jonathan Zimmermann), Dennis Hopper (Tom Ripley), Lisa Kreuzer (Marianne Zimmermann), Gérard Blain (Raoul Minot), Nicholas Ray (Derwatt), Samuel Fuller (the American), Peter Lilienthal (Marcangelo), Daniel Schmid (Igraham), Sandy Whitelaw (doctor in Paris), Jean Eustache (friendly man), Lou Castel (Rodolphe), Wim Wenders (bandaged man)

Synopsis: Jonathan Zimmermann is a framemaker. He is Swiss but runs a small shop in Hamburg and makes little money—a concern since he knows he has leukemia and wants to leave his wife Marianne and son Daniel enough on which to get by.

In New York, Tom Ripley, an American with a mansion near Hamburg, secures another painting from the artist Derwatt. Tom has been getting good prices for the art because Derwatt is living as a recluse and the public thinks he is dead.

At a Hamburg auction house where Marianne works, the Derwatt painting is sold. Tom is introduced to Jonathan, who knows Tom's bad reputation and refuses to shake hands, saying rudely "I've heard of you." Tom feels slightly insulted. When Raoul Minot asks Tom if he knows someone not known in the crime world who could assassinate a couple of American Mafia men, Tom thinks of Jonathan. Knowing about Jonathan's illness, Tom spreads a rumor that he has taken a turn for the worse. Jonathan becomes paranoid. He refuses to believe his doctor when the doctor tells him there is no change in his condition.

Raoul proposes to Jonathan that he kill two Mafia men for a huge sum of money. Jonathan says no but can't get the offer out of his mind. He could give the money to his family. Raoul tells Jonathan he has arranged for him to see a specialist in Paris, where the first murder is to take place. Jonathan agrees to go to Paris but says he won't commit the crime.

The results from the Paris specialist, are bad. Jonathan agrees to the murder. He follows a man through the métro, shoots him in the back, and kills him. He can't believe what he has done. But he feels giddy and proud. He returns to Hamburg.

Tom hangs around Jonathan's shop. He becomes friendly with him and envies his ability to work with his hands. Tom is beginning to feel like he's in a daze.

Raoul wants Jonathan to kill a man from a second, rival Mafia faction on a Munich train. Jonathan gets on the train although he says he won't commit the crime. Four Mafia men get on. When the one Jonathan is to kill discovers him in the bathroom preparing a garotte, Jonathan is involved in a fight he can't win. But suddenly Tom appears and kills the man. A second Mafia man appears. They push him and the dead man out the train. Jonathan thinks Tom and Raoul are in cahoots, but Tom insists not.

Marianne doesn't understand where Jonathan got all his money. She knows he is lying to her. She moves out with Daniel. Meanwhile, the Mafia has tracked Raoul down, bombing his place in Paris. Tom picks up Jonathan and brings him to his mansion. A Mafia man turns up and they kill him. Near the house, they spot an ambulance. Raoul is a prisoner inside. Jonathan and Tom toss the Mafia leader to his death down a long flight of stairs. They hug.

Marianne arrives. She tells Jonathan the Paris hospital reports were fake. He had guessed it. She drives Tom's car, following Tom in the ambulance to the shore. Jonathan sleeps. At daybreak, on the beach, Tom blows up the ambulance. He is surprised to see Jonathan and Marianne drive off and leave him. Jonathan dies. Showing no emotion, Marianne gets out of the car. Derwatt waits for Tom in New York.

The American Friend

Wim Wenders's *The American Friend* is—with the possible exception of emerging French cult favorite *Diva* (1982)—the most dazzlingly daffy suspense-psychological thriller to be imported to the United States within memory. Based on *Ripley's Game,* an exceptional 1974 entry to the devilish Tom Ripley series by Patricia Highsmith, author of *Strangers on a Train,* it was the first film of the West German cinema renaissance to be truly accessible to American audiences. That it was Wenders (who looks like a long-haired Buddy Holly), rather than the late Rainer Werner Fassbinder or Werner Herzog, to break through first is not surprising, since his work is much more influenced by Western culture (films, rock music) than that of his countrymen. The popularity of *The American Friend* in America outside of the art house circuit is understandable. First of all, it was made for $1.2 million, the total cost of Wenders's six previous films, allowing for a fairly polished production. It was made in color (a first for Wenders), and instead of using arty, subdued, sleep-inducing colors that would blend into one another and into the subtitles, he went for splashy, flashy, gaudy kaleidoscopic colors (especially blinding reds) that keep our eyes open and moving. There are musical references to familiar songs by the Kinks, Byrds, Bob Dylan, and the Beatles, and the morbid, ominous score by Jürgen Kneiper is obviously influenced by Bernard Herrmann, composer for some of Alfred Hitchcock's most popular films. The picture is set partly in America, English is the dominant language, Dennis Hopper costars, and well-known American directors Sam Fuller and Nicholas Ray have supporting parts. The story of an ordinary, somewhat dull man who gets manipulated by strangers into a murder plot that has nothing to do with him (actually committing the murder himself) rings of Hitchcock. In fact, the relationship between Tom, a slightly bonkers criminal, and Jonathan (fine German actor Bruno Ganz) is very reminiscent of that between Bruno (Robert Walker) and Guy (Farley Granger) in *Strangers on a Train* (1951). The nail-biting Paris métro and Munich train sequences also remind one of Hitchcock. While Wenders's story, characters, and methods of building suspense are, in part, indebted to Hitchcock, his brutal, sharply edited action sequences recall Fuller's hard-biting B films; and his use of the frame as an arena for tension and to expose character isolation recalls Ray: it is through his character placement (spatial relationships) and his strategic use of one-shots and two-shots that we see how an invisible wall builds between Jonathan and Marianne (a strong portrayal by Wenders's wife, Lisa Kreuzer), while, simultaneously, Jona-

In a Paris hotel room the restless Jonathan contemplates the unimaginable: his committing murder. Typically director Wenders isolates Jonathan in the frame, for he is alone in the world.

than and Tom become increasingly comfortable in each other's presence. (It's fitting that Jonathan is a *frame*maker.)

In the film's production notes, Wenders discussed the essence of *The American Friend:* "A sinister story grows out of a small, harmless lie, a pleasant self-deception, and there is no escape. It could happen to anyone. Jonathan's life is turned upside down. Jonathan himself is wrung inside out. Is he the person he always thought he was, or is he someone else too?" Before Jonathan commits his first murder, there is a revealing camera shot: the camera begins on Jonathan, moves away, and travels in such a way that when it comes back on Jonathan it is as if the Jonathan of the first shot is looking at his own reflection in the mirror (is he?); as if he had stepped outside of his body and is watching another, more courageous and reckless person—his real self?—inhabit it. This picture, in part, is about an individual who strips off his shackles (of living the correct life) and, rather than changing, bares his real self.

When we meet Jonathan, he is a quick study, someone you know completely after five minutes. He knows everything about himself, too, including that he will continue to live a predictable, uneventful life until the moment of his imminent death. Enter Tom Ripley, a ghoulish sort who exploits painter Derwatt (whose works are more valuable because he is supposedly deceased) and Jonathan, two men who are, in truth, dead. Tom is a wicked angel of sorts, a Mephistopheles who gives Jonathan a chance to sin (although Tom wouldn't consider killing mafiosi sinful) during the final moments of his life. This is Jonathan's last chance to do something unconventional and exciting, and he can't dismiss the opportunity. Highsmith writes: "The idea was curiously exciting and disturbing, a bolt from the blue, a shaft of

colour in his uneventful existence, and Jonathan wanted to observe it, to enjoy it in a sense." Of course Jonathan goes along with the murder-for-money plan, offered him by Raoul Minot but initiated by Tom, who gave Raoul his name. And Jonathan's orderly life goes topsy-turvy: Jonathan becomes unpredictable ("You're crazy," Marianne concludes); his wife, who has supported him in illness, becomes his accuser; his worst enemy becomes his best friend and confederate; his good marriage disintegrates; a decent, saintly man becomes a cold-blooded murderer.

"Wenders is charting the breakdown of identity in a situation of extremity," wrote David Ansen of *Newsweek,* "and he underscores his theme by showing us a world—Hamburg, Paris, New York, Munich—where the cityscapes themselves have lost all national identity." It is a world of displaced people: an American (Tom) and a Frenchman (Raoul) do a number on a Swiss man (Jonathan) in Germany; the Swiss man kills Americans in France and Germany; Tom's a cowboy who lives not in Texas but in New York and Hamburg; Jonathan goes to an American hospital in France; Jonathan sings English songs; English, French, and German are spoken. The cities we see all look alike and blend into one another (Tom is in Germany in one scene and New York the next as if he'd gone down the block)—just as Tom and Jonathan eventually blend into each other.

A recurrent theme in Wenders is that men have a common bond: they will attract while their women are repelled. He best explored this theme in *Kings of the Road* (1976), in which a drifter and a suicidal man whose marriage has just come crashing down unite and, though apparent opposites, become friends while on their aimless journey. He explored this "buddy" theme again in *The American Friend.* Ironically, actors Bruno Ganz and Dennis Hopper had a relationship on the set that paralleled that of their characters in the film. Ganz, a serious stage actor who spent hours each night trying to figure out his character's motivations in upcoming scenes, was annoyed by Hopper's seemingly lackadaisical approach to

The American gangster, played by director Sam Fuller, searches for his missing henchmen aboard the Munich train. Directors Nicholas Ray, Gérard Blain, Peter Lilienthal, Daniel Schmid, Jean Eustache, and Wenders, too, took parts in the film.

Loners Jonathan and Tom become confederates following the second murder. Tom reveals that the simple, spiteful reason he involved him in Raoul's murder plot was because he had been insulted by Jonathan's disdainful words "I've heard of you" when they had been introduced.

his role, meaning Hopper did very little preparation. Their resentment of each other built to such a point that there was actually a full-scale drunken fistfight between the two. After the fight, the two actors became close friends and Ganz decided that in films Hopper's approach was probably the more suitable. How Tom and Jonathan become close is another matter. Immediately we realize that both Tom and Jonathan are loners, as Wenders isolates them in his frame. It doesn't matter that Jonathan is married, because when the chips are down for the first time in his life he cannot talk openly to Marianne: he is alone. Tom and Jonathan are both friendless, and in need of a friend. Significantly, they are also both aliens. Tom is a cowboy in Hamburg, a cowboy in New York, a man without a country; he travels back and forth across time (zones) and vague boundaries of the living and dead, the real and unreal. Even his mansion in Germany is out of place: it has a Russian design. Jonathan is Swiss and living in Germany with a German wife. He is a craftsman in the jet age; a simple man who lives in a world of high technology and high-rise buildings. He is also a dying man in a world of the living. Tom envies Jonathan because he knows how and approximately when he will die, while Tom sees his own life as open-ended (symbolized by his endless travel) and meaningless. Jonathan is attracted to Tom because he represents freedom from family responsibilities, morality, and a dull life; he admires Tom's skill in carrying out criminal activities; he envies Tom for not being afraid to die.

Patricia Highsmith was reported to be dissatisfied with Wenders's film. Although I am equally fond of both the book and the film, I can understand Highsmith's discontent. Thematically, there is a big difference between the two. Highsmith wanted to write, she says, "about what's going on in a person's head when . . . in the middle of problems or a crisis." Her books are concerned with "the effect of guilt on heroes." The guilt that Jonathan struggles to overcome (and does with some success) in *Ripley's Game* is the result of his breaking, in his own mind, a religion-based code. Not that he himself is religious or believes in a soul, but in his eyes his Catholic wife Simone (Marianne in the film) has come to personify the religious code. If he were to let her know he broke that code he is sure she will be driven away. This is his *greatest* fear. Jonathan lies to Simone about how he has suddenly come into large sums of money because he is positive she would never accept money "tainted" by men's deaths, even if they were scoundrels. Consequently, the lies ruin the marriage. The final irony is that once Jonathan is dead and Simone knows the truth, she still takes the "tainted" money to start a new life for herself and their son. The book ends: "Simone was just a trifle ashamed of herself, Tom thought. In that she joined much of the rest of the world. Tom felt, in fact, that her conscience would be more at rest than that of her husband, if he were still alive."

Conscience, guilt, and morality are important to Highsmith. Wenders doesn't deal with these themes at all. God, after all, doesn't exist in his world. Men can play gods themselves, determining the courses of each other's lives and determining whether one lives or dies (though they are unable to reverse Jonathan's illness), and not have to face as enormous a moral responsibility as Highsmith's heroes. Wenders is concerned with existentialist themes and with male bonding and friendship. (In Highsmith, Tom befriends and helps Jonathan more out of guilt for having gotten him into a messy situation than because he grows to admire him.)

Tom Ripley is, according to Tom Milne of the *London Observer,* "the quintessential Wenders hero, the loner traveling through alien lands in quest of himself, of friendship, of some meaning to life." This also sounds much like Hopper's hippie cyclist in *Easy Rider* (1969). He is tormented, drunken, confused, and spacy, blurting existentialist rhetoric into his recorder: "I know less and less about who I am." Highsmith's Ripley knows himself very well, is at peace with himself, and is even impressed by his own ability to shift so easily back and forth between life with the leisure class and life with those weird characters who inhabit the sordid world of crime. He is married, has a beautiful villa in France, is cultured, speaks several languages, and lives the good life: fine clothes, money, cocktails, caviar, art, music (he plays the harpsichord), shopping, buying presents for Heloise, puttering in the garden, taking expensive trips, having quaint dinner parties with neighbors. He's a conceited fellow: he might feel sorry for

Only at the end, when his death is imminent, does Jonathan realize that Marianne won't desert him if she knows the truth.

Jonathan because of his illness or his dull life, but he'd not envy him just because he "can make things with his hands." Book and film critics have described Ripley as "amoral," but Highsmith wouldn't agree. Tom has guilty feelings about all his crimes, it's just that he always finds a way to make the guilt tolerable (one way is to rationalize that he hurts no one who matters). Highsmith would think her Ripley a rapscallion, or maybe a Nixon "dirty trickster."

I can better see Bruno Ganz as the Jonathan described in the novel. But Jonathan's reasons for carrying out actions are different in the book than in the film. In both Jonathan deceives himself when he thinks his purpose for committing crimes is to be able to leave money to his wife and son after he is dead. Soon it's obvious that Jonathan really wants to do something daring before he dies. At this point the film and book take alternate routes. In the film we realize that Jonathan has taken on his dangerous assignment in part to satisfy a suicidal wish—he places a pillow over his head one night and aims a gun at it but can't pull the trigger. He is afraid of waiting for inevitable death from leukemia. In the book, taking this job is Jonathan's way of seeing how he'll face up to the real thing, death, and he comes to the realization that "money has ceased to matter." What does matter is that "he hasn't lost his self-respect, only Simone." In fact, by joining forces with Tom and eliminating mafiosi, he has *gained* self-respect before dying. Like Tom, he learns to justify the murders of bad people so he won't consider himself immoral. That makes him a worthy candidate for heaven. In the film Jonathan doesn't bother to justify his actions: there's no one he must answer to. (Marianne's morality is not based on religion but on a strict marital code based on trust and truth.) It is important for Wenders's Jonathan to prove himself in a crisis situation. It is also important that he leave behind a legacy, not to his wife but to his son Daniel (male bonding). This legacy is not the money but the exciting story in which he has just taken part.

Barbarella

1968   France-Italy Paramount
Director: Roger Vadim
Producer: Dino De Laurentiis
Screenplay: Terry Southern, Brian Degas, Claude Brule, Jean-Claude Forest, Roger Vadim, Clement Wood, Tudor Gates, Vittorio Bonicelli
Based on the book by Jean-Claude Forest
Adapted from the comic strip by Jean-Claude Forest
Cinematography: Claude Renoir
Music: Bob Crewe and Charles Fox
Editor: Victoria Mercanton
Running time: 98 minutes

Cast: Jane Fonda (Barbarella), John Phillip Law (Pygar), Anita Pallenberg (The Black Queen), Milo O'Shea (the concierge), David Hemmings (Dildano), Marcel Marceau (Professor Ping), Ugo Tognazzi (Mark Hand), Claude Dauphin (President of Earth)

Synopsis: It is 4000 A.D. Beautiful astronaut Barbarella is sent by the President of Earth on a mission to find Durand-Durand, an evil scientist who disappeared years before carrying the secret of the ultimate weapon—the Positronic Ray.

Barbarella's spacecraft is thrown out of orbit and crashes on the planet Lytheon. She is taken captive by a group of strange children who set their sharp-toothed killer dolls on her. Just in time, Barbarella is rescued by Mark Hand, a bearded catch man responsible for rounding up these wild children. She asks how she can repay him, and he requests that she make love to him. She would like to make use of the exultation transfer machine in their lovemaking, but goes along with his wishes to make love in a bed instead of just touching hands. She has never loved this way before and finds it an exhilarating experience.

Her ship fixed by her lover, Barbarella resumes her flight, only to crash into the ground and end up far below in Labyrinth. Here she meets the handsome, blond Pygar, whose white wings make her believe he is an angel. In reality he is the last of the ornithanthropes. The Black Queen, the great tyrant of Sogo, has destroyed his sight and his will to fly. Barbarella also meets the elderly Professor Ping, who promises to fix her ship. He tells her to seek out Durand-Durand in Sogo. But of all those exiled to Labyrinth by the Black Queen, only Pygar has the ability to take her there—and he refuses to fly.

Pygar rescues Barbarella from the queen's Black Guard. She rewards him by making love to him in the old-fashioned way. Afterward, she sings and he flies. He takes her to Sogo, a city built upon the mathmos, a living liquid that feeds on all the city's evil.

The beautiful Black Queen and her vicious concierge arrest Barbarella and Pygar, whose wings are nailed to a cross. Put in a cage with birds that attack her, Barbarella is rescued by Dildano, who is planning a revolt against the queen. They make love. She agrees to help in the revolution if Dildano will help her find Durand-Durand.

The concierge captures Barbarella and tries to kill her on his Excessive Machine, but she short circuits the machine. She realizes the concierge is Durand-Durand. He locks her in the Chamber of Dreams with the Black Queen. The queen helplessly watches Durand-Durand coronate himself—his first step to ruling the universe. There is a revolution. Durand-Durand sends Dildano and Ping into oblivion with his Positronic Ray. The queen unleashes the mathmos, which gobbles up Durand-Durand and all of Sogo. But the mathmos won't eat the innocent Barbarella and Pygar, and the queen survives by staying in their protective bubble.

Pygar flies the two women toward the ship Ping fixed. Barbarella asks Pygar how he can forgive the Black Queen for all she's done to him. He smiles: "An angel has no memory."

A publicity shot of Jane Fonda in one of Barbarella's outlandish costumes. Such revealing garb is one of the major reasons the picture retains its cult status; such stills—at once silly and sexy—have long been popular among memorabilia collectors.

At almost every press conference promoting a new Jane Fonda film, some spiteful reporter will sneak in a snide question about *Barbarella* in hopes of seeing her squirm. Obviously, they assume she'd like to burn every print of this picture, made before her politicization, in which she spends all her screen time in various states of undress and plays a character who is rescued time and again by men, whom she then rewards with sex. But while Fonda admits to many mistakes in her past, she insists that *Barbarella* isn't one of them. "I like it—it's fun," she'll tell the reporter succinctly, and then turn the tables on him: "Why? Don't you?" or "Why don't you?" Not wishing to admit to having been as much offended by Barbarella's sexual escapades the tenth time he saw the film as the first, and not daring to debate this intimidating actress over whether Vadim exploited her, the reporter invariably backs down sheepishly. That's too bad, because it would be interesting if Fonda were pressured, just a bit, into elaborating her warm feelings for the picture many consider the flimsiest of her career.

Fonda is the screen's most compelling star and has been since she stopped making the fluff that twice earned her the Harvard *Lampoon*'s Worst Actress award and stunned everyone with back-to-back tour-de-force performances in *They Shoot Horses, Don't They?* (1969) and *Klute* (1971). For discriminating moviegoers who believe pictures should be enlightening as well as entertaining, her films, post Roger Vadim, comprise an oasis in Hollywood's cinematic wasteland.

Jane Fonda's best, most personal films have bucked the tide and dealt with serious political themes. Her apparent philosophy: if social-issue films can help improve society, then viewers will feel less need for escape. That's not to say Fonda categorically dismisses comic book films in the

Barbarella mold, with their cardboard characters, exaggerated situations, absurd humor, and simplistic good vs. evil, black-white storylines; certainly her later comedies *Fun With Dick and Jane* (1979), *9 to 5* (1980), and even *The Electric Horseman* (1979) have had comic book ingredients. But if Jane Fonda continues to like *Barbarella*, it's not because it's escapist fare but because she still admires her character.

In most Roger Vadim films, offscreen sex goddesses (from the young Bardot to Fonda '69) portray women who are sexually naïve, and thus perfect prey for lustful male characters who wish to coax them out of their clothes and into beds. Their sexual innocence, which is expressed by their matter-of-fact nudity and a willingness to believe that the men who look them up and down are only trying to guess their heights, is meant to turn audiences on. Male audiences. Contrary to what many would think, rather than being annoyed by Barbarella's naïveté, Fonda is still attracted to this character trait. Consider that her women in *Julia* (1977), *Coming Home* (1978), *The China Syndrome* (1979), and *Rollover* (1981), as well as in *The Electric Horseman* and *9 to 5*, whatever their intelligences, are distinguished by their initial ignorance of the situations in which they involve themselves. Fonda sees them as being typical of many women who venture alone through a male-controlled universe. What makes them heroic is that they don't let their ignorance keep them back. They move forward into dangerous waters, usually stepping on people's feet, always igniting a time bomb of sorts. Although confused, they speak loudly and boldly, moving from jittery to smooth as their confidence builds— unlike Warren Beatty's mumbling fact-finders—and ask questions even at the risk of revealing their lack of knowledge. Fonda's putting her foot in her mouth is a constant source of

Not the most popular movie couple of their time, Fonda and Vadim survey the futuristic sets.

humor. When mocked, these women don't back down but push aside their embarrassment and move forward until they thoroughly understand their situations. Once educated, they usually triumph. Barbarella is like these women in most respects, but she does not overcome her naïveté—perhaps because the filmmakers didn't wish to tamper with Jean-Claude Forest's defined comic strip character. Barbarella is the only one who doesn't either grow up or grow wiser.

Few would argue that *Barbarella* is as witty as Vadim intended, but the fact that Barbarella was given (supposedly) funny lines in the first place, at a time when only Barbra Streisand was trusted with one-liners, must be appreciated by Fonda. Always an underrated comic actress, Fonda deftly handles such intentionally overwritten fare as "A good many dramatic situations begin with screaming," upon hearing a

In a scene influenced by The Wizard of Oz *(1939), Barbarella threatens to melt the wicked Black Queen's face (she has been calling Barbarella "Pretty Pretty") if she doesn't free Pygar.*

scream, and "This is really too poetic a way to die," upon being locked in a cage with starving birds. Unfortunately, Vadim wants to achieve pure camp by having such lines delivered straightforwardly. Parody is wonderful if well done, but settling for camp is lazy. I'd prefer it if Fonda were more subtle: Vadim should have had her deliver such lines under her breath, perhaps like W. C. Fields or Robin Williams's Popeye.

Critics of the film might guess that Fonda would object to her character's willingness to give her body to all males who give her assistance. But the point is that it is always Barbarella's choice that she gives these men physical pleasure—and, besides, *she ends up using their bodies to give herself sexual satisfaction.* Fonda likes Barbarella because she gives sex of her own free will, and, in turn, turned-on audiences like *Barbarella* because in it Fonda took off her clothes of her own free will. In 1968, when an actress made it to star status, she automatically rejected all roles that called for nudity. But Fonda broke with convention; she was a major actress who sought out roles that required her to disrobe. The result was a *Barbarella* cult of curious people stimulated by the prospect of seeing a star so uninhibited. The political Fonda is too conscious of her public image to again play such a role. This has made *Barbarella* a curiosity piece, and pinups of her in the picture, and in the Vadim segment of *Spirits of the Dead* (1969), in which she plays a temptingly dressed libertine, have become collectors' favorites.

When Fonda was married to Vadim and lived with him in Paris, we couldn't really decide if it was indeed Fonda's choice to play Barbarella, a Barbie doll for adults. Though it's hard to imagine, back in 1969 we thought she was trapped in a Svengali-Trilby relationship with her husband-director, much like the one we envision between John and Bo Derek. At the time, Pauline Kael wrote that Fonda was "married to a superb example of the Jamesian villain, a sophisticated European (a Frenchman of Russian origin) who is redolent of shallow morals, who is the screen's foremost celebrant of erotic trash, and who has the scandalous habit of turning each wife into a facsimile of the first and spreading her out for the camera." We had seen how Vadim had orchestrated the careers of former wives Brigitte Bardot and Annette Stroyberg Vadim. And now *Life* magazine reported that Vadim had been so inspired seeing Fonda walk around their villa topless that he wanted the whole world to share her physical attributes. But if we look farther back, we see that Fonda herself helped cultivate her sex kitten image. In her first film, *Tall Story* (1960), a comedy directed by her godfather, Joshua Logan, she wears tight cheerleader sweaters and low-cut dresses. Two scenes are unbelievably torrid, even by 1980s standards: a heavy-breathing Fonda, in a dress that shows much cleavage, and an aroused Anthony Perkins smooch on a couch and discuss genetics; later the turned-on but fully clothed pair stand interlocked in a tiny trailer shower, expanded chests pressing and Fonda licking her lips. Other Hollywood films—from *The Chapman Report* (1962), cast as a frigid housewife (and using her direct-facing-the-camera-as-if-being-interviewed speaking style for the first time), and *Walk on the Wild Side* (1962), as her first hooker, to *Barefoot in the Park* (1967) and *Cat Ballou* (1965)—promoted her sex image. Besides these, she traveled to Europe to make erotic

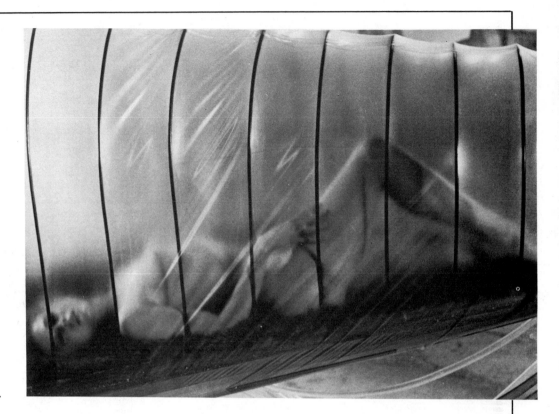

The standard Vadim tease: It's impossible to be certain if Fonda is truly nude behind the glass. Such moments abound in the film.

films, first for René Clément, and then for Roger Vadim, who knew how to exploit her sexuality to the nth degree. Marriage came later.

Barbarella begins with Fonda's famous strip out of her space suit while floating in the air. But the title letters block the view. And the rest of the film is one big tease, as viewers try to glimpse parts of Fonda's anatomy and Vadim frustrates them. She's nude or seminude all right, but only when she is in long-shot (as when she crawls through her ship after having made love to Mark Hand) or when her back is turned (as when she speaks to the President on her ship's monitor), or when she's under Pygar's feathers or Durand-Durand's pleasure machine. True, both the kids' toothy dolls and the people-eating birds bite away at Barbarella's clothes, but predictably she's rescued before much damage is done. All the sex other than the hand-to-hand contact between Barbarella and Dildano is done offscreen, so the most erotic moment in the film turns out to be when Barbarella reaches under Pygar's loincloth and pulls out the gun hidden there. It's all tease, and *that* is the disappointing essence of Vadim. You leave the theater thinking you saw Fonda nude throughout, but after reflecting a bit, you aren't sure you saw her nude at all. That was also what happened after seeing Vadim's notorious Bardot films.

It was two years after Monica Vitti starred in *Modesty Blaise* (1966) that Vadim ventured into the pop-art world for his own sex fantasy, adapting *Barbarella* from Forest's incomprehensible comic strip. (The strip's about ten notches below *Playboy*'s "Little Annie Fanny," if that's possible.) Seven writers, including Forest, Vadim, and Terry Southern (who contributed two scenes) churned out an embarrassingly lame, unambitious script. Problems abound. For instance, having Dildano, Ping, and all the revolutionaries killed by Durand-Durand's Positronic Ray is out of tune with a picture

that for the first hour and a half seems not to take itself seriously. Moreover, their deaths make the potentially climactic revolution a dud. Certainly the relationship between Barbarella and the Black Queen should have more substance. Since they're not at each other's throats very often, perhaps they should be attracted to each other—that would give the picture needed spice. Vadim isn't averse to lesbian encounters: Annette Vadim and Elsa Martinelli are drawn to each other in his vampire film *Blood and Roses* (1961); ex-wife Bardot and Jane Birkin make love in the raw in *Don Juan* (1973). The one unforgivable problem with the picture is that Barbarella has little to do with what transpires. She may lift Pygar's spirits so he can fly, but otherwise she is a bystander, while the revolution takes place and while the Black Queen does in Durand-Durand, by releasing the mathmos. Some heroine! How terribly she compares to Val Lewton's damsels in distress who move the story along and also get themselves out of trouble.

This whole production (the much-publicized futuristic, erotically designed sets; music; dialogue; storyline; direction; special effects) lacks imagination. It's also full of examples of poor judgment, such as having Marcel Marceau do nothing but deliver dialogue—that's like hiring Olivier to do mime. Only the scene with the evil children and their spooky dolls—reminding one of the *Village of the Damned* (1960)—is the least bit exciting. But even here there is a problem. In this and other scenes, Vadim subjects his heroine to ghastly tortures while she is either nude or having her clothes ripped off. If this weren't such an innocuous film, feminists (like Jane Fonda) might want to complain that the director is trying to stimulate libidos by showing women subjected to physical abuse. At the very least this is irresponsible, and the Jane Fonda of later years makes certain that the content of her films is, above all else, responsible.

Basket Case

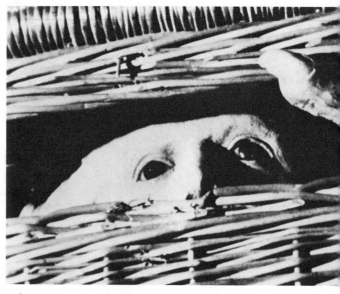

Belial peeks out of his mobile home.

1982 Analysis Releasing (Midnight bookings
were initially handled by Libra Films)
Director: Frank Henenlotter
Producer: Edgar Ievins
Screenplay: Frank Henenlotter
Cinematography: Bruce Torbet
Special effects: Kevin Haney and John Caglione
Music: Gus Russo
Editor: Frank Henenlotter
Running time: 93 minutes (the edited version is slightly shorter)

Cast: Kevin VanHententryck (Duane Bradley), Terri Susan Smith
(Sharon), Beverly Bonner (Casey), Lloyd Pace (Dr. Harold Needleman), Diana Browne (Dr. Judith Kutter), Robert Vogel (hotel
manager), Bill Freeman (Dr. Julius Lifflander), Joe Clarke (Brian
"Mickey" O'Donovan), Dorothy Strongin (Josephine), Ruth Neuman
(aunt), Richard Pierce (Mr. Bradley), Kerry Ruff (detective)

Synopsis: It's night in Glens Falls, New York. Dr. Julius Lifflander
knows someone is following him. He runs into his home and tries
to call the police. The line is cut. The lights go out. There are
strange sounds. He fires his gun at the shadows on his wall. A
grotesque hand grabs him. He is ripped apart.

Duane Bradley checks into a fleabag hotel in Manhattan. Brian
"Mickey" O'Donovan, drunk as usual, notices that Duane carries a
wad of money. Everyone notices he carries a wicker basket. Duane
secretly talks to the basket's occupant. Duane walks up to room
number 7, meeting Casey, a prostitute, and Josephine, a wacky
storyteller, on the way. He buys fast food and tosses it in the
basket. Whatever is in there gobbles it up. It communicates with
him telepathically.

Duane and his basket pay a visit to Dr. Needleman. Duane
takes off his shirt to reveal an enormous scar that covers his
right side. Needleman realizes that he operated on him when he
was a teen-ager. He becomes frightened. Duane is very taken with
the nurse Sharon. They make a date for the next day.

Duane falls asleep in a movie. A guy steals his basket and opens
it. His face is mangled. That night, Sharon leaves work. Needleman
is alone. Duane opens up his basket. The door to Needleman's
office is ripped off the hinges. Soon his body is ripped apart. By
Belial, a misshapen little semihuman creature with fangs and claws.

Duane has a date with Sharon. They kiss at the Statue of Liberty.
Back in the hotel room, Belial knows what's happening. He's
jealous. He tears apart the room. All the weird people from the
hotel investigate. They find nothing. O'Donovan steals Duane's
money and returns to his room. Belial, who can crawl on the
outside of the building, rips O'Donovan apart and retrieves the
money. Duane returns. He realizes Belial's jealousy provoked his
outburst. He tells Belial not to worry—they'll always be together.

They were born in Glens Falls. Siamese twins. Belial was attached to Duane's side. Their father considered Belial a monster
because his wife had died giving birth. He hired Needleman and Dr.
Judith Kutter to help family doctor Lifflander detach Belial. They
tossed Belial in a garbage bag. They thought he was dead, but he
survived and grew stronger. He killed the father. An aunt raised
Duane and Belial. Belial wanted revenge on the doctors.

There are more incidents in the hotel. Casey screams when she
sees Belial in her bed, reaching for her breast. But she is not hurt.

Belial and Duane visit Dr. Kutter. Belial rips her apart. She
screams when about ten scalpels wind up in her face.

That night while Duane dreams, Belial rapes the sleeping Sharon.
He tries to quiet her when she screams, maybe killing her. The
outraged Duane takes him back to the hotel. As the residents look
on, Belial grabs Duane's crotch. Duane screams. They fly out the
window. Belial hangs from the hotel sign. He holds Duane, but by
the neck. He can't help but strangle him. They fall to the pavement,
both dead.

I know. A lot of you turkeys didn't expect me to show.
I'm not what you call a *public* kind of guy. But this is
different. This is premiere night. This is one of the top 10
movies of the decade. This is sick and grotesque and hilarious.
This will totally gross out Cherry Dilday if I can con her into
going. We're talking classic cinema here. We're talking No. 1
on the Joe Bob Briggs Best of '82 Drive-In Movie list.

We're talking *Basket Case.*

—Joe Bob Briggs
Dallas Times Herald (7/9/82)

In the year of *E.T.*, Joe Bob Briggs, the refreshingly
irreverent guru of the drive-in crowd down in Texas, was
one of many critics talking up *B.C.*, a stunningly
creative little horror gem that provided a needed spark
to the Midnight Movie scene. Featuring the sensitive
psychotic Belial (B.C.), the most endearing movie "monster"
since *Mighty Joe Young* (1949) when he's not ripping people
apart, this surprisingly smooth mix of terror, strong violence
(which, except in one scene, will offend few), and quirky humor
("What's in the basket—Easter eggs?") was "the midnight
classic of the year!" according to *Heavy Metal;* "the sleeper
of the year!" according to *Heretic;* "the terror-cult sensation
of the year!" according to *Fangoria;* "a rare picnic for horror fans"
according to the *San Francisco Chronicle;* "the best of the year
so far" according to the *East Village Eye.* It got a particularly glowing review in the *Detroit Free Press:* "It's like *E.T.*,
as written and directed by a psychopath," wrote Diane
Haithman. "Admittedly, *Basket Case* is not for everyone—
but the fact that one horror film can be so different and so
much superior to another [*Halloween III*] goes to show that
even schlock horror fans are looking for more than blood.
They need a character they can love—even if he has to be
kept locked and chained in a wicker basket." Even Rex Reed,
who along with Joe Bob Briggs "discovered" *B.C.* at the
Cannes Festival of 1982, was impressed enough to declare it
"the sickest movie I've ever seen."

Basket Case was a joint venture by director-writer-editor Frank Henenlotter and producer Edgar Ievins, two Greenwich Village horror movie fanatics who, according to Ievins, simply "wanted to make a movie so we'd get money to make another movie." Previously Henenlotter had done a few 8 mm films for his own pleasure (*Son of Psycho, Lurid Women*); the closest he'd come to making something commercial was *Slash of the Knife,* a 16mm short that had the distinction of being considered too offensive to play as a companion piece to John Waters's *Pink Flamingos* (1972). Ievin's film experience had been limited to experimentation with stop-motion photography (one of *Basket Case*'s delights) and work on *Stalking the Wild Asparagus,* a project that was never completed. Together, Henenlotter and Ievins rounded up enough investors to finance a film called *Ooze.* But when that film was abandoned in the planning stages due to investors' fears it couldn't compete with similar Hollywood products, Henenlotter wrote *Basket Case,* a picture designed specifically for a shoestring budget.

I spoke to Ievins, who didn't want to reveal exactly how low the budget was until he had sold the film to cable. "I don't want them to say here's twenty-five bucks, now you've made a profit." Ievins did admit that filming had to be shut down six times when funds ran out, requiring frantic searches for additional investors. "Sometimes we'd arrive on the set with less than thirty minutes of film in the camera. So we'd do a lot of rehearsing because we couldn't have retakes. And we had to forget about *cover shots.*" Of course, they couldn't pay for studio space, so they went out on location, to Ievins's friends' houses in Glens Falls, New York, friends' lofts in New York City, and a welfare hotel in mid-Manhattan. (The hallway-stairs scenes are particularly fascinating.) "We can't mention the name of the hotel, because they threatened to sue if we did," says Ievins. "They were worried about the health board seeing footage." Henenlotter and Ievins would have liked to use 35 mm film, but that was impossible. Ievins: "We used 16 mm strictly because of economic factors. It was cheaper. Our theory was that if the picture was good enough, we'd get money to blow it up to 35 mm. Bruce Torbet, our cameraman, did a great job because he lit everything in such a way that it would look correct once blown up to 35 mm—which was different than lighting a 16 mm film that you don't expect to blow up. The film is grainy, but I'm happy to say it doesn't detract. Torbet, who hates horror movies and low-budget films, was our technical director-wonder. He made things work on bubble gum and Scotch tape, about the only resources we had."

Henenlotter and Ievins were also fortunate to hire Kevin Haney and John Caglione, protégés of Dick Smith, to do the special effects. They are quite remarkable: even when they look silly or cheap, they have charm. The very lifelike, misshapen Belial was made out of foam and latex. He looks a bit like Dick Smith's embryo in *Altered States* (1981). There were two full-bodied models, as well as the teen-age Belial, and there were a couple of pairs of his hands. Haney built the cable-operated version of Belial, Caglione the teen-age version, and both worked on the stop-motion model. Henenlotter did the stop-motion scenes himself. At no time can you see how Belial is operated (no visible wires, etc.), a fact which pleases the filmmakers considerably.

The picture took six months to shoot. It was sold to

Their lovemaking interrupted, Duane has a hard time keeping Sharon calm once Belial makes his presence known.

Analysis Releasing, which worked out a deal with Libra Films to handle Midnight bookings, a task it had done so well with *Eraserhead* (1980). But Analysis and Libra made a big mistake. They decided to trim the picture's violence, causing a furor among horror cultists who were waiting for the director's version they'd read such fine things about (in publications like *Fangoria* and *The Gore Gazette*). "Their decision to cut the film," reflects Ievins, "was admirable and in a way flattering. They wanted to reach the art house audience first. But whereas *Eraserhead* is an art film, *Basket Case* is a monster movie. It should have been geared for the horror-cult audience first. It must prove its worth with its target audience. You must deliver. You can't have a musical without songs. We needed violence. The thing that worried me was that audiences who saw the edited version were taking it so seriously. The cuts actually made the film more violent. The excessiveness of the violence is what made it cartoonish. People'd scream and then they'd laugh. It was a cathartic experience. It would loosen up the crowd to laugh at our silly jokes. The film we made was punctuated for horror. After the trimming, it was like having jokes without punchlines." *Basket Case* limped along in its edited version for several months before the deleted footage was restored in most cities. Almost immediately, attendance zoomed; and soon there were lines down the block (as all top Midnight Movies should have), and some repeat viewers could be seen carrying wicker baskets.

I saw the complete *Basket Case* at a Midnight showing at New York's Waverly Theater, the original Midnight home for both *The Rocky Horror Picture Show* (1975) and *Eraserhead.* The capacity audience was very young, less festive than found at *Rocky,* less apprehensive than found at *Eraserhead,* but equally curious. There were only a few repeat viewers. Some, including myself, were braced for the gore (after all, the picture is dedicated to Herschell Gordon Lewis), and most, including myself, didn't expect anything special, despite the rave reviews. In fifteen seconds of screen time—during which time Dr. Julius Lifflander finds himself trapped in his home

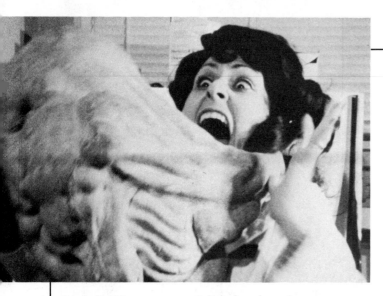

Dr. Judith Kutter reacts to Belial's brutal act of vengeance. This is the pose of all Belial's victims once his teeth and claws go to work.

by an unknown terror—the entire audience is laughing at Lifflander's situation and at the ridiculousness of his hysterical actions, while feeling some of his fear. A few more seconds pass. Lifflander backs against the wall, doomed. A hideous, deformed hand with clawlike fingers reaches up, grips his head, and pulls it down off the screen; blood shoots everywhere; the head reappears and Lifflander's face is a deeply gashed, bloody mess; the hand grabs it again. The entire audience cheers. No one was repulsed—and everyone was impressed with the nifty direction. Everyone, including myself, had been won over. And Ievins is correct: there is tremendous gore—what Belial does to Dr. Needleman, Dr. Kutter, and Brian "Mickey" O'Donovan is truly gruesome—but unlike other gore filmmakers (Herschell Lewis in particular), Henenlotter has made the gore effective enough to please "splatter" fans but at the same time made it so excessive that it's funny. It's great gore, but it's also peculiarly amusing. Importantly, it's not meant to gross viewers out.

What I find most impressive about *Basket Case* is that it never loses momentum. Scene after scene of this oddball story is interesting, well written for tension and humor, cleverly directed, and well acted. Adding to our enjoyment, Henenlotter has assembled one of the strangest groups of actors/characters to ever grace a horror film. Duane and Belial seem almost normal in a world of mad doctors and lowlifes of the type who occupy the Hotel Broslin (Josephine, O'Donovan, the clerk). The three positive influences on the twins are their kindly aunt (young Belial sits in her lap while she reads out loud), prostitute Casey (played by cult favorite Beverly Bonner), and Sharon—and even they are peculiar. "Terri had a tough assignment playing Sharon," says Ievins. "In a film filled with bozos, she had to play it so audiences could identify with her. Females like the scene where she accuses Duane of not visiting New York's tourist sites. In most films, it's the man putting the woman on the spot." Sharon's wig, which the audience I was with was quick to point out, makes her "look like a 1960s All American girl. Miss Iowa. The typical horror movie victim."

Kevin VanHententryck does a great job as Duane Bradley, sympathetic hick from upstate New York. I particularly like the scene where, drunk, he tells Casey the story of his youth (she, of course, doesn't believe his twin is in the wicker basket)—half laughing, half crying. He's not as funny as Terri Susan Smith or any of the hotel residents, but he makes an appealing lead. Of course, no one can match little Belial. There've been a lot of strange hotel/inn/boarding house boarders in horror movie history—Claude Rains in *The Invisible Man* (1933), Henry Hull in *The Werewolf of London* (1935), Laird Cregar's Jack the Ripper in *The Lodger* (1944), and Michael Rennie's alien in *The Day the Earth Stood Still* (1951) immediately come to mind—but none are as weird as "the very small, very twisted, and very mad tenant" (as the publicity sheets say) in room 7 of the Hotel Broslin. When he paces back and forth plotting his next crime, he reminds me of gangster Edward G. Robinson, cigar in mouth, pacing while plotting his next heist. "Belial has a personality," writes Diane Haithman. "Besides his annoying tendency to murder, he's jealous, sulky, possessive, witty—and he even can be grotesquely cute."

The filmmakers handle Belial quite interestingly. For one thing, as Ievins points out, "We make fun of everyone in the film, including Sharon in the reception room scene, but never do we make fun of our monster—he's treated more caringly than the humans." For almost the entire film, we sympathize with Belial because a great wrong was done to him in his youth. We don't mind his doing away with such despicable characters as Lifflander (almost called Pillsbury), Kutter, and Needleman, or even thief O'Donovan. After all, he has the good taste not to harm Casey, a decent person. Suddenly, in the film's most controversial scene—to which the audience I was with acted negatively ("How obligatory!")—he rapes (and possibly kills) Sharon. "This scene was not meant to be enjoyable," says Ievins. "It's meant to be disturbing and haunting. We knew that it had elements that would help make the film a success or limit the audience. Because it adds a new twist—the monster has gone *too* far. Everyone, even Duane, is outraged." Personally, I hate the recent trend which has nude women being raped by monsters—*Humanoids From the Deep* (1980) and *Forbidden World* (1982) are two offenders—and I think it's a big mistake to have had Belial rape Sharon. It's a mean thing to do to a nice character. The filmmakers' intentions may have been honorable, but there's *no* excuse for having a woman raped by a monster on the screen. I'm disturbed by the sight of him perched on her bloody crotch, moving up and down. This is one scene that could have been more subtle, that would have been helped by editing. When he was looking up toward his hotel window, I thought Belial had been contemplating suicide ("He's too much in control to kill himself," says Ievins). Better that than what he's really contemplating. At least, it's not clear that Sharon is killed: "We deliberately had her continue to breathe throughout," says Ievins. "We're guilty of not making her breathing more obvious."

So when Belial is hanging from the Hotel Broslin sign, both strangling and trying to save Duane ("Hey, are you okay up there?" asks a dimwitted hooker), our feelings toward the monster are ambivalent. The beast hurt the beauty, we rationalize, so he deserves to die. Still, he's such a pathetic creature. . . . As for the film, despite the rape, it deserves to play on the Midnight circuit for, as Ievins hopes, "ten years."

1954 United Artists release of a Romulus-Santana production*

Director: John Huston
Associate Producer: Jack Clayton
Screenplay: John Huston and Truman Capote
From the novel by James Helvick
Lighting Cameraman: Oswald Morris
Camera Operator: Freddie Francis
Music: Franco Mannino
Editor: Ralph Kemplen
Running Time: 92 minutes

Cast: Humphrey Bogart (Billy Dannreuther), Jennifer Jones (Gwendolyn Chelm), Gina Lollobrigida (Maria Dannreuther), Robert Morley (Petersen), Peter Lorre (O'Hara), Edward Underdown (Harry Chelm), Ivor Bernard (Major Ross), Bernard Lee (C.I.D. Inspector), Marco Tulli (Ravello), Mario Perroni (Purser), Aldo Silvani (Charles), Saro Urzi (Captain), Juan De Landa (Hispano-Suiza driver), Manuel Serano (Arab officer)

Synopsis: Peterson, O'Hara, Ravello, and Major Ross shuffle off to prison. Their great caper has failed. Six months before, they were waiting in a small Mediterranean seaport for passage to Africa to pull off a land swindle and acquire uranium deposits. American Billy Dannreuther was arranging the deal. He needed the money. He suspected Petersen had Nazi Major Ross assassinate Paul Vanmeer, a colonial officer who was aware of the swindle, and he worried that Petersen would double-cross him and kill him.

While waiting for the *Nyanga* to sail, Billy and his Italian wife, Maria, became acquainted with British passengers Gwendolyn and Harry Chelm, who were going to Africa to live on a coffee plantation. Anglophile Maria loved Billy but fantasized about running away with Harry, who falsely appeared to be a man of wealth and position. Meanwhile, Gwendolyn was excited by Billy, and the two carried on a mild flirtation. O'Hara overheard Gwendolyn say that Harry was wealthy and was going to Africa to invest in land that contained uranium. Billy realized Gwendolyn was a habitual liar, but O'Hara believed what he heard and reported back to Petersen. Thinking Billy would double-cross him with Harry, Petersen insisted he and Billy fly immediately to Africa. However, on the way to the airport there was a car crash.

Everyone thought Billy and Petersen were killed. Gwendolyn told Harry she had loved Billy. While O'Hara tried to convince the weeping Maria that she should take Billy's place in the venture, Ravello revealed the swindle scheme to Harry, hoping he'd put up the money. But then Billy and Petersen returned.

The *Nyanga* sailed. Petersen stole Harry's dispatch case to see if Billy had told the truth when he said Harry had no wealth. He unhappily discovered Billy was correct. Harry became furious at the thievery and swore to tell authorities about the land swindle. Maria unsuccessfully tried to seduce him to get him to reconsider. Then Major Ross tried to kill him but Billy prevented it. Gwendolyn had Harry locked up for his own good, but he slipped overboard.

The *Nyanga* broke down and Billy, Maria, Gwendolyn, Petersen, O'Hara, Ravello, and Ross rowed a small boat to the African shore. They were arrested by an Arab dictator who demanded to know why they were there. Before the dictator could torture Petersen and find out about the swindle, Billy got the Arab to release them. Petersen paid the Arab money, and Billy promised to introduce him to his friend Rita Hayworth.

Back in the small Mediterranean town, a colonial inspector asked them questions about Paul Vanmeer. Just when Petersen thought he had convinced the inspector of his innocence, Gwendolyn revealed the truth. Petersen, O'Hara, Ravello, and Major Ross go to prison.

Billy and Maria, still without money, are happily back together. A telegram from Harry cheers the grieving Gwendolyn. He has bought the land with the uranium deposits.

Beat the Devil is often regarded as a British film. Location filming was done in Italy with an American-British-Italian crew; studio work was done in London at Shepperton Studios. It was released by Independent Film Distributors (in association with British Lion) in a 100-minute version in England on November 24, 1953, almost four months before it played in New York.

Beat the Devil

The remarkable fascination of *Beat the Devil,* certainly the fifties' most peculiar A-budget film, has as much to do with its background as with its zany characters, performances, and tone. How James Helvick's novel made it to the screen is part of the film's legend; fittingly, there are many versions of the story. According to most sources, Humphrey Bogart happened upon the book while searching for a project along the lines of *The Maltese Falcon* (1941). I assume he sensed its potential for being adapted into a straight but witty film, full of adventure, danger, and romance. Again he could play a tough, morally ambiguous hero who sidesteps his way through a corrupt world of greedy, double-dealing rogues, outrageous flirts, and pathological liars. Since old pal John Huston wrote and directed *Falcon,* naturally Bogart sent him the book. When Huston agreed to both write and direct the film, Bogart gave the go-ahead to the project, which would ultimately cost his production company Santana about half of the $1 million budget. Bogart then went off to make a couple of films with director Richard Brooks, while Huston tried to hammer out a script with Peter Viertel and Anthony Veiller, with whom he'd worked before.

It is likely, however, that events happened in a slightly different manner. For instance, it's probable that it was Huston who initiated the project. As stated in Joe Hyams's *Bogie* (New American Library, 1967), Huston was living in Ireland at the time, James Helvick was his neighbor, and Helvick was in great need of money. Realizing he couldn't afford to

The film opens with the villains already in custody and grumpy: O'Hara and Ravello march behind Major Ross and Petersen.

Neither Bogart's Sam Spade nor Philip Marlowe would dress like his Billy Dannreuther as he lazes with Maria on their hotel balcony, the Mediterranean in the background.

finance the filming of his friend's book, Huston sent Bogart a copy in a successful attempt to get him to put up the money. Moreover, Helvick was paid to be the original script collaborator with Huston. It was only when Helvick proved unsuitable that Huston put loyalty aside and hired veterans Viertel and Veiller. Only they didn't do any better. After three months, which Huston spent in Ireland, Viertel in Switzerland, and Veiller in Venice, the Huston-Viertel-Veiller script arrived at Bogart's home in America. His oft-quoted reaction: "It stinks." Huston couldn't deny it. Then either Huston or Bogart, depending on which source one trusts, wanted to call off the film but the other convinced him to stick with it. After all, production was already set to begin in Italy, script or no script.

It is not clear whether location filming was originally intended to take place in Rome, where Huston resided for a time, or if Ravello was set from the beginning, but soon cast and crew (including Italians who never would understand Huston's directions) assembled in this small coast town. Panic set in again and Huston and Bogart, worrying that their small black-and-white film couldn't compete with the lavish spectacles and gimmicky productions being churned out back in Hollywood, contemplated ordering a 3-D lens from America—but sense prevailed for a minute or two and that idea was scrapped. Getting a scriptwriter was a more pressing need. Luckily, Huston obtained the service of twenty-eight-year-old Truman Capote, who happened to be in Rome and available. Huston always took credit for his "brainstorm" in hiring Capote, but David O. Selznick, who had given up pleading with Huston to abandon the project because he thought it might damage Jennifer Jones's career, is the one who deserves credit. *Memo From David O. Selznick* (Viking, 1972) includes a cable he sent Huston in Rome on January 30, 1953; it reads in part:

> Once again, I do urge you to consider calling in Capote. . . . I know of very few writers other than Capote whose work is of the sort that I know would appeal to you. He can also be quite fast, but only if he is whipped every day. . . . Also, he is easy to work with, needing only to be stepped on good-naturedly, like the wonderful but bad little boy he is, when he starts to whine.

Selznick was correct about Capote's originality; not long after he joined the project, he proceeded to change *Beat the Devil.*

with Huston's blessing, from a straightforward adventure tale into a sly, one-of-a-kind spoof of all international intrigue pictures.

Capote was to begin rewriting the Viertel-Veiller script the day he arrived in Ravello, which may have corresponded to the day shooting was set to begin. However, production was held up several days due to a nearly fatal car accident involving Huston and Bogart, who bit through his tongue and loosened several teeth. A bit later Capote replaced him in the hospital, victim of an abscessed tooth that made his face swell up hideously. But he kept writing through the pain and confinement, earning him the respect of Huston. He also won over Bogart by defeating him in an impromptu wrestling match during one of their many drunken nights together. For the entire shooting period, Capote and Huston wrote scenes at night that were to be shot the next morning. Not told of the picture's switch in tone, the cast was understandably confused by what was expected of them. One actor would play a scene as comedy, another actor would be serious. Still this didn't affect Gina Lollobrigida, who, as critic David Shipman points out, *always* "switched from comedy to drama without varying her approach." What did trouble her was learning her lines phonetically for the picture she hoped would make her a big star in America.

When Huston promoted *Beat the Devil,* he warned critics and ticket buyers "that its greatest risk is in someone's considering it important. You can't get more trivial." But the majority of critics didn't care what he had to say and vigorously complained that it was self-indulgent and frivolous. Exhibitors were not keen on the picture either. A theater owner in Sault Ste. Marie, Michigan, took out an ad which began:

> Personally if you don't see this picture you are not missing much. The picture at the Temple did not come up to our expectations, we would like to discontinue it, but are forced to play it until Wednesday. Please accept our apologies.

As it turned out, most people, including Bogart (who had enjoyed making the picture but didn't like seeing his large investment go down the drain) detested *Beat the Devil.* It did exceptionally poor business. However, immediately and unexpectedly, a coterie rallied behind it and it became known as "a cult film" long before that term became fashionable. In fact, this was several years before the Bogart cult was established in France, upon the release of *Breathless* (1961), with its Bogart-idolizing Jean-Paul Belmondo character, and in Cambridge, Massachusetts, when *Casablanca* (1942) began turning up regularly at the Brattle Theater.

When United Artists rereleased *Beat the Devil* in 1964, at the height of the Bogart revival, it used the slogan "the picture that was ten years ahead of its time." In truth, American films have never caught up with *Beat the Devil.* It has a distinctly Continental flavor: open air cafés, villas, balconies that look over town squares, hotel rooms warmed by sea breezes, statues along Mediterranean cliffs, characters lounging in house robes, and most important, characters with manners (bad manners perhaps, but manners nevertheless). The emotional, involved, chatty people in this film could mingle easily with those in a Jean Renoir film, particularly *Rules of the Game* (1939). Whatever their failings and degrees of pomposity, they believe in living life to its fullest.

Appropriately, this offbeat film opens with a band playing slightly off key—a musical metaphor for what will come. Looking humiliated in their handcuffs, cutthroats Petersen, O'Hara, Major Ross ("the Galloping Major"), and Ravello (obviously named after the town) shuffle past. Six months before, and at first sight, Gwendolyn realized that they were "desperate characters" ("Not one looked at my legs") and a disparate group as well. Indeed, the key to much of the film's humor is that the various characters involved are a mismatched conglomeration, a motley group who somehow have gotten thrown into the same adventure. They come in all shapes and sizes, have strong accents that betray their varied nationalities, and have conflicting personalities. It makes even less sense that the dignified Petersen pals around with wild Nazi assassin Major Ross than it did that Gutman (Sydney Greenstreet) became surrogate father to Wilbur (Elisha Cook, Jr.) in *The Maltese Falcon*. Even the married couples don't seem to belong together: the imaginative Gwendolyn and the dullard Harry; the emotional Maria and the glib,

The Nyanga *has broken down, so Billy rows toward the African shore. Once smitten with Billy, Gwendolyn is now fed up with him and longs for her missing husband, Harry.*

The other prisoners watch Petersen get into hotter water by lying to and accidentally insulting the African dictator.

laid-back Billy. And the individual characters conflict with the established film personae of the performers who play them. What's Bogart, for instance, doing in a fancy robe and ascot instead of a trenchcoat? What's the former Duke Mantee, Dr. X, Mad Dog Earle, Sam Spade, and Philip Marlowe doing playing a non-man-of-action named Billy? And why have Bogart and Bacall given way to Bogart and . . . Lollobrigida? (Actually, they make a splendid team—as do Bogart and Jennifer Jones.) In fact, what's he doing playing a *married* man? Then there's Jennifer Jones, once the sainted Bernadette but now a compulsive liar (on par with *Falcon*'s champion deceiver Brigid O'Shaughnessy). Wearing a blond wig (!), gabbing nonstop, flirting with Billy, knitting, exercising (while Maria paints), Jones turns in a bravura performance that equals her only other comic role of note in Ernst Lubitsch's *Cluny Brown* (1946). Jones's characters almost always were driven by their hearts and libidos, but Gwendolyn Chelm (what a name for a romantic lead) is activated by her fertile mind. Peter Lorre is also blond in this film, and since it was made during one of his many plump periods, he looks amazingly like Truman Capote! The best of all character actors, he was always a delightfully fussy companion to rotund Sydney Greenstreet, who played characters who enjoyed good conversation; and here, as a probable Nazi war criminal who insists his name is O'Hara, Lorre works well with the Humpty-Dumpty-like Robert Morley, who plays, as usual, a man who likes to hear *himself* talk. The bad guys are a silly lot, whether trying to close an overstuffed suitcase, bad-mouthing Billy behind his back, or marching across the deck of the *Nyanga* while singing "Blow the Man Down" and deeply inhaling what Petersen calls "Neptune's mixture." "Good morning, Mrs. Chelm!" the smiling Petersen calls when he spots her exercising on the upper deck; then he turns to his three cohorts and snaps "Let's hope she breaks her neck." A fun group.

The four bad guys—Petersen and his cohorts—want wealth and power, which obviously have always avoided such losers.

Only by purchasing the African land that contains uranium deposits can they hope to realize their dream—but they might as well go after the Maltese falcon, considering how little chance *they* have of accomplishing anything. What the four "good" people—Billy, Harry, Gwendolyn, and Maria—have in common with Petersen and his accomplices is that they too are dissatisfied with their present lives and desire something better. With a straight face, Billy tells Gwendolyn he wants wealth so he won't be dull, listless, and have a bad complexion—yet he's a good loser (as most Bogart characters are) when Harry sneakily buys the land with uranium. He likes a good joke even if it's on him. Harry wants to be considered the aristocrat he pretends to be—yet he's willing to switch places with Billy, whom he called "a middle-aged roustabout," and pull off the uranium swindle to make big bucks. Gwendolyn wants the exciting Billy—yet she ends up with her dull, yet more gallant, husband ("I wouldn't marry a ninny") and couldn't be happier. On the other hand, Anglophile Maria ("Emotionally I'm English") is impressed by the sophisticated Englishman Harry and bored with American Billy—but she also comes to her senses and returns to Billy's reliable arms and a life of chance. As in most Huston films, characters fail at their missions, yet they accomplish a great deal in another direction and reach some sort of fulfillment.

Billy, Maria, Harry, and Gwendolyn treat each other's infidelities so lightly that it seems unlikely that anything could shake them up. Yet these and all characters in the film are time and again stunned by other characters' actions. Repeatedly, the humor comes from characters doing double takes or becoming speechless in reaction to what other characters are saying or doing: Billy and Maria are bemused into silence by O'Hara, who endlessly philosophizes about nothing; Harry is shocked by crazy Major Ross's pro-Hitler diatribe; Petersen is flabbergasted when Gwendolyn tells him how Harry is going to Africa to learn about *sin*; Harry can't believe Gwendolyn telling everyone on the *Nyanga* that he has mental problems, etc.

Beat the Devil is filled with many more delectable moments between the wonderfully attitudinizing characters. Still, on the whole, I am not as taken with the picture as those who lionize it. Although its cultists would surely argue against it, I'd prefer a little more coherence, especially in regard to the uranium-deal subplot. I'd also like a few more exciting moments like the one when we, Billy, and Gwendolyn think Major Ross sits at a playing player piano when he's elsewhere trying to murder Harry. This is a creepy bit worthy of Eric Ambler or Graham Greene. Billy's laughter at the end ("This is the *end*," he cackles as he reads Harry's telegram—and not "If this doesn't beat the devil!" as was originally intended) is reminiscent of Walter Huston's laughter at the end of the John Huston-directed *The Treasure of the Sierra Madre* (1948). Here it implies that *Beat the Devil* is an in-joke between those who made this "lark" (Huston's term) and those who accept it in the spirit in which it was made. I certainly accept its geniality and forgive its self-indulgence because somehow it's not pretentious. But I can't help wishing it were something more, and not as trivial as Huston wanted. Still it's so disarming and so popular with film connoisseurs that I sometimes worry if it's one of those films that's better than I think.

Bedazzled

1967   Great Britain 20th Century-Fox
Director: Stanley Donen
Producer: Stanley Donen
Screenplay: Peter Cook
From an idea by Peter Cook and Dudley Moore
Cinematography: Austin Dempster
Music: Dudley Moore
Editor: Richard Marden
Running time: 107 minutes

Cast: Peter Cook (George Spiggott, a.k.a. the devil), Dudley Moore (Stanley Moon), Eleanor Bron (Margaret Spencer), Raquel Welch (Lilian Lust), Michael Bates (Inspector Clarke), Howard Goorney (Sloth)

Synopsis: Diminutive Stanley Moon is a short-order cook in a London Wimpy's. He loves waitress Margaret Spencer but is too shy to tell her so. Disconsolate because his prayers for help with his romance have gone unanswered, Stanley sends Margaret a suicide note and attempts to hang himself. He is interrupted by George Spiggott, a dapper man who proves to the flabbergasted Stanley that he is the devil. Stanley accompanies George to his scandalous Rendezvous Club in Soho, where he meets the Seven Deadly Sins and watches George perform mischief. George admits that in these nonheroic times he has lost his spark. Stanley agrees to sell George his soul if he will help him win Margaret. George will grant him seven wishes.

Stanley is turned into an articulate intellectual. He invites Margaret to his pad, where they discuss art and music and how much they both like to feel things. Stanley takes Margaret's hint and puts his arms around her. She screams for help.

Next, Stanley becomes a wealthy tycoon who lavishes priceless presents upon his wife Margaret. Only she is more excited by the physical advances of a young stud.

When Stanley is awakened by Lust, who curls up in his bed, he asks George to make him irresistible to women. He becomes a pop singer whom Margaret and other screaming women idolize. However, when Dremble Wedge (who looks like George) and the Vegetation start singing, Stanley is soon forgotten by the fans.

Stanley wants to be a fly on the wall in order to hear all Margaret is saying about him. She speaks fondly of him to the inspector who is investigating Stanley's disappearance. When the inspector asks her for a date, Stanley buzzes him. The inspector sprays him and he falls to the floor. George, also a fly, rescues Stanley.

Stanley's next wish is that Margaret love him, be at home in the kitchen, and be the mother of two children. Unfortunately, it turns out that Margaret is married to Stanley's best friend, who looks like George. Because her husband is such a wonderful man, Stanley and Margaret find it impossible to cheat on him. She calls off their affair.

Finally, Stanley asks that he and Margaret both become warm, loving, and outgoing. They are transformed into nuns of the Order of Leaping Berelians.

George tells Stanley that he will return his soul in hopes that this gesture will earn George entry into heaven. However, God refuses George because he broke his contract with Stanley for selfish reasons. George asks Stanley to temporarily sign a new contract; then he can let him have his soul back for better reasons. Realizing that George has never fully delivered on his promises, Stanley refuses. He decides to approach Margaret without the devil's help. George will stick around to tempt him.

George tells God that he'll make the world so noisy and disgusting that "even you'll be ashamed of yourself." God laughs and laughs.

F redric Brown's classic horror anthology *Honeymoon in Hell* (Bantam, 1958) contains a delightfully diabolical one-page story called *Millennium.* Conducting his daily one-wish-for-one-soul bartering, Satan becomes wary when a kindly looking little man enters his chamber. Could this be the person he had hoped, maybe even prayed, would never come? The one in billions who would make the Ultimate Wish, the ultimate, *unselfish* wish that would doom the devil to a thousand years in chains and put him out of business for eternity? Since the chance of this being that person is so slim, Satan agrees to accept the man's soul and then contemptuously asks what deed was desired from him in return. The scared little man says: "Well . . . I wish that, without any change whatsoever in myself, I become the most evil, stupid, and miserable person on earth." Satan screams. End story.

The devil should certainly worry about making transactions with the likes of Brown's altruist or, say, Mother Teresa, but Stanley Moon isn't the type who could cause problems. This simpleton is not capable of making a wish as creative as Brown's hero; and anyway he is so flawed to begin with (and later so corrupt that he begins to enjoy some of the devil's misdeeds) that even if he makes that ultimate, unselfish wish there is no guarantee a saintly population would result. Still, I was hoping that by the end of *Bedazzled*, Dudley Moore and Peter Cook's Faust tale in mod clothing, Stanley would wise up to the fact that a pact with the devil is a losing proposition and make an unselfish wish that would send the devil, a.k.a. George Spiggott, off screaming in defeat. As it turns out, Stanley comes closer than one might expect: "I want to be a warm, loving, outgoing person and Margaret the same." Unfortunately, an inferiority complex (which the devil surely knows keeps 99.99 percent of the people on earth from having their foremost wish be unselfish) prevents Stanley from requesting that the rest of mankind become even more warm, loving, and outgoing than he; instead he asks more for himself: to be young,

Publicity shot. Stanley, a millionaire in this wish-fantasy, is angered that his wife is affectionate with everyone (including his best friend) except him.

George illustrates how God liked to sit around while those He considered beneath Him were, literally, beneath Him, singing endless praises.

white (??), and in perfect health. Appropriately responding to Stanley's selfishness, George devilishly tricks Stanley for the umpteenth time, making both Stanley and Margaret nuns in the Order of Leaping Berelians.

As usual, Stanley has fallen into the devil's trap. This isn't surprising because his main objective is not to outwit the devil—which is exactly what Brown's hero intended. Like Dudley Moore's other "little men"—in *30 Is a Dangerous Age, Cynthia* (1967), *10* (1979), and *Arthur* (1981)—all he cares about is winning the woman he idealizes, so he's unprepared for the devil's ambushes. *Bedazzled* is a comedy, but its point is serious: in a world seemingly abandoned by God, man wants the devil to exist; man does not trust himself having free will and free choice. Happily, Stanley finally turns down the devil's offer to help him further in his romantic conquest of Margaret, and makes his own feeble effort to win her heart. Stanley never decides to defeat the devil, but at least he resists temptation. He had learned the priceless lesson that the devil, for no reason other than to be mean, will not grant wishes that will work out. As Takashi Shimura realizes in Akira Kurosawa's *Ikiru* (1952), the best Faust variation on film, a person's own actions are what provide fulfillment in life; that which is provided by those who have ulterior motives *never* meets expectations. Stanley has figured out that the devil's greatest pleasure is to build up one's expectations—he once told Stanley that Stanley's great-great-great-grandfather left one million pounds—and then let the person down with a thud—he next told Stanley, who had thought he was a wealthy heir, that Stanley's relatives had frittered away the fortune and there was nothing left. George would be a great carnival barker: he could certainly get the curious to pay to see what's inside the tent.

There really is no need to defeat or destroy the devil found in this film. He's not such a bad sort, and is certainly a more lenient devil than the world deserves. By no means is he as obnoxious or self-impressed as George Burns's God in *Oh, God!* (1977) and, especially, in *Oh, God! Book Two* (1980). As played by Peter Cook in Carnaby Street cape and Ben Franklin glasses, he has his own aggravations and insecurities—we even sympathize with him because God's treatment of him seems unjust. He is also clever and charming, and at times (almost) compassionate. He even feels guilty over some of his more spiteful tricks. His so-called crimes against humanity, like ripping out the last page of Agatha Christie mysteries, scratching record albums, making grocery bags tear open, setting wasps loose on picnickers, and calling up women and revealing to them their husbands' infidelities, are more worthy of a fraternity prankster than Satan. So we can forgive him—especially since he proves to be the best friend Stanley ever had. In fact, he serves Stanley the same way Dan Ackroyd does John Belushi in *Neighbors* (1981): he causes him untold aggravation yet simultaneously gives him the first breath of life, of excitement, he has ever enjoyed. He lets Stanley have the chance to be, in turn, articulate, rich, a pop singer women lust after, a fly on the wall who can spy on Margaret, someone Margaret loves desperately, and that warm, loving, outgoing person—and then he lets Stanley out of the

Raquel Welch, on her way to superstardom, plays Lilian Lust, who tempts Stanley with her bust.

contract, meaning Stanley got a free ride. Never mind that Stanley didn't get exactly what he desired when the devil granted him these experiences. Even considering the devil's trickery, I'd bet Stanley's glad he went through what he did.

Because of the success of James Bond and the Beatles, America imported a great amount of British product from the midsixties to the early seventies. Spy films, Hammer horror films, lumbering epics, lightweight comedies. There were Vanessa Redgrave and Julie Christie; there were also Judy Geeson, Lulu, Linda Hayden, and Susan George. Blond women in their late teens and early twenties who wore miniskirts and were full of pep. And when they weren't making romance, they always seemed to be shopping or climbing on and off buses while the soundtrack blared with dreadful music, obviously composed by admirers of Herb Alpert, the 1910 Fruitgum Company, and Dave Clark Five instrumentals. Their mismatched lovers were eccentrics or losers or window washers or spoiled rich boys who must prove themselves worthy to win these women they adore. Stylistically, the worst comedies were characterized by that bad music, too-fast editing, and an inordinate amount of jump cuts, à la the French New Wave but without rhyme or reason.

Bedazzled has become dated, but when it was released we considered it unique among the British imports, and much better than the other comedies that made it to America at that time. It combined the absurdity and breezy style of the Richard Lester films that were extremely popular in America

Margaret donates money to George's worthy cause: the National Society for the Promotion of Depraved Criminals.

in the sixties; the mixture of ridiculousness and sophistication of the early Peter Sellers/Alec Guinness/Ian Carmichael/Alastair Sim films; the verbal outrageousness and slapstick of the later Peter Sellers; the lowbrow comedy of the *Carry On* series; and, of course, the irreverent satire and parody of *Beyond the Fringe,* the revue that had a long run in London and on Broadway and made Americans aware of Dudley Moore, Peter Cook, and (in a small role) Eleanor Bron. The film's not all that funny, but as Andrew Sarris wrote,

> If *Bedazzled* does indeed need a defense, it must be recorded that there is more than a little exhilaration in the spectacle of clever people saying and doing whatever comes to mind without fear of pressure groups or the philistinism of the masses. Mere cleverness is not necessarily enough for the screen but it does deserve recognition and encouragement in this difficult period of transition.

For those not curious to see the scantily clad Raquel Welch gyrating in Stanley's arms—playing Lilian Lust, "the Babe with the Bust," during the era before she proved "I'm an actress"—the delight in seeing *Bedazzled* is to catch a nostalgic glimpse of the once-wonderful comedy team of Peter Cook and Dudley Moore. They don't do much visual comedy (what there is, however, is unexpectedly wild), but much of their verbal repartee is brilliant. Much humor in *Bedazzled* comes not from what they say but how they say it; how adeptly they change voice nuances and intonations and conversational mannerisms as their characters move from class to class. As a team they can drawl like lazy-lipped British aristocrats or banter like ex-burlesque comics Abbott and Costello (C: I'm not mad, my brother's mad./A: Who told you?/C: My brother.):

STANLEY: You're a nut case.
GEORGE: They said the same of Jesus, Galileo . . .
STANLEY: They said the same of a lot of nut cases, too.

Such moments are delightful. Unfortunately, the majority of the comic vignettes, which were strung together (and directed a bit too casually by Hollywood vet Stanley Donen) as if they were part of a revue, aren't particularly clever. I'd say the Moore-Bron dialogues are more on the quality level of Stiller and Meara than, as they should be, Nichols and May—although when Stanley and Margaret discuss Brahms in Stanley's hip room ("This room is you!" she tells him) it recalls the famous Nichols and May "Bach to Bach" skit. The only routine I find thoroughly witty is the one by Stanley and Margaret when they feel too guilty to cheat on her husband, his best friend, because he's such a wonderful man ("He's an example to us all," weeps Stanley. "It would kill him if he knew," weeps Margaret). But all the sequences have their moments: the articulate Stanley pretentiously discusses "the fruitlike qualities of the French horn"; during an insufferable billiards game, a stuttering old man takes forever to spout out an incomprehensible opinion on world politics, whereupon Cook says, "That's very easy for *you* to say" (variations on this gag have turned up in many films since); Cook's Dremble Wedge, a New Waver ahead of his time, wins fans by emotionlessly singing "I don't care, I don't want you, I don't love you, leave me alone"; nuns scrub the grass of their monastery and do flips on trampolines.

Nuns aren't the only once-sacred targets of Cook and Moore's provocative satire. They also shoot down vicars ("He's one of ours," declares the devil); the English police ("I have mixed feelings about rape," shrugs Inspector Clarke); the British upper class; the prime minister; Lyndon Johnson; and even Julie Andrews. But what's most remarkable is that God receives such harsh treatment. In the opening scene, we realize that God has long stopped bothering to answer prayers of the common man, and allows the devil to intercept messages directed to him. We learn from George that God has a "God complex" and enjoys his power: he insists that his angels sit around admiring him, dance around him, and continuously sing his praises. We can understand why George wanted "to change places" with God, which resulted in his being cast from heaven. God will only be good, George contends, "when people make the choice between good and evil"; since George believes people will never make this choice, we must conclude that God will never be good. We finally meet God when George requests reinstatement in heaven, and we come to agree with George that God is a tyrant. (He doesn't even allow people to undress in privacy.) It may be George who makes the vicious threat at film's end, but it's God who comes off second best in George's statement: "I will make the world so noisy and disgusting that even *you* will be ashamed of yourself!" (What we have are two spiteful characters whose petty feud causes misery among mortals.) God's heinous laugh in response to the threat is unnerving— it's a laugh most of us would associate with Satan. Considering that *Bedazzled* came out not long after John Lennon was forced to publicly retract his "The Beatles are more popular than Jesus" remark in order to stop a boycott of Beatles records on many U.S. radio stations, as well as organized Nazi-like burnings of Beatles records and magazines, it's amazing Moore and Cook attempted and got away with using material I'm sure many people considered blasphemous.

Perhaps the highlight of the film and its most tasteless moment: Margaret, Stanley, and George are nuns of the Order of Leaping Berelians, about to do somersaults on a trampoline.

1953 Columbia
Director: Fritz Lang
Producer: Robert Arthur
Screenplay: Sydney Boehm
From a book by William P. McGivern

Cinematography: Charles Lang
Music: Mischa Bakaleinikoff
Editor: Charles Nelson
Running time: 89 minutes

The Big Heat

Cast: Glenn Ford (Dave Bannion), Gloria Grahame (Debby Marsh), Jocelyn Brando (Katie Bannion), Alexander Scourby (Mike Lagana), Lee Marvin (Vince Stone), Jeanette Nolan (Bertha Duncan), Peter Whitney (Tierney), Willis Bouchey (Lt. Wilkes), Robert Burton (Gus Burke), Adam Williams (Larry Gordon), Howard Wendell (Commissioner Higgins), Chris Alcaide (George Rose), Michael Granger (Hugo), Dorothy Green (Lucy Chapman), Carolyn Jones (Doris), Ric Roman (Baldy), Dan Seymour (Atkins), Edith Evanson (Selma Parker)

Synopsis: Policeman Tom Duncan commits suicide. His widow Bertha reads a letter he wrote and calls Mike Lagana, the man who runs the town.

Bertha tells homicide detective Dave Bannion that her husband killed himself because of ill health, that he had been an honest cop. Bannion believes her. But then barfly Lucy Chapman says that Duncan wasn't sick, that he was about to divorce his wife to marry her. Lucy says she will talk to reporters. Now suspicious, Bannion questions Bertha again, asking how Duncan could afford a second house in Lakeside. She becomes furious. When Lucy Chapman is tortured and killed, Lieutenant Wilkes tells Bannion to stay off the case. He has gotten orders from high up.

Nevertheless, Bannion questions Tierney, the bartender at the Retreat, where he had talked to Lucy. Bannion sees him make a phone call afterward. That night, Bannion's wife Katie picks up the phone and hears obscene words directed at her by an unknown person. Bannion takes the phone and listens to the man threaten him. He is told to drop out of the case because important people are involved.

Bannion is so incensed he goes to Lagana's mansion, realizing that Lagana directs all shady business in town, although he is considered an important civic leader. He threatens Lagana to leave his wife alone, and beats up Lagana's bodyguard when he tries to throw him out. Katie tells Bannion not to back down from the case.

Katie goes to get a babysitter for daughter Joyce. A bomb explodes in Bannion's car and she is killed. His life ruined, Bannion asks friends Al and Marge to look after Joyce. He sells the house and moves to a hotel. When Wilkes and Commissioner Higgins won't help solve Katie's murder, Bannion resigns from the force to investigate on his own. Off the record, Wilkes offers help, as does Bannion's partner Gus. Bannion trusts no one.

At the Retreat, Bannion confronts Vince, Lagana's righthand man. Vince flees. His moll Debby Marsh tries to be friendly to Bannion, but he is cold to everyone.

When Vince finds out Debby talked to Bannion, he throws hot coffee in her face. Realizing she will be killed, she goes to Bannion's hotel. He is friendlier this time but won't speak of Katie to her when she asks.

With the help of Selma Parker, who works for a man on Lagana's payroll, Bannion tracks down Larry, the man Lagana hired to help Vince kill Lucy. He also planted the bomb that killed Katie. Bannion puts the word out that Larry squealed—Larry is killed trying to leave town.

Lagana decides to kidnap Joyce. He has the corrupt commissioner order the police detail away from Al's apartment building. But Al's army buddies and Wilkes and Gus make entry by Lagana's men impossible.

Wanting to help Bannion, and afraid he will kill Bertha and be arrested for murder, Debby shoots Bertha. Upon her death, Duncan's letter will now be mailed, revealing Lagana's corrupt practices.

Debby goes to Vince's apartment. She throws hot coffee in his face. He shoots her. Bannion captures him, but does not kill him. Wilkes arrests him. Debby's friendship and sacrifice have had a profound effect on Bannion. He no longer feels blind hate. As Debby dies, he tells her about Katie.

With Lagana, Vince, and Commissioner Higgins in jail, Bannion returns to his job on the force.

Estes Kefauver's historic congressional hearings on organized crime, which were televised live on a daily basis by NBC and CBS in March 1951, educated a naïve American public about the staggering sphere of influence maintained by underworld kingpins like Frank Costello. They also made the public hungry for stories, factual and fictional, about conspiratorial alliances between ganglords/racketeers—who invariably had become respected civic leaders—and politicians/law enforcers/labor. As a result there was a wave of exposé films, among them Robert Wise's *The Captive City* (1952), Phil Karlson's *Kansas City Confidential* (1952), Karlson's prototypical *Phenix City Story* (1955), Karlson's *Tight Spot* (1955), *New Orleans Uncensored* (1955), *Miami Exposé* (1955), *Slaughter on Tenth Avenue* (1957), *Chicago Confidential* (1957), *New York Confidential* (1957), and *The Case Against Brooklyn* (1958). Like Robert Aldrich's *Kiss Me, Deadly* (1955), Fritz Lang's *The Big Heat* is a transitional film that links the hard-hitting exposé films of the fifties (which were foreshadowed in 1948 by Abraham Polonsky's *Force of Evil*) and film noir, the dominant style of forties melodrama. True, Lang's film doesn't have the entangled relationships, the femme fatale who leads an unsuspecting hero down the wayward path, or the low-key photography that were hallmarks of film noir. But while it coolly surveys the all-inclusive political/police corruption of a small city, it is equally concerned with the corruption of a decent man's soul. This is pure film noir. So is the film's pervading pessimism; its ferocious violence; its lone hero in a corrupt universe; its hero making but one mistake—underestimating his opposition (as much as they do him)—from which there is no recovery; and, most importantly, its intertwining traits: fatalism and paranoia.

Dating back to his German films like *Destiny* (1921), Lang's characters have the misfortune to live in a preordained world. If they make the wrong decision, take the wrong fork in the road, or end up at the wrong place at the wrong time, they risk falling into a bottomless pit, a nightmare world where they have no control over their futures. Witness the sad fates of nice guys Spencer Tracy in *Fury* (1936), who is lynched for a crime he didn't commit, and Henry Fonda in *You Only Live Once* (1937), who is gunned down by police after being driven by wrong information to commit murder. These men are sorry victims of circumstances. Like them, Dave Bannion is a prime candidate for falling into fate's trap. For he also acts impulsively, taking wife Katie's supporting advice to "lead with your chin," rather than considering the possible consequences for himself and his family. It pays to be cautious in Lang's world.

When Bannion accidentally topples daughter Joyce's play castle, it should be a warning to him and an ominous sign to us that his actions (continuing his investigation) will inadvertently lead to the destruction of his happy home. Sure enough, Katie is killed by a bomb meant for him, Joyce is sent to stay with friends Al and Marge, and Bannion moves into a bleak hotel room after vacating his house—as if to confirm to himself that his life has hopelessly fallen apart. (At this point, he has no intention of picking up the pieces.) But compared to some Lang heroes, Bannion gets off easy. Fortunately for him, the film doesn't end here. On a hate binge (Lang's heroes often blindly seek revenge) that precludes thinking rationally, Bannion moves deeper into fate's trap by going after Larry, Vince, and Lagana, and attempting to strangle Bertha Duncan. He assumes he's fated to die or end up in jail and acts accordingly. But unexpected godsend Debby Marsh intervenes and thwarts his worst efforts. Because of her, he loses his chance to kill Bertha (Debby kills her instead) and his desire to kill Vince (Debby's friendship has soothed the savage beast). Thus he avoids imprisonment, possible execution, or being destroyed by his conscience (Edward G. Robinson's unhappy end in Lang's 1945 film *Scarlet Street*). Ford's Bannion avoids his downfall, fate's final trap. He successfully walks the tightrope over Lang's ever-present bottomless pit. He has been tempted and tested, and has emerged triumphant; from now on he can determine his own life's course.

The Viennese-born Lang fled Germany not long after propaganda minister Goebbels, who had just banned the director's *Das Testament des Dr. Mabuse* (1932) because of its pro-Republic slant, said Lang was being considered to head Hitler's film division. (Hitler was a great admirer of Lang's 1927 silent classic *Metropolis*.) If *M* (1931), which was made before Hitler came to power in Germany, dealt with paranoia in a significant way, then the films Lang made after coming to America are those of a man who seems to be constantly looking over his shoulder. On an obvious level, Bannion's

Bannion's world is shattered when Katie dies in an explosion.

paranoia stems from the murder of Lucy Chapman after she talked to him and before she could talk to reporters; the orders he gets from high in the police department to abandon his investigation; his realization that people are avoiding his questions or lying outright; his realization that his actions are being monitored by unknown persons; the threatening phone call to his home; the death of his wife from a bomb planted in his car; his discovering that the policemen assigned to protect Joyce have been ordered away; and his being followed up the stairs in Al's apartment building (a false alarm). (Lang underscores the paranoia by keeping certain backgrounds in shadows and by keeping the camera on individuals after Bannion has questioned them and left so we glimpse their true reactions to him.) But a study of Lang reveals that the paranoia his men feel comes from more than just reading clear signs that things are out of the ordinary. They sense that their immediate surroundings are malevolent. Lang's men, Bannion included, are like spies (sometimes they are spies) who are on secret missions in enemy or, as in *The Big Heat*, enemy-controlled territory, where seemingly no one can be trusted.

Lang's films are about the territorial imperative, about how inhabitants of an environment react to trespassers. It's not so much the good guy versus the bad guy in Lang (although the trespasser is usually the hero) as it is the alien versus a faceless (paranoia!) mob of residents. What's so frightening is that there is no way to predict if the mob will side with the alien: criminals, as well as lawmen, want childkiller Peter Lorre dead in *M* (1931); vigilantes lynch innocent Spencer Tracy in *Fury*; a sympathetic jury frees outlaw-hero Henry Fonda in *The Return of Frank James* (1940). Whether the alien is good or bad, innocent or guilty makes no difference. There's no such thing as justice in Lang's world, which is why men like Bannion are justified in feeling paranoid. Bannion, a scared trespasser in a no-longer-friendly town, is, according to Lang (who seems to be describing the reactionary Dirty Harry), "the eternal man trying to find justice, the vigilante who steps in when established law and order fails. Through him, right prevails in spite of overwhelming odds."

So where is the faceless mob Bannion must confront? What's terrifying is that *The Big Heat*'s "mob"—Lagana's *mob*sters, in this case—isn't just causing havoc on some isolated street, but has actually come to power, just as Lang remembers Hitler's thugs coming to power in Germany in the early thirties. A Hitler-Lagana analogy is appropriate because Lang sees both as ex-street criminals who maintain a group of terrorist thugs to do their dirty work while their own hands appear clean. Lang is revolted by their hypocritical sense of moral superiority now that they have risen to power and prominence in society. Lagana's criminal hierarchy has the same unstable control of the community as Hitler's regime did at an early stage. As Lagana's oppression grows, it seems to Bannion that everyone acts, as Atkins says, "like scared rabbits." However, as the cynical Bannion discovers with surprise, he is not alone in his fight: there is a resistance, just as there was in Germany. Those who are willing to help Bannion are the unlikeliest people in town: barfly Lucy, crippled Selma, kept-woman Debby, and Al's ex-war buddies who don't even know Bannion. There is indeed a war on the homefront. There are also ongoing battles in the *homes* of the

The Big Heat *is about territoriality. In their respective homes, their "castles," the men regard chairs as their thrones—usually the women stand. (TL) In a large house that was paid for with dirty money, Bertha Duncan cares little that her husband has just put a bullet in his head. (BL) In his mansion Lagana angrily rises when Bannion accuses him of corruption. (BR) In his modern apartment Vince winces in pain because the badly scarred Debby, in whose face he had thrown hot coffee, has just returned the favor. (TR) In his modest home Bannion shares everything, including a happy life, with Katie.*

individual characters. The tension in *The Big Heat* comes from continuous powerplay: each character makes his home or work place his power base. These characters become territorial and defiant; the villains become arrogant. Heartless Bertha in her large house, Lagana in his mansion, Vince in his flashy modern high-rise apartment (Lang was once an architect), smirking Tierney (shot in closeup from below) in his Retreat, fat Atkins in his used car lot's office, and Al and Marge in their inexpensive apartment all take power stances they'd be reluctant to take elsewhere.

In *The Big Heat,* the more expensive the home or place of business, the more corrupt the owner (Tom Duncan owned *two* homes despite a small income). So we run the gamut from Lagana's palatial estate to law-abiding Bannion's modest one-story house. Lagana may act like a feudal lord but Bannion feels just as kingly. Katie is his queen and their perfect marriage, in which *everything* (food, drinks, cigarettes, housework) is shared, is a storybook romance. We only see

Katie at home (she is killed the minute she goes out), so it's clear Lang wants her to be symbolized by the home; Bannion sells it once she is dead. When Larry, Lagana's man, calls Bannion's home and makes obscene remarks to Katie, Bannion reacts furiously because the sanctity of his home has been violated: in a sense there has been a rape. When one character enters, or merely telephones the home of an enemy, it is tantamount to an act of aggression, an invasion. Therefore, Bannion feels it necessary to pay Lagana back in kind for the call, by visiting his home. Realizing that Lagana is repulsed by having a low-salaried civil servant, a working-class cop, walking on his lush carpets, Bannion scoffs, "I've violated your immaculate home, is that it?" That's exactly what Bannion intended. Interestingly, those people without a home or business of their own, who have the least to lose, are the ones who cause Lagana's downfall: Bannion, once he has no home or job, Debby, Lucy, and Selma. Fittingly, Bertha is killed in her home, Lagana and Commissioner Higgins are arrested at their homes, and Vince is captured in his apartment. The good guys have reclaimed the city.

In the sixties, at the height of auteurist frenzy, revived interest in Fritz Lang's brilliant career resulted in a re-evaluation of *The Big Heat,* which had received no better than mixed notices in 1953. It quickly became a cult favorite of film connoisseurs and now ranks with *Kiss Me, Deadly* as the best crime drama of its era. Briskly paced, moodily photographed by Charles Lang, Jr., and brilliantly scripted by Sydney Boehm, *The Big Heat* is a truly exciting, intriguing political film, brimming with clever twists, sparkling touches, and wonderfully offbeat characters. The performances are first-rate down to the smallest parts (including Carolyn Jones as the barfly Vince burns with his cigarette). The only time star Glenn Ford has been better is in *The Blackboard Jungle* (1955). An actor who always "talks" with his hands, Ford as a righteous avenger (Lang's oft-used theme being "hate, murder, and revenge") speaks with clenched fists this time around. Also memorable are Lee Marvin's well-dressed, fun-loving, emotionally—and intellectually- –arrested sadist; Alexander Scourby's slimy ganglord; and Jocelyn Brando, effectively portraying a "dream" homemaker, mother, and wife.

Best of all is the great Gloria Grahame, who gave special meaning to such terms as "fallen woman," "femme fatale" (which she definitely is not in *The Big Heat*), and "tarnished lady." At first Debby Marsh is like Grahame's character in *Human Desire* (1954), who walks on a couch in high heels while vainly admiring her legs. Debby leads a useless life of leisure: she sleeps six days and on the seventh day she shops. She's a nonstop talker, but we forgive her because she only seems to be searching for someone with whom she can carry on a polite conversation or who can be straight man for her constant wisecracks. She's too smart, too funny, too brave, and too good to be Vince's woman, but until she meets Bannion she believes Vince is typical of all men. When Vince throws hot coffee in her face, she realizes she deserves better treatment; ironically, at the same time, her disfigurement forces her to stop being vain. She says in William P. McGivern's book, "A girl with only looks to keep her from being a bum can't afford to lose them."

Debby thinks back to her past when she was poor. She envies Katie, who chose a good man instead of a bad man with money. She wishes she had done the same, because she thinks her past life with Vince has made her unworthy of men like Bannion. When she goes to Bertha's house to kill her, she wears a mink just like Bertha's. Her words, "We're sisters under the mink," tells us she considers herself just as good and just as bad as Bertha. But Bannion knows she's much better. When Debby is dying, she no longer wears the mink (another symbol for selling one's values); it becomes her expensive blood-stained pillow. Because now Bannion is willing to talk to her about Katie, Debbie realizes he has come to regard her as being in Katie's class. This makes her happy because (her dying words) "I like her. . . . I like her a lot." As Molly Haskell writes in *From Reverence to Rape* (Holt, 1974), "Jocelyn Brando's madonna and Gloria Grahame's whore gradually merge and, with the death of the former, and the atonement of the latter, are symbolically fused." Debby's death scene, like Katie's, is deeply moving. *The Big Heat* is an extremely brutal film; what sets it apart are such moments of genuine tenderness.

Blood Feast

1963 Box Office Spectaculars
Director: Herschell G. Lewis
Producer: David Friedman
Screenplay: A. Louise Downe
Cinematography: Herschell G. Lewis
Music: Herschell G. Lewis
Editors: Robert Sinise and Frank Romolo
Running time: 70 minutes

Cast: Thomas Wood (Pete), Mal Arnold (Fuad Ramses), Connie Mason (Suzette), Lyn Boulton, Scott H. Hall, Toni Calvert, Astrid Olsen

Synopsis: A homicidal maniac has done away with several young women in brutal fashion. He has always taken away parts of their bodies. Homicide detective Pete Thornton has no clues.

Dorothy Freemont arranges for Fuad Ramses to cater a party for her daughter Suzette. Since Suzette is studying Egyptology, she is happy Fuad will prepare an Egyptian feast that hasn't been done for five thousand years. It will be in two weeks, which will give Fuad time enough to get the last of his ingredients. In his back room, Fuad has a statue of the "mother of veiled darkness," the goddess Ishtar. He is preparing the ancient blood rite for her. The solution he mixes in a huge vat, which contains the parts of the dead women. Fuad is the murderer!

Tony and Marcy make love on a beach. Fuad attacks them. He slices off the top of Marcy's head and takes her brain for his solution. The only thing her parents can tell Pete about their daughter is that she belonged to a book club. This makes Pete stop and think. Some of the other victims belonged to a book club. Including the one whose tongue Fuad rips out that night.

Pete attends his weekly Egyptian studies lecture with his girlfriend Suzette. The lecturer tells them about the cult for Ishtar, and how virgins were sacrificed on an altar.

Pete rushes to the hospital. The maniac has struck again, hacking away most of the skin on Janet Blake's face. She is dying, but manages to tell Pete the killer was old and had wild eyes. She also says he said something that sounded like "Etar." Pete can't understand why that sounds familiar.

Suzette's best friend Trudy also belongs to the book club. She orders the book Ancient Weird Religious Rites by Fuad Ramses. Fuad kidnaps Trudy and brings her to his store. He whips her and collects her blood, the last ingredient in his solution for his goddess.

Despite the kidnaping, the party is still on. Pete calls Suzette to tell her he'll be late. Meanwhile Fuad arrives with his food. Before he will serve the feast to the guests, he insists Suzette come into the kitchen with him. He has her lie on a counter, his altar, and say a prayer to Ishtar. He is ready to stab her with his knife. She is to be sacrificed. This takes forever because she can't take him seriously.

Pete calls up the lecturer and gets information about the cult of Ishtar. He figures out Fuad is the murderer. He discovers Trudy's chopped-up body at the catering store. He rushes to Suzette's party. Dorothy Freemont interrupts Fuad just as he's about to stab her daughter. Fuad escapes just as the police arrive. Pete chases him. Fuad climbs into the back of a garbage truck. He is crushed, just like the garbage he was.

A maniac has viciously murdered ten young women in two weeks time. He has invariably carried off parts of their bodies. The last three victims have had a leg hacked off, brain removed, and tongue yanked out (the cause of death), respectively. Pete, the officer in charge of the homicide investigation, offers to drive pretty Suzette Freemont (some name!) home one night so she won't risk danger. Along the way, he pulls his convertible into a secluded area for some nookie-nookie. When Suzette gets the shivers, Pete assures her that the

NOTHING SO APPALLING IN THE ANNALS OF HORROR!

You'll Recoil and Shudder as You Witness the Slaughter and Mutilation of Nubile Young Girls — in a Weird and Horrendous Ancient Rite!

AN ADMONITION
If You are the Parent or Guardian of an impressionable adolescent DO NOT BRING HIM or PERMIT HIM TO SEE THIS MOTION PICTURE

Box Office Spectaculars
Presents

Introducing
CONNIE MASON
YOU READ ABOUT HER IN PLAYBOY

BLOOD FEAST

MORE GRISLY THAN EVER IN BLOOD COLOR!

Produced by David F. Friedman   *Directed by* Herschell G. Lewis

This weather-beaten, grisly poster inspired one amateur songsmith to invent a theme jingle (with music from "Camptown Races") for Blood Feast: *"Writhing victims of a madman's lust, doo da, doo da . . .*

murderer isn't lurking about, that she's safe with him. Then he jokes: "On second thought, you may be safer with the killer than you are with me!" Talk about tasteless . . .

When you talk about tasteless cinema you must begin with the self-professed "Wizard of Gore," Herschell Gordon Lewis. This notorious exploitation filmmaker from Chicago was the perpetrator of a whole slew of money-making grotesqueries, most of them made prior to *Night of the Living Dead* (1968), the picture generally and mistakenly regarded as the first horror film with gore. Lewis's pictures, which cost around $30,000, made use of buckets of his patented blood solution (made up in a cosmetics laboratory) and featured uncommonly repulsive violence: slashings, stabbings, whippings, impalings, eye gougings, dismemberments, and scalpings ad nauseum. Characters died with their eyes open; blood gushed. If you detest horror films that show how many shocking ways a creative sadist can do away with young women, then Lewis is the man to blame. His women are

dunked head first into boiling oil, have boulders dropped on them, their eyes pulled out and squashed, their nipples sliced off (with milk shooting out—*chocolate* milk to show it's all done in fun, ha ha). He's paved the ugly way with such "gore" classics as *Blood Feast;* his best film, *2000 Maniacs* (1964)—an obvious influence on Tobe Hooper's *The Texas Chain Saw Massacre* (1974); *Color Me Blood Red* (1965)—last of his "blood" triology; *The Gruesome Twosome* (1967); *A Taste of Blood* (1967); *The Wizard of Gore* (1971); and *The Gore-Gore Girls/Blood Orgy* (1972), with Henny Youngman. "His films are impossible to defend; thus he automatically becomes one of the great directors in film history," writes John Waters in *Shock Value* (Delta, 1981). Waters, who titled his *Multiple Maniacs* (1970) as a tribute to *2000 Maniacs,* willingly takes position number two (naturally) behind his idol on the Tasteless Filmmaker chart. The equally generous Lewis, whom Waters interviewed in his book, maintains that they should be rated even: "The difference is simply that in your films, people eat defecation [*Pink Flamingos* (1972)]; in mine the audience is simply exposed to it."

Lewis's career began with commercials and business films. From there he graduated to soft-core "nudies," which he filmed in Chicago (he made the first Chicago films in forty years) or down at the local nudist camp. This man, who has an M.A. in journalism and a Ph.D. in psychology, and who has taught on the university level, churned out such films as *Living Venus* (1961), *Nature's Playmates* (1962), *Daughters of the Sun* (1962), *B-O-I-N-N-N-G!* (1962), *Goldilocks and the Three Bares* (1963), and *Bell, Bare, and Beautiful* (1964). All done in 35 mm, they were stiff competition for Russ Meyer's 16 mm "nudies" output. One, *Lucky Pierre* (1962), which Lewis claims has "the seven ugliest girls that ever appeared," is considered a pioneer film of the foolish genre. All were profitable and were booked for several years.

When Lewis figured the "nudies" were on their way out and more graphic sex films were on the horizon, he looked for another type of film that wasn't being made in Hollywood. He settled on pictures that contained ultraviolence. Producer and partner David Friedman, inspired by a performance of the Grand Guignol in Paris, went along with the decision. Their first film was *Blood Feast,* made in Miami in four, six, or nine days (Lewis gives a different number each interview). Containing some of the most violent images in screen history, it somehow slipped by the censors. It opened in Peoria, and by the second day there were overflowing crowds despite a torrential downpour. It then went on to do astronomical business in drive-ins and grind houses throughout the country, with business particularly strong in the South: this set the trend for future Lewis films. In an interview with Todd McCarthy and Charles Flynn for *Kings of the Bs* (Dutton, 1975), Lewis said: "Everyone was surprised at the business this picture did, including myself. There were many people who wouldn't see it. There were a great many who wanted their money back. There were others who saw it five or six times, which also bewilders me, because I'd never call *Blood Feast* a good production."

In *The Golden Turkey Awards* (Perigee, 1980), Harry and Michael Medved nominate Lewis as candidate for "Worst Director of All Time." From their description of his work, which is quite difficult to see currently, I'd deduce that the Medveds bluffed having seen any of his films (e.g., they call the elderly maniac in *Blood Feast* "youthful"). But if you would want to make a case that Lewis is among the worst directors in history, go no further than *Blood Feast*. This is certainly one of the most inept pictures of all time. The acting is ghastly, casting abominable, scoring (by Lewis) miserable, camerawork clumsy. Even *Playboy* playmate Connie Mason wears too much clothing, but for a needless insert where Suzette lounges by the pool in a bikini. "She never knew a line," Lewis told Waters. "Not ever. Nor could she ever be on the set on time. . . . I've often felt if one took the key out of Connie's back, she'd simply stand in place. Acting was simply not one of her talents." I particularly like the way she holds her arms while in front of the camera, as if she were freezing.

I stop laughing at *Blood Feast*'s *badness* about ten minutes into the film, around the time I start to get a migraine from the characters' infernal voices (Fuad, Dorothy Freemont, and Dr. Flanders are the worst culprits) and the irritating score, which utilizes a booming timpani and "soap opera" organ. But *Blood Feast* could be a delight for camp enthusiasts. Because the film was done tongue in cheek, it's hard to say how much of the humor was intentional. But it's safe to conclude that with this bunch of actors and technicians at work, there was no way a good film could result. It's just remarkable how awful *every* scene is. (This observation comes from someone who admits that *2000 Maniacs,* despite its offensive aspects, has some style and is genuinely nerve-wracking.) Particularly memorable: the way Lewis's camera lingers on a Zenith radio in the opening sequence; the wacky, horribly acted scene in which Dorothy makes catering arrangements with Fuad, who besides talking like a cross between Bela Lugosi and a chorine in a Gold Diggers movie, is obviously reading from cue cards; the way Tony tells the ill-fated Marcy "PROVE that you love me!"; the scene where an hysterical Tony, distressed over Marcy's death, shouts out indecipherable inanities, while Pete stands inches away calmly taking notes with his pencil and pad; the way Marcy's mother Molly cries loudly at the police station, but mysteriously interrupts her weeping each time another character must talk into the microphone; the living room conversation between Suzette and Dorothy, in which Mason can be seen *reading* her awful dialogue; the scene where a hospital doctor looks at a patient who has had "half her face hacked away clear to the bone" and admits "it's one of the most brutal cases I've ever seen"—I wonder what his most *most* brutal case was; the scene after Fuad is dead, when Pete tells the whole story to his partner—as if viewers couldn't understand how he was able to solve such a mystery. A word on Mal Arnold. Blah! Mal Arnold, a Miami actor, in *Blood Feast* gives the worst acting performance in a horror film since the old man (Felix Lucher) in *Frankenstein's Daughter* (1959). Lewis doesn't know what happened to him after making this film. Could they have forgotten he was in the back of that garbage truck? (I could have sworn that the print of *Blood Feast* I saw years ago ended with a dedication to the Miami garbage department—but the print I saw of late has no such acknowledgment. Was I mistaken?)

I can understand those people who enjoy *Blood Feast* for its camp value. I only question those who thrill to the no-holds-barred violence; laugh and cheer while Lewis lovingly pans up and down hacked-up, bloody bodies—just as John Waters lingers on fire in *Pink Flamingos;* smile during Fuad's protracted whipping of Trudy's bare back and when he collects her dripping blood in an urn; and applaud shots of a face with a gouged-out eye, and a head with its top lopped off. These are the people who write letters to Lewis, wanting to know how he did his special "splatter" effects. They care most about the film's "highlight": when Fuad pulls the tongue out of the woman's mouth. (He hired a woman named Astrid Olsen, who worked at Miami's Playboy Club. One reason he picked her was because she had a mouth big enough to hold a sheep's tongue—purchased in Tampa, and so spoiled on shooting day that Pine-Sol was doused on it—cranberries, gelatin, and Lewis's blood solution.) It is very convincingly done, which is why it's so popular. For me it's easier to take than the frighteningly realistic thumb amputation in *2000 Maniacs.* There is a growing cult for "gore" films and Lewis, now living in semiretirement, has become a god to gore fans. When it comes to adoration of Lewis, I can only think of Suzette's remark regarding Ishtar's death cult: "How could . . . people follow such a vile cult?"

The Egyptian head on the wall seems to be taking part in this jolly conversation between Pete and Suzette—or laughing at the horrendous emoting of Thomas Wood and ex-Playboy playmate Connie Mason. Throughout the film Mason holds herself as if she were freezing.

Fuad mutilates Marcy on the beach. Questioned by police, Marcy's parents will recall what they consider to have been her most interesting characteristic: She belonged to a book club.

Blood Money

1933 20th Century Pictures production released
by United Artists
Director: Rowland Brown
Associate Producers: William Goetz and Raymond Griffith
Screenplay: Rowland Brown
Cinematography: James Van Trees
Editor: Lloyd Nosler
Running time: 65 minutes

Cast: George Bancroft (Bill Bailey), Judith Anderson (Ruby Darling),
Frances Dee (Elaine Talbert), Chick Chandler (Drury Darling),
J. Carol Naish (Charley), Blossom Seeley (singer), Etienne Girardot
(Bailey's coworker). Joe Sawyer (Red), Sandra Shaw, Paul Fix

Synopsis: Bill Bailey is a bail bondsman who has influence with
judges, the police, and lawyers. He is an exuberant man, playing a
daily game of pool, visiting his lover and friend Ruby at her
nightclub.

Rich girl Elaine Talbert is arrested for shoplifting. Bailey takes a
fancy to her, although he is wary of her fascination with crime. He
pulls strings and gets her charge dropped. They start to date. He
wants to remain friends with Ruby but she sends him on his way.

Ruby reluctantly accepts Bailey's help when her younger brother
Drury is wanted by the police for robbing cash and bonds from a
bank. He is guilty, but there is no evidence. Bailey gets Drury to
give himself up, saying that he will quickly get him out on bond.
This is accomplished.

At the racetrack, Drury meets Elaine. He falls in love. She is
thrilled because he is a bankrobber. They start seeing each other on
the sly. Bailey informs Drury that the D.A. is ready to press
charges. Drury will do as Bailey suggests: skip town. He sends
Elaine to Bailey's with some stolen unregistered bonds, to cover
the amount of the bail.

Bailey finds the bonds are registered and worthless to him. He
thinks Drury double-crossed him. So he talks to the cops about
Drury. Ruby thinks Bailey has finked to the police because Drury
stole Elaine away from him. She calls him a bloodsucker. He kicks
her out.

Drury is arrested. Ruby asks mobster chieftain Charley for help
in breaking Bailey. Charley's gangsters get to work. Everyone out
on bond skips town, leaving Bailey to pay their bills. It is arranged
for the police to look into Bailey's safe. They find the registered
bonds that incriminate Bailey in the bank robbery.

Bailey gives all the details about the vice in the city to the paper.
Police begin raids.

Ruby fears for Bailey and tells Charley to call off his men. He
tells her it is too late. He has decided to assassinate Bailey, now
under police guard. Before his daily pool game, an eight ball with
an explosive inside will be substituted.

Drury discovers that Elaine had switched the bonds and had
given Bailey the registered ones. He slaps her. He smuggles a note
to Ruby informing her Bailey was framed. She gets in a taxi and
rushes to the pool hall. The game is winding to an end. Only the
eight ball with the explosive remains. Just as Bailey is about to hit
it with the cue ball, he hears a crash. He goes outside. Ruby's taxi
has run into a fire hydrant. She is shaken up. He can no longer act
mad at her. She tells him about the eight ball.

Elaine comes to see Bailey because she thinks he's the only man
who understands her. She sees Bailey and Ruby in a cozy posture.
She turns away. She goes up to a woman who is crying. She'd
answered an ad in the paper for a job, but the man had tried to
molest her. Elaine excitedly takes her ad and goes to meet the man
of her dreams.

A real curio, Rowland Brown's *Blood Money* has been
one of the most exciting finds of the last few
years. Like Brown's first directorial effort, *Quick
Millions* (1931), it was out of circulation for
many years (perhaps since the thirties) before someone discovered a print around 1970. Not that repertory theater
owners were so eager to book it. It had only a minor, but
enthusiastic, underground reputation (as it has today) when I
first saw it at 1977's Filmex (L.A.'s film festival). I have only
been aware of a few subsequent screenings. So chances are
that only those who have been on the lookout for it have seen
it. Chances are better that the majority of avid movie fans
haven't even heard of it. That's because *no* film history text
has mentioned it, not even in passing. And director-screenwriter
Brown, whose oeuvre seems ideal for auteurist study, has
been strangely and sadly overlooked. Only Leslie Halliwell's
reference volume *The Filmgoer's Companion* concedes his
existence, and then it merely offers this brief description:
"American director whose career waned curiously after a
promising start." Cult interest in *Blood Money* coincides
with unsatisfied curiosity about Brown. Those aware of his
small but fascinating body of work realize he should at very
least be a footnote in cinema history. But that will not make
up for what should have been: alone, *Blood Money* and
Angels With Dirty Faces (1938)—for which he wrote the
original story for Michael Curtiz's direction—prove that he
had enough talent, plus a unique vision of contemporary
society, to have become regarded as one of the top filmmakers
of his era *if* he had simply done more.

Brown's odd film career began in the silent days when he
sold a one-act play to Universal. It was never filmed, thus
becoming the first of many unrealized projects that would
characterize his career. Universal hired Brown to be a gagman
for Reginald Denny and later assigned him to write *Points
West* (1929) for cowboy idol Hoot Gibson. Brown was more
interested in modern, urban subjects than westerns and wrote
a story called "A Handful of Clouds," about the rise and fall
of a gangland chieftain. Warner Bros. filmed it as the talkie
The Doorway to Hell (1930), with Lew Ayres. It did tremendous business, perhaps sparked by Warner production head
Darryl F. Zanuck's ads that implied it was a fictionalization
of the life of Al Capone. Because of this success, Fox offered
Brown a chance to both direct and write a feature—double
duty given very few men in those days. *Quick Millions* was
about honest trucker Spencer Tracy becoming a powerful
mobster and crooked politician before being taken for that
proverbial "ride." After collaborating with Gene Fowler on
two good films, George Cukor's *A Star Is Born* precursor
What Price Hollywood? (1932), and *State's Attorney* (1932),
starring John Barrymore, he wrote and directed his second
film, *Hell's Highway* (1932), in which Richard Dix played
a bank robber sentenced to a brutal southern prison farm.

After a couple of aborted projects, Brown made *Blood
Money,* the third film for Darryl F. Zanuck's newly formed
20th Century Pictures. Whether or not it made money depends on which source you read, but it was certainly an
artistic success. By this time, Brown had a reputation in
Hollywood for being able to draw an incisive, believable
picture of the criminal world—almost, thought some, as if he
had firsthand knowledge. At age thirty-two Brown seemingly
had a spectacular career ahead of him, especially with the

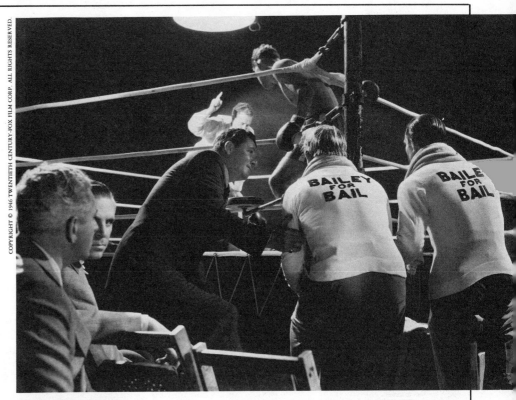

(R) This publicity shot is of the scene where viewers first see Bill Bailey. He is at the fights; as usual, he is making money off losers. (Below) Ruby Darling (Judith Anderson's film debut) and Bill Bailey are an enjoyable, unusual screen couple: lovers and friends.

gangster cycle in full swing. But for some reason Brown went to England, where he worked on several projects as a writer. They had nothing to do with gangsters. Two farces, *Leave It to Blanche* (1934) and *Widow's Might* (1934), came to fruition, but the third, an adaptation of "The Twelve Chairs," which he was also to direct, was never made. When Alexander Korda wanted him to direct *The Scarlet Pimpernel* (1935), it appeared that Brown would make it to the big time despite having left Hollywood at an inopportune time. But soon after, Brown was relieved of his coveted post. Once back in America he was set to direct his story *The Devil Is a Sissy* (1936), which contained familiar Brown subjects—tenements, juvenile delinquents, crime. But here he was again replaced, by W. S. Van Dyke. Now David O. Selznick—who had produced *What Price Hollywood?*—wanted him to be script doctor on William Wellman and Robert Carson's script for *A Star Is Born* (1937). When he informed Selznick that the script needed no rewrite, he was quickly fired. However, Monogram hired him to write and direct *Boy of the Streets* (1937), its major release of the season. Brown's story was used, but again he was replaced as director.

Brown would win an Academy Award nomination the following year for his original story *Angels With Dirty Faces*, about two punks who grow up in the tenements, one to be a priest (Pat O'Brien) and the other a gangster (James Cagney). Of course, this film is regarded as a classic today, but then, even with the Oscar nomination, it didn't help Brown find work. But for coauthoring screenplays for *Johnny Apollo* (1940), about a cynical young man (Tyrone Power) who follows in gangster dad's footsteps, *Nocturne* (1946), a weak George Raft mystery, and Phil Karlson's fine B film *Kansas City Confidential* (1952), the rest of Brown's career was completely undistinguished. It goes without saying that numerous projects he initiated fell through.

In 1963 he died of a heart attack.[*] Facts about his personal life are obscure. Did he have underworld ties? Was he blacklisted for being difficult to work with (having once punched out a producer)? Did he have personal problems that prevented him from completing much of his work? Why did he go to England when his career was blooming? How could the imaginative director of *Blood Money* never get offered a studio contract? The more one looks at *Blood Money*, the more one asks these questions.

Angels With Dirty Faces concludes with the classic scene in which Cagney, at O'Brien's urging, pretends to go "yeller" when he's about to be executed. By doing this he stops

---

*Much of this biographical information was taken from an article by Don Miller, "Notes on the Blighted Career," in *Focus on Film* (no. 7, 1971).

Thief Drury and kinky Elaine prepare to skip town and have their honeymoon.

teen-agers (the Dead End Kids) from idolizing him and wanting to be just like him, without respect or fear of the law. The irony is that we viewers, let in on the secret, believe that this gangster was brave to the end, and that he had no regrets about his life in crime—even if it ended with him strapped in the electric chair. Likewise, *Blood Money* and other Brown works are unique because they refuse to moralize about participation in crime. A person has no obligation to lead the clean life—there is no such thing in Brown's world. A person's only obligation is to watch over the young (as Ruby and Bill look after Drury), to give them some guidance, and to be there when they do something wrong—which they will—and try to ameliorate the bad consequences. In Brown's cities, business runs smoothly because criminals, law enforcers, politicians, and citizens each recognize the others' domains. Crime is a business. There is little difference between criminals and coppers; Ruby in fact insults Bailey by saying he's started acting like a cop. Everyone commits crimes: politicians who accept graft, police who use selective law enforcement, judges who allow themselves to be influenced by powerful citizens like Bailey. Some crimes (robbing banks, committing murder) demand that the culprit be thrown in jail. People who commit such crimes are losers ("I make all my money off losers!" Bailey laughs)—but no one but a judge can condemn them. It's all part of the game, the way things are done. (Once all police jobs are taken, men must play on the other side.) Once you get caught (as does Drury), you just shrug your shoulders: no regrets, you knew the rules, fair's fair. Some crimes are not illegal, and you'll not get tossed in jail for committing them. Bill Bailey, for instance, takes advantage of all people in trouble, not showing any more sympathy for a kindly old lady whose teen-age son committed a crime than he would for a hardened criminal. He philosophizes: "For every Barnum, there's a Bailey," meaning that for every sucker born there's a vulture like him waiting to exploit their misery.

Crime is treated casually by all people in *Blood Money*. It's a way of life, one of the few that pays dividends in the Depression. The only crime for which a person must be ashamed and for which there must be retribution is double-cross. Drury's jumping town while out on bail is fine (Bailey recommends it) because it is the law that is victimized, but when Bailey thinks Drury failed to send him money (unregistered bonds) to cover the bail Bailey paid, then he has the right to retaliate. Just as Ruby has the right to try to break Bailey when she assumes he's sold out Drury to the police because he's jealous of Drury's affair with Elaine. Of course, everything turns out to be a misunderstanding—it was Elaine who failed to deliver Drury's money to Bailey. What's interesting is that everyone forgives and forgets—there is no retaliation, but a return to the status quo. And, even stranger, Bill will not reform. He and Ruby merely make up. In other films that would mean the man has learned the error of his ways and will give up his old lifestyle to please the woman. But Ruby, no angel herself, doesn't want that: "You'll always be behind the eight ball, and I'll always be pulling you out." Tomorrow morning, Bill will surely be back at his office taking some kind old lady's deed to her home in lieu of bail for her son, knowing full well that the ungrateful lad will hop the next train out of town and he'll get the property. A guy's gotta make an honest living, doesn't he?

Before the days of James Cagney and Edward G. Robinson, George Bancroft was the top actor in gangster films. He was Bull Weed in Josef von Sternberg's *Underworld* (1927), probably the first talkie gangster film. Then he had leads in such noteworthy films as *The Docks of New York* (1928), *Thunderbolt* (1929), and *Ladies Love Brutes* (1930), no doubt Elaine Talbert's favorite film. Trying to attain his earlier fame, Bancroft does a good, sturdy job as Bill Bailey. He plays him like Wallace Beery would, but not with Beery's heart of gold. He's no softy, except with Ruby. Bancroft gets good support from Judith Anderson, making her screen debut as Ruby, Chick Chandler as the always smiling Drury,

Red (L), played by veteran character actor Joe Sawyer, isn't concerned that his gal set him up for the cops. All criminals who know bail bondsman Bill Bailey know they'll soon be walking the streets again.

and especially Frances Dee, jolting us by the second in a role far removed from the ingenue parts she was being offered at this stage of her career. Small roles are also inspiringly cast.

Blood Money has much going for it: good acting, a solid storyline that ends in the exciting climactic pool game, and tremendous dialogue, full of humor and punch. (Lines always have two meanings.) But what makes the film so extraordinary is that it's flooded with creative, offbeat touches. *Nothing* is done in the standard way. For instance, Bailey is introduced in an unusual manner: there's a radio ad for his bail bond firm ("a friend in need"); Red, an arrested man, acts cockily because he knows Bailey will soon bail him out; Bailey's assistant wakes a judge and his wife in the middle of the night (spilling ink on the bedsheets) to get Red released—and the judge signs the court order obediently because "Bailey has a lot of influence" ("a lot of nerve," says his tired wife); butchers (cooks?) take Bailey's order for one hundred turkeys for the poor: "poor judges, poor lawyers, poor law officers." In just a few seconds we know all about Bailey and we haven't seen him as yet. The strong friendship (distinct from their love) between Bailey and Ruby is certainly unusual. So are certain set pieces: the Hawaiian luau, where curvaceous, scantily clad maidens dance a wiggly pre-Production Code hula; the greyhound races, where men who look like bellboys parade the dogs, and men in the grandstands (Drury) pay for the company of foxy-looking dames; the mobster gathering at Ruby's, where weird-looking men and women gangsters puff on cigars and cigarettes; the golf club where Bailey and Drury sit in adjoining phone booths and each tries to call Elaine; the nightclub where Blossom Seeley belts out two wonderfully dramatic numbers (and Brown wisely lets his camera linger). Most remarkable are Brown's odd assortment of characters: the tiny, smiling mother who happily gives Bailey the deed to her house, and her slimy woman-beating son Tony; Bailey's elderly assistant; the department store owner who sits on a whoopy cushion; Ruby's hip, beautiful black maid, a lot different from the Hattie McDaniel–Louise Beavers prototype; and of course, the barfly who wears a monocle and men's clothing, and who, when offered a cigar by Bailey, gives it a whiff and returns it, saying "Why, you big sissy!" But none of these compare to the outrageously sexy Elaine Talbert. During this era there were several rich female characters in films who were excited by crime, but Elaine is like no female in film history. ("I've always wanted to meet a girl who likes onions," says Bailey.) She has a crime mania, and is also a kleptomaniac, a nymphomaniac, and a masochist. She is turned on by anything daring: the hula dancers she gets instructions from (". . . Almost savage, isn't it?"), being on the lam ("This will be the most exciting honeymoon a girl ever had"), associating with criminals ("People you know are guilty of everything," she says to Bailey in the way of a compliment). Here's a woman who is looking for a man to give her a good thrashing ("I'd follow him around like a dog on a leash"), who likes being kissed hard ("You hurt my lip," she tells Drury), who tells Bailey "I love you when you're angry," and who, in her final scene, goes off to meet a stranger who she hopes will molest her. Like director Brown, this is a screen character who was certainly several decades ahead of her time. Just like Brown, she has, as Bailey tells her father, "imagination"—a quality that made contemporaries both fascinated and fearful.

A Boy and His Dog

1975 An LQJaf presentation
Director: L. Q. Jones
Producer: Alvy Moore
Screenplay: L. Q. Jones
From a novella by Harlan Ellison
Cinematography: John Arthur Morrill

Music: Tim McIntire
"Topeka" music by Jaime Mendoza-Nava; "When the World Was New" by Richard Gillis
Editor: Scott Conrad
Running time: 87 minutes

Cast: Don Johnson (Vic), Susanne Benton (Quilla June Holmes), Tiger (Blood), Tim McIntire (Blood's voice), Alvy Moore (Dr. Moore), Jason Robards (Lew Craddock), Helene Winston (Mez), Charles McGraw (the preacher), Hal Baylor (Michael), Ron Feinberg (Fellini), Mike Rupert (Gary), Don Carter (Ken), Michael Hershman (Richard)

Synopsis: It is 2024 A.D., several years after World War III. Phoenix, Arizona, is a wasteland. Bands of marauders, rovers, battle for food found in the tops of buildings that were bombed out and almost entirely covered by desert sands. What "civilization" there is is below in one of the downunders. Neither Vic, a solo in his early twenties, nor his partner Blood, a dog who communicates with him telepathically, wants to go below. Blood finds women for Vic to rape. Vic provides Blood with food.

Blood sniffs out a woman, but rovers have reached her first and have killed her after raping her. Vic argues with Blood about his inability to find women. Blood wants to go "over the hill," to paradise. Vic promises that they'll go once Blood finds a woman for him.

Fellini, a brutal king, leads his group of scavengers through the desert. On impulse, Vic steals some of their food. He is observed by unseen people. They agree that Vic will be right for their purposes.

Vic and Blood watch the nightly films in a makeshift theater. Blood sniffs out a woman dressed as a solo. At first, Vic doesn't believe him, but he follows her to an abandoned YMCA. When she strips, he knows Blood was right. He starts to rape her, but her friendly conversation confuses him and he stops. She says her name is Quilla June Holmes. Marauders know about her, too. Vic and Blood put up a fight to save her. Blood is injured. Quilla June seduces Vic. Much to Blood's chagrin, they make love. She tells Vic he should come live with her in Topeka, a downunder. Vic is afraid to go below. She conks him on the head and flees. Vic decides to go after her. Blood says he will wait for him a little while.

Topeka is an agrarian community run by a ruthless, impersonal Committee: Lew, Dr. Moore, and Mez. It had sent Quilla June above to lure Vic to them. They want him to impregnate thirty-five virgins because the men in Topeka have trouble breeding. But he is surprised when they hook him up to an artificial insemination machine. They plan to kill him afterward. Quilla June is angry that she has been denied entry to the Committee after performing her task. She frees Vic so he can help her, her boyfriend Gary, and others to overthrow the Committee and take over the dictatorship. However, the other rebels are killed by Michael, a robot in farmer's garb. Vic shoots Michael and he and Quilla June escape. She tells him how much she loves him. Vic is her one hope for survival.

They find Blood. He hasn't eaten in days and will soon die unless Vic provides him with food. Quilla June says it's too late to save Blood, and Vic should go with her if he loves her. He looks at Blood. He looks at Quilla June.

Vic and Blood go off into the sunrise. Having eaten, Blood feels much better. Vic was touched that Quilla June picked him to be with. Blood remarks, "She had marvelous judgment—if not particularly good taste." They laugh at the pun, and the boy and his dog walk toward paradise.

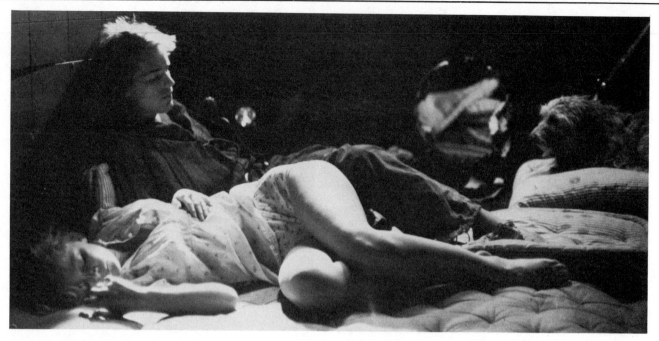

After fighting off marauders, Vic, Blood, and Quilla June find shelter in an abandoned building. Much to Blood's disapproval, Vic and Quilla June (played by once hot stars Don Johnson and pretty Susanne Benton, who'd been a WAC secretary in the 1970 film Catch-22*) will spend the night having sex.*

This picture has nothing to do with the 1946 Academy Award–winning short *A Boy and His Dog,* about a barefoot country boy who rescues a mistreated hound from its cruel owner. Nor does it in any fashion resemble the famous pre–World War II dog stories of Albert Payson Terhune (e.g., *Lad: A Dog; Buff: A Collie; His Dog; A Dog Named Chips*)—although Blood's calling Vic *Albert* in both Harlan Ellison's novella and L. Q. Jones's film adaptation is meant to be an ironic comment on Terhune's wholesome tales. Despite its heartwarming title, which conjures up nostalgic images of grassy fields, mysterious woods, and rippling brooks—as well as of Roddy McDowall, Tommy Rettig, and Jon Provost with Lassie, Lee Aaker with Rin Tin Tin, David Ladd with the dog of Flanders, and Tommy Kirk with Old Yeller—the Ellison-Jones *A Boy and His Dog* is a violent, sexy, sometimes vulgar black comedy far removed from kiddie fare (although teenagers with phony I.D.'s are perhaps its biggest fans).

A Boy and His Dog was first published in 1969, in Great Britain rather than Ellison's native America. (He expanded it slightly for its first American printing in 1974.) By this time Ellison was already a cult figure, known for being an opinionated, obsessive, fussy intellectual; an undeniable talent who had shaken up the polite science fiction establishment with stories overflowing with sex, four-letter words, violent imagery, antisocial heroes, and left-wing politics. He epitomized the *modern* science fiction writer—he was also the type who'd walk out on interviewers who introduced him as a "science fiction writer." Many of Ellison's stories won sf prizes, and true to form, *A Boy and His Dog* copped the prestigious Nebula. Several studios took notice. Ellison subsequently turned down big money from Warners and Universal to adapt his story. Warners wanted him to make the downunder sequences less anti–Middle America; worse, *both* studios wanted

Blood to literally talk to Vic, moving his lips the way Francis the Talking Mule used to. Ellison insisted that Blood communicate with Vic telepathically, which was logical in context of the story and their unique relationship ("because Blood and I think alike," Vic explains to Quilla June, "and have a feeling for one another"). Ellison had given up on the story becoming a movie when he was contacted by L. Q. Jones, the character actor who had gained limited fame as one of Sam Peckinpah's redneck villains (the one who always groveled in the dirt with Strother Martin). Jones and fellow character actor Alvy Moore, best known for his stint on television's *Green Acres,* had formed a production company specializing in low-budget horror movies and wanted to purchase the rights to *A Boy and His Dog,* which would be their fourth production. For some reason, Ellison was impressed by their latest film, *Brotherhood of Satan* (1971), an improvement upon their *The Devil's Bedroom* (1963) and *The Witchmaker* (1969) but muddled and amateurish. And when they told Ellison that he would be screenwriter and that Blood would communicate telepathically, a deal was made. As it turned out, Jones made his debut as director when the one he hired had to be replaced. Similarly, he became screenwriter when Ellison, who promised to whip off a script, had writer's block for the better part of a year. In an interview conducted by Don Shay for *Cinefantastique* (Vol. 5, No. 1), Jones talked about adapting Ellison:

> To begin with, it's a fascinating story, and gorgeously written—not a wasted word in it. And I find that each time I read it again, there's one word which I've missed in context and it'll shed light on what he tried to say about the other things. The picture is a picture of sensation. What's it like to be really dirty? What's it like to be really lonely? You've got to learn to hate, and you've got to learn to fight—all this is built into it. It's the way he wrote it. Harlan writes more visually than he

does with words. So what I was trying to do was find out what he meant, or what he saw, and then translate it into something. That's why it took me a year to write it.

The best part of *A Boy and His Dog* is the wicked, rat-a-tat-tat dialogue between Vic and Blood, which Jones took almost word for word from Ellison's novella. It is made up of quick arguments (Blood refuses to track women for Vic's sexual lust until Vic finds food to satisfy Blood's constant hunger), threats to walk out on each other (Vic also threatens to give Blood swift kicks to the rump), insults, apologies, naïve statements from Vic, martyristic remarks from Blood—all delivered with an undercurrent of tremendous affection (let's call it "love") and need for one another. Vic and Blood are almost like a comedy team cast in an absurdist play, with the ignorant, musclebound macho boy playing the foil for the conceited, wise, cynical mutt. Blood comes across as a vicious variation on Cleo, Jackie Cooper's memorable dachshund from the fifties TV comedy series *The People's Choice,* whose every snide thought about his master's foibles could be heard by viewers. But whereas Cleo, with floppy ears and droopy eyes, was always cute, friendly, and sympathetic, Blood is merely cute; his attitude, as Ellison writes, is "insolently humble." It's amazing what a good actor Tiger, of *The Brady Bunch* fame, is, particularly in those scenes when Blood is ignoring Vic after being hurt by one of his insults. Tim McIntire, who was a dynamic Alan Freed in Floyd Mutrux's *American Hot Wax* (1978), properly provides Blood with a biting "adult" delivery, which one might think ideal for a Mr. Belvedere portrayal or *The Man Who Came to Dinner* but few would be smart enough to give to a shaggy pooch. It works because it keeps viewers from being *too* sympathetic toward Blood, who is, after all (despite his vicious streak, blatant misogyny, and various irritating peculiarities), a victim. Basically Blood is an old-timer, who has much to offer (wisdom, experience, companionship, historical knowledge) but fishes for reassurance from Vic that he's not obsolete in a world of stupid scavengers, where only the fittest survive.

The post-apocalyptic world (Phoenix, Arizona, 2024 A.D.) that Jones presents is pretty much how Ellison describes it (although there wasn't enough money to build a deserted city through which Vic could follow Quilla June). An enormous blue sky is in marked contrast to the bleak, battle-scarred, garbage-strewn landscape. It is a world of constant danger, of living in dirt and dust (which, of course, Jones got used to when he was working with Peckinpah), of searching for food to eat, women to rape (which critics find most unpleasant about the film), and a place for the night in the bombed-out buildings that barely jut out of the sand. I suspect that when director George Miller made *Mad Max* (1980), he was influenced by this post–World War III vision because he, too, created a world in which bands of brigands roam the countryside in search of women to rape and other sustenance. This was confirmed in Miller's sequel, *The Road Warrior* (1982), in which we see a brigand leader much like *A Boy and His Dog*'s Fellini. Each is treated like a king by his followers; each keeps one on a leash. The vision of post–World War III Arizona is indeed intriguing, especially when action takes place in a makeshift movie house—where men and their dogs watch action movies double-billed with cowboy stag films—or in one of the dangerous buildings below the surface. (When

(*Above*) *This still of Vic forcing stranger Quilla June to strip has often been used by feminists to illustrate what they believe is the sexist nature of the film. (Below) Mez and Lew are two of the clownish yet coldhearted members of Kansas's Committee.*

we see Vic spying on Quilla June as she undresses in the bombed-out YMCA, it is as if we are the ones watching a stag film.) Unfortunately, the story shifts to Topeka, a downunder. Not that the downunder sequence is bad—it isn't—it's just that more scenes are needed above ground to satisfy our curiosity (perhaps another action sequence would be sufficient). Besides, Blood doesn't tag along.

Jones greatly changed the downunder sequence of Ellison's novella. For one thing, the small town becomes more of an agrarian community. It also becomes more repressive in nature, as the Committee automatically executes ("Send them to the farm") all who display a "lack of respect, wrong attitude, and failure to obey authority." (This is surprising, since Jones is far more politically conservative than Ellison.) Other changes:

The moviehouses of the future will have armed guards instead of ticket takers. Here Vic barters with canned goods so that Blood can watch the movies too. According to director L. Q. Jones, a sequel called A Girl and Her Dog *was planned but called off when Tiger died.*

Ellison's impersonal, mobile green box-like guard becomes Michael, a robot henchman with a smile on his metallic face (when Vic destroys him, Lew shrugs, "Let's get another Michael out of the warehouse—no smile this time"); Jones has Vic strapped to an insemination machine whereas Ellison had the townspeople arrange for him to actually have intercourse with Topeka's maidens; and Jones's nightmarish vision of a community without sun, where loudspeakers blare and everyone wears hideous clownish makeup, replaces Ellison's dull, peaceful hometown.

The biggest change Jones made has to do with Quilla June, and is, I suspect, the reason for much of the feminist antagonism toward the film. In the novella, the first time Vic and Quilla June have intercourse it is because Vic rapes her. She was a virgin. Although she becomes sexual putty for Vic at this point and willingly has sex with him, over and over and over again, we do not forget that she did not initiate the sex. In the film, Quilla June manipulates would-be rapist Vic until she is no longer in danger of his taking her against her will. Then *she* seduces *him*. This wouldn't be so bad in itself, but once she turns out to have been bait for Vic to be taken prisoner by the Committee, we think back to the seduction: In our eyes, Vic, committer of a dastardly act in the novella, is now a victim of a conniving, treacherous Mata Hari. All that comes after—Quilla June tries to get on the Committee so she can become part of the dictatorial command; she tries to *use* Vic again, to help in the revolution; we learn that she is not a virgin (she has a boyfriend named Gary) and is willing to use her body to move herself upward; she tries to get Vic to leave Blood behind and go off with her—is meant to justify Vic's killing her so Blood can have food. In the novella, she doesn't deserve her sad fate: she is neither mean nor self-serving. It's just that Vic and Blood love each other and she—being female—is odd man out. The novella's treat-

ment of Quilla June is much more acceptable—there is no need to whitewash Vic and Blood's murder, to, in fact, make it a joke (I laugh, but I feel guilty about it)—by making Quilla June into such a bitch, no pun intended.

Jones was most interested in the "love story" of Vic and Quilla June. But I'd rather look at the film as another entry in the "buddy"-picture genre. Quilla June, the soft woman with an apple, embodies civilization ("When Blood visits he can have his own room") and the sex and sin therein. The natural order is: a man, his rifle, and his hunting dog. Love is pure only when it is not soiled by sex (contact with women)—it is pure between a boy and his dog. This noble partnership between man and animal reminds me of "That Mark Horse," a wonderful short story by Jack Schaefer, author of *Shane,* about a rodeo cowboy who bemoans the lost respect of his horse. I love the concept of *respect* between man and animal (not love, not affection, not need), and *A Boy and His Dog* is one of the few examples of a film or story that deals with it. That is why I like this picture that many critics have attacked with good reason. (I also like its fine, nonelectrical score; the splendid performance by the once-promising Don Johnson [a favorite among gays] exuding boyish country charm, like a regular on *Hee! Haw!* only with a shotgun by his side; and the great dog character.)

Jones didn't know how to promote the film (at one time he wanted to call it *Rover Dog*) and it didn't catch on with the mass audience. However, it did attain a loyal following, about half of them being Harlan Ellison cultists, and won a Hugo award. Tiger won a Patsy as best animal actor in a film. This gave Jones hope that he could eventually find an audience. Although an attempt by both Jones and Ellison to turn *A Boy and His Dog* into a pilot movie for a possible network series failed, in 1982 Jones went ahead with plans for a second release with a new ad campaign.

Breathless

(À Bout de Souffle)

1959 Impéria Films (distributed in 1961
in the U.S. by Films-Around-the-World)
Director: Jean-Luc Godard
Producer: Georges de Beauregard
Screenplay: Jean-Luc Godard
From a story idea by François Truffaut
Cinematography: Raoul Coutard
Music: Martial Solal
Editor: Cécile Decugis and Lila Herman
Artistic Supervisor: Claude Chabrol
Running time: 89 minutes

Cast: Jean-Paul Belmondo (Michel Poiccard, a.k.a. Laszlo Kovacs),
Jean Seberg (Patricia Franchini), Daniel Boulanger (police inspector),
Jean-Pierre Melville (Parvulesco), Liliane Robin (Minouche), Henri-
Jacques Huet (Antonio Berrutti), Van Doude (journalist), Claude
Mansard (Claudius Mansard), Michel Fabre (plainclothesman), Jean-
Luc Godard (informer), Jean Domarchi (drunk), Richard Balducci
(Tolmatchoff), Roger Hanin (Carl Zombach), Jean-Louis Richard
(journalist), François Moreuil (cameraman), Philippe de Broca

Synopsis: Michel Poiccard is a petty crook who wants to be like
the gangsters Humphrey Bogart played in the movies. With the help
of his girlfriend he steals a car in Marseilles. He drives off without
her. He speeds along a country road, muttering to himself and
pretending to shoot his gun at people he passes. He pulls over to
the side and a motorcycle cop stops. Michel casually kills him. The
newspapers report that the Paris police are looking for the murderer.

In Paris he steals money from the purse of a model. He then
looks for Patricia Franchini, an American girl he met recently in
Nice. He finds her walking the streets hawking the *New York Herald
Tribune.* He tells her that he doesn't enjoy sleeping with other
women. He wants her to run off to Rome with him. He is jealous
when she keeps an appointment with an American journalist. Michel
follows her around in a stolen car. The journalist has arranged for
her to interview Parvulesco, a famous novelist. He worries that she
considers having an abortion—the baby she carries is probably
Michel's. She tells the journalist: "I don't know if I'm unhappy
because I'm free or not free because I'm unhappy."

Patricia returns to her tiny apartment and finds Michel in her
bed. During his lengthy visit, they talk, they flirt, she discusses
books, he talks about dying, she slaps him, he proposes they sleep
together, she keeps refusing. She isn't sure if she loves him. She
tells him that she thinks she's pregnant by him. "You should have
been more careful," he replies. They sleep together.

When other contacts fall through, Michel arranges to pick up
money from his friend Antonio so he can leave Paris with Patricia.
He is spotted on the street by an informer who tells the police.
Meanwhile Patricia carries on a philosophical interview with
Parvulesco.

Police question Patricia about Michel. When the inspector tells
her "Careful, one doesn't joke with the Paris police!" she admits
she knows Michel and promises to call the next time she sees him.

Michel beats up a man who tinkers with his car. He knows there
is a dragnet out for him because of newspaper reports and from
having seen the police tail Patricia. He takes her to the cinema. They
neck. He and Patricia hide out, waiting for Antonio to deliver
money. Patricia calls the police and tells them where Michel is. She
doesn't want to go away with him. She tells Michel about her call,
saying he has just enough time to escape. "Because I'm mean to
you, it proves I don't love you!" she insists. He tells her he doesn't
care if he goes to prison. He makes no effort to escape.

Antonio drives up with the money and a gun. He forces the gun
on Michel when he sees the police arrive. Trapped, Michel has no
choice but to run. He is shot in the back by a police bullet. Patricia
stands above the dying man. He calls her a *dégueulasse* (bitch).
She doesn't understand what the word means. He dies. She rubs
her finger over her bottom lip, just like Bogart and Michel used to
do.

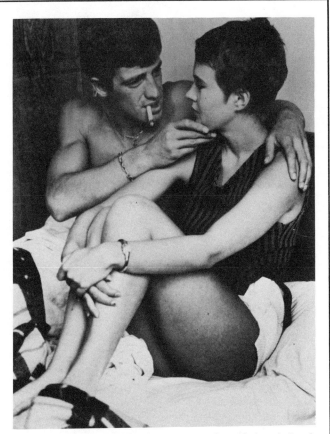

*French youth found them electrifying: Belmondo/Michel and
Seberg/Patricia in the classic apartment interlude.*

t's hard to overestimate the impact Jean-Luc Godard had
on all of us excited by cinema back in the sixties and
early seventies. In that turbulent era when American
youth rejected all conventions, even conventional
"entertainment" cinema, Godard became God for film
fanatics, filmmakers, and college students who didn't belong
to a fraternity or sorority or drive a Ford. Sure we *enjoyed*
Truffaut's pictures more—many people hated Godard films—
but Godard's complex, intellectually provocative films were
required viewing. The era's most controversial filmmaker (as
much for his radical politics as for his revolutionary style),
and the films' supreme political theorist, he gradually did
away with the traditional narrative structure, all "logic," by
using every "alienation" technique imaginable. He wasn't
interested in telling a story but in showing us how film—a
series of *images* (filmed and edited in a particular manner) that
appear on a screen—can be used to express a filmmaker's
polemics, to educate or propagandize, and to stimulate viewers into political discourse. By the late sixties he was using
his frame—a battleground for emotions in his early films—as
an arena for characters who are in the midst of politicization
and who take part in dialectical discussions about such political issues as capitalism, mechanized society and dehumanization,
revolution, the role of students in political movements, and
worker exploitation. Or he'd have a representative of a particular class look directly at the camera and explain his political
overview—several times if what he says is complicated or
needs to be stressed. Or he'd pan his camera for minutes at a
time on a seemingly endless traffic jam (Godard uses cars as a

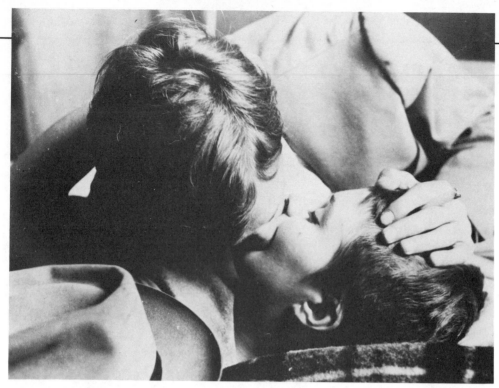

Neither Michel nor Patricia could be called emotional or sensitive, yet rarely has a film had so much passion.

symbol for capitalism). It was all extremely exciting. Filmmakers like Brian De Palma and Jim McBride (who in 1983 remade *Breathless*) borrowed from Godard with some success; Haskell Wexler did it best in *Medium Cool* (1969). University film departments added Godard courses. Everyone had their favorite political Godard films—mine were *La Chinoise* (1967) and *Weekend* (1967)—but even then, the Godard film for which we felt the most emotion was his least political, *Breathless*. So it's not at all surprising that *Breathless* is the Godard film theater owners continue to show when they want to be assured a good turnout.

Truffaut had already made *The 400 Blows,* Chabrol *The Cousins,* Malle *The Lovers,* and Resnais *Hiroshima, Mon Amour* (all 1959), but with the release of *À Bout de Souffle* Godard gave definition to the term *la Nouvelle Vague,* opening all paths for his contemporaries to explore. Looking back, Andrew Sarris calls it "the most important film of the New Wave" and "the most passionate," and Amos Vogel, in *Film as a Subversive Art* (Random House, 1974), contends that "the modern cinema could not exist without this film." In 1959 Jean Cocteau called it "a masterpiece," and Jean-Paul Sartre, undoubtedly excited by the film's existential viewpoint, hailed it as "an extraordinary triumph." And when *À Bout de Souffle* came to America in 1961 as *Breathless,* Penelope Gilliatt expressed the view of many critics: "Jean-Luc Godard makes a film as though no one had ever made one before."

Godard had only $90,000 to work with on *Breathless*. Godard knew that he couldn't afford to make a *polished* film, according to the rules. Luckily he didn't want to. *Breathless* breaks with all technical conventions. There are no transitions between scenes or between two shots in a scene. There are no establishing shots. There are no matching shots. A character's in one place, then he's somewhere else. Godard dared use jump cuts—the bane of existence for low-budget filmmakers—as a stylistic device to convey a chaotic atmosphere and to express the reckless nature of his youthful Michel and Patricia—just as Richard Lester's anarchic style in

A Hard Day's Night (1964) would perfectly express the Beatles. Godard's characters jump through time and space and it seems perfectly natural. It was fine to film a person from the back of the head, move the camera a bit and again shoot the back of the head. There were no lights, no makeup, no sound equipment (all sound was dubbed in later); dialogue was delivered to the actors right before a scene was shot; scene logistics were conceived on the spot; cameraman Raoul Coutard often hid in a mail barrow or sat in a wheelchair and, with camera in lap, rolled down the street following the actors (all filming was done on location). Godard told *Cahiers du Cinema:*

> *À Bout de Souffle* was the sort of film where anything goes: that was what it was all about. Anything people did could be integrated in the film . . . I said to myself: we have already had Bresson, we have just had *Hiroshima, Mon Amour.* A certain kind of cinema has just drawn to a close, maybe ended, so let's add the finishing touch . . . What I wanted was to make a conventional story and remake, but differently, everything the camera had done. I also wanted to give the feeling that the techniques of filmmaking had just been discovered or experienced for the first time.

Although Godard's technique and storytelling methods were extraordinarily different, he did retain a fairly conventional gangster movie framework. Truffaut is credited with providing Godard with his story idea (Michel is the son of the lovers in Jean Vigo's 1934 classic *L'Atalante*), but Godard's inspiration came from a newspaper item: a motorcyclist killed a policeman and hid out with his girlfriend, who later betrayed him. It seemed like an ideal premise from which to pay homage to early gangster films (*Breathless* is dedicated to Monogram Studios, home of the B melodrama). Godard:

> What caused me a lot of trouble was the end. Should the hero die? To start with, I intended to do the opposite of, say, *The Killing* [1956]: the gangster would win and leave for Italy with his money. But as an anticonvention it was too conventional. . . . Finally I decided that as my avowed ambition was

to make an ordinary gangster film, I had no business deliberately contradicting the genre: he must die. . . . After a certain time I realized that *À Bout de Souffle* was not all that I thought. I thought I had made a realistic film . . . but it wasn't that at all. . . . Although I felt ashamed of it at the time, I do like *À Bout de Souffle* very much, but now [in 1962] I see where it belongs—along with *Alice in Wonderland*. I had hoped it was *Scarface* [1932].

Breathless was not all producer Georges de Beauregard had hoped for either. He had only financed the picture because Truffaut and Chabrol, Godard's former staffmates at *Cahiers* in the fifties, had promised they would collaborate on the project. Instead they'd gone home and left Godard, making his feature debut, on his own. On premiere night, the producer and the director fought in the lobby because de Beauregard accused Godard of deliberately trying to ruin him. Neither men, nor stars Jean-Paul Belmondo and Jean Seberg, realized that *Breathless* would become the sensation of the year in France, breaking box office records, making Godard the enfant terrible of the cinema, and turning Belmondo and Seberg into idols of French youth.

French fans appreciated Godard's technical daring; his originality; his Paris street photography; his score, which mixes jazz and Mozart; his many movie references and in jokes (e.g., for his alias Michel assumes the name of American cinematographer Laszlo Kovacs) and his intriguing concept, which Richard Roud points out in *Jean-Luc Godard* (Doubleday, 1968), that "the world is just a bad movie"; his willingness to interrupt his fast-moving gangster tale (the Frank Tashlin influence?) for a remarkably erotic, extended (seemingly improvisational) bedroom conversation between Michel and Patricia and for a drawn-out scene in which Patricia interviews novelist Parvulesco; and his inclusion of politically motivated swipes at automobiles and telephones (often they're in disrepair; both are instruments of death: a Volkswagen runs over a pedestrian and Patricia's phone call results in Michel's being killed). But what excited the alienated French youth most was that they could identify with casual lawbreaker Michel Poiccard and his disloyal girlfriend Patricia Franchini, lovers who act impetuously without regard to consequences.

Antihero Michel wears sunglasses and dresses spiffily in suit, tie, and hat (tough guy garb in Monogram's forties films), but he's as much of a punk as that motorcyclist-killer Godard read about. Without conscience, he deflates tires, robs parking meters, takes money from a model's purse, steals cars, mugs a guy in a men's room, and kills a cop. He never plans his crimes, and he has no reason for committing them other than his own hyperactivity. He must keep busy: driving cars (turning down hitchhikers because they're too ugly), playing with guns, smoking and rubbing his thumb over his bottom lip like Bogart, reading about himself in the newspaper, chatting incessantly (even when alone), making phone calls, peering at his reflection, getting himself into trouble with the law. He lives for the second, without memory of the past or thought of the future: in the bedroom centerpiece he thinks nothing of asking Patricia to have sex with him even though she rejected him a couple of moments before. He accepts that he only has a short time to live (the Bogart poster he admires is an ad for 1956's *The Harder They Fall,* Bogart's last film) and not only the inevitable demise of relationships (a recurrent Godardian theme) but also inevi-

Breathless has always been popular on college campuses. I made this crude poster, showing Michel accompanying Patricia down the Champs-Élysées while she hawks the New York Herald Tribune, in 1971 for my film society at the University of Wisconsin.

table betrayal: "To betray," reflects Patricia; "I think that's very bad." "No," corrects Michel. "It's normal." (Why then does he call her a bitch when she betrays him?) What France's youth thrilled to is that Michel follows the words of a slogan scrawled on a wall he passes: "To Live Dangerously Till The End." A combination Humphrey Bogart and James Dean. Though speaking of his own philosophy, Purvulesco sums up Michel: "His greatest ambition is to become immortal, then die." Which is exactly like Martin Sheen's casual young killer (deserted by girlfriend Sissy Spacek) in *Badlands* (1973), one of many pictures indebted to *Breathless*. It is appropriate that Michel admire Bogart, who became a major cult figure in France as a result of this film. For one thing, he is also a tough guy who has wit and the heart of a sentimentalist. Equally important is that ex-prizefighter Belmondo is the one movie hero other than Bogart whose face (so battered and ugly that it's beautiful) reflects that he has experienced *life in a harsh world*. Belmondo had been in several earlier films, but it was *Breathless* that turned him into the "male Bardot" as the French press called him, and made him an international star: the greatest, most interesting, sexiest European rogue-hero of the sixties.

Godard chose the beautiful, dimpled Jean Seberg to be his hard-bitten free-spirited American expatriate because of her performance in Otto Preminger's *Bonjour Tristesse* (1958), in which her character feels nothing about a death she causes. Seberg refused to accept the part until Godard (whose misogyny was more blatant in his early films) agreed that Patricia wouldn't rifle the pockets of the dead Michel at the end. An uncommitted woman who would drop out of the Sorbonne in her senior year, who contemplates an abortion, who never sees anything through to the end, would surely break off with Michel (no use going to prison with him), but she wouldn't want him dead, just away from her, and she wouldn't take advantage of his death by stealing his money. Nor would she feel guilty about causing his death. Molly Haskell writes of this enigmatic heroine:

> Sexually she's a whore, emotionally a virgin. Something is missing: a conscience, a soul? . . . She's not even malevolent. Her cruelty lies in her indifference, in the equal ease with which she can make a life-or-death phone call to the police—or not make one.

Jean Seberg, born in Marshalltown, Iowa, was considered a flop in America as a result of poor public and critical reaction to her first two films, *Saint Joan* (1957), which she made at seventeen after being discovered by Preminger in a much-publicized nationwide talent search, and *Bonjour Tristesse*. But *Breathless* made her the darling of the French. A lovely, sexy, natural performer, she would become the first American actress to work regularly, and successfully, in France. Back home, she would gain critical acclaim only in *Lilith* (1964). In America, the status of *Breathless* as a cult film for years had to do primarily with Belmondo, Godard, and the picture's importance in the New Wave. But Seberg's cult reputation has grown considerably (along the lines of Frances Farmer's) since her suicide in 1979 and since startling proof has surfaced showing that the FBI, angered at her support of the Black Panthers, systematically tried to ruin her by planting false accusations in the press that she was carrying the baby of a Panther lover. (Following her death, a Broadway musical and television movie were quickly planned.) Seberg is one more very good reason to seek out *Breathless:* it's worth the price of admission to see her walk down the Champs-Élysées, Belmondo at her side, singing out *"New York Herald Tribune!"*

Michel pummels a man he finds fooling with his car. Scenes like this, with characters dressed similarly, could be found in every cheapie Monogram crime film in the forties.

The Bride of Frankenstein

1935 Universal
Director: James Whale
Producer: Carl Laemmle, Jr.
Screenplay: William Hurlbutt and John L. Balderston
From the novel by Mary W. Shelley

Cinematography: John D. Mescall
Music: Franz Waxman
Editor: Ted Kent
Running time: 80 minutes

Cast: Boris Karloff (The Monster), Colin Clive (Baron Henry Frankenstein), Valerie Hobson (Elizabeth Frankenstein), Ernest Thesiger (Dr. Septimus Pretorious), Una O'Connor (Minnie), E. E. Clive (the burgomeister), Elsa Lanchester (The Monster's Bride/Mary Shelley), Douglas Watson (Percy Bysshe Shelley), Gavin Gordon (Lord Byron), Dwight Frye (Karl), O. P. Heggie (blind hermit), John Carradine (hunter), Walter Brennan (neighbor), Joan Woodbury (little queen)

Synopsis: Mary Shelley tells her husband, Percy, and friend Lord Byron, that she has only told part of her story about scientist Henry Frankenstein and the Monster he created. The Monster had become a murderer because of the criminal brain Frankenstein had accidentally given him.

The peasants think the Monster lies dead in the blazing windmill, following his confrontation with Frankenstein. But he fell through the floor and landed safely in water below. Hans, the father of a little girl the Monster accidentally drowned, searches for the Monster's remains and is killed. The Monster also kills Hans's wife. Minnie, Frankenstein's nervous housekeeper, tells the townsfolk that the Monster lives, but no one believes her until corpses are discovered.

Frankenstein recovers from his battle with his Monster. His new bride, Elizabeth, tells him he did the devil's work in creating an artificial being from dead matter. Dr. Pretorious visits Frankenstein. He was a doctor of philosophy at Frankenstein's university but was booted out. Although Frankenstein insists he has learned his lesson, his curiosity forces him to go with Pretorious to his lodgings, where Pretorious shows Frankenstein several miniature figures he has created by growing them from seeds. But he has been unable to create a being of normal size. He wants Frankenstein to be his partner. Frankenstein refuses, saying "This isn't science. It's more like black magic." Pretorious reveals he wants to create a woman. Then he can create a race of monsters. Frankenstein realizes that Pretorious is power hungry and mad.

The Monster flees through the forest. As always he looks for friendship. He frightens a sheepherder. Her screams result in townspeople chasing him. The Monster is arrested and chained in the police dungeon, but he breaks free and kills one of his guards. He runs into the forest and takes refuge in a blind hermit's house. The hermit doesn't realize he is a Monster. He teaches him how to talk and say words like *bread, drink, friend.* Both forget their loneliness. But hunters discover the Monster in the house. They force the hermit to leave. Again the Monster is alone and miserable.

Fleeing the townspeople, he comes upon Pretorious, who has hired murderers Karl and Ludwig to rob graves. Pretorious pretends to be his friend by giving him liquor. The Monster kidnaps Elizabeth. This forces Frankenstein to help Pretorious build a Bride for the Monster. Karl kills a young woman for her heart, but doesn't tell Frankenstein that he got it through murder. Pretorious keeps the impatient Monster quiet by keeping him drunk.

The Bride is created. The Monster is excited. He hopes she will be his friend. But she pulls away from him, horrified by his looks, although her own aren't much better. The Monster is hurt and angry.

The Monster, who has already killed Karl, orders Frankenstein from the laboratory, locking him safely outside with Elizabeth. He tells Pretorious that he must stay with him and the Bride. Pretorious has underestimated the Monster. The Monster pulls a lever. There is an explosion. The castle crumbles. The Monster, the Bride, and Pretorious are killed. Frankenstein and Elizabeth hold each other.

A poignant, tragic moment. The Monster hopes he has found a friend and companion—he will be sadly disappointed. Jack Pierce's makeup on Lanchester and Karloff was remarkable; unfortunately it left permanent scars.

The gatherings that took place summer nights at Lord Byron's estate in Switzerland in 1816 were the artistic equivalents of the summit conferences of World War II. In addition to Byron himself, they were attended by intellectual physician John Polidori and neighbors Percy Shelley and his nineteen-year-old bride, Mary Wollstonecraft Shelley. These meetings were significant because of long philosophical discussions among the three men (while Mary listened intently), and because Byron was at work on Canto III of his *Childe Harold* and Shelley on his *Hymn to Intellectual Beauty* and *Mont Blanc*. Yet they are better known for a particular June night when the four challenged each other to write the best horror story. The surprising winner of the contest was Mary Shelley. She concocted a frightful story about a scientist named Victor Frankenstein who created a horrible monster out of dead matter and (while his creation went on a murder spree) became so guilt-ridden because of what he considered his own blasphemy that he withdrew into a life of constant self-torment. That Shelley called her book *Frankenstein (or, the Modern Prometheus)* instead of simply *Frankenstein* is significant. (Not coincidentally, Byron wrote *Prometheus* at this time, and Shelley soon after wrote his epic poem *Prometheus Unbound*.) Her work is no simple story of a mad scientist and his monster gone amok. It is about the philosophical implications of man defying God's laws (both Frankenstein and his articulate creature offer their views on the subject), the great burdens he places on himself for daring this, and his moral responsibility when the monster turns killer.

James Whale's classic *Frankenstein* (1931), the first sound and third film version of Shelley's novel, is indeed about the scientist (here called Henry, not Victor) feeling guilty for tampering in the unknown, for creating a "baby" who has no chance in this world, for unleashing a killer. He is the one who suffers. He is the modern-day Prometheus. It is his film. In Whale's splendid sequel *The Bride of Frankenstein,* however, the Monster relieves Frankenstein of his overwhelming burden by becoming responsible for his own heinous actions. *Bride* is the Monster's film.

Bride (which had shooting titles *The Return of Frankenstein* and *Frankenstein Lives Again!*) ingeniously begins with a recreation of the conversation in which Mary Shelley (played by Elsa Lanchester) discussed her horror story with Percy Shelley and Byron. (The lesser-known Polidori has been discarded.) Before continuing her story, which will be what takes place in *Bride,* she refers back to what happened in the first part of her tale, the content of the original film. She tells the men that she had written "a moral lesson": "There is punishment for those who emulate God." Although this statement does express the theme of the first film, it is extremely misleading, because it can mistakenly be understood as implying that Henry's sin was to create an artificial life form instead of leaving all creation up to God. (After all, such an endeavor is indeed portrayed as sinful in countless horror stories, including many derivatives of *Frankenstein.*) I don't believe the real Mary regarded Frankenstein's life-giving act as criminal and deserving of punishment, although she did realize that Frankenstein would feel both terror and shame as a result. For here was the daughter of feminist Mary Wollstonecraft (who died in childbirth) and radical religious philosopher William Godwin; she was the wife of a man who welcomed Prometheus's defiance of God's supreme authority and considered it unjust

Frankenstein (L) stands back warily while the diabolical Pretorious introduces the Monster to his unreceptive bride.

that God sentenced the Titan to endless torture for going against His law and helping man. It's probable that Mary Shelley admired Frankenstein's attempt to create life, to discover the secret of life, particularly because his initial purpose was to benefit mankind. Frankenstein's sin in the original film is *not* that he went against God's laws but that once he became a creator he competed with God for sovereignty. There is a revealing moment in *Frankenstein* when the Monster looks up and spots sunlight flickering into the dark chamber in which his creator keeps him. How beautifully Boris Karloff conveys the new being's newfound feelings of warmth and wonderment as, with a half-smile, he shuffles directly under the light. Suddenly, and seemingly without reason, Frankenstein blocks out the light. He jealously refuses his creature any knowledge (symbolized by the sunlight) that he didn't offer himself, as well as any contact with the God who sent this sun ray. It is for *emulating* our jealous God in the sense he won't allow others to use divine powers in his domain—rather than for *defying* God—that Frankenstein deserves condemnation.

Frankenstein's real crimes are against society. Moreover, they begin even before he has brought life to his Monster. His self-imposed isolation from fiancée Elizabeth, his friends, and the townspeople is itself a perversion, because he becomes an outsider, an outcast, an elitist. (Ironically, it is the Monster who seeks love, companionship, and camaraderie with the masses.) Even more important, as Lester D. Fried-

man points out in *The English Novel and the Movies* (Ungar 1981), "it is his refusal to provide the parental responsibility due his offspring that seals his fate. . . . Frankenstein is an irresponsible researcher, for he fails to take human consequences into account." Frankenstein should oversee his "child's" introduction to the townsfolk, its "coming out" into society. But caught up in his own grief, he neglects his fatherly responsibilities and abandons his creature, leaving it to make its own way in a world repulsed by grotesquery. Consequently, the Monster-child ends up murdering almost everyone who rejects him.

Following the prologue, *Bride* flashes back to the end of *Frankenstein,* when the scientist and the Monster confront each other near the windmill. It is a significant scene because here, finally, Frankenstein faces up to his responsibility. He is like George in Steinbeck's *Of Mice and Men* (published in 1937), who kills the feeble-minded Lennie (a child in a powerful man's body whose unintentioned murder is very similar to the Monster's murders) rather than let the mob devour his friend. (Although the Monster isn't Frankenstein's friend, to him it represents man's highest achievement, regardless of its criminal activities.) They struggle to the death— the Monster's—and the windmill (symbol of Frankenstein's great dream, as it was Don Quixote's) comes crashing down in flames. Although Universal's desire to make a sequel to the mammoth hit *Frankenstein* resulted in the Monster's resurrection (giving further credence to the theory that the Monster is a Christ figure), Henry had done his duty. Therefore, in *Bride,* there is no need for him to continue with his suffering. Now we can fully concentrate on the Monster's misery.

There are many reasons why *Bride* is better than its predecessor, not the least being that it deals with the Monster's need for female companionship, which is central to the second half of the novel. In Shelley's book, the Monster tells his creator: "I am alone and miserable; man will not associate with me; but one as deformed and horrible as myself would not deny herself to me. My companion must be of the same species, and have the same defects. This being you must create." When Frankenstein destroys his female creature before bringing her fully to life, the Monster is furious and dedicates himself to making his creator's life miserable. On his wedding night Frankenstein discovers his bride Elizabeth has been killed. He pursues her slayer endlessly, and dies from the ordeal. Before voluntarily going off to the coldest region on earth to die also, the Monster explains the reason for his suicidal wish: he will never be able to love a woman. "I shall no longer feel the agonies which now consume me, or be the prey of feelings unsatisfied, yet unquenched." *Bride,* like the film *Frankenstein,* fails to properly indicate the Monster's guilt from having committed murders, a guilt often expressed in Shelley's book ("Polluted by crimes, and torn by the bitterest remorse, where can I find rest but in death"), but at least it deals with the Monster's desire for a mate. In other ways it differs radically from the second half of Shelley's book. Never mind. It's a superlative, wonderfully imaginative horror masterpiece. Only *Mad Love* (1935), directed by Karl Freund, Whale's cameraman on *The Kiss Before the Mirror* (1933), is as stylized. Those who don't consider *King Kong* (1933) the greatest of the monster films almost invariably choose *The Bride of Frankenstein.*

As good as *Frankenstein* is, it is bleak, cold, and depressing. There is little music, little wit. It is much like a silent film. *Bride* had a higher budget and its production values breathe life into the story. Most impressive is Franz Waxman's full score, complete with church bells upon the Bride's birth. The claustrophobic castle and laboratory set of the original film are balanced here by great spacious, candlelit chambers with shiny floor and columns, all covered by mysterious shadows. And how wonderful is the expressionistic forest the Monster runs through, as the camera pans. We see a dark gray, cloudy backdrop in the distance, peasants with torches (on its way to becoming a horror movie cliché) massed on the horizon, and the Monster maneuvering around the trunks of trees (we never see branches or leaves) that are scattered about the hilly foreground. (Some shots of peasants against the sky remind one of Sergei Eisenstein.) Neither James Whale nor his skilled cameraman John Mescall strived for realism; they wanted viewers to know at all times that this was the visualization of the *story* Mary Shelley is telling in the prologue.

Director Whale, whose other classics include *Journey's End* (1930), starring Colin Clive, *Waterloo Bridge* (1931), *The Old Dark House* (1932), with Karloff and Ernest Thesiger, *The Invisible Man* (1933) and the best of the Dumas films, *The Man in the Iron Mask* (1939), was an outstanding, under-rated director who treated horror films with respect and gave them elegance. In *Bride* he displayed a bold, macabre sense of humor. How devilish he is when he has a silly farm wife reach into the windmill for her husband's hands and accidentally pull the Monster from the debris; or when he has a beautiful sheepherder (obviously one of Universal's starlets) become so terrified at seeing the Monster in the woods that she plummets into a nearby stream. There are other humorous touches: having one of Pretorious's miniatures be a replica of Henry VIII, who was played by Elsa Lanchester's husband Charles Laughton in *The Private Life of Henry VIII*

It is the hermit who teaches the Monster to talk. His vocabulary consisted of forty-four simple words that director Whale found in test papers of Universal's child actors. The Monster was given the mental age of a ten-year-old, and the emotional age of a fifteen-year-old.

(1933); having Karl complain about grave-robbing: "This is no life for murderers." It was also a nice twist to have the same actress play the Bride and Mary Shelley (a bride in 1816), further emphasizing that we are watching Shelley's story. Interestingly, Whale originally intended to have Karl kill Elizabeth and have it be her heart placed in the Bride, so the bride of Frankenstein would also be the Bride of the title. That idea was scrapped when it was decided that Henry would survive. (Why does the Monster spare Henry and Elizabeth? Perhaps to make his last gesture a noble one.)

Of course, the film benefits tremendously from imaginative casting. The weaselly Dwight Frye. The overly hysterical Una O'Connor. Elsa Lanchester, who had a comedy background. Ernest Thesiger, Whale's friend, who looks like a caricature of mad scientists, is unforgettable as Pretorious, one of the oddest scoundrels of the horror genre. Here's a weirdo who fancies he looks like the devil ("A slight resemblance or do I flatter myself?"), toasts "a new world of gods and monsters," and civilly tells Henry his one weakness is gin and the Monster his one weakness is cigars. He is indeed Satan in his relationship to the Monster (Adam, in the novel), tempting the first male of an artificial race with a female (Eve). For Henry, he serves as an example of what he could have become if he hadn't rid himself of his God complex.

Whale was fascinated by actors with angular faces: Clive, Thesiger, O'Connor, Lanchester, and Karloff all are given tremendous closeups, from straight on and in profile. Particularly effective is the creation scene, which appropriately takes place during a terrifying electrical storm. It's all shot with strange camera angles, with Clive (an excellent actor) and Thesiger standing at angles themselves; Whale cuts wildly from closeup to closeup of the two scientists, who *both* become increasingly loony as the experiment progresses. Then the Bride appears. Elsa Lanchester, who beat out Brigitte Helm and Phyllis Brooks for the part, is marvelous in this brief appearance. In a white shroud, on two-and-a-half-foot stilts that make her movement birdlike, she half-wobbles, half-glides across the room. In profile, her stitches are barely noticeable because of her wild hairstyle, inspired by Nefertiti. She almost steals the film from Karloff and Thesiger.

But it is Karloff's touching performance that makes the film great. What an actor he was. Wearing a forty-eight-pound uniform, standing on stilts, covered with bluish-green greasepaint, and almost hidden beneath genius Jack Pierce's patented makeup, Karloff still comes through. His sensitive eyes always manage to express the Monster's feelings. Here is a creature who comes across as a stray dog, beaten and burned in the past and paranoid, but desperate for kindness. He loves beauty, music, people. Karloff can be mean when the script calls for it, and he can be tender, as Karloff himself was, as when he pats the Bride's hand and asks hopefully, "Friend?" Or when in the famous vignette with the blind hermit, he comforts the overjoyed man who has finally been sent a friend by God. His Monster can even be amusing, as when he smokes, drinks, and learns a vocabulary. At all times, viewers empathize with him—we understand his misery and his longings. The Monster speaks in *Bride* for the only time in the Universal series, but it was unnecessary; with Karloff in the part, the Monster is eloquent even when silent.

Les Enfants du Paradis

1945 France Pathé Consortium Cinema (U.S. release in 1947)
Director: Marcel Carné
Producer: Fred Orain
Screenplay: Jacques Prévert
Cinematography: Roger Hubert
Music: Maurice Thiriet and Joseph Kosma
Pantomime Music: George Mouqué
Editors: Henri Rust and Madeleine Bonin
Running time: 188 minutes

Cast: Jean-Louis Barrault (Baptiste Deburau), Pierre Brasseur (Frédérick Lemaître), Arletty (Garance), Marcel Herrand (Pierre-François Lacenaire), Pierre Renoir (Jericho), Maria Casarès (Nathalie), Étienne Decroux (Anselme Deburau), Fabien Loris (Avril), Louis Salou (Count Edouard de Montray), Jeanne Marken (Madame Hermine), Gaston Modot (blind man), Pierre Palau (stage manager of the Funambules), Marcel Péres (director of the Funambules), Jean Lanier (Iago)

Synopsis: The setting is Paris in the 1840s. The Boulevard of Crime is crowded. People entertain on the streets and in the mime theater, the Funambules. Frédérick Lemaître, an aspiring actor, wants to get a job there. He is diverted by seeing a beautiful woman, Garance. She is Truth in a street exhibition. Frédérick flirts with her. She is mistress to Lacenaire, a criminal who writes comedies. He is a cynic who hates man and wages war on society. He doesn't love Garance, but he wants her.

Garance and Lacenaire stop in front of the Funambules. Outside Anselme Deburau urges everyone inside; his foolish son Baptiste sits outside and dreams. Lacenaire steals a man's watch and leaves Garance to take the rap. The police want to arrest her, but Baptiste says he saw what happened. He does a remarkable mime act showing how a man stole the watch.

Frédérick is hired to play a lion in the Funambules. Because of his success outside, Baptiste performs mime inside. He becomes a big star. Baptiste and Frédérick become friends. At Baptiste's rooming house, Frédérick seduces the landlady, Madame Hermine. Baptiste goes to a tavern. He asks Garance to dance with him. Avril, Lacenaire's companion, tries to scare Baptiste off, but Baptiste wins their fight. Baptiste takes the homeless Garance home with him. They kiss passionately. He is too shy to make love to her. He flees her room. In the morning Frédérick and Garance meet again. She invites him to her room. They will live together.

Garance works at the Funambules in a skit Baptiste writes. Having lost her to Frédérick, Baptiste contemplates suicide. He is miserable. So is Nathalie, the director's daughter, who wants Baptiste to love her. Frédérick and Garance realize they don't love each other. A count has been watching Garance every night. He wants to possess her. She turns him down, but takes his card. Lacenaire robs a debt collector in a room he got from Madame Hermine by using Garance's name. The police want to arrest her for being his accomplice. In desperation, she shows them the count's card. She will not go to prison, but she will have to become mistress to the count.

Years pass. Lacenaire goes to prison. Garance and the count travel. Baptiste and Nathalie are married and have a son. Frédérick becomes a great actor at the Grand Theater. Garance realizes she loves Baptiste. Back in Paris, she goes every night to see Baptiste perform. There she meets Frédérick. He tells Baptiste she is in town. Baptiste becomes emotional—he loves only her. Garance tries to stay away from him, rather than break up his family. Lacenaire meets Frédérick. He'd kill him if Frédérick didn't give him money—but Frédérick willingly does so. Lacenaire reunites with Garance and is disappointed she is unchanged. His bleak view of man is changed by the two incidents. The count thinks Garance is in love with Frédérick. He insults him into fighting a duel. But Lacenaire pulls back a curtain to reveal Garance and Baptiste kissing. Lacenaire kills the count before the duel knowing he'll be arrested. Garance and Baptiste sleep together. She leaves him to go back to the count, who she doesn't realize is dead, so that he won't kill Frédérick. Baptiste runs after Garance past Nathalie and his son. He is unable to pass through the great crowd. Her carriage disappears from view.

Children of Paradise

Nothing's more humbling than revealing that your all-time favorite film is *Night of the Living Dead* (1968), *Rock 'n' Roll High School* (1981), or *Bedtime for Bonzo* (1951), only to have someone respond that his or her favorite is *Les Enfants du Paradis*. The most prestigious picture on any revival house schedule, *Children of Paradise* is one of the glories of the cinema, arguably France's greatest film between Abel Gance's *Napoléon* (1927) and the New Wave—the romantic's delight, the sophisticate's cult favorite.

Children of Paradise was the fifth film made by Marcel Carné in collaboration with Jacques Prévert, the remarkable Marxist-surrealist-influenced scenarist-poet. France's top creative team from 1935 to 1946, their *Quai des Brunes* (1938) and classic *Le Jour se Lève* (1939), had established Jean Gabin's tough, doomed hero persona and made him the country's top romantic idol; *Les Visiteurs du Soir* (1942), with a devil who resembled Hitler, was an allegorical attack on Nazism. *Children of Paradise*, like *Les Visiteurs*, would be one of the cornerstone films of *le cinéma d'évasion*—the French film industry's brave response to the German occupation. It's amazing that an epic, especially one that celebrates a free France, could be made under the noses of the occupation authorities. The Vichy government forbade any film to be more than 2700 meters in length. *Children of Paradise* ended up almost double that. (It has been screened as two separate films.) Over two years, secret filming took place in garages and alleys. Members of the French resistance were able to hide from the Gestapo during the day because they were among the eighteen hundred extras the film employed. The production was so elaborate that a five-hundred-foot set was built, recreating the Boulevard du Temple: twice the set was shipped between Paris and Nice, the two cities where filming took place. "We were in Nice shooting our big exterior scenes," Carné told Marie Portal in an October 1944 interview, "when the Allied troops landed in southern Italy. The authorities ordered us to return to Paris. When I went to the Ministry of Information to protest, I was told that they knew from the best sources that there had been a landing at Genoa. It's unbelievable, but it's true! The outcome of it all was that we had to stop work for two months." Of course, the Liberation was welcomed; but Robert Le Vigan, who was originally cast as Jericho, the old clothes man, disappeared when he was suspected of collaboration with the Nazis and was replaced by Pierre Renoir; Arletty would spend a brief time in prison for collaborating and be placed under surveillance for a year—but this wouldn't take place until after *Children of Paradise* had been completed.

Children of Paradise opened in Paris in March 1945, and broke all records by playing nine months to great crowds. It was quickly hailed as France's *Gone With the Wind* (1939): an

The children of the theater. In a self-pitying mime conceived by Baptiste (R), Frédérick wins the stoical Garance's heart away from him—just as it happened in real life.

epic, a recreation of a bygone nineteenth-century period (Louis Philippe) and setting (the Boulevard of Crime), a romance about a woman who is coveted by all men who see her. But there were greater reasons the French held it so dearly. Made during the occupation, it was an affront to the Nazis. That the film takes place exactly one hundred years before it was filmed indicates the filmmakers wanted their French viewers to see parallels between the French in the film and the French in occupied Paris: as Prévert realized, the historical events on which the film is loosely based took place between 1827 (approximately) and 1836 (the year Lacenaire was executed). The film is a wonderful tribute to a people who have never been controlled by authority: lovers, mountebanks, rogues, criminals, artists, the poor who crowd the inexpensive "gods" (paradise) of the theaters, and the performers (children) who entertain them. The French, the picture states, can be dictated to only by love of country, memories, dreams, and their *hearts*—most of all it is the *heart* to which the *French* person responds, which is why Prévert and Carné think the actor is so vital in French society: he or she has the "ability to make people's hearts beat faster at exactly the same time every evening." The character of the French people cannot be altered by an invader. The French withstand poverty in the nineteenth century of the film, and the filmmakers believed correctly that they could outlast the occupation. The film is a cry for a return to the past ("Those were easy, happy days,"

sighs Garance; "life was sweet"), for liberty ("The one thing I really love is my freedom," asserts Garance), for solidarity between artists and their public (expressed by Frédérick's love affair with his audience); for solidarity between all French people. It reaffirms that there is beauty in life; and, through cynic Lacenaire's self-sacrifice, that humanity (all those in Balzac's *La Comédie Humaine* except counts, policemen, teachers, brutal fathers, and other authority figures) has goodness. It indicates that as long as the French do not betray each other, have love in their hearts (surrealists believe *love* is stronger than all else), seek beauty and truth, and maintain their superegos (*everyone* looks in mirrors), they cannot be defeated.

At the *heart* (naturally) of the film is Garance, a fictional female who is loved by several historical personages, Baptiste Deburau, Frédérick Lemaître, and Pierre-François Lacenaire. (The count is *probably* based on an historical figure as well.) The men see her as an angel, a dream, a vision of beauty, Venus. She is symbolized by birds, flowers, and the moon. She herself is the symbol of Paris, or maybe she is Paris. Beautiful, freedom-loving, full of memories, as tolerant (even as proud) of its gutter dwellers as of its elite, the lover of every man—the betrayer of none; in whose presence (as the moon's) hearts begin to flutter. Most important: she is a survivor, a stoic beauty (the perfect description of Sphinx-like Arletty) who remains unchanged ("I am free") despite becom-

Baptiste's father once thought his son a simpleton, but now that Baptiste has proved to be the greatest mime in Paris, he is eager to perform with him.

ing mistress to a dictatorial man of another class. Only when one realizes Garance is other than a beautiful woman can one clearly see the film as a political propaganda piece.

Perhaps François Truffaut derived his "stolen kisses" concept from *Children of Paradise.* People desire only those they cannot have. Frédérick and Baptiste are first attracted to Garance when she is mistress to Lacenaire. Lacenaire doesn't decide he wants Garance until he realizes he is losing her. Baptiste becomes passionate about Garance while she is mistress to Frédérick. Meanwhile Nathalie is passionate about Baptiste. Typically, when Garance and Frédérick live together, they love others: Garance loves Baptiste, and Frédérick loves the theater audience. Lacenaire, Baptiste, and Frédérick lose Garance to the count. Garance does not love the count, and he cannot convince her to truly give herself to him. (Since Garance is more a reflection of the mirrors she constantly gazes into than she is a real person, it is questionable whether she could really give herself to anyone.) Baptiste marries Nathalie, but he still loves Garance. Baptiste ("I shall never forget the light in your eyes") and Garance ("He has beautiful eyes") finally spend one night of love together; but come morning Garance departs rather than breaking up Baptiste's family. She does not know that Lacenaire has murdered the count, a "crime of virtue." In *Children of Paradise* all lovers end up alone—that is tragic, but for those who live—"I'm not beautiful, I'm alive," said Garance; "Life is beautiful," said Frédérick—there is no tragedy. As Garance told herself: "You have no right to be sad, you are one of the happy ones in spite of everything, because someone really loved you." To be French, as if there were an initiation rite, one must survive the breakup of one's greatest love affair. Great romances cannot live long—they are too consuming. So losing one's true love is to be expected and accepted—as Frédérick and Garance realize, and perhaps (but don't bet on it) Baptiste will discover in time. Jealousy is also a constant companion of the romantic. ("Jealousy belongs to everyone," states Lacenaire,

"even if women belong to no one.") It's nothing to be ashamed of—it just must be put to better use than the count makes of it (he kills his rivals); for instance, Frédérick uses the feeling to help him play Othello. The tragedy we find in the film is that some men need to be loved by a woman (Garance) and are jealous of men with whom she has innocent relationships, yet cannot give love themselves. Lacenaire sees that such men as the count and himself are misplaced in a world where people must have hearts (in order to give love): he kills the count and awaits the gallows for himself. Lacenaire, with his death, thus becomes one of several characters who fulfill prophecies in the film (Frédérick predicted he'd be a great star, Jericho predicted Nathalie would marry the man she loved) but what changes him from a blackguard to a noble man is that his other predictions, which relied on man being coldhearted, did not pan out (Garance did not betray him; she did not change when she became rich; Frédérick willingly gave him money). The point is, fate plays a hand in life's drama, but the players can improvise if they have the will to change their destinies.

Balzac's Paris, as presented by Carné and Prévert, is a giant carnival (complete with carnival music on the soundtrack). Chaos is the order of the day. Prostitutes, pickpockets, barkers, old-clothes peddlers, dandies, pretty girls, men with trained monkeys, beggars, and entertainers fill the Boulevard of Crime. In the Funambules, the poor sit on each other or hang from the rafters and shout toward the stage. Tumblers, jugglers, a man in a lion suit, and Pierrots pass before them. Backstage, costumes are changed, gongs clang, rival families fight, and the director makes threats, levies fines, and develops an ulcer. At the Grand Theater, hammy Frédérick makes up dialogue to confuse his fellow actors and enrage the authors he loathes, runs into the audience (the actor and audience are one) and there continues his performance, and wins a standing ovation from his wild admirers. Crime is in the street—Lacenaire makes sure of that—art imitates life and vice versa. Baptiste's mime acts include thievery and murder; Frédérick plays a criminal and later, as Othello, a murderer. Everyone in this world seems to know everyone else—it is very incestuous. Everyone is a performer: Baptiste is a mime ("He's not acting," observes Garance; "he's inventing dreams"); Frédérick an actor; Lacenaire a showman ("You talk all the time," Garance compliments him; "it's like being in the theater"); the blind man (who's not really blind) a charlatan; Jericho a Greek chorus of sorts. Only Garance does not put on an act of any kind: she is Truth when she is first seen; she can't bear lying, even to the count.

The opulent visuals of Carné and cinematographer Roger Hubert are perfectly suited to the subject matter. The elaborate sets are rich in detail and historically accurate (lithographs and woodblock prints of the period were studied), the costuming both decorative and expressive, and the truly magnificent performances by Jean-Louis Barrault, Pierre Brasseur, and Marcel Herrand thoroughly flamboyant. The theatricality of the visuals is set up by the ironic, philosophic, symbolic dialogue of Jacques Prévert. In *Film Comment* (Nov.–Dec. 1981), Marc Mancini described Prévert's style:

> It is true that Prévert's poetry is remarkable for its cinematic nature, but his scripts are equally noteworthy for their melding of ornate structure and the language of the street—a poetic

realism Prévert helped forge, and which seems the most obvious characteristic of the great scripts of pre-War France. Prévert's dialogue sounds tight and convincing; yet when examined closely, it is far too clever, far too incredible for any character to speak. Parallelisms, contrasts, contradictions, alliteration, rhythmic repetitions—all the arsenal of visual and musical tropes later available to Prévert the poet would be born in his screenplays. Above all, Prévert favored two devices which most certainly came from surrealist poetry. The first—lists of words in seemingly random order—establishes a rhythmic effect and compresses a multitude of images into a few lines, like some kinestasis of words. . . . A second device for which Prévert is well known is the pun—verbal surprises, the weapons of the mind (or a screen character) charmed by surrealist affinities between sound and thoughts.

I highly recommend that everyone, especially admirers of *Children of Paradise,* read Prévert's script. It will certainly make the complex film a bit clearer. Also, you'll discover almost an hour's worth of material that is not in the final version of the film. The most important change from script to film is that in the final scene, when Baptiste futilely chases after Garance through the large street crowd, the movie does not include a moment in which Baptiste clubs Jericho on the head and kills him (the death of the third person who cannot love others). The real Baptiste was tried for manslaughter for killing a man who insulted him and his wife on the street: it was this event that first interested Prévert in writing a film about Baptiste Deburau.

I'm glad that the Jericho death scene was eliminated. It would really have made the glorious ending depressing. What's most strange about this picture is that although everyone's life seems to be in ruin at the end (except for Frédérick's), you leave the theater feeling happy.

(T) In one of Carné's many crowd scenes Garance is accused of being a pickpocket. The Parisians never appreciate her and always condemn her of wrongdoing, yet to Carné she is the heart and soul, the very essence of the French people. (Above) The count proposes to Garance. Not wanting to relinquish her cherished freedom, she refuses . . . for now. (R) Thinking Garance secretly loves Frédérick (made up as Othello), the count challenges him to a duel. Infuriated by the count's arrogance, Lancenaire pulls back the curtains to reveal Garance and Baptiste embracing.

1971 Warner Bros.
Director: Stanley Kubrick
Producer: Stanley Kubrick
Screenplay: Stanley Kubrick
From a novel by Anthony Burgess
Cinematography: John Alcott
Electronic music: Walter Carlos
Editor: Bill Butler
Running time: 137 minutes

Cast: Malcolm McDowell (Alex), Patrick Magee (Mr. Alexander), Anthony Sharp (Minister of the Interior), Warren Clarke (Dim), Aubrey Morris (Deltoid), James Marcus (Georgie), Michael Tarn (Pete), Godfrey Quigley (prison chaplain), Michael Bates (chief guard), Adrienne Corri (Mrs. Alexander), Philip Stone (Dad), Sheila Raynor (Mum), Carl Duering (Dr. Brodsky), Paul Farrell (tramp), Michael Gover (prison governor), Miriam Karlin (Cat Lady), David Prowse (Julian), John Clive (stage actor), Clive Francis (Joe), Madge Ryan (Dr. Branon), Pauline Taylor (Dr. Taylor), John Savident (conspirator), Margaret Tyzack (conspirator)

Synopsis: It is the not-too-distant future. Young Alex, our Humble Narrator, and his three "droogs"—Dim, Georgie, and Pete—spend their nights practicing ultraviolence: beating, raping, robbing, and terrorizing citizens. After drinking some milk plus at the Korova bar, they go out and brutally beat a drunk tramp. Later they come upon a rival gang about to give the old "in-out in-out" to a nude woman they've abducted. The gangs have a brutal fight. Alex and his droogs race their Durango 95 over country roads, playing Hogs of the Road. Wearing masks with long noses they play Surprise Visit on wealthy writer Mr. Alexander. They beat Alexander and beat and rape his wife—while Alex sings "Singin' in the Rain." Alex caps off the evening by sitting in his room in his parents' flat listening to Beethoven, his one true love.

Alex's father and mother go off to the factory but Alex stays home from school. He is visited by the sneering truant officer Deltoid, who warns him that the next time he gets into trouble he'll be sent to prison. Alex picks up two teen-age girls. He brings them home for some quick in-out in-out. His droogs are angry with him because he smacked Dim for disturbing him during a Beethoven selection the previous night. The three violently rebel, but Alex quelches the revolt. He is still leader.

The four droogs play Surprise Visit on a snobbish lady who has a lot of cats. Alex kills her. He tries to escape before the police arrive. But Dim smashes him with a milk bottle. He is arrested. Deltoid is delighted.

Alex is sentenced to a lengthy prison term. The only way to get released is to convince the new Minister of the Interior, whose conservative law-and-order party has just come to office, to let him be the first subject of the controversial Ludovico technique designed to restrain the criminal impulse.

For two weeks Alex endures Dr. Brodsky's Ludovico technique. He is given a shot, then forced to watch movies of awful violence. His eyes are clamped open and drops of some liquid are constantly dropped into them. Beethoven is played in the background. Violence begins to make him nauseated. Alex is released from prison. He is incapable of hurting a fly, he will turn his cheek if struck; but he cannot bear listening to Beethoven's Ninth. Alex returns home. His parents have given his room to a lodger. He walks the streets. The tramp he once beat up recognizes him and with his tramp friends beats him up. Police disperse the crowd. The cops are Dim and Georgie. They beat and almost drown Alex. He seeks refuge in a nearby house. It is Mr. Alexander's house. Mrs. Alexander has died. Now manic, Alexander only recognizes Alex as the poor boy who endured the Ludovico technique. Liberal Alexander considers Alex a victim of the modern age. He wants Alex to help embarrass the party in office. Alex agrees to help. When Alex unthinkingly sings "Singin' in the Rain" Alexander realizes who he is. The crazed man locks him in a room and puts Beethoven's Ninth on full blast. Alex attempts suicide. He survives. Alexander is taken to prison. The government has condemned the doctors for what happened to Alex. His parents want him to come home. Alex agrees to further help the minister in return for certain favors. He has evil thoughts once again. He knows he has been cured.

A Clockwork Orange

In 1961, British novelist Anthony Burgess wrote *A Clockwork Orange* (Norton, 1963), "partly as exorcism from my own experiences": During a London blackout in World War II, three AWOL GI's raped, robbed, and brutally beat his wife; she lost the baby she carried and suffered internal bleeding that contributed to her death at age forty. In 1964, Mick Jagger wanted to play Alex, leader of a gang that rapes a writer's wife, but no producer dared finance an adaptation of such a violent-sexual-political book because of possible trouble with British censors. So it remained available until Stanley Kubrick decided it would be his highly anticipated followup to *2001: A Space Odyssey* (1968). Since no date is given for the events in the futuristic *Clockwork,* perhaps Kubrick wanted to show what was happening back on earth while Poole, Bowman, and H.A.L. were out in space.

Whereas *2001* had been the most controversial film of the sixties, *A Clockwork Orange* was the most fiercely debated film of the seventies. But whereas most critics (Andrew Sarris was in the minority) thought *2001* a masterpiece that firmly established Kubrick as the English-language film's most important director—the controversy wasn't about *2001*'s quality but about interpretation—critics either hailed *Clockwork* for its originality, its surrealistic/futuristic design, its technical virtuosity, its view that all politicians are hypocrites, and its serious attempt, as Vincent Canby wrote in *The New York Times,* "to analyze the meaning of the social climate that tolerates it"; or ripped into it for having a bleak outlook on man that was decidedly "fascist" (Fred M. Hechinger, also in the *Times*), for "catering to the thugs in the audience" (Pauline Kael), and for being "an ideological mess, a paranoid right-wing fantasy masquerading as an Orwellian warning" (Roger Ebert). Although the picture did superlatively at the box office (after *2001,* the college-age audience wouldn't dare miss the next Kubrick film) and walked off with the New York Film Critics prestigious Best Film award, so many heavyweight critics condemned the film that Burgess, Kubrick, and even Malcolm McDowell had no choice but to join in the discussion.

While Burgess conceded that the film was a "radical remaking of his novel," he expressed great satisfaction with it: "It's very much a Kubrick movie, technically brilliant, thoughtful, relevant, poetic, mind-opening." According to Burgess, the film was "not a Bible of violence" as some of its detractors suggested, and the ultimate destructive act shown "is dehumanization, the killing of the soul." Burgess believed that his book and the film were Christian parables that expressed two basic points: "If we are going to love mankind, we will have to love Alex as a not unrepresentative member of it"; "it is preferable to have a world of violence undertaken

Alex and his droogs visit the Korova bar, which contains decor that angered feminist viewers.

in full awareness—violence chosen as an act of will—than a world conditioned to be good or harmless." I offer these thoughts:

1. It was not the *strength* of the violence that caused some critics to term the film *fascistic*. True, they found the gratuity of the violence and the justification for violence to be highly objectionable (as well as the comical atmosphere when violence is being perpetrated). Yet, while they were less than thrilled that this picture helped create a moviegoers' *cult of violence*, the major reason they considered the picture "evil" was Kubrick's heartless, superintellectual, superorderly, antiseptical, antihuman, antifemale, antisensual, antipassion, antierotic treatment of his subject. In his cold world of the future, all emotional stimuli, from drugs to Beethoven, are lumped together as being harmful; all art (classical music, theater, literature, paintings, sculpture, and film) is pornographic.

2. The film is technically brilliant, relevant, and, I suppose, mind-opening (it initiated brief legislative debate over forced "volunteerism" of U.S. prisoners in scientific experimentation designed to eliminate the criminal instinct). Who knows if it's poetic? It is more thought out, in a conniving sort of way, than it is thoughtful.

3. Christian training teaches the individual to be good and to turn the other cheek (to be harmless). Until the altruistic "true Christian" emerges, this training—though more benign, hopefully, than the Ludovico "brainwashing" technique—is a *conditioning* process meant to subdue one's baser instincts.

4. Stanley Kubrick is an obsessive individual whose films invariaby take several times longer to complete than those of other directors. His mania for perfection is well known: for *The Shining* (1980), he actually had someone type, not photocopy, all Jack Nicholson's many, many single-spaced pages that repeated the one line: "All work and no play make Jack a dull boy." Kubrick insists on absolute control over every aspect of the production. According to McDowell (who liked him), he is a military man. His actors—his puppets—are rehearsed incessantly from early morning to late afternoon on each scene before he turns on the camera. This goes on for months. With few exceptions (McDowell

Alex picks up two teen-age girls at the local record shop. (One album available is the soundtrack to 2001.) In the Burgess novel these girls are just ten, and Alex rapes them.

is one of them), his actors perform in the Kubrick method, giving mannered, emotionless performances, creating caricatures instead of characters. So I'd say that Kubrick has a lot of nerve to make a film against dehumanization.

5. None of us will dispute Burgess's theme: "When a man cannot choose, he ceases to be a man." However, the question arises: does Alex act violently because of free choice (making a rational decision) or because he follows his instincts? There is a difference. On the one hand, I sense that the smart Alex acts as despicably as he does to insult the society he detests ("Alex," writes Pauline Kael, "is not so much an expression of how this society has lost its soul as he is a force pitted against the society"). But I also see his brutal acts as being impulsive; child games meant for a moment's pleasure. Since his acts seem to be reflexive, conditioned by past violence, he already is a *clockwork orange* (human on the outside, mechanized on the inside) before he is subjected to the Ludovico technique and has his ability to act on his free will (or his impulses) restrained.

6. Christians might be able to love Alex if he were a representative of mankind. But in the world Kubrick shows us, "others are lesser people," according to Kubrick (and we agree), "and in some ways worse people." This version of mankind, totally alien to us, is not worthy of our love. Anyway: it's only preferable to have "a world of violence undertaken in full awareness" if we all play by the same rules, if we are all predators and not prey.

7. Never mind about other Christians, what makes Burgess assume Kubrick shares his love of man? Kubrick loves the individual's ability to fight off conformity, but he certainly doesn't love man: "One of the most dangerous fallacies which has influenced a great deal of political and philosophical thinking is that man is essentially good, and that it is society which makes him bad"; "I'm interested in the brutal and violent nature of man because it's a true picture of him"; "man isn't a noble savage, he's an ignoble savage. He is irrational, brutal, weak, silly, unable to be objective about anything where his own interests are involved."

The film is like a Sunday sermon where the fellow up on the pulpit suddenly realizes there is no moral lesson that applies to his listeners. If the film ended with Alex dying as a result of being driven to suicide, the lesson would have been: those who sin will eventually be paid back in kind. If the film had ended where the original edition of the Burgess novel did—it was a chapter longer and had Alex contemplating settling down with a wife and family—the lesson would have been: left to his own devices, and with a little Christian training (from the prison chaplain), a person will eventually reform and choose the right path. But because it ends where it does, those who listen to the sermon would be more worried about Alex's return to their streets with an evil gleam in his eye than they'd be concerned about a moral lesson. The reactionary-making lesson Kubrick teaches paranoid individuals is that you can't cure the habitual thrill criminal. Since Kubrick doesn't believe that an improved society will prevent the creation of more Alexes, viewers are left to decide what to do with future criminals once our jails are full of political prisoners. (Of course, viewers should say

"First of all our jails shouldn't contain any *political* prisoners . . .") Because Alex is meant to embody our savage, anarchic impulses, Kubrick figured that we'd identify with him and suggested that was the reason many of us felt discomfort watching him maul people. He wanted us to "come to grips with our savagery," and "not feel guilty about enjoying it" on the screen. But we didn't buy it. In 1971 there was a pacifist generation—not the punk generation who today has made *Clockwork* one of the most-in-demand revival-house and Midnight Movie selections. We were more inclined to identify with Alex's potential victims. We were, however, manipulated by Kubrick into *accepting* Alex in relation to his world; he wins our admiration, Kubrick realized, "in the same way that Richard III gradually undermines your disapproval of his evil ways."

It's hard to dislike Alex with Malcolm McDowell in the part. He's extremely energetic, handsome, and witty, as dynamic as the young James Cagney was when he played punk hoods back in the thirties. His Alex is more clever, honest, intelligent, and interesting than any of the adults he meets in his cruel world. Just in case McDowell's presence didn't do the trick, Kubrick made several alterations in

As if illustrating the concept of filmmaker as rapist, Kubrick holds the camera while directing Alex's two rampages. (T) While crooning "Singin' in the Rain," Alex prepares to rape Mrs. Alexander. (B) Alex lifts the sexual sculpture that he'll use to kill the Cat Lady.

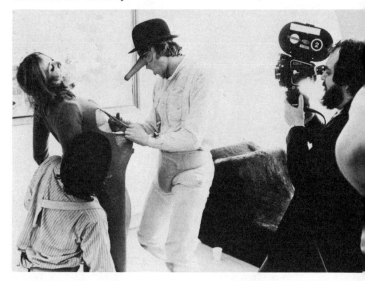

Burgess's story that would put us more on Alex's side. In the novel, he rapes two ten-year-old girls whom he coaxes into his room; in the film, the girls are teen-agers who willingly participate in the sex. The Cat Lady in the book is a feeble, eccentric old lady; in the film she is a physically fit, snobby rich bitch who Kubrick wants us to believe deserves what she gets. Kubrick eliminated a book sequence in which Alex murders a helpless fellow prisoner. Without exception, every victim in the film is more repulsive than in the book. Kubrick makes their abuse at Alex's hands more palatable by making them grotesque, mannered, snobbish figures (Deltoid and Alexander, the film's two liberal forces, are thoroughly obnoxious). Kubrick uses other distancing devices: extreme wide angles, slow motion, fast motion, surreal backgrounds, songs that counterpoint the violence. Notice how the violence Alex perpetrates is very stylized, but when it comes time for Alex to endure violence (a bottle to the head, police brutality, the Ludovico technique), it is much more realistic. In fact it is torturous for him and for us. Poor Alex, we think. Our hostility is directed toward everyone else but him: he is like an alley cat who is declawed before being returned to the streets. As Pauline Kael complains, "the movie becomes a vindication of Alex."

Kubrick has also been charged with altering the book in such a way as to deliberately insult women. In the book, the female the rival gang wants to rape is only ten. She is fully clothed. In the film, she is a big-breasted woman who is totally nude. The Cat Lady becomes a yoga dabbler, wearing a leotard, and is caught by Kubrick's camera in a very compromising position. For no reason her studio is filled with perverse sculptures and art of nude women. In the book she is killed with a sculpture of a woman. In the film she is killed when Alex slams a sculpture of a penis and testicles into her mouth. Unlike in the book, Alex has pictures of naked women on his wall (in Burgess, the hoods have only an impulsive need for sex; in Kubrick it is central to their lives, as their long-nosed masks and codpieces attest). One disturbing image is Alex's snake slithering toward the vagina of one of the naked models. Feminists were even more outraged by the decor in the Korova milk bar, which features sculptures of nude women in obscene poses. One sculpture of a woman leaning back on her hands is used as a male footrest; if you pull a lever located under the crotch area of a second sculpture, milk plus will spurt out of its nipples. But the most disturbing image of all occurs when, preceding the rape, Alex shoves a little ball into Mrs. Alexander's mouth: we realize that the actress playing the part had to participate in Kubrick's humiliating fantasy.* "If Oscars were awarded for Best Achievement in Misogyny," seethed Beverly Walker in *Women & Film* (No. 2, 1972), "*A Clockwork Orange* would surely have been last year's winner. . . . Because he has genius for this sort of thing, he has accomplished the near impossible: he has made an intellectual's pornographic film."

---

*Because such scenes are stylized, the violence doesn't offend us—although it should—and the "sexual" content is exciting rather than repulsive. In the book, interestingly, the sex and violence is not offensive, but it's also not exciting. That's because Burgess's use of Nadsat (teen-age slang) to describe the action makes it seem as if we're struggling through a foreign language—it's a powerful "distancing" tool. So one (Kubrick) uses distancing techniques to titillate, while the other (Burgess) uses them for the opposite effect.

Mr. Alexander and his liberal friends wait for the blaring Beethoven symphony to drive Alex, who is locked in an upstairs bedroom, into committing suicide.

The Minister of the Interior reviews prisoners while looking for a subject for the Ludovico treatment. Alex waits in anticipation. The high-stepping guard brings up the rear.

My own charge is that once Alex is arrested and the look of the film shifts away from dreamlike pop art, the picture becomes excruciatingly dull. I could have watched an infinite number of space travel scenes in *2001*, but I cannot stand the pacing in *Clockwork* once Alex hits prison. It's Kubrick at his most irritating: everyone talks loudly and sermonizes; that obnoxious militaristic prison guard keeps marching around, stamping his feet, and shouting; we keep having to watch forms being signed in triplicate; everything is ritualistic. I've long been worried that some day Kubrick will film a scene showing a cool black entering an all-white gym—the ritualistic handshakes could go on forever and ever. . . . Knowing Kubrick, he'd have everybody stammer.

Cutter's Way

formerly titled *Cutter and Bone*

1981 United Artists
Director: Ivan Passer
Producer: Paul R. Gurian
Screenplay: Jeffrey Alan Fiskin
From the novel *Cutter and Bone* by
Newton Thornburg

Cinematography:
Jordan Cronenweth
Music: Jack Nitzsche
Editor: Carline Ferriol
Running time: 109 minutes

Cast: Jeff Bridges (Richard Bone), John Heard (Alex Cutter), Lisa Eichhorn (Maureen Cutter), Valerie Duran (Ann Dusenberry), Stephen Elliott (J. J. Cord), Arthur Rosenberg (George Swanson), Nina Van Pallandt (woman in hotel), Patricia Donahue (Mrs. Cord)

Synopsis: Richard Bone is a handsome, overage beach bum living on a yacht in Santa Barbara. George Swanson wants him to sell yachts, but instead Bone picks up a few bucks as a gigolo, sleeping with the middle-aged wives of prospective buyers. Bone's best friend is Alexander Cutter, who lost an arm, an eye, and a leg in Vietnam. Cutter resents Bone because while Cutter was off fighting, Bone had, as always, walked away from possible danger and commitment. But Cutter's real resentment is against the rich men who sent him to fight such a meaningless war. Cutter spends his nights drinking and insulting everyone around him. His neglected wife, Mo, stays at home and drinks. Bone would like to sleep with her, but she disrespects him too much.

After leaving a woman in a hotel, Bone drives home. His car stalls in an alley. A big car pulls up behind him. A figure, wearing sunglasses and a strange hat, gets out and dumps something in the trash. The next day, police tell Bone that the man had brutally murdered a young hitchhiker named Vickie Duran. Bone says he could never identify the man, because it was too dark.

At a street parade, Bone spots oilman J. J. Cord, one of the most powerful men in the area. He automatically says "That's him!" Later he retracts his statement. But Cutter hopes to convince him that Cord was the killer. He provides evidence that Cord often picked up hitchhikers and that he was in the vicinity where Vickie was killed.

Cutter enlists the help of Valerie Duran, Vickie's sister, to try to convince Bone to trap Cord. Mo is furious with them for playing around with real danger. The three type up a blackmail note. Bone backs out of delivering it, but Cutter proceeds with the plan. If Cord agrees to pay, they will know they have the right man. Cutter reports that Cord will soon deliver a message to Bone, whose name is on the letter.

Mo kicks Cutter out of the house. At a weak moment, she agrees to sleep with Bone. Bone leaves in the middle of the night, breaking his promise to Mo. He learns the next morning that the house was blown up and Mo has been killed. Bone says Mo may have killed herself after he left. Cutter thinks Bone is egotistical, that Cord did it, thinking Bone was in the house. The bomb was the message. At a polo match, Cutter spots Cord wearing a polo hat. He threatens him. Mourning his dead wife, whom he loved, he moves into George's guest house. He tells Bone that Cord took control of the marina by force years before, from George's father and mother. Since Cutter lies constantly, Bone doesn't know whether to believe him.

Cutter decides to kill Cord. He is obsessed with Cord's guilt. He gives Bone permission to back out, as Valerie has already done. But Bone goes with Cutter when they crash Cord's party. Cord's guards capture Bone. Meanwhile, Cutter steals Cord's horse. He eludes Cord's men and charges the house, crashing through the window of the room in which Cord and Bone stand. He lies on the floor dying, his gun pointed at Cord. Bone assures Cutter "It was him!" He too holds the gun. He asks Cord "It was you?" Cord disdainfully puts on his sunglasses and answers "What if it were?" Making a true commitment, Bone pulls the trigger.

Cutter and Bone premiered in New York in late March 1981 and was promptly lambasted by New York's three dailies, all three network critics, and *Variety*. Soon after, Richard Schickel in *Time,* David Ansen in *Newsweek,* and critics for New York's weekly papers wrote glowing reviews and urged readers to rush to the film before it was too late. But it was already too late. In a wave of post-*Heaven's Gate* (1980) panic, United Artists, which had been willing to gamble only a paltry $63,000 on publicity, pulled the plug and shelved it after four days of weak box office. Fortunately, its enterprising "art" division, United Artists Classics, which is also responsible for turning another John Heard starrer *Head Over Heels* (1980)—reedited as *Chilly Scenes of Winter* (1982)—from a box office disaster into a cult and modest commercial success, was buoyed by the late-coming critical raves and took over its distribution. Promptly changing the title to *Cutter's Way* so people would no longer assume it to be a comedy about surgeons, it quickly entered the picture in Houston's Third International Film Festival, where it won the Best Picture, Best Director (Ivan Passer), Best Screenplay (Jeffrey Alan Fiskin), and Best Actor (John Heard) awards. A week later it was the prestigious closing feature at Seattle's Film Festival. Given a new ad campaign geared for the art house audience, which stressed its mysterious character relationships rather than its murder mystery, *Cutter's Way* (an equally confusing title that likely has to do with Alexander Cutter's form of morality) reopened in the summer of 1981, first in Seattle and then in Los Angeles, Boston (where *Head Over Heels* and still another Heard film, 1977's *Between the Lines,* had their principal cults), and New York. By this time the word had gotten around and *Cutter's Way* became a cause célèbre, even going into the black during long runs in first-run theaters.

Admittedly, I was slightly disappointed in *Cutter's Way* when I first saw it. I agreed with those who complained it was boring in spots, confusing, and had three of the most infuriating lead characters in cinema history. But as I have come to learn, it is a picture that demands several viewings to be judged fairly, simply because it takes that long to break bad viewing habits. *Cutter's Way* can be enjoyed only by those willing to accept certain facts: a movie with a whodunit needn't be about the mystery (the less impressive 1980 film *True Confessions* is another case in point); lead characters needn't be crowd pleasers; ambiguity can be intentional, and also profound. *Cutter's Way* is an original, endlessly fascinating work, one that involves you in the lives of real people. It is uncompromisingly written, eerily photographed (by Jordan Cronenweth), marvelously cast and acted, erotic, sinister, and disarmingly emotional. A picture that shifts directions at every turn, it begins in classic noir style, with its darkness, rain-soaked streets, and violent murder. Thereafter we're in bright California sunshine. Yet in leisurely, luxurious California the sensation of menace is even more pervasive. What starts out on a seemingly pessimistic course, as an elegy to the hopeful sixties, ends on an ironically hopeful note: Bone kills villain Cord, sealing his own doom, but, more importantly, signifying that morality has emerged triumphant.

Czech émigré Ivan Passer, Miloš Forman's screenwriter on *Loves of a Blonde* (1965) and *The Firemen's Ball* (1968) before both fled their native country in 1968 upon the Russian invasion, somehow zeroes in on distinct American types ignored by Ameri-

(R) Only Cutter would use a real gun at an amusement park shooting gallery. Bone and Valerie are used to this kind of display from him. (Below) The sad Mo was the last holdout to give in to Bone's charms.

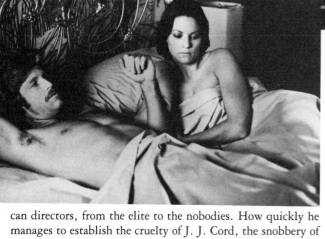

can directors, from the elite to the nobodies. How quickly he manages to establish the cruelty of J. J. Cord, the snobbery of Cord's thick-skinned socialite wife, the opportunism of Valerie, the hurt that the woman in the hotel (Nina van Pallandt) feels when Bone insults her sexual prowess, and the peculiar character traits of Cutter, Bone, and Mo. Remarkably, he gets us to understand these characters through their posturing; then he lets their words confirm our suspicions about them. What's most fascinating for me (and I think other recent viewers feel similarly) is that my feelings for Cutter, Bone, and Mo (and for the actors' performances) change each time I see the film, depending on my moods and tolerance levels. Passer, Fiskin, and actors John Heard, Jeff Bridges, and Lisa Eichhorn are to be commended for causing this reaction. For each of the three also fluctuates between love and disgust for the other two, depending on his/her moods and tolerance levels.

In *The Third Man* (1949), Alida Valli sums up Orson Welles's Harry Lime for Joseph Cotten: "He never grew up—the world just grew up around him." This is certainly how Mo might explain Cutter, *her* good man gone sour, but in truth this statement applies to all three. They fill a serious void in the cinema: nowhere else can we find representatives of a large part of the American populace—people in their twenties and thirties who wish society would allow them to become "adults" at their own paces, rather than having adulthood and adult responsibilities thrust on them once they reach a certain age. Cutter, Bone, and Mo have not made the dramatic transition from young people to adults. They are too irresponsible to even take care of themselves: none has a real job, there's no food in the refrigerator, Cutter's driver's license has expired and his insurance has lapsed, they choose to live in permanent squalor, and I wouldn't be surprised if each has some uncontrolled infection or social disease

(it's a sexy film, but touching any of these people seems like a dangerous proposition). They are children of the sixties (they'd have been something back then, when vital and in their primes) who wanted to improve the *real world* for the time they'd be adults and be ready to live in it. But the wishful thinking of the sixties was smothered by the dark reality of Vietnam, and what somehow rose from the ashes was an equally poisonous America run by rich bastards like oil tycoon J. J. Cord, the symbol of their frustrating defeat. No wonder these three want to delay "growing up" even longer.

On one level, Cutter, Bone, and Mo are a less sophisticated (yet smarter) equivalent of the Marsha Mason–Joan Hackett–James Coco triumvirate in Neil Simon's *Only When I Laugh* (1981). They too are people who thrive on martyrdom, who feed off each other's infirmities and find security in each other's inability to accomplish anything. How else could they stand each other's company? John Heard's cripple is one you wouldn't mind pushing down the stairs. Having worse manners than the one-legged, one-armed, one-eyed pirates he resembles, Cutter drinks, curses, insults, and intentionally embarrasses everyone in sight (making sexual remarks to Mo in front of Bone and George, implying Bone is a racist while blacks stand nearby). He always puts himself on public display ("I'm a cripple," he reminds his angry neighbor), making sure everyone suffers from his presence. A nonstop talker, philosophizer, and complainer, his raspy, abrasive voice is hard to take. So is his suicidal bent and his obsession with getting back at those fat cats who sent *him* to war to protect *their* concerns.

Richard Bone, Cutter's Ivy League chum, is as much of a cripple, although his body is intact and kept in loverboy shape. Jeff Bridges's screen persona is that of an idealist who bravely battles corruption and conspiracy in America, but in *Cutter's Way* he plays an opposite. In sport jacket and seedy mustache, his posture is that of a coward. He'd rather believe that the reason he walks out on women who are sexually attracted to him is that he has a great ego, rather than that he is afraid of personal commitment. Whereas Cutter's voice is always irritating, Bone's is always calming, as if he were trying to ward off a fight. His words too are always defensive, as he tries to rationalize why he must back off from whatever Cutter wants to involve him in.

A sense of melancholy surrounds Mo. She's still beautiful, but the beauty in her life has been lost. She is worn out and, like Dorothy Malone in *The Tarnished Angels* (1957), who also is

committed to staying with a broken man, is too weak to fight
the fates or accept responsibility for not improving either her
man's or her own lot. Like Nina van Pallandt's unhappy rich
woman who hires gigolo Bone, she has anesthetized herself. She
doesn't want to feel the pain that the wives of crippled war vets
must deal with. But it doesn't work. Lisa Eichhorn, who was
sweet as the English shopgirl in *Yanks* (1979) and inspiring as
the Jewish resistance fighter in the TV film *The Wall* (1982),
is stunning as Mo. A bottle at her lips, in an open dirty kimono
that reveals a bare breast, she waits for Cutter to start living
again. Again we learn so much from the voice: Eichhorn's is
high and tinny yet full of rage, quivering with sadness, cracking
with fear, bristling with sarcasm, gritty with courage.

Mo does indeed have courage. In fact, she and her two men
have numerous good qualities, the most significant being their
loyalty to each other. The problem is how to get these three to
blossom, to strive for their potential greatness. None will make
the initial attempt to rise from their failed existences. Each waits
for the others to take the first step. They stick around with each
other because they sense that only the others can uplift them
from their hurt and depression. If one cared, then they'd all
care. They need each other. Cutter chooses Bone for his best
friend rather than the nicer George Swanson because Bone doesn't
coddle him. And now that he's a cripple himself, Cutter sees
Bone as his lone hope for the future—if he can get Bone to put
up a fight for "justice." Bone sticks by Cutter because he truly
hopes Cutter will goad him into making that genuine commitment to something worthwhile—the same reason Humphrey
Bogart accepts Claude Rains's persistent jibes in *Casablanca*
(1942). Mo and Cutter need each other to rekindle their capaci-
ties for genuine love. And they need Bone because he is their
moral conscience, and because they sense (as Mo says in the
novel) that he has a touch of greatness.

At the end of Newton Thornburg's riveting book (which
Robert Mulligan and Mark Rydell also had considered adapting),
J. J. Wolfe (the book's Cord) ambushes Bone (killing him),
proving that he killed Vickie Duran and was responsible for
Mo's death. (In the novel, Cutter survives but has a mental
breakdown following Mo's death and is institutionalized.) In
the film it's questionable whether Cord killed Vickie or Mo, but
as Cutter ("Cord is responsible for everything") realizes and Bone
learns, Cord has such horrific arrogance (which equates with
power and amorality) that he's likely used many teen-age girls as
sexual disposals, crushed their skulls, and dumped their used,
dead bodies in the trash. He's the type who thinks he can get
away with anything. After all, in the *real world*, the rich
and powerful needn't worry about paying for such insignificant
crimes. In the *real world*, the law leaves men like him alone,
and amateurs like Cutter, Bone, and Valerie know better than
to tangle with him. Unfortunately for Cord, Cutter refuses to
live in the *real world*.

Critics have usually grouped Cutter, Bone, and Mo as a
threesome of "crushed romantics" from the sixties. But that's
not correct. Despite being a cripple, Cutter has remained the
true romantic. He still believes in heroes, as his talk of the
Three Musketeers, Purple Hearts, and Babe Ruth indicates.
Bone tells George, "Alex says there's a shortage of heroes." So at
the end there's Cutter filling the gap, playing the part ("Mo
would have approved—she liked to play dress up"), galloping
on a white steed past an enemy army (Cord's men), past the
moat (the swimming pool), through the court's throng (the
party guests), across the drawbridge (the steps of the house), and
into the evil king's castle (Cord's house). It's a glorious moment.
Cutter's gallant gallop is the impetus Bone needs to make his
commitment. As Cord arrogantly stares at Cutter and Bone
instead of ducking for cover (just as the arrogant Nazi Conrad
Veidt ignores Bogart's pointed gun in *Casablanca*), Bone holds
his dying friend's hand and together they aim the gun at Cord.
Their symbiotic relationship has been replaced by one in which
Cutter and Bone are interchangeable. Bone (let's forget that he'll
probably be tossed in prison for life) can carry on after his
friend's death, just as Cutter wanted. In Bone, Cutter has his
body back. Bone has traded the lady's razor he held the first
time we saw him for a weapon to kill an evil king. So it's
apparent that Cutter's romanticism was contagious. By pulling
the trigger, Bone is also willing to accept moral responsibility
for the first time—he has learned Cutter's way. The seeds of
renewed protest against America's power elite have just sprouted.

Dark Star

1975 Jack H. Harris release
Director: John Carpenter
Producer: John Carpenter
Screenplay: John Carpenter and Dan O'Bannon
Cinematography: Douglas Knapp
Special Effects: Dan O'Bannon and Bill Taylor (uncredited)
Set Design: Dan O'Bannon
Music: John Carpenter
Editor: Dan O'Bannon
Running time: 83 minutes

Cast: Brian Narelle (Doolittle), Andreijah Pahich (Talby), Carl Kuniholm (Boiler), Dan O'Bannon (Pinback), Joe Sanders (Powell)

Synopsis: It is the twenty-first century. For twenty years the scoutship *Dark Star* has journeyed in space, bombing unstable planets to make colonization possible. A television communiqué from earth arrives ten years after it was sent. The military officer apologizes for the crew's bad luck. Captain Powell is dead. Because of budget cutbacks, nothing can be done to prevent radiation leakage.

There are four crew members aboard. Doolittle, Pinback, and Boiler spend most of their days in the cramped control room. Doolittle has become a bit "spacy" from the years in isolation. He just wants to find planets to blow up. The ship sets course for a new star that needs blasting. Doolittle visits the fourth man on the crew, Talby, who sits in a bubble on top of the ship dreaming about the Phoenix asteroid which circles the universe every 1.23 trillion years. Doolittle tells Talby how he misses surfing back in Malibu.

There is little to do aboard the *Dark Star*, especially since Doolittle, Pinback, and Boiler have long ago lost interest in speaking to one another. The astronauts are constantly treated to music played by their computer, who speaks in a sexy, yet motherly, voice. The computer also talks to the bomb, when she wants it to return to its bay rather than explode.

The ship passes through an electrical force field and there is a malfunction with the laser in the emergency airlock. The astronauts don't realize this.

Pinback has taken an alien aboard to be the ship's mascot; the alien refuses the food Pinback offers and escapes from its chamber. It traps Pinback on a small ledge in an elevator shaft. When the elevator starts to move, Pinback grabs onto it and wriggles into a door at the bottom. The elevator explodes. Angry and disheveled, Pinback marches after the alien and shoots it with an anesthetic gun. It deflates.

The ship arrives at the planet that must be exploded. The bomb is set to go off. Meanwhile Talby locates the malfunctioning laser. But he is temporarily blinded by the beam and steps in front of it. There is a fire and damage is done to the computer, which tells the men to abort the bombing or the ship will explode. But the bomb won't be talked out of it. Doolittle gets advice from Captain Powell who, it turns out, is frozen below in suspended animation. Outside the ship, Doolittle gets the bomb to go back into the bay.

When Doolittle attempts to enter the ship, Talby flies out. He gives chase. The bomb decides that it is god. It detonates. The ship explodes. Doolittle cannot save Talby, but Talby is happy because he has become part of the Phoenix asteroid which is passing by. Doolittle climbs on top of a piece of the ship's debris and "surfs" toward the planet in the distance.

The Dark Star *destroyed, Doolittle uses a piece of debris to "surf" through space.*

Even before the release of *Halloween* (1978), John Carpenter's *Dark Star* and *Assault on Precinct 13* (1976) had strong underground reputations, particularly among aficionados of low-budget films. Interestingly, the cults for the two films had nothing to do with Carpenter, as yet unknown, and were quite separate from each other: *Assault*'s was fervent and had spread to Europe (particularly England), where the picture had done well in festival competition; *Dark Star*'s was affectionate—it centered around an appreciation for someone who could make an ambitious film on a shoestring budget— and was mostly confined to SF film fans and independent filmmakers in America. When *Halloween* took off and almost immediately became the most profitable independent film in history, critics and moviegoers were finally inspired to seek out the quickly heralded director's two earlier works. *Assault,* a violent film about a group of cops and prisoners who spend a night barricaded in an isolated jailhouse that is surrounded by a murderous-suicidal youth gang, has enough action, suspense, and technical skills to make it superior low-budget fare. Yet, if you've heard the hard sell on the film, you'll likely be disappointed. It has rightly been called an homage to Carpenter-idol Howard Hawks's *Rio Bravo* (1959), but it's also just one more variation on George Romero's *Night of the Living Dead* (1968), as is quite apparent in those scenes where faceless gang members crash into the building. On the other hand, the quality of the soft-peddled *Dark Star* may surprise you. It is hip, irreverent, lively, provocative, funny, and daring. And despite being influenced by Stanley Kubrick's *2001: A Space Odyssey* (1968), *Dr. Strangelove* (1964), *Silent Running* (1972), and fifties science fiction films about space exploration, Carpenter made a film that is like no other.

Carpenter was a cinema student at the University of Southern California when he began *Dark Star*. In fact, it was to be his thesis film, made in 16 mm and lasting about forty-five minutes. Already known in some circles for having edited, written the music for, coscripted, and helped Jim Rokos direct the student short *The Resurrection of Broncho Billy,* which won an Academy Award in 1970, Carpenter hoped that a film of his own would further convince some studio to invest in a feature he'd direct. Or perhaps they'd let him

Distorted wide-angle view of the Dark Star *cockpit where Pinback (foreground), Doolittle, and Boiler have been sitting for many years beyond their breaking points.*

make an expanded version of *Dark Star,* what Warners had let George Lucas do with *THX-1138* (1971), originally a short he'd made at USC. But Carpenter dropped out of school and took the flim with him, scrounging for money to complete it. When he had shot footage for the short, he was given money by a Canadian investor to add on another forty minutes so it could be distributed commercially as a full-length feature. The new footage was shot in 35 mm. The completion money, which allowed the original 16 mm footage, comprising the beginning and end of the final film, to be blown up to 35 mm, and for special effects to be added, was provided by Jack Harris, an exploitation distributor. By giving Carpenter and partner Dan O'Bannon, who cowrote, edited, did special effects and set design, a set amount of money, Harris gained ownership of the film. But when Harris became financially strapped, he sold the rights to Bryanston, which had gained some notoriety as the distributor of such films as *Deep Throat* (1972) and *The Texas Chain Saw Massacre* (1974). Bryanston managed to get *Dark Star* bookings, but due to a poor ad campaign misdirected toward the "counterculture audience" and the fact that there hadn't as yet been an SF boom, the picture did little business. Bryanston went bankrupt, partly as a result of *Deep Throat* court cases, and the picture became very hard to see until several years later, when it was picked up by Atlantic Releasing.* (Today it turns up frequently at revival houses and is a popular videocassette.) In an article written by James Stevenson for *The New Yorker* (January 28, 1980), Carpenter reflected back on his strange luck with the film:

In 1970 I started to make a feature film. It was the kid in the log cabin going out with his friends to make a movie again. I had a thousand dollars from U.S.C. . . . It began on the sound stage at U.S.C. and ended on the sound stage in Hollywood four years later. It cost sixty thousand dollars. I raised the money from my parents, friends, investors. We'd make ten minutes and show that, try to get some money, then make ten more. Five years after we started, the film . . . was released in multiple run in L.A. *Dark Star* was one of the most difficult, brutalizing, devastating, and satisfying experiences of my life. It was not successful. It was a weird little science fiction movie, with a lot of imagination and energy but a cardboard spaceship. I wanted it to be slick and professional, with suspense and a sense of humor; it was youthful, naive, and innocent. It was exactly what I was. . . . I thought, I have created this work—don't I have any credibility? I had *no* credibility. I never got a job. . . . *Dark Star* was the end of youth for me. It didn't work.

But for viewers looking for something unusual, it does work. In 1970–1974, Carpenter was obviously much like the innovative astronaut Doolittle, who fills up two rows of hanging bottles with varing amounts of water to create a makeshift vibraphone, and uses a floating piece of the exploded ship's debris as a surfboard to glide through space. When making *Dark Star,* Carpenter used everything at his disposal to complete a "legitimate" film (as much "art" as Doolittle's music), despite having little money for production values. Smartly, Carpenter wasn't afraid to call attention to his limited financial resources, to let viewers know that he was "just making do." He takes O'Bannon's shoebox sets and creates a sense of claustrophobia; fills the soundtrack with a wide range of music, from classical to rock to country to intentionally boring string music to his own trademarked

---

* Much of this background information comes from an interview with Carpenter that was conducted by Jordan R. Fox for *Cinefantastique* (Summer 1980).

pulsating Moog synthesizer sound (a less tense version than played throughout *Halloween*); uses interesting opticals and animation effects; builds an eighty-foot shaft and flips his camera on its side to make Pinback's elevator-hanging scene seem believable and exciting; allows for a monster that is no more than a beachball with claws because he can use it for humor as well as suspense; varies the visuals by including several sequences in which characters appear on television monitors and seem to be addressing the viewer; and gives voices to the ship's computer (a sexy but motherly female) and the bomb about to be detonated (a fussy male), thereby adding two characters to the film. Carpenter's work, so impressive in *Halloween*, TV movies *Someone Is Watching Me!* (1978) and *Elvis* (1979), and much of *The Fog* (1980), has sadly and surprisingly gone downhill as his goal has apparently shifted to impressing viewers with gratuitous violence and visual virtuosity, at the expense of subtlety, atmosphere, characterization, and good taste. So it's a pleasure to rediscover the young unknown Carpenter who was interested in completing personal projects rather than catering to an undiscriminating mass audience hooked on violence and elaborate, indulgent special effects. The intelligence so evident in *Dark Star* is nowhere to be found in such later shallow efforts as *Halloween II* (1981), which he coproduced and cowrote with Debra Hill, *Escape From New York* (1981), and *The Thing* (1982), pictures he obviously made to build fortunes and fame.

Carpenter's version of *The Thing* is about an alien creature that systematically takes over the bodies and minds of men who work at an arctic research station. The problem is that from the start these men who have been living together in what amounts to a Siberian prison camp are presented as dehumanized by their ordeal. Who cares if dehumanized characters are further dehumanized? For *The Thing* to have been effective and have had an emotional impact as well as shock value, the characters needed to be more sympathetic, more *human*. However, in *Dark Star*—as long as the story does not become one about an alien takeover—it is appropriate that we are introduced to characters who have already become dehumanized through years of isolation, claustrophobia, and flying through infinite space. The gist of the film is the "pre-story," or how the men got into their "weirded-out" states. Just as in Francis Ford Coppola's *Apocalypse Now* (1979), when Martin Sheen happens upon a wacked out, leaderless battalion in a trench the Armed Forces have no doubt forgotten about, what is important is how these men got this way (dehumanized), rather than what will become of them. (In *The Thing*, it would have been wise to have given a pre-story before bringing on the alien.) Until the very end of *Dark Star*, almost every visual, clip of dialogue, and bit of action (other than the journey itself and the appearance of the electrical force field that causes the laser to malfunction) relates to the past. As the film begins, Captain Powell is already dead, the ship has already become radioactive, the toilet paper has run out, Talby has retreated to the bubble on top of the ship, Doolittle has gone gun crazy, there is an alien on board. Constant references to Powell, a series of tapes of Pinback showing his mental deterioration over the past few years, scenes in which the astronauts show they have long been sick of each other and have lost the ability to communicate with each other, the computer's monotonal instructions and questionable selection of music for the men's "listening

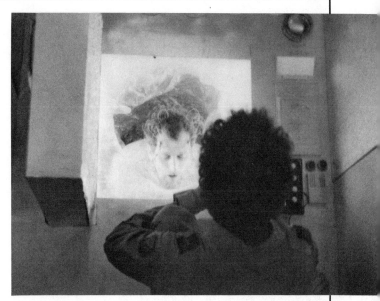

Hoping to stop the bomb from blowing up the ship, Doolittle asks Captain Powell, in a suspended state, for advice.

pleasure," and regular panic situations, all tell us why these men are in their sorry states. This is all presented humorously, but not merely for laughs. There are elements from the theater of the absurd; there is much satire: no doubt in the twenty-first century our government will be just as callous toward our astronauts on missions as it was to our modern-day foot soldiers in Vietnam.

There is much in *Dark Star* that strikes the funnybone: the quick shot of the three astronauts sitting in their cramped control room shaking furiously and "grooving" to the rock music they listen to; Pinback kibitzing Doolittle while the latter tapes a telemessage for home base, making sure it's known he's unhappy sitting next to the unfixed seat where Captain Powell was electrocuted; the computer trying not to lose her temper while requesting, once again, that the obstinate bomb return to its bay; the irony in the timing (everything in space takes years to occur, yet when the ship is in danger, the computer informs the men that they have only seconds to save themselves); Doolittle's phenomenological discussion with the bomb; and Doolittle's surfboard ride through space as "Benson, Arizona" is sung in the background. The highlight of the film is Pinback's sequence with the alien he brought aboard to be the ship's mascot ("I thought you were *cute*," he gripes at feeding time). The way the alien slithers about, hides in every nook and cranny, jumps out of the darkness or drops from the ceiling, makes noises upon attack, and reveals it has intelligence, leaves little doubt that O'Bannon was the one who provided the concept for Ridley Scott's *Alien* (1979), although Walter Hill and David Giler got full script credit.

Before Wayne Wang's *Chan Is Missing* (1982) became the darling of critics because of its success on a minuscule $20,000 budget, *Dark Star* was the low-budget film most often pointed to as an inspiration to aspiring independent filmmakers. It should still be looked at, especially by science fiction fans and filmmakers. It is an impressive film, surprisingly nonindulgent for a new director, and worthy to be called "the poor, poor, poor man's *2001*."

Daughters of Darkness

Also known as *Le Rouge aux Lèvres (Blood on Red Lips)*

1971 Belgium-France-West Germany-Spain Maya, Roxy Films, and Mediterranea Films production released by Gemini Releasing in association with Maron Films
Director: Harry Kumel
Producers: Paul Collet and Alain C. Guilleaume
Screenplay: Pierre Drouot, Harry Kumel, and J. J. Amiel
Cinematography: Edward van der Enden
Music: François de Roubaix
Editors: Gust Verschueren and Denis Bonan
Running time: 87 minutes (some European prints may run 96 minutes)

Cast: Delphine Seyrig (Countess Elisabeth Bathory) Danièle Ouimet (Valerie Tardieu), John Karlen (Stefan Chiltern), Andrea Rau (Ilona Harczy), Paul Esser (Porter), George Jamin (The Man), Joris Collet (butler), Fons Rademakers (Mother)

Synopsis: Valerie and Stefan make passionate love on a train. Two hours earlier, they were married in Switzerland. They are heading for England, where Stefan's mother lives. When they miss their boat, they check into a seaside hotel in Ostend, Belgium. Off season, it is completely deserted.

A red car pulls up driven by a young girl named Ilona. Her middle-aged mistress checks into the hotel. The concierge is surprised that she looks exactly like a woman who checked in thirty years before. Her name was the same as well: Elisabeth Bathory. Elisabeth spots Stefan and Valerie dining. She thinks them perfect and tells them so. Ilona is jealous of how Elisabeth looks at Valerie. She wants to die, to be set free. She's also thirsty.

In nearby Bruges, a fourth girl has been murdered and had her blood drained from her body. When Stefan sees the corpse, he can't hide his enjoyment. This worries Valerie. A retired detective follows them back to Ostend. He tells Elisabeth that similar murders took place thirty years before.

Elisabeth becomes acquainted with the young couple. She and Stefan recall the murders of Elisabeth Bathory three centuries before. Valerie is upset to see her husband speak so delightfully of torture. She goes to her room. She undresses. When she looks on the balcony she sees the nude Ilona. She screams. Elisabeth tells her she imagined seeing Ilona. That night, while Stefan and Valerie make love, Elisabeth and Ilona watch from the balcony.

Stefan finally calls his mother, who happens to be a man. He is upset that Stefan has married but tells him they'll figure out what to do with her once they arrive in England. At night Stefan brutally beats Valerie with a belt. She tries to leave him, but Elisabeth stops her at the train station. Valerie is disgusted when Elisabeth tells of her love for her. But she listens when Elisabeth says Stefan thinks of Valerie only as a slave.

At Elisabeth's instruction, Ilona seduces Stefan. He pulls her into the shower. She panics and falls on an open razor and is killed.

Elisabeth takes control. They bury Ilona. Racing back to the hotel to beat the sunlight, Elisabeth runs over the snooping ex-detective. She and Valerie sleep together. Valerie tells Stefan she is like a different person when with Elisabeth. She can't control herself. The three dine together. Elizabeth tells Valerie to kiss Stefan. She obeys but is repulsed. Stefan slaps Valerie. The two women fight him and kill him by hitting him over the head with a heavy glass bowl. They drink the blood that flows from his wrists.

With the body of Stefan in the trunk, Elisabeth and Valerie drive away. They can't wait to sample life's pleasures. But the morning sun gets into Valerie's eyes. The car crashes and Elisabeth is impaled on a sharp limb.

A young couple at a resort listens to a strange woman tell them how perfect they are, and how they will be great friends. But though she sounds like Elisabeth, she looks like Valerie.

T his Belgian-made English-language vampire film, which director-writer Harry Kumel termed "a gothic fairy tale for full-grown adults," is among the most stylish of horror films and might very well be the most perverse. Twentieth Century-Fox originally was set to both finance and release the picture: its executives had been impressed by Kumel's prize-winning *Monsieur Hawarden* (1968), about a mysterious baroness who lives as a man outside Amsterdam, and probably figured he'd tell an equally intriguing tale of the historical "bloody countess," Elisabeth Bathory. But a disagreement over distribution resulted in 20th's changing its mind and Kumel desperately searching for a new backer. Gemini Pictures agreed to let *Daughters* (then titled *Blood on Red Lips*) be its first picture as long as Kumel was willing to make changes in his screenplay to make it more commercial. (The result? Gemini's J. J. Amiel got cowriter credit.) We who detest studio interference that forces a writer or director to alter *his* movie, may protest Gemini's insistence that the picture contain more nudity and violence than Kumel intended, as well as including the telephone scene between Stefan and his male "mother" that suggests a macabre homosexual relationship between the two. (Critics dispute whose idea this scene was.) But it is precisely because *Daughters* is an utterly bizarre, kinky film that it has such allure.

In its publicity releases, Gemini used a four-word slogan: "Vampirism, lesbianism, homosexuality, sadism!" Simple enough, and more accurate than the ad Gemini ran in *Variety*. According to this ad, Judith Crist considered *Daughters* "Exquisite!" What Crist actually stated in her *New York* magazine review was that "the exquisite {Delphine} Seyrig has . . . landed in a horror of a movie." (Gemini would have done better quoting *Variety* itself or, strangely enough, *The Christian Science Monitor,* which gave *Daughters* mild endorsements.) Most New York–based critics agreed with Crist. Luckily, the only review I read at the time was in *The New York Times,* where Howard Thompson, whom I remember going out on the limb only once before, to praise *The Nutty Professor* in 1963, asked temptingly, "Want to see a fascinating vampire picture?"

I didn't think *Daughters* a horror masterpiece then—and I still don't—but I greatly appreciated its oddness, its daring stylistic impositions, its spellbinding character interaction. And that Kumel had clearly made an art film, not the exploitation film Gemini wanted. As it drifted off into temporary obscurity over the decade, it remained distinct in my memory while countless horror films, some better, blended into one another. As it turned out, others couldn't forget this film either, and in the early eighties it reemerged, at revival houses, even at the Museum of Modern Art. It is a flawed film to be sure, but of all the horror films that have strived for high camp, only Roman Polanski's *The Fearless Vampire Killers* (1967) and George Romero's *Night of the Living Dead* (1968) have so masterfully combined traditional horror elements with outrageous, often ludicrous wit; only Paul

Male vampires in movies usually need to drink a victim's blood before gaining control, but female vampires such as Elisabeth use subtler methods—as Valerie discovers.

Bartel's cult item *Private Parts* (1973) and Paul Schrader's *Cat People* (1981) can approach its sexual perversity, but neither matches the eroticism that pervades every scene of *Daughters*. Moreover, it is that rare horror film with social relevance: it more than expressed feminist themes at a time when mainstream movies weren't so brave; it actually had a decidedly antimale attitude, despite being made by men.

Until *Personal Best* (1982) and *Lianna* (1983) came along to tastefully, in my opinion, and fairly graphically depict loving, sexual relationships between women, lesbians as central characters could only be found in porno flicks and vampire films (maybe because audiences accepted the notion that lesbians were as perverted as bloodsuckers). There is a famous, extremely sensual scene with vampire Gloria Holden and streetwalker Nan Grey in *Dracula's Daughter*, which was filmed way back in 1936, that has strong lesbian implications. In 1961, when Roger Vadim made his haunting vampire film *Blood and Roses*, in which Elsa Martinelli comes to possess the angelic Annette Vadim, there was no longer the need to be merely suggestive. And as films became more explicit and sensational, female vampires and their female victims could be seen cavorting in the nude (often with blood dripping from fangs onto bare bosoms) in films all over Europe: in England, in Hammer Studios films like *The Vampire Lovers* (1970), with Ingrid Pitt, and its semisequel *Lust for a Vampire* (1971); in France, in Jean Rollin's softcore sex-bloody horror films; in Spain, in Jesus Franco films like *Vampyros Lesbos* (1970), a title that needs no translation.

In America, Stephanie Rothman directed the tongue-in-cheek *The Velvet Vampire* (1971). Despite having a bright, sunny look unique to vampire films (her vampire loves the sun, the plants that fill up her desert home, her dune buggy, and sex), Rothman's film has striking thematic and plot similarities to *Daughters*. It too is about a female vampire with a sense of humor who breaks up the male-dominated marriage of a young couple by first showing the wife how faithless and worthless he is, then seducing her, and finally killing him. What's most remarkable is that in both films the lesbian couplings are preferable to those involving men. In *Daughters* the mistress-slave relationship of Elisabeth and

Ilona ("I want to be free") has become unfulfilling for both women, yet it comes across as being more caring, tender, and even respectable than the one we imagine between sadistic mama's boy Stefan and his obviously diabolical "mother" (a cameo by Dutch director Fons Rademakers). And Valerie finds being with Elisabeth much less debasing than being with Stefan, whose attitude is "I'm a man, and she's mine."

As the film begins and Stefan and his bride of a couple of hours are in the middle of some heated lovemaking in a train, she inquires if he loves her. He answers negatively. At the time we think he is only joking, but already we dislike his cruelty. Soon after, we see that he is deceiving his wife by telling her he has been unable to get through to his mother. When he finally calls his mother and we see a red-lipped, deep-voiced, orchid-sniffing queen on the other end of the line, saying "I can't wait to see our new flower," we can only guess what horrors Stefan is bringing Valerie to. We get some indication perhaps when Stefan beats Valerie with a belt for no reason. When she questions his obvious delight in viewing the mutilated girl in Bruges, his sadism becomes psychological: he turns her question around and makes *her* feel guilty by accusing her of enjoying pointing out his perversity; when she seeks forgiveness and tries to unbuckle his belt, in an effort to seduce him on the bus, this manipulator rejects her advances. With Elisabeth's help, Valerie comes to understand that Stefan wants her to be "a slave, a thing, an object of pleasure." Therefore she'd rather be with Elisabeth, who truly loves her and promises to bring her happiness ("There's so much of life still to taste"). At the last moment, Rothman stops short of having her velvet vampire and the young wife become lovers, but Kumel allows Elisabeth and Valerie to get into bed together. Still, *both* films confirm an important point about *female* vampires in the cinema: unlike their male counterparts, who must win a woman's "undying" love by hypnotizing them into submission and drinking their blood, females can win over a woman completely through the unbeatable combination of will power, mind control and sex

After being beaten with a belt by Stefan, Valerie lies awake thinking how she can escape her sadistic husband.

While being unfaithful to Valerie, Stefan inadvertently causes Ilona's gruesome death. He looks up from her corpse to see Valerie and Elisabeth looking at him.

appeal. As we see again in Tony Scott's *The Hunger* (1983).

Just as there was an historical Dracula, Vlad the Impaler, there was indeed a Lady Dracula. Elisabeth Bathory was a Hungarian countess who got it into her head that she could preserve her youth and beauty by bathing in an elixir: the blood of young virgins. So between 1600 and 1610 she kept a "herd" of female virgins in the dungeons of her Castle Crejthe, murdering between six and eight hundred for her daily baths. When King Mathias II got wind of these atrocities he had her walled up in her castle for life. "How did the story end?" asks Stefan in *Daughters*. "Who knows?" replies Elisabeth knowingly.

The legend of "the bloody countess" was the subject of several horror films that came out at about the same time as *Daughters*. (Most did not use the name Bathory, however.) I've never come across Jean Grau's *Legend of Bloody Castle* (1972), with Lucia Bose; Paul Nashy's *La Noche de Walpurgis* (1970), with Paty Shepard; or Nashy's sequel *El Retorno de Walpurgis* (c. 1970), with Maria Silva; but Hammer's handsomely produced *Countess Dracula* (1972) plays quite often. What's most interesting about Ingrid Pitt's obsessive Bathory (called Elisabeth Nadasdy) is that she hates women—they are her competition. She kills women to satisfy her vanity, believing beauty will help her win love and favors from men. On the other hand, Delphine Seyrig's lesbian Elisabeth, who is confident but not vain, has no use for men. She has no fear of the retired detective: she runs past when he wants to question her (dismissing him with "I have no time for you right now") and later she casually runs him over with her car. She despises Stefan most of all: she manipulates him into Ilona's love trap; after he accidentally kills Ilona, she throws his clothes at him disdainfully, ordering him to get dressed; she bosses him around while he digs Ilona's grave in the sand, submissively working on his hands and knees; and when the hole is big enough she rolls Ilona's corpse into it without even the common courtesy of allowing him to climb out first.

Seyrig, a Lebanon-born French actress who won critical

raves in the early sixties in two landmark films by Alain Resnais, *Last Year at Marienbad* (1962) and *Muriel* (1963), must have delighted in playing this strange role. Seyrig is an ardent feminist: artistically, she sought out films in the seventies that were to be directed by women; politically, she was extremely active in a move to change antiquated rape laws in France. How she must have loved giving Stefan, the epitome of the male chauvinist pig, his just rewards. Also I'm sure she enjoyed playing Elisabeth in the manner of her friend Marlene Dietrich. Thus the ironic, wry humor, and the smile even when insulted or feeling melancholy; and the wild, magnificent wardrobe. In fact, Seyrig's initial appearance recalls Dietrich in Sternberg films (Sternberg and Kumel were friends as well). At an angle we see only part of her visage: the sanguine lips stand out because of the white-caked facial makeup; the face is delicately framed by a black veil and the wings of a high fur collar. And she is as mysterious as Dietrich. Oddly, we never become positive that Elisabeth has become a vampire in the classic sense, although her beauty at the age of about four hundred certainly indicates she is. But we never see fangs and she denies she is a vampire when she admits to most everything else. Is this woman only *pretending* to be Elisabeth Bathory?

Kumel gets effectively offbeat performances from his entire ensemble, including John Karlen, who was only hired because he was Gemini's Howard Zucker's friend, former Miss Canada Danièle Ouimet, and the pouty, wistful Andrea Rau. But as mentioned, Kumel's strength is his audacious style. Most directors fade to black, a few fade to white, Kumel fades to blood red. The film may contain numerous horror conventions—mist, too loud suspense music, and vampires who cast no reflexions, don't drink alcohol, and spend time peering into bedrooms from balconies—but nothing is handled conventionally. How cleverly he uses sound, music, his wonderful sets (including a deserted hotel that predates the one in Kubrick's 1980 film *The Shining*), colors (especially red, of course), clothes, character placement, and weird camera angles (often he shoots from above, or at a great distance to visually convey the terrible isolation *each* character feels). He knows how to create moods without relying on dialogue; it is the dialogue that establishes the film's humorous tone. The film can be intentionally silly, as when Elisabeth says "It's a great day to be alive"—upon her return from burying Ilona and running over the detective; then it can be utterly outrageous, in a macabre sort of way, as when Stefan and Elisabeth, with her arms draped over him and massaging his chest, almost reach simultaneous orgasms while detailing for the aghast Valerie the tortures used by Elisabeth Bathory in the seventeenth century; it can be surreal, as in the magnificent shot of Elisabeth surrounding Valerie with her cape as they stand on a cliff, the full moon shining behind them; it can recall the dreamlike quality of Nicolas Roeg's *Don't Look Now* (1973), as when Stefan and Valerie visit Bruges and see the girl's corpse; and it can be downright horrifying, as when Ilona is killed by falling on Stefan's razor. Harry Kumel never became a major director, but this one film proves he had great talent. *Daughters* may be a wicked film, as some critics and viewers have complained, and it is no gem, but it is sexy, imaginative, amusing, and undeniably fun. It is a curiosity piece that viewers who have tired of the latest trend in horror films surely should seek out.

The First Nudie Musical

1976 Paramount (later distributed by World Northal)
Directors: Mark Haggard and Bruce Kimmel
Producer: Jack Reeves
Screenplay: Bruce Kimmel
Cinematography: Douglas H. Knapp
Music and Lyrics: Bruce Kimmel
"The Lights and the Smiles" is sung by Annette O'Toole;
"Where Is a Man" is sung by Valerie Gillett
Choreography: Lloyd Gordon
Editor: Allen Peluso
Running time: 90 minutes

Cast: Stephen Nathan (Harry Schecter), Cindy Williams (Rosie), Bruce Kimmel (John Smithee), Leslie Ackerman (Susie), Alan Abelew (George Brenner), Diana Canova (Juanita), Alexandra Morgan (Mary La Rue), Frank Doubleday (Arvin), Kathleen Hietala (Eunice), Art Marino (Eddie), Hy Pyke (Benny), Greg Finlay (Jimmy), Herb Graham (Frankie), René Hall (Dick Davis), Susan Stewart (Joy Full), Artie Shafer (actor), Jerry Hoffman (Schlong)

Synopsis: To keep Schecter Studios in business, young producer Harry Schecter makes low-budget exploitation films like *Cheerleaders in Chains, Teenage Sex Mutants, Stewardesses in Cages,* and *Kiss My Boots.* His retired father thinks he is still making legit pictures. Greedy investors Eddie, Benny, Jimmy, and Frankie want to turn the studio into a shopping center because Harry's films haven't been making money. Inspired by his secretary Rosie, Harry decides to make the first pornographic musical to save the studio. The investors agree to give him the money, but if he can't make a hit movie in two weeks, the studio is theirs. To make sure Harry doesn't succeed, they insist that the director be twenty-three-year-old novice filmmaker John Smithee—Benny's stupid, virginal nephew.

Harry and Rosie hold auditions, looking for actors who "can screw and carry a tune." Mary La Rue, a prima donna with a crush on Harry, agrees to play the female lead. George Brenner, who tries to pick up every female and is turned down by everyone, wins the lead male role. Also hired are Cuban dynamo Juanita Juanita, who is accompanied by chain-carrying boyfriend Arvin, who makes sure no one touches her; Susie, a virgin from Indiana, who agrees to play the ingenue as long as she can wear clothes during her nude scenes; and porno vet Joy Full, who wins her part by lying on the ground and simulating an orgasm. Dick Davis, musician and pervert, is hired to write the musical numbers.

It becomes obvious that John can't direct the nude actors without giggling and making nonsensical remarks. Harry sends him out for doughnuts each day and directs the film himself. John doesn't realize Harry directed the scenes he sees each day in the projection room—he thinks he did them while in an artistic fervor. Harry sends John to Wanda's, where he loses his virginity to a half-dozen prostitutes.

Mary La Rue causes one porno actor to quit, forcing Harry to hire a "stunt cock" for the scene. She fights with John when he knocks over all the dildo-garbed male dancers with a crane during her "Dancing Dildoes" number. She constantly exchanges insults with Rosie, who is jealous of the attention Harry pays her. When she kicks George out of bed during a scene, Harry fires her. When George gets a black eye from a transvestite mugger he tries to pick up, that means there are no dancing leads in the finale. Harry convinces Rosie to be the girl dancer, and John convinces Harry to be the male dancer.

Come . . . Come Now, the first nudie musical, premieres. After the final number, "Let 'em Eat Cake (And I'll Eat You)," in which Rosie and Harry dance and sing, there is great applause. The film will be a smash. John is surrounded by admiring critics, George by girls who want dates, Susie by agents, and Juanita by men whom Arvin scares away. Harry tells Rosie that he's going to make a movie about a hot-shot producer who marries his secretary. They walk down the street kissing.

"I won't do this scene until those damned dancing dildoes know their steps. I'm an actress!"

Mary La Rue

The *First Nudie Musical,* a minor but often amusing parody of both porno and "Let's-put-on-a-show!" musicals, flopped at the box-office in 1976, when Paramount didn't know how—and barely tried—to market it for the youth market. Even good word of mouth and voluntary promo appearances on its behalf by hot television star Cindy Williams (making Paramount's TV brass very uneasy) failed to attract an audience. It has only been through later showings in revival houses and on pay television that the picture has found the cult that eluded it years before. The major creative force behind *First Nudie* was Bruce Kimmel, who codirected, wrote the screenplay and songs, and played first-time director John Smithee (a tame name in the real porno world, where one director's moniker is Abe Snake). Kimmel, who looks as if he could be Peter Bogdanovich's baby brother, was an aspiring L.A. playwright, stage director, and actor (who specialized in schlemiel roles like Mr. Whipple's assistant on "Don't Squeeze the Charmin!" commercials) when he hit upon the idea of making a porno spoof with music. Then Alan Abelew, who along with other *First Nudie* leads Cindy Williams and Diana Canova had worked with Kimmel in Los Angeles Community College theater productions, introduced him to Mark Haggard, director of such porno films as *The Love Garden* and *The All-American Girl* (both about 1974). Like Kimmel, Haggard had decided that the way to break into mainstream movies was to make an X-rated—but not hardcore—musical.* So the two men joined forces and concocted the first X-rated musical comedy which, in turn, would be about the making of the first XXX-rated musical comedy. The picture would spoof porno films, satirize the world of porno filmmaking, and pay homage to and borrow plot elements from *Babes in Arms* (1939), and other Busby Berkeley putting-on-a-show-while-fighting-the-clock vehicles.

Although they had no script or complete story outline, they tried to find a producer on the basis of their gimmick and a cassette of Kimmel singing his original songs such as "The First Nudie Musical," "Orgasm," "Lesbian Butch-Dyke," and "Perversion." They were always rejected.

With the help of producer Jack Reeves, Kimmel and Haggard raised enough money to make the film independently. Kimmel got $3,000 to write the script: it took him a week. Writing in *Filmmakers Newsletter* (April 1976), Haggard recalled:

---

* *The First Nudie Musical* eventually was given an R rating.

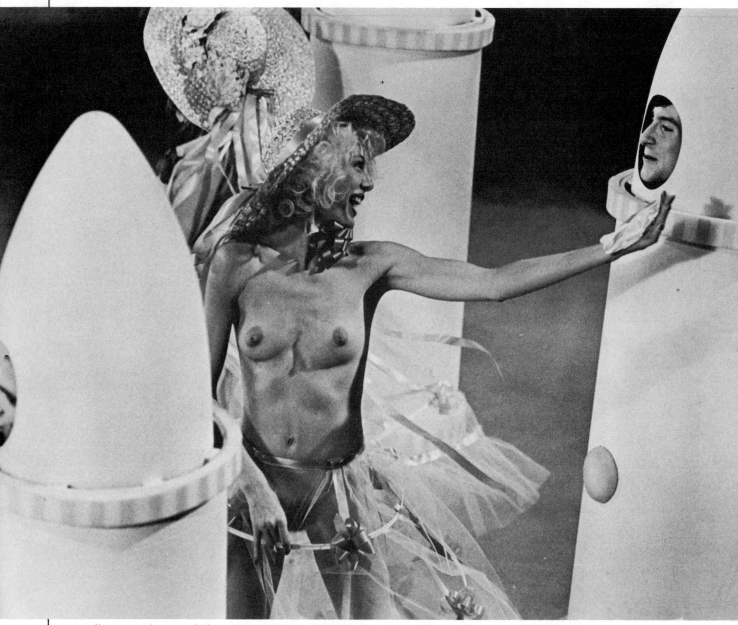

Joy Full sings to the giant dildo inhabited by George Brenner during the film's "Dancing Dildoes" showstopper.

You see, the producers never really believed in the finished script. They believed in the *idea*, the *gimmick*, but they were simply unable to visualize the movie we wanted to make from a reading of the script. . . . We became very obstinate and refused, steadfastly, to change *anything*. . . . This obstinacy didn't make me or Bruce well-liked, but . . . we succeeded in preserving the integrity of our concept. . . . At any rate, the money was raised from a variety of private investors, including Texas oilmen. . . .

The trouble really began when the producers started consulting industry professionals about our budget. The unanimous opinion . . . was that it was impossible to shoot our script in three weeks [on the projected budget]. . . . One group of producers offered to step in and take over the film, claiming that Bruce and I didn't know what we were doing. Of course,

where low budgets were concerned, I *did* know what we were doing.

Having filmed *The Love Garden* and *The All-American Girl* in a total of eight days on minimal budgets, Haggard was able to finish on schedule and keep the film close to its estimated budget. Considering that *The First Nudie Musical* was made in eighteen days for between $125,000 and $150,000, it is truly impressive. At times the picture may *look* cheap, but that seems appropriate for a film about low-budget filmmaking. The film has many flat spots, but significantly, there is never a moment when the cost-cutting makes the picture seem amateurish.

Paramount bought the rights to the completed *The First*

Nudie Musical and it looked as if it was going to gear it for the enormous youth market. At the time, an excited Haggard wrote, "I just hope Paramount handles the picture correctly and I see a profit on my percentage. And I think I will."

But it wouldn't be so easy. Paramount test-marketed the picture in such cities as Houston, Dallas, Los Angeles, and Portland, then shelved it. (World Northal would buy the rights a few months later but wouldn't have much success with it either.) Paramount blamed poor box office for its decision to abandon the project, but Hollywood insiders had another explanation: the studio was afraid viewers of its hit television series *Laverne and Shirley* would take offense at the wholesome Cindy Williams being in a raunchy film. That Paramount didn't get behind its film was certainly the main reason it never found its audience, but I think its awful title was the reason individuals initially stayed away from it and gave the studio the excuse to dump it.

It's rare that a title has caused me to skip a film. I have let curiosity take over and lead me into theaters showing everything from *Sidelong Glances of a Pigeon-Kicker* (1970), *The Texas Chain Saw Massacre* (1974), and *I Eat Your Skin* (1971), to *Wrestling Women vs. the Aztec Mummy* (1965). *Mama's Dirty Girls* (1974), and *Tongue* (1975), but the title *The First Nudie Musical* kept me away. In the first place, I really resented a title which called attention to the filmmaker's gimmick. This hinted that they were trying to make quick bucks, hoping to attract viewers via a novelty before the bad reviews came in. What if the first 3-D film, *Bwana Devil* (1952), had instead been titled *The First 3-D Film*? Besides, the gimmick itself didn't seem so unusual. Anthony Newley's X-rated *Can Hieronymus Merkin Ever Forget Mercy Humppe and Find True Happiness?* (1969), another film about the making of a film, certainly had a lot of nudity, and songs to boot. And I was sure there must have been at least one *hardcore* porno film of the early seventies that had musical numbers. But even if the title was accurate, so what? It surely wasn't an original idea to make an X-rated musical; it's just that

Juanita tells boyfriend Arvin that he should learn to control his jealousy.

Codirector Bruce Kimmel (L), Cindy Williams, and Stephen Nathan are the naughty but generally wholesome leads. In 1981 Kimmel (as director and star) and Williams would team again for the innocuous horror parody The Creature Wasn't Nice.

everyone who thought of it knew better than to proceed with the idea. (Kimmel and Haggard may have turned out a better film on the subject than anyone else could have, but they still didn't make much money.) There have been no musical comedies set in outer space, but there's no need for them, either.

Another gripe I had was that the word "nudie" was long outmoded by 1976. "Nudies" were those awful pictures Russ Meyer and other exploitation cameramen-directors made back in the fifties at nudist camps, where a lot of naked families and maidens with braided hair played bouncy games of volleyball and went horseback riding. Perhaps the use of the word "nudie" caused me to fret that this film might be about a group of nude go-getters who get together and decide to "Hey, let's put on a show!" in order to save their colony from being taken over by land developers. The film's title, which should have attracted a hip, young audience, was instead a turn-off, because it projected thoughts of a time gone by when even adult films were innocent. I believe that the picture would have attracted a large audience upon its initial release and would now be a fixture on the Midnight Movie circuit if they had used "The First X-rated Musical" as a subtitle or a promotional slogan.

Ironically, when I finally saw *The First Nudie Musical,* I realized that the title perfectly reflects the innocence of the filmmakers—and it is this innocence when dealing with supposedly perverse, adult material that gives the picture its charm. It makes sense that when Bruce Kimmel spoke to nude actresses on the set, he really did have to look toward the ceiling, just like his character does in the same situation. And it's not surprising to learn that the reason the dildoes look like vibrators in the "Dancing Dildoes" number is that Kimmel wasn't positive what dildoes are. Probably the most remarkable thing about this movie, considering its subject matter, is that it is totally inoffensive, which leads one to believe it might have done better if it had not been. Rather

The climactic "Let 'Em Eat Cake (And I'll Eat You)" number features full frontal nudity. Nevertheless, it's a letdown.

than filling the screen with sexist humor (or sick humor), Kimmel left his women alone: there is frontal female nudity but there are totally nude men as well; jokes about female breasts ("That's a great pair of knockers you've got there," says jerk John) are shown to be immature and are balanced by references to the male anatomy. And again, though there is much matter-of-fact nudity and four-letter words fill most sentences, we are never turned off by it all. It's all done in fun, rather than to shock or be exploitative. (However, I would prefer the film to be more erotic.)

Kimmel's comic weakness is with dialogue (not to mention the trite lyrics to his songs), but he makes up for it with humorous characterizations and situations (like mixing virgins with porno vets in the film within a film). Comic highlights include John sitting down in a heavy chair *before* pulling it forward to Harry's desk (the camera focuses on Harry's sick face as he realizes he's dealing with a moron, and we *hear* the chair bouncing and scraping against the floor); John, wearing directorial garb appropriate for Erich von Stroheim, explaining to the cast how he will direct (he will always use a camera) and randomly throwing every four-letter word imaginable into his speech to prove he's the right man to direct porno films; the appearance of Schlong, whose below-the-frame "stunt cock" has males and females alike agog ("Ees jost so beeeg," Juanita repeats several times as Arvin pulls her away). Besides John, with his manic bray and five-year-old's mentality ("I've got dibs on the crane," he tells the cameramen), and Cuban firecracker Juanita (a wild

role that may surprise Diana Canova fans), the character I like best is George Brenner, played by Alan Abelew. Acting like God's gift to women, he constantly sings "So touch me, I'm you" and tries to smooth-talk every woman he meets. "That's a beautiful name—Jane," he says. "Why do I have the feeling if my name were Fungus you'd think it beautiful?" replies Jane, becoming one of many who don't take the bait. And George never takes a hint; after being mugged by an ugly transvestite he tries to pick up, George yells, "You didn't even tell me your name, you creep." All the other characters have their funny moments. As the wisecracking Rosie, Cindy Williams, who refused to play Mary La Rue because she didn't want to do nude scenes, is her usual adorable, spunky self—a naughty girl-next-door. Too often, however, the directors have her say or sing something bitchy or dirty while she's smiling and she begins to become irritating. Stephen Nathan, who created the role of Jesus in *Godspell,* is only adequate as Harry. Too much of Harry's and Rosie's time is spent *reacting* to others' crazy antics instead of *participating* in the zaniness.

The First Nudie Musical should have ended with a bang. Unfortunately, the climactic "Let 'em Eat Cake (And I'll Eat You)" number loses its impact after the first time Harry and Rosie sing their dirty lines and smile. Also their tap dancing leaves a lot to be desired. At the end, everyone applauds, *Come . . . Come Now* is a hit, and the filmmakers will have money to go on to bigger and better things. It was wishful thinking on the part of the real filmmakers.

1956* Japan-America Embassy release of a Toho production
Directors: Terry Morse and Ishiro Honda (original footage)
Producer: Toho International, Inc.
Executive Producer: Tomoyuki Tanaka
Screenplay: Takeo Murata and Ishiro Honda
From an original story by Shigeru Kayama
Cinematography: Masao Tamai and Guy Roe (American footage)
Special effects: Eiji Tsuburaya, Akira Watanabe, Hiroshi Mukoyama, and Kuichiro Kishida
Music: Akira Ifukube
Editor: Terry Morse
Running time: 80 minutes

Cast: Raymond Burr (Steve Martin), Takashi Shimura (Dr. Yamane), Momoko Kochi (Emiko Yamane), Akira Takarada (Hideto Ogata), Akihiko Hirata (Daisuke Serizawa)

Synopsis:** Steve Martin, American correspondent for United World News, lies injured in a Tokyo hospital, along with countless other victims. The city has been destroyed. He greets Emiko, the daughter of famous paleontologist Dr. Yamane. She tells Steve "We're all living on borrowed time." Steve flashes back on past events.

Steve had come to Tokyo to meet his scientist friend Dr. Serizawa. He was met by Tomo,† a government official, who informed him that when he was flying over the ocean a ship had been wiped out. There had been a blinding flash and the ocean had burst into flame. Then eight other ships were obliterated. Only a few men were rescued. Covered with strange burns and suffering from shock, they soon died. At a meeting of scientists, Dr. Yamane and others decide to question the natives of Odo Island, where for centuries there had been a legend about a great monster of the land and sea: Godzilla.

Steve and Tomo went to the island. At night, during a storm, some natives were killed and huts crushed. Screaming natives claimed they had seen Godzilla. Odo natives came to Tokyo to testify, spurring Yamane to lead a scientific expedition to the island. He discovered that the land was radioactive. Suddenly Godzilla, a four-hundred-foot beast, appeared over the mountain. The people ran to safety. Emiko fell but was pulled to her feet by young seaman Ogata. Although she was engaged to Serizawa, she and Ogata were in love.

Back in Tokyo, Yamane announced that Godzilla had been wakened from two-million-year sleep by the atomic-bomb testing in nearby Bikini Atoll. Godzilla is radioactive.

Godzilla emerged from Tokyo Bay. He destroyed a train and a bridge, killing many people. Guns had no effect on him. When he next came from the water, the military had put an electric barrier around the city. He ripped down the wires and walked through Tokyo, spewing his atomic breath, crushing all buildings in his path. Steve was hospitalized when a ceiling fell on him. He tells Emiko that it looks hopeless for mankind. She confesses that Serizawa has invented an Oxygen Destroyer, which when placed in water could destroy the monster.

After much soul searching and arguing with Ogata and Emiko, Serizawa agrees to use his Oxygen Destroyer. But he says that it must never be used again.

Ogata and Serizawa take the weapon into the ocean where Godzilla waits. Ogata emerges from the water and climbs aboard the navy ship where Steve, Emiko, and Dr. Yamane stand. He expects Serizawa to follow. But Serizawa remains below once he detonates his weapon. With the oxygen gone, Godzilla is killed. Serizawa tells Emiko and Ogata to be happy together. He cuts off his own oxygen, committing suicide rather than suffer the guilt of having created such a terrible weapon and possibly be tempted to use it again. All on board weep for the gallant man. Steve realizes that Serizawa gave his life so the world can begin anew.

---

* The Japanese-language film was titled *Gojira*. It was released in 1954, and played in a subtitled version in the United States in 1982. It was made by Toho Studios and directed by Ishiro Honda (sometimes called Inoshiro Honda). It runs 98 minutes and has the same stars as *Godzilla* except for Raymond Burr. The film's chronology is the same.
** This is the synopsis for *Godzilla, King of the Monsters*, not *Gojira*.
† I assume this is the correct spelling. This character is not listed in the film's credits.

Godzilla, King of the Monsters

I admit nostalgic affection for Ishiro Honda's flying reptile film *Rodan* (released in America in 1957) because it scared me into screaming "Japanese! Japanese!" in my sleep when a kid. But even with the popularity of campy (as in *bad*) movies, I am at a loss to explain the cult in America for Japanese monster movies—not just for the likes of *Godzilla, King of the Monsters; Rodan,* and Honda's *Mothra* (1962, U.S. release), which are considered the cream of a poor crop, but also for all those silly, terribly dubbed cheapies that play on the Early Show and on weekends opposite cartoons. Members of this odd group can correctly name the winners and losers in *War of the Gargantuas* (released

Godzilla, the embodiment of the A-Bomb dropped on Japan in 1945, emits its atomic breath.

in America in 1967), distinguish among the faces of Ghidra—the Three-Headed Monster—and list the films containing the absurd Gamera, an atomic flying turtle. They resent Kong's narrow victory in the American-release version of *King Kong vs. Godzilla* (1963) and would prefer seeing the original Japanese version, which, I am told, has Godzilla the victor over the American favorite.* And, unlike most American science fiction fans, they love *Godzilla, King of the Monsters.*

It may be surprising to some that in Japan *Gojira,* as the non-Americanized version is called, is regarded with the same awe and pride as Americans feel toward *King Kong* (1933). (Ironically, *King Kong* was the major influence on Eiji Tsuburaya, Toho's special effects master.) Not only did the first Japanese monster film cost thirty times that of the average Japanese film of the day, and break all records during its much ballyhooed November 1954 premiere engagement (a *Gojira* radio play had heightened anticipation), but it also received much serious critical attention in its native country. As Joseph L. Anderson and Donald Richie point out in *The Japanese Film* (Tuttle, 1959), even those who criticized "the picture's exploitation of the atom-bomb scare, praised it for an 'intellectual content usually lacking in foreign pictures of the same genre.'" It won many awards, including the Japanese Film Technique Award for Tsuburaya. In *The Japanese Fantasy Film Journal* (No. 13, 1981), Ed Godziszewski writes:

> To this day it remains the undeniable favorite of nearly all the monster films in Japan and is considered in Japan by many to be the second greatest Japanese film ever made, next to Kurosawa's *The Seven Samurai* [1954]. Because of *Gojira's* success, Toho produced a wave of science fiction and fantasy films until the mid-70's, when soaring costs and dwindling audiences brought the production of these films in Japan to virtual standstill. Despite this, thousands of fans turned out for a screening of *Gojira* during the 1979 Godzilla 25th Anniversary Festival, a testimony to its enduring popularity. *Gojira* was, and still is, the King!

The New York Times critic Bosley Crowther was one who resented the American distributors' claim that Godzilla was "King of the Monsters." In 1956 he wrote angrily, "One might remotely regard him as a symbol of Japanese hate for the destruction that came out of nowhere and descended upon Hiroshima one pleasant August morn. But we assure you that the quality of the picture and the childishness of the whole idea do not indicate such calculation. Godzilla was simply meant to scare people."

Viewings of *Gojira,* which finally had its American debut in subtitled form in the summer of 1982, and *Godzilla, King of the Monsters* reveal conclusively that the nuclear bomb theme was foremost in the minds of both the Japanese filmmakers and the American distributors who altered it for American release. Kong, of course, is king, but Crowther was wrong in thinking Godzilla was simply meant to scare viewers. What makes the picture interesting—even though it isn't that enjoyable or exciting (the Honda version is so somber it is dull)—is that unlike all those giant creatures found in

---

*With *King Kong vs. Godzilla,* Godzilla became a Japanese folk hero. In future films, Godzilla would *protect* Japan from attacks by Mothra, Ghidra, the Smog Monster, Megalon, et. al.

Raymond Burr gave his least interesting movie performance in the American version of the film, yet next to his killer in Hitchcock's Rear Window *(1954), this is probably his most memorable cinema role.*

American SF films of the fifties, Godzilla was not just a bad consequence of foolhardy nuclear testing. This merciless monster who kills and destroys with machinelike precision, impersonally and indiscriminately, is meant to be the embodiment of the five-ton atomic bombs that immediately killed 210,000 people when dropped on Hiroshima and Nagasaki. This horror film gave Americans one of their first opportunities to see Japanese fury and disgust over what America did to them in August 1945.

When the war ended, Allied Occupation forces in Japan regulated the film industry, destroying more than half of the pictures made, and heavily censoring others. Naturally, for a time, Japanese directors didn't bother to make films with war themes. Beginning around 1950, however, with the Occupation forces long gone, many films were made with antiwar messages, in angry reaction to the American-made war films that were being imported for the first time and the outbreak of the Korean conflict, which Japan wanted to stay out of. The tone of films such as *Vacuum Zone* (1952), *Five Scouts* (1950), and Honda's *Eagle of the Pacific* (1953) was not anti-American as one might suspect but anti-imperialistic and antimilitaristic, with World War II Japan the target. But filmmakers wouldn't continue to ignore what they felt was America's crime against humanity. First came *Children of the Atom Bomb* (1953). This was followed by Hedio Sekigawa's widely seen *Hiroshima* (1953)—containing documentary footage of the Bomb's aftermath—which epitomized the anti-American films of the period. Anderson and Richie write: "The picture was financially successful . . . and opened the way for the spate of other films supposedly expressing the American terrorization of Japan."

Early in 1954, Toho Studios' executive producer Tomoyuki Tanaka became excited by the fine American film *Beast From 20,000 Fathoms* (1953), about a dinosaur that is awakened by nuclear blasts and rampages through New York. Wanting to do something similar, Tanaka conceived a project titled *The Big Monster From 20,000 Miles Beneath the Sea.* That title was changed to *Gojira,* which was the nickname of a gigantic man on the Toho staff. Meanwhile, the giant octopus which

This lobby card was meant to draw parallels between Godzilla and King Kong, who also destroyed a train back in 1933. Another lobby card had Godzilla being attacked by planes, reminding viewers how Kong met his death.

Tsuburaya had envisioned as the monster became a combination Tyrannosaurus and Allosaurus, with a multiplated dorsal fin down its back. Two men alternated wearing the one-hundred-pound, virtually airless Gojira suit (accumulating blisters, getting muscle cramps, losing twenty pounds, and even fainting in the process); also two small Gojira puppets were used, including one that emitted a smoky spray, simulating Gojira's atomic breath. Because of all the special effects, including the building of many miniatures which Gojira crushes throughout the film, the picture took six months to complete. Two years later it was released in America, in a newly edited version.

The most obvious difference between Honda's version and that turned out by American Terry Morse is that an American character, correspondent Steve Martin, appears in the U.S. film. In cleverly edited scenes, he appears to talk to Japanese characters from the Honda version—but of course their faces are never shown in the same shot. Martin also serves as narrator. Therefore much of the dialogue can remain in Japanese—giving the production surprising authenticity—because Steve translates the words for us or asks his Japanese sidekick (also an actor hired by Morse) to translate for him. Because of Martin's presence, a Japanese newspaperman from the original version thus became obsolete and his footage was eliminated. In one scene, Martin also takes the place of a Japanese television announcer of the original who sees the monster approaching through the streets of Tokyo and has no way to escape from its path—Martin, like the Honda character, just keeps talking into his microphone as the monster gets closer and closer. Raymond Burr, as Steve, has to react to people and events filmed two years earlier. And he bungles

it. His emoting is so nonexistent that at times it's hard to believe he knows he's making a horror film. His expression changes only twice: when he takes out a pipe and when he is expecting to die and wipes the sweat from his forehead. Burr was hired for only one day's work, but it's amazing how much he's subjected to as the character he plays is hustled around from one location to another by Serizawa's aide. It's little wonder Burr looks nauseated in his final screen moments.

The American version makes two deletions that arouse suspicions regarding the covering up of references to damage done by the A-Bomb: a young woman (Emiko?) says that she doesn't want to be a victim of Gojira, "not after what I went through in Nagasaki"; a doctor detects that a little girl has radiation poisoning, and though she is sitting up now, he indicates she is doomed. Ironically, Morse also makes changes that identify Godzilla with the deadly powers of the A-Bomb that fell on Japan. Honda has the few ship survivors disappear after their rescue. In the Morse footage these men, who we're told have been exposed to radiation burns, die mysteriously from the aftereffects. Martin speaks of the pervasive "odor of human flesh" in Godzilla's wake and describes the rubble as "a smoldering memorial to the unknown"—the unknown being both the incomprehensible bomb that ended the war *and* what lies ahead in the terrifying atomic (and nuclear) age. Morse retains the scene where the ship and crew are destroyed by a blinding flash of light that initiates a fire—certainly a sign that Godzilla has A-Bomb powers; he also leaves in Honda's scenes in which the monster emits its atomic breath (rather than only showing it kill by trampling and using its claws), and in which the monster glows, indicating it is radioactive. Oddly, Morse has Steve tell us that

Tokyo is evacuated before Godzilla's attack, which hints that the citizens of Hiroshima and Nagasaki were prepared for some kind of attack. Knowing this wasn't the case, Honda didn't have the city become deserted and inadvertently stuck Morse with footage that makes no sense in the American version: after Godzilla leaves, the hospitals are filled with his victims—people who were supposed to be out of town.

Early in the Morse film, Emiko surveys the hospital victims and worries "We're all living on borrowed time." This is the kind of gloomy statement made at the *end* of the Honda version by Dr. Yamane; like Edmund Gwenn at the conclusion of *Them!* (1954), in which bomb-testing creates giant ants, Yamane predicts future monsters if scientists keep experimenting with deadly weapons. On the other hand, Morse's film ends optimistically (after all, *his* film is being shown to the people who dropped the Bomb and won World War II), with Steve mumbling something about how "the whole world could wake up and live again."

In Morse's film, Dr. Serizawa, the inventor of the Oxygen Destroyer, the ultimate weapon that is even stronger than the A-Bomb (Godzilla), doesn't know if he should use it to destroy the monster. We are told he has a moral "responsibility no man has faced." Of course, here Morse is overlooking the fact that the inventors of the A-Bomb, who had gone on to create the H-Bomb, had faced the same decision as Serizawa—unfortunately, they hadn't the foresight to destroy the formula for the Bomb after it was used in Japan. Consequently, nuclear testing has proliferated. Serizawa is a Japanese Robert Oppenheimer, the deeply-troubled man who created the bomb and later disavowed further bomb testing. Like Serizawa, he concluded that people are just fooling themselves when they say they are creating bombs to be used for peaceful purposes. In Honda's film, Serizawa (who lost his eye in the war) says, "Man is weak. As long as I live, I may be tempted to use it." That he uses his Oxygen Destroyer to put an end to Godzilla is philosophically confusing because it almost backs up America's much disputed claim that it used the A-Bomb in Japan to quickly end the war and stop the killing. But that he destroys his formula and kills himself we can respect: these are drastic acts which Honda, if not Morse, wishes those scientists around the world involved in bomb experimentation would consider. Obviously, none of these scientists saw *Godzilla*.

Godzilla, King of the Monsters, like *Gorija*, can be taken too seriously. It does have its camp elements. For instance, when Serizawa and Ogata fight in Serizawa's lab over the Oxygen Destroyer, and we are in the midst of the most serious scene in the picture, the men suddenly turn to watch a television set that is on for some reason. (In Morse, the many singers we see on the set are supposedly singing a prayer of mourning. Significantly, in Honda, they sing a song about future *peace*.*) Equally amusing is when Yamane (played by Kurosawa's great actor Takashi Shimura) sends Ogata and Serizawa into the ocean, where they will detonate the ultimate weapon in mortal combat with the seemingly indestructible monster; his advice? "Be careful."

---

* Even though American science fiction films had antibomb themes (while exploiting the Bomb at the same time), they were not antimilitaristic. Nor did they seriously support a goal of world peace, which in the McCarthy era was considered by the film industry to be a communist goal that was supported in the United States only by those sympathetic to Russia.

1977 New World release of a Yasny Talking Pictures-II production
Director: Michael Pressman
Producer: David Irving
Screenplay: David Kirkpatrick and Mark Rosin
Cinematography: Jamie Anderson
Music: Craig Safan
Editor: Millie Moore
Running time: 90 minutes

Cast: Claudia Jennings (Candy Morgan), Jocelyn Jones (Ellie Jo Turner), Johnny Crawford (Slim), Chris Pennock (Jake), Tara Stroheimer (Pam Morgan), Bart Braverman (Freddie), Buddy Kling (Mr. Sherman), Tom Rosqui (Jason Morgan), Eric Boles (Johnny), Stefan Gierasch (Robert Simon), Don Elson (Mr. Smith)

Synopsis: Using dynamite, Candy Morgan breaks out of a Texas prison. On the same day, Ellie Jo Turner is fired from her job as bank teller. As her boss is firing her, Ellie Jo watches Candy enter the bank and threaten to ignite a stick of dynamite unless she gets money. Ellie Jo gladly fills her bag. After Candy flees, Ellie Jo is still excited by the event.

Ellie Jo says good-bye to her boyfriend Freddie and hitchhikes out of Alpine, determined to have a fun-filled life. Candy gives the money she stole to her father so he can keep his farm. She then takes the backroads out of town. She gives Ellie Jo a ride. Ellie Jo convinces Candy that they should team up and rob more banks.

On their first caper, Candy's dynamite fizzles and the women only manage to escape because of fast driving and by throwing one stick of good dynamite into a chasing patrol car. (The police escape with no injuries.) Ellie Jo feels bad about causing Candy such bad luck and offers to leave. Candy says "We're in this together."

The women purchase dynamite from a handsome mining operator named Jake. Candy gets the price down by seducing him. He gives them a shotgun and wishes them luck.

Candy and Ellie Jo pull off several successful heists. They become known as the "Dynamite Women" and are wanted for murdering a guard—something they have never done.

When Ellie Jo is stopped at a grocery store counter for shoplifting, the two women rob the store. They also take another shoplifter, Slim, as a hostage. He becomes their friend. That night the three check into a ritzy hotel. While Ellie Jo and Slim make love, Candy seduces Johnny, a bellboy. They all end up nude in the bathtub. The hotel clerk informs the police that the bankrobbers are present. But Johnny helps them escape.

The robberies continue. Now Slim serves as a "professional hostage": at each bank the women pretend he is a customer they will blow up if they don't get money. After robbing one bank for the second time, the three dine at a fancy restaurant. Mr. Smith, that day fired as the bank's manager, spots them and chases them out. The experience unnerves Slim. He decides to walk out on Ellie Jo, but changes his mind so they can pull off one last job together.

They go into hiding at a deserted cabin. But the manager recognizes Slim and calls the police. While in the woods Ellie Jo tells Slim she loves him. Cops step out of the bushes and gun him down. Candy kills both cops and pulls Ellie Jo away from her dead lover. They escape. Having lost their money in the cabin, they need to pull off one more job. They are ambushed in town, but somehow escape. Candy is wounded.

Followed by the police they head for the Mexican border. They are trapped in a barn. Candy tells Ellie Jo to go on without her. Ellie Jo says "We're in this together!" They roll their car at the police. It explodes. During the diversion, the women hop on two horses and gallop to freedom in Mexico.

The Great Texas Dynamite Chase

In casual attire and dynamite in hand, Candy (L) and Ellie Jo pull off a daring bank robbery.

The Great Texas Dynamite Chase, one of many New World sexploitation films that hit it big in drive-ins and small-town America in the seventies, contains an extremely erotic scene in which bankrobber Candy Morgan seduces Jake, a handsome mining operator she met about ten minutes earlier. While he lies on a pile of hay, she sits a few feet from him, giving off body heat. Her unbuttoned blouse is tied at her waist, she wears short shorts, her legs are spread wide. Without waiting for an invitation, Candy removes her blouse. "My god!" Jake exclaims, as he looks at his godsend. Now, these might have been the words in the script, but it's obvious that Chris Pennock, the actor playing Jake, believes what he's saying. For as the many fervent fans of the late Claudia Jennings can attest, she had the most beautiful body of any leading lady making movies in the seventies. Males should know better than to admit going to a movie for the specific purpose of seeing a beautiful actress naked, but no one bothered to deny that was the primary attraction of a Claudia Jennings picture. Jennings, the much heralded 1970 Playboy Playmate of the Year, whose attitude was "everyone must understand that today nice girls do take off their clothes," shrugged and gave her fans what they wanted. In all her starring films (at least the ones that were released), she spent time in the nude: on the beach in her debut film, *Jud* (1970), in a swamp in *Gator Bait* (1976), on the floor in *Deathsport* (1978), on a bed (!) in *Group Marriage* (1974). When she wasn't undressed, there was a good chance she'd be in an unbuttoned blouse, a see-through minidress, or, as in *Gator Bait*, tight cut-off jeans and an open vest with nothing underneath. Her appreciative fans made Jennings the Queen of the Drive-In Movies, a.k.a. the Queen of the Bs.

But while Claudiaphiles considered her nude scenes (which were more passionate than steamy) the highlights of her R-rated action films, these were not the only reason Jennings became as popular as she did, particularly with women. Although John Simon praised her fully-clothed performance in 1970's off-Broadway production of *Dark of the Moon,* she was an actress of limited range—the less experienced Jocelyn Jones certainly betters her in *Dynamite Chase*—but one can't dispute that she had something *very* special. Call it screen presence, star quality, or charisma, a term critics usually reserve for actors. She had that perfect body, but she also had strikingly intelligent eyes, a self-assured expression, and infectious vitality. Her films weren't the best around, yet her women were almost always interesting and appealing; and I'm sure that's because much of Jennings came through. They had a desirable blend of courage, confidence (without being obnoxiously cocky), skills (driving fast, shooting straight, loving hard), and strength in the face of adversity; and though they usually weren't educated, they were the sharpest people around. On the one hand they fit the mold of Erskine Caldwell's flirtatious, skimpily-dressed, sexually promiscuous country-nature girls. A lusty combination of woman Tina Louise and nymphet Fay Spain in *God's Little Acre* (1958). But Jennings's women were more cognizant of sexual politics; they knew that their bodies were their best weapons in their quest for justice and power and respect in a world of leering, addle-brained misogynists. They were also distant cousins of Jennifer Jones's *Ruby Gentry* (1952) and of the sexually liberated Russ Meyer heroines of *Lorna* (1964), *Mud Honey* (1965), and *Vixen* (1968), who also were extremely popular with female viewers. But Jennings's women were less conniving, less selfish, more sensible, wiser, and being "modern women," more aware of their responsibility to better the socioeconomic standing of their sex.

We admire Jennings's women because they sought lifestyles and occupations that were both challenging and daring. Jennings is a roller derby star in Vernon Zimmerman's *The Unholy Rollers* (1972), probably her best film; the driver of a semi in Mark Lester's *Truck Stop Women* (1974); the lawyer for and a member of a group of lovers who deliberately test the country's marital laws in Stephanie Rothman's satirical *Group Marriage*; a racer of superspeed cars in *Deathsport*; a seller of illegal alcohol in *Moonshine County Express* (1977), my favorite Jennings film; and a bankrobber in *Dynamite Chase.* Looking for excitement, her characters seem to enjoy the battles they invariably have with the bad guys whose feet they're stepping on: the mob in *Truck Stop Women,* prudish

Slim tells Ellie Jo that he's leaving because their lifestyle is too dangerous. But he'll change his mind.

citizens' groups in *Group Marriage,* a corrupt politician and sheriff in *Moonshine County Express,* etc. We marvel at their strong defiance, their refusal to be broken by the powerful people out to destroy them. They are winners. The women Claudia Jennings played are genuine heroines, smart, independent, brave women of action who did not appear in A films of the seventies despite all those rumors about improvement in women's roles. (Surprisingly, such women could be found on television, albeit on the comic book level.)

It was on the morning of October 3, 1979, just ten years after she had first appeared as *Playboy*'s Playmate covergirl, that Claudia Jennings, at the age of twenty-nine, was killed in a head-on collision with a truck on the Pacific Coast highway in Malibu, California. Considering how important she was to a segment of the movie audience, it was sad how brief her obituaries were in the nation's dailies—*if* her death was mentioned at all. So it was good to see a long, moving tribute to her in *Film Comment*'s November–December 1979 issue, written by critic Todd McCarthy, coeditor of *Kings of the Bs* (Dutton, 1975). McCarthy had gone to high school with Jennings (then Mimi Chesterton) in Evanston, Illinois, had dated her and, I sense, developed a lifelong crush on her. He cast her as the lead in his prize-winning short *Mimi,* and a dozen years later he headed New World's publicity force on *The Great Texas Dynamite Chase.* Included in his article:

> The first thing that struck me was the similarity of Claudia's death to that of Françoise Dorleac, another beautiful star that flashed across the movie sky all too quickly. The second thing was that her life and career, now that they were over, fit the contours of a Harold Robbins novel. It was all there: the modest beginnings, the sudden vault to fame based on beauty and sex, the toughness, the boyfriends, the glamour, even the inner sense of irony and perspective that was nonetheless dominated by the thing she had become. Despite my rejection of

the notion of suicide,* I shudder to think that perhaps she had come to the same realization as her most cynical detractors—that she was indeed washed up. Where, after all, can a Queen-of-the-Bs sexpot go once she's hit thirty? All the answers are depressing.

Claudia Jennings never had the chance to make a top-grade mainstream film, yet she did leave behind a respectable screen legacy. But *The Great Texas Dynamite Chase,* which Jennings's underground following ranks with *The Unholy Rollers* as her most enjoyable picture, is surprisingly disappointing. One of the countless low-budgeted cops-chase-heroes/heroines-on-dusty-southern-backroads pictures that have been made since *Thunder Road* (1958) and the peak drive-in era, it lacks the excitement, humor, and even the sweaty rednecks that can be found in most films of the genre. Worse, Jennings gives an uncharacteristically lackluster performance. Following an injury received in a getaway sequence, Jennings had to spend time in a hospital, where she dropped twenty pounds, and she relied on painkillers to get her through subsequent filming. According to Todd McCarthy, Jennings felt too bad to enjoy finishing the picture—and it shows. At times she appears to have no energy, and her sense of humor, much in evidence in her other films, is virtually nonexistent.

So it is that bright-eyed Jocelyn Jones (the daughter of character actor Henry Jones) steals the film. Her Ellie Jo is extremely likable, tough but vulnerable, enthusiastic (how she loves watching Candy rob the bank that just fired her), pretty, and so sexy (in halter tops, or nude but for a slim chain around her hips) that we don't mind when Jennings isn't on the screen. Of course, Jones benefits from having a better part than Jennings. Ellie Jo is a woman who seeks a better life than the humdrum one she had in Alpine; who wants to be on the other side of a bank teller's window for a change; who goes through emotional crises; who learns the meaning of loyalty and female camaraderie. Candy, who has no real goal in life but to become rich, doesn't change one bit from beginning to end: that makes for too predictable a character. I'd like to have seen Jennings and Jones reunited when both were in peak form and both had good characters.

It's odd seeing Johnny Crawford, once the emotional boy on *The Rifleman* (1958–1963), as well as a young pop singer (he even has a "Greatest Hits" album), all grown up and flexing muscles. And doing nudity yet. Unfortunately, Slim is a thankless role. Not only does the appearance of this character halt the interaction between Candy and Ellie Jo before it really gets started, but it also signals a foolish change in the film's tone. At the beginning, when he helps Candy and Ellie Jo pull off robberies, Slim contributes to the film's lighthearted sense of mischief. Suddenly, he starts to worry about their safety and the picture becomes serious. Then in a very bloody scene that is totally incongruous with the rest of the picture, Slim is gunned down by police. What happened to the comedy we've been watching for eighty minutes?

---

* Earlier in his article, McCarthy had said, "Jennings had recently lost out [to model Shelley Hack] for the job of Kate Jackson's replacement on *Charlie's Angels* after having been led to believe she might get the part. But she was too tough . . . too level-headed to be plunged into depression over not winning a role."

A lurid publicity photo of sexy stars Jocelyn Jones and the late but not forgotten Claudia Jennings.

Probably the biggest problem with *Dynamite Chase,* however, is that its storyline lacks complexity. Obligatory car chases and idiotic southern cops abound, but the writers didn't bother to insert a dramatic conflict. Nothing has to be resolved. It would have been ideal to have had a powerful villain, rather than a lot of faceless policemen, in pursuit of Candy and Ellie Jo, because until the end we never worry about the women. Perhaps this villain could have been the owner of all the banks, including the New World Bank (an in-joke of the filmmakers), that Candy and Ellie Jo attempt to rob. In that way their robberies could be acts of revenge. This would work because Candy and Ellie Jo need a better purpose to rob banks than simply to have fun and become wealthy. Only at the end, when the two are fighting for survival, can we really empathize with them.

And only when Candy and Ellie Jo pull off an escape Butch Cassidy and the Sundance Kid would have been proud of—sending an exploding car into a crowd of policemen and riding horses across the border—do we have a scene that is pure "dynamite."

1958 Metro-Goldwyn-Mayer
Director: Jack Arnold
Producer: Albert Zugsmith
Screenplay: Lewis Meltzer and Robert Blees
From an original story by Robert Blees
Special material: Mel Welles
Cinematography: Harold J. Marzorati
Title song: Jerry Lee Lewis and Ron Hargraves;
sung by Jerry Lee Lewis
Editor: Ben Lewis
Running time: 85 minutes

Cast: Russ Tamblyn (Tony Baker/Mike Wilson), Jan Sterling (Arlene Williams), John Drew Barrymore (J. I. Coleridge), Mamie Van Doren (Gwen Dulaine), Diane Jergens (Joan Staples), Ray Anthony (Bix), Jackie Coogan (Mr. A), Charles Chaplin, Jr. (Quinn), Burt Douglas (Jukey Judlow), Jody Fair (Doris), Michael Landon (Steve Bentley), Lyle Talbot (William Remington Kane), William Wellman, Jr. (Wheeler-Dealer), Texas Joe Foster (henchman), Carl Thayler (Petey), Jerry Lee Lewis (himself), Florida Freibus (Mrs. Staples), James Todd (Jack Staples), Phillipa Fallon (poetess)

Synopsis: Tony Baker enrolls in Santo Bello High. He has come from Chicago and is living with his married aunt Gwen. He immediately makes an impression on everyone at the school by acting disrespectfully to the principal, flirting with English teacher Arlene, carrying a huge wad of money around, and putting the move on Joan Staples, the girlfriend of J. I. Coleridge. Tony informs J.I. that he is replacing him as head of the rowdy Wheeler-Dealers. When J.I.'s gang threatens Tony, Tony pulls out a switchblade and chases them away.

At home, Gwen tries to get Tony to make love to her, but he resists her advances. He is more interested in trying to get a date with Arlene. She believes that he has a nice streak despite the awful way he acts. But she won't date him—she'd rather reform him.

The principal is informed that marijuana cigarettes have been found in the school and that there is a serious drug problem. The commissioner is waging a war on drugs. Tony discovers that Joan is hooked on marijuana. When J.I. won't acquire joints for her until she comes up with the money, Tony tells Joan that he'll supply the money if she'll introduce him to the contact. Joan starts dating Tony. At a pool party they find out that a classmate, Doris, has become a heroin addict.

Tony buys grass from Jukey Judlow, who tells him he can buy it in quantity from someone at the car rally. That person turns out to be J.I. Tony tells J.I. he wants to purchase heroin and cocaine so he can sell it. He wants to meet Mr. A.

During the car race, Joan gets high on grass and pushes the peddle on Tony's car. Grass falls from Tony's hubcaps just as police drive up. Everyone is arrested. Joan's parents are angry with the police for arresting ''innocent'' children. Mr. A bails out Tony. His man Bix drives Tony to meet him. Mr. A turns out to be the pianist at the local hangout. Tony sees Doris in the next room. She is in agony with withdrawal—Mr. A will give her a fix if she'll join his upstate prostitution ring. Mr. A will not sell Tony heroin and allow him to become one of his dealers unless he can prove he is legitimate. Tony pretends to shoot up and fools him. The deal will be made later that night.

Stoned and needing more grass, Joan waits in Tony's room. She discovers that he has tape-recorded the conversation with Mr. A. Having no time for explanations, Tony goes to make the money payment and asks Arlene to watch over Joan. But J.I. and Jukey show up at the house and slap around Joan, Arlene, and Gwen. They learn of the tape recording and call Mr. A to warn him that Tony (whose real name is Mike Wilson) is an undercover agent. Tony meets Mr. A at the hangout. Tony's police–contact–Quinn, who has gotten a job as a waiter, recruits Steve Bentley and the Rangers (a club with football types) to help Tony. When Mr. A tries to shoot Tony, Tony throws heroin into his face and there is a big fight. Quinn is shot, but Mr. A and Bix are eventually captured.

J.I. and Jukey are sent to reform school, Mr. A and Bix go to jail. Joan only smokes real cigarettes now. Gwen, who isn't really Tony's aunt, is no longer after every man in sight because her husband has come home. The jobs of Arlene (teacher) and Mike Wilson (police officer) are not over.

High School Confidential

No filmmaker has had a more schizophrenic career than Albert Zugsmith, a one-time journalist turned producer and sometimes director. It's hard to believe that the same man who cast Mamie Van Doren in no less than six films and allowed Zsa Zsa Gabor to play *two* parts (one Stalin's mistress!) in a single film, *The Girl in the Kremlin* (1957), was producer on two of Douglas Sirk's finest pictures and paved the way in 1958 for Orson Welles to be given another chance to direct films in America. Zugsmith has contributed such class productions as Sirk's *Written on the Wind* (1957), and *The Tarnished Angels* (1958), based on Faulkner's *Pylon*; Jack Arnold's *The Tattered Dress* (1957) and *The Incredible Shrinking Man* (1957), among the most intelligent of fifties SF films; Arnold Laven's *Slaughter on Tenth Avenue* (1957), a hard-hitting racketeering exposé; and Welles's classic *Touch of Evil* (1958). But film devotees admire him just as much for his low-budget exploitation films aimed at teen-agers, college freshmen, soldiers on leave, and the gang down at the bowling alley: *High School Confidential, The Beat Generation* (1959), *College Confidential* (1960), *The Private Lives of Adam and Eve* (1960), *Sex Kittens Go to College* (1960), *Girls Town* (1960), all with Mamie Van Doren; *Teacher Was a Sexpot* (1960); *Platinum High School* (1960); *Confessions of an Opium Eater* (1962); Russ Meyer's *Fanny Hill* (1965); *Movie Star, American Style, or LSD, I Hate You!* (1967); *The Incredible Sex Revolution* (1967); etc. The titles alone are to be appreciated.

Sliding back and forth between A and B films, with an occasional Z thrown in for good measure, Zugsmith explored such touchy subjects as male impotence (*Written on the Wind*), miscegenation (*The Night of the Quarter Moon*, 1959), racial prejudice, juvenile delinquency, sexual promiscuity, alcohol and drug (marijuana, cocaine, speed, LSD, opium, heroin) dependency. He considered his films "moral essays" and defended his use of lurid plot elements: "I don't make movies without a moral, but you can't make a point for good unless you expose the evil."* Zugsmith was aware of the times, so his leading ladies were almost always sexy blondes who looked enticing in tops several sizes too small: Van Doren, the poor man's Jayne Mansfield; Jan Sterling, who appeared in several Zugsmith films; Janet Leigh, who was never sexier than in *Touch of Evil*; Zsa Zsa Gabor; Dorothy Malone, who was in both Sirk films; Tuesday Weld; Diane Jergens; Yvette Mimieux. His leading men ranged from Rock Hudson, Charlton Heston, and Jeff Chandler (Universal's biggest actor until Hudson emerged) to Mickey Rooney, George Nader, and Steve Allen. Not to be overlooked was his strange male

*''From *Rock Around the Clock* to *The Trip*: The Truth about Teen Movies'' by Richard Staehling. *Rolling Stone*, No. 49 (December 27, 1969)

The picture opens with Jerry Lee Lewis riding onto campus and belting out the title song, and the obviously overaged high school students breaking into an impromptu jitterbug.

repertory company, which included John Drew Barrymore, Jackie Coogan, Charles Chaplin, Jr., and bandleader Ray Anthony.

Zugsmith's teenpix were able to compete with the product of other top exploiters of the period, most notably Allied Artists and American International Pictures (where Roger Corman was making his name), because they contained everything the discriminating drive-in crowd ordered: fist fights, hot rod races, rock 'n' roll, wild dancing, drugs, teens out for kicks, sex, hip jargon, and WASPish characters in deep trouble. *High School Confidential*, Zugsmith's first picture after his move from Universal to Metro, isn't in the league with such A "teen problem" films as *The Blackboard Jungle* (1955) and *Rebel Without a Cause* (1955)—which influenced the whole genre—but it makes no such pretentions. For what it is, a fast-moving, tongue-in-cheek glimpse of the turbulent youth scene, it is great fun. Partly because of the action, partly because of the *three* blondes, partly because of the dialogue. In 1958, the teen-age lingo used in the film was meant to be alien to viewers not directly involved in the scene; today, the lingo—a great source of amusement—seems foreign once again because it's so outmoded. Still, a wave of nostalgia has to sweep through all of us who remember when teens said things like "flip out," "swingingest," "nowhere," "square," "(*fill in any word*)sville," "That's the way the ball bounces," "Tough toenails," "You're dragging your axle in waltz time," and "I'm putting it down" (Tony puts his hand out, palm up) and "I'm picking it up" (Petey lays his hand in Tony's and they shake); and when beat existentialist poets recited such lines as "Tomorrow's a drag; the future's a flake."

It was the era of such pictures as *I Was a Teen-age Frankenstein* (1957) and *I Was a Teen-age Werewolf* (1957), starring Michael Landon (who has a small part in *High School Confidential*). So it would have been a natural to call this picture *I Was a Teen-age Narc*. But I suppose they didn't want to let on right away that Tony (energetically played by Russ Tamblyn) was working undercover in Santo Bello High. We get hints that Tony isn't the teen-age punk his classmates think him to be: he drinks milk, turns down the sexual advances of his aunt, is civil to All-American boy Steve, refuses Joan's marijuana cigarette, and looks upset about addict Doris's distress. Also he looks too old to be in high school (his alibi is he's flunked three times). But we keep waiting and waiting for him to make contact with someone in law enforcement or with the principal so that we can know for sure he's on the right side. (After a while one begins to wonder if Tony truly is a punk who will be reformed by his teacher Arlene at film's end.) Instead, Tony spends his time racing his convertible, fighting with switchblades, "grazing for grass" and trying to make big drug deals, flirting with Arlene, showing disrespect for his principal, smoking stogies in school, and, most suspiciously, helping Joan buy marijuana. Having Tony act in such a way actually serves the picture well once we find out that Tony is really Mike Wilson, narc: teen-age viewers can see that squares aren't the only ones who are antidrugs.

High School Confidential was banned in a number of countries (from Greece to New Zealand) indicating that not everyone believed the antidrug message strong enough to offset the unflattering portrait of American youth. Realizing that "a lot of people will hate this picture and not get the point," Zugsmith added a prologue to British prints of the

Tony (L) makes a play for Joan, ignoring the fact that she's J. I.'s gal.

film, and apparently to some prints that were distributed in America. Prints I've seen begin with Jerry Lee Lewis, piano in a pickup, belting out the title song to jitterbugging students. In *Rolling Stone* (December 27, 1969), Richard Staehling writes about this scene:

> The film starts with a close-up of a man behind a desk looking directly into the camera; it looks as though he's about to endorse a candidate for office. Instead, we are informed that he is a member of a narcotics control board [of the Los Angeles Medical Association] who wishes to endorse the film. It seems the film we are about to see is "not pleasant," but will bring forth some of the hard-hitting facts about drugs and their use in high schools. The gentleman urges us to study *High School Confidential* closely, and be ever on the alert for such problems in our schools.

Mr. A holds a gun on Tony while Bix examines his arms for needle marks. Finding none, he realizes Tony is a narc!

Oh, well—Dr. Frank Baxter endorsed *The Mole People* (1956).

I don't think Zugsmith was particularly concerned with the drug problem in American high schools; still, as the *Variety* critic wrote at the time: "Although the presentation seems to exploit to the fullest every facet of this evil situation, it does so skillfully and with compelling effect." Considering that the very controversial *The Man With the Golden Arm* (1955) was made only three years before, I'm surprised at how daring the heroin aspect is. The scene in which Tony pretends to shoot up by inserting the needle in a rubber ball he has hidden in the crook of his arm is chilling. Especially with Doris nearby in the throes of withdrawal. There really is little about drugs in the film that can be laughed at. Zugsmith and his talented director Arnold (known best for an outstanding series of SF films in the fifties) include much intentional campy humor, but the drug angle is treated cautiously. Today's viewers may sneer at Tony's "If you flake around with the weed, you'll end up using the harder stuff," but as drug-abuse workers would suggest, Tony's only mistake is implying it happens to everyone rather than to a small minority; importantly, the film points out that people who end up on heroin were initiated into the drug scene through marijuana, and that many who sell marijuana in a big way also deal in hard drugs. We can't dislike Tony—although in real life, narcs will win no popularity contests—because he is sincere in wanting to stop a bad problem.

I'm a bit surprised considering twenty-two years had passed about the similarities between *Reefer Madness* (1936) and the infinitely superior *High School Confidential* in regard to the antidrug propaganda expounded. Both films express the theme that problem children don't necessarily come from problem homes. Also, even nice teen-agers can become drug users and abusers. In both films, some preachy fellow tells adults about how the "evil weed" has ruined the lives of teen-agers elsewhere—in *High School Confidential* we are told of a once thriving school in middle-America (Indiana) that has literally gone to pot—warning their listeners that "it can happen here." Interestingly, in both films we see that the main dealers aren't users themselves—they know better. And that the dealers set up business, through a network of pushers, around schools, in local hangouts, because there they can find naïve kids out for kicks. We also "learn" that where there is wild music, there is usually drugs: Dave O'Brien, who goes insane from smoking grass in *Reefer Madness*, plays a mean piano; drug kingpin Mr. A plays a mean piano in *High School Confidential* and also uses a jukebox business as his front. The major mistake made by the makers of both films—if they were indeed serious about getting the teens in their audience off drugs, which I doubt they were—is that they show that people who turn on usually have a very envious sex life with beautiful, willing partners like Joan. At least the filmmakers give us an impression in the last shot of the film, in which Joan sits next to Mike (formerly Tony) in his convertible (Arlene is next to her and Gwen smooches with her husband in the back) that she is still willing to be Mike's girl even though she no longer carries joints in her bra ("Joan only smokes ordinary cigarettes now," claims the Russ Meyer–like narrator). Even nice girls can have fun—of course, blondes have the most fun of all.

Gwen protests when she discovers J. I. and Jukey manhandling Joan and Arlene in Tony's bedroom. She, too, will be roughed up. In this scene Mamie Van Doren is as modestly dressed as she ever is in this picture.

A case can be made that the last shot signifies that teen-agers like Joan are being guarded on one side by teachers and on the other side by law enforcers. I also think the shot implies that Arlene and Mike have become surrogate parents for Joan, because her own parents do little to protect her from the real world. Surrogate father or not, Tony will probably date both Arlene and Joan. The relationship between Tony and Arlene is most peculiar. Arlene spends most of the picture trying to reform him, when in fact it turns out he needs no reforming. So all her judgments about teen-agers based on Tony go down the drain. We also figure, wrongly, that Tony makes a play for Arlene as part of his plan to either impress the school big shots by dating a teacher or to just be plain pushy. But at the end, we can conclude that there is a legitimate attraction between the two. Zugsmith is an exploitation director supreme, and I wish he would have further exploited the relationship between the young Tony (Tamblyn was twenty-four) and that somewhat older Arlene (Sterling was thirty-four).

Who in their right mind would place a young undercover agent in a house with nymphomaniac Gwen while her husband's away? No one. Nevertheless, we can forgive Zugsmith for including this unnecessary character, for it lets Mamie Van Doren strut her stuff. I've always liked Van Doren—especially when she married flakey baseball pitcher Bo Belinsky—and it's fun watching her walking around in semiobscene outfits, rolling around on Tony's bed as if she were a cat in heat, biting into Tony's apple with the thoughts of Eden in her naughty little head, drinking herself into a stupor, even being slapped around in classic cheap-dame style. She was called a five-and-dime imitation of Marilyn Monroe and Jayne Mansfield, but she was one of a kind. There is absolutely no way Tony, moral or not, could have resisted *her* advances. Of Gwen's classic verbal duel with Arlene, Richard Staehling marvels, "Spiffed out in a white cashmere sweater at least four times too small, Mamie tells [the] superstraight young teacher: 'Don't tell me you never rode in a hot rod or had a late date in the balcony.' It is one of the finest moments in the history of teen-age flicks, and indicative of Zugsmith's modus operandi."

His Girl Friday

1940 Columbia
Director: Howard Hawks
Producer: Howard Hawks
Screenplay: Charles Lederer
From the play *The Front Page* by Ben Hecht and Charles MacArthur

Cinematography: Joseph Walker
Music: Morris W. Stoloff
Editor: Gene Havlick
Running time: 92 minutes

Cast: Cary Grant (Walter Burns), Rosalind Russell (Hildy Johnson), Ralph Bellamy (Bruce Baldwin), Gene Lockhart (Sheriff Pinky Hartwell), Helen Mack (Mollie Malloy), Porter Hall (Murphy), Ernest Truex (Bensinger), Cliff Edwards (Endicott), Clarence Kolb (Mayor), Roscoe Karns (McCue), Frank Jenks (Wilson), Regis Toomey (Sanders). Abner Biberman (Louis), Frank Orth (Duffy), John Qualen (Earl Williams), Alma Kruger (Mrs. Baldwin), Billy Gilbert (Joe Pettibone), Pat West (Warden Cooley), Edwin Maxwell (Dr. Egelhoffer)

Synopsis: Tomorrow Earl Williams is to be hanged for shooting a black policeman. Chicago reporters Murphy, Endicott, McCue, and Wilson play poker while waiting for the execution; fussy Bensinger sits at his desk. The *Morning Post* has been pressuring the governor to give Earl a reprieve because of insanity, but the governor has resisted. To the *Post*'s managing editor, Walter Burns, Earl is just part of a major story.

Walter's star reporter is Hildy Johnson, who has just gotten her divorce from him. She tells him that she is quitting the paper to marry Bruce Baldwin, an Albany insurance man who will give her the home, family, and attention Walter never did. Walter tries to get Hildy to realize she would never be happy away from the paper.

Walter wants to break up Hildy and Bruce before they're to take a train with Bruce's mother to Albany. He tells Bruce he'll buy an insurance policy if Hildy gets a story on Earl Williams. Knowing better than to trust Walter, Hildy takes Bruce's ticket money for safekeeping. Walter's friend Louis picks Bruce's pocket.

Hildy interviews Earl Williams, who turns out to be a confused little guy who didn't know what he was doing when he pulled the trigger. She manipulates him into saying he used the gun after hearing speeches about "production for use." Her story impresses the tough reporters.

The reporters treat Hildy like one of them, but they treat Mollie Malloy, a streetwalker who is Earl's one friend, like trash when she tries to tell them that they had written lies about her having an affair with Earl.

When Hildy finds out Bruce was arrested because Walter had Louis plant a stolen watch on him, she tells Walter off and quits. But when Earl shoots Egelhoffer, a psychiatrist, with Sheriff Pinky Hartwell's gun, and escapes, Hildy can't resist pursuing the story. Meanwhile, Bruce is arrested for "mashing" with Louis's girlfriend Evangeline.

Pettibone tries to deliver a reprieve from the governor. The crooked mayor and Pinky offer him a bribe not to deliver the reprieve until Earl has been executed.

Hildy and Walter hide Earl in Bensinger's desk. When Bruce's mother informs the reporters that Bruce said they were hiding Earl, Louis picks her up and carts her off. Their car crashes into a police car. The reporters demand to know where Earl is. To divert their attention, Mollie jumps out the window and is injured. Hildy, with Walter's assistance, writes the story about Earl. With the money Walter gave him, Bruce goes to the train station to wait for her. When the mayor and Pinky discover Earl they handcuff Hildy and Walter. But Pettibone walks in and reveals he was offered the bribe. The handcuffs come off. Earl gets his reprieve.

Walter and Hildy decide to remarry. Meanwhile Bruce is arrested for carrying counterfeit money.

*In a publicity pose both Cary Grant
and Ralph Bellamy lay claim
to Rosalind Russell.*

Most directors resent insinuations that their film's are merely variations on each other or, worse, replicas of other directors' pictures. Yet Howard Hawks never worried about critics realizing that many of his pictures weren't true originals. He found no reason to apologize for remaking his silent *The Road to Glory* (1926) as a 1936 talkie, or his 1941 comedy gem *Ball of Fire* as *A Song Is Born* in 1947. He even boasted that he was able to rework *Rio Bravo* (1959) twice: as *El Dorado* (1967) and *Rio Lobo* (1970), his last film. As a matter of fact, *Rio Bravo* itself was conceived as an angry response to Fred Zinnemann's *High Noon* (1952). Similarly, Hawks made *The Dawn Patrol* (1930) after William Wellman's *Wings* (1927), *Scarface* (1932) after Wellman's *The Public Enemy* (1931), and *The Big Sleep* (1946) after Edward Dmytryk's Philip Marlowe flick *Murder, My Sweet* (1944). *Red River* (1948), in which scenes and shots pay tribute to the westerns of pal John Ford, was essentially *Mutiny on the Bounty* (1935) out west. So Columbia had no hesitation in asking him to remake *The Front Page* (1931), Lewis Milestone's adaptation of Ben Hecht and Charles MacArthur's rowdy newspaper play of 1928. And what Hawks produced was not only an improvement on Milestone's film but the fastest moving, most hilarious of all screwball comedies.

Actually Hawks wouldn't agree to the project until he figured out a way to give it a twist. Wanting to hear the dialogue, he asked a woman who happened to be in the room to read the part of Hildy Johnson, the role played by Pat O'Brien in the Milestone film and Osgood Perkins on the stage. Hawks became excited by the reading and asked Charles

Lederer, the rewrite man on the Milestone film, to devise a screenplay with Hildy Johnson as a *female* caught in a romantic triangle: *His Girl Friday*.

Hawks immediately recognized that with Hildy as a woman the story takes on a new, interesting dimension: the characters play for higher stakes. In *The Front Page*, Walter (Adolphe Menjou) wants Hildy to remain with the *Morning Post* instead of marrying Peggy *and* taking a high-paying ad agency job. This is as much out of spite (as Peggy points out) as out of fear of losing his ace reporter. (In the play, there is additionally a subtle homosexual bond between Hildy and Walter.) In *His Girl Friday*, Walter, who has become the *lead* male character, *needs* Hildy (as all Hawks's heroes are incomplete without women of equal intelligence, wit, and strength of character) because he loves her and because she is a crack reporter—not necessarily in that order. In the Milestone film Hildy is merely torn between remaining with the *Morning Post* and taking the ad agency position—although he wrongly believes that Peggy won't marry him if he stays a reporter and under Walter's control. But in the Hawks film Hildy (one of this director's many independent-minded working women) must decide between marrying Bruce to be taken care of always (as only insurance men can do) and the inviting combination of earning her own living using her work skills and remarrying Walter. In the Milestone film there can be a compromise that pleases everyone: Hildy can marry Peggy and remain in Walter's employ. But Hawks makes the choice decisive: if she marries Bruce, then she will permanently give up Walter and reporting; one man must cancel out the other.

The men in Milestone's film are identical to the snide, sarcastic, self-serving cutthroats who populated the venal newspaper world on the stage; because women (Peggy, Peggy's mother Mollie) can't penetrate the males' cynical circle, they are relegated to secondary-character status. The yapping, card-playing reporters in *His Girl Friday*, while not so heartless, are cousins of the vulturous crew created by Hecht and MacArthur. Louis and his buxom blond companion, Evangeline, who'd fit in with the petty criminal element down at the race track, are out of Damon Runyon. Walter, Hildy, and Bruce are pure Howard Hawks.

Adolphe Menjou's Walter Burns (played by Lee Tracy on the stage) is insensitive, unscrupulous, and an all-out woman hater. Cary Grant's Walter Burns is a smart aleck who is out for a good time, a good story, and Hildy at all costs. But he is not cruel or as arrogant. A suitable Hawksian hero, he lives at a pace far more hectic (he shaves in his office) than Menjou. He's also more physical in his movements. (Grant is so frantic with his jabber and actions that it's surprising he's not improvising.) He is fabulous in *His Girl Friday*, and I imagine one reason is that he enjoyed the novelty of the part. Very often Grant played an excitable man who is completely befuddled by weird characters and situations that suddenly disrupt his solid world. In *His Girl Friday* he had the rare opportunity to be the aggressor, the agitator who systematically keeps everyone else off balance. Also different is that he's playing one of the few screen heroes who loves a woman *because he truly knows everything about her*—Hildy's not a *mystery* woman—and wins her because he understands her. Bruce, who speaks of Hildy's "unexpectedness" mistakenly appeals to her heart and loses her—Walter, who knows her, appeals to her work vanity ("This isn't just a newspaper story—it's a career") and she's his.

Rosalind Russell's Hildy is certainly someone worth fighting over, which is more than can be said about Pat O'Brien's incarnation ("I'm a rotter and that's all I ever want to be"). She is a match for Walter and can even tell him off and get away with it; she ends up staying with Walter because *she* wants to. The male Hildy is so weak-willed that he eludes Walter by sneaking out a window; he ends up staying with Walter because Walter tricks him. Russell's Hildy comes across as a great reporter: a topnotch interviewer, someone willing to put herself on the line for a story, a writer whose talent is envied by the male reporters. Hawks shows Hildy at work, but Milestone figured that a male reporter's talent would be taken for granted and didn't bother. Russell even comes across as being more physically fit than O'Brien. Many movie critics have little appreciation for this film star who chose vehicles to be directed by technicians rather than by stylists who geared their films for the theater crowd. But in *His Girl Friday,* Russell is dynamic playing the most fascinating of the era's many wisecracking girl reporters. She's unabashed as this bawdy, cigarette-smoking, aggressive, unladylike female and it's a shame she wasn't offered such parts more often. It seems incredible that Russell was offered Hildy only after the part had been rejected by Irene Dunne, Jean Arthur, Claudette Colbert, and Carole Lombard.

In *The Front Page*, Peggy dissolves into the woodwork. She is inconsequential. But playing Bruce with umbrella in hand and good manners, Ralph Bellamy further established himself as a top comic foil—enduring all that Walter dumped on Hildy in the earlier films without losing his temper or comprehending what's going on. That Walter realizes Bruce looks like actor Ralph Bellamy explains why he feels it's required to treat Bruce so rudely (after all, *Ralph Bellamy*

Hawks often used overlapping dialogue, and in this scene Hildy and other reporters, gab at the same time. Three or four microphones were strategically placed over the crowded set in such scenes, but since all of them registered on the same soundtrack, only one could be on at a time. Therefore the sound mixers had the task of switching the various mikes on and off as different characters spoke. Some takes took thirty-five mike switches.

Hildy is more interested in prisoner Earl Williams (her work) than her jailed fiancé Bruce (her social life). To make such scenes visually striking Hawks dressed Russell in a suit with stripes and placed her next to crossing wires and bars.

is always treated in such a slipshod manner). Bruce may be a better Joe than Walter (as Walter readily admits) but we recognize that he's not Hildy's type. So whereas we'd advise the original Hildy to go off with Peggy (who says she is the "fresh air" getting him out of "the sewer"), we'd advise the female Hildy to stick with Walter, who is her ideal match, and to leave Bruce for Bruce's own good.

Milestone staged most scenes of his film as if they were small battles. Hawks wasn't satisfied. What is most impressive about *His Girl Friday* and is the reason the film maintains its furious pace is that Hawks uses his soundtrack for constant verbal wars—as usual, Hawks uses overlapping dialogue and the frame as an arena for physical combat. We are presented with nonstop power play in which each of the numerous combatants consciously endeavors to gain the upper hand and a piece of territory (the frame) through bullying tactics, lies, insults, and manipulation. For instance, if one person says something funny or unleashes an insult, someone else must neutralize it or top it with a joke or insult of his or her own. Those people who can talk without taking time to breathe, or bothering to listen to anyone else's words, are at a decided advantage. Those like Bruce, Bruce's mother, Earl, Mollie, Pettibone, and Bensinger, who can't get in a word edgewise and react to insults, don't stand a chance. When characters like Bruce or Mollie or Bensinger wander in where stronger characters hold forth, they are quickly dispatched. Only someone as dominating as Walter, Hildy, the mayor, or the reporters as a unit, can walk into an occupied space and take over. Even when Hildy interviews Earl Williams, it's the strong dominating the weak. This scene, surely, is the most important in the film. It establishes Hildy as a skilled professional and shows that she is a champion manipulator: she puts words into Earl's mouth. From this, we can forgive Walter for trying to manipulate Hildy—Walter and Hildy are equally underhanded when after something they want, making them perfect for each other. O'Brien's Hildy *never* interviews Earl!

His Girl Friday, which has been of particular interest to feminist critics, is not so much a traditional battle of the sexes as it is about sexual differentiation. The characters, like audience members, have been taught that men and women are supposed to act in certain ways, and they play out their male-female roles accordingly. But Hawks repeatedly shows us that when people let down their guard they take on some traits of the opposite sex—and stop paying attention to others' genders. The reporters may be tough-talking poker players, but when no one is watching, they suddenly become as gossipy as a women's bridge group. When they sneak a look at Hildy's article on Earl Williams, they're more like traditional snoopy female neighbors than hard-hitting reporters. They may be as insensitive as stone walls when Mollie spills her heart out to them, but once she's out of the room they reveal the guilt and embarrassment she's made them feel. They may pigeonhole Mollie as being a certain type of woman, but they put no such restrictions on Hildy and readily accept her unconventional (for a woman) traits. Walter also believes that women are exactly how society defines and molds them, but when it comes to Hildy, he instinctively throws out such guidelines. Acting like the traditional male, he promised Hildy a house on the day he proposed because he believed *all* women want a home; but once

Pettibone (center) has turned up with the governor's reprieve for Earl Williams, so Hildy and Walter inform the crooked mayor and sheriff (R) that they'll soon be the ones in handcuffs.

married he never bothered to make the purchase because he figured *Hildy* didn't really care about having one. To get Bruce's sympathy he uses feminine wiles and pretends to cry, as he suspects all women do; yet when Hildy weeps he is surprised: "You never cried before." He accepts her for the person she is, and doesn't treat her as he probably would if he sat down and reminded himself that she is a woman. ("*Bruce* treats me like a woman," says Hildy.) When the going gets tough—a time when other male heroes would send their women to a safe place—Walter pleads to Hildy: "This is war—you can't desert me now."

Hildy, too, believes that there is a certain way a woman should act and live. When Walter tells her she's a newspaperman, Hildy replies as if all newspapermen should be *men*: "I want to go somewhere and be a woman." She thinks that she should have a home, a family, and a husband who will give her security. But we see that being a newspaperman is in her blood; how excited she is when working on a major story ("Can't you see this is the biggest thing in my life?" she tells Bruce). She is decidedly feminine, regardless that she proposes to Bruce, doesn't accept Walter's alimony, tackles Cooley while on the dead run, takes Earl's gun away, and inhabits a world where there are no other women. She likes Bruce's compliments, but can take Walter's insults and dish them out as well. If there is one difference between men and women according to Hawks, it is implied in the difference between Hildy and the male reporters: she manages to retain her *humanity* while the men, as a matter of course, forfeit theirs.

Most American critical analysis of Howard Hawks's tremendous career took place in the sixties, thirty years after he was canonized in France. Because *His Girl Friday* was nearly impossible to see until the mid-seventies, it has been less written about than some of his other work. For most who see it for the first time, it is a wonderful surprise.

Last Tango in Paris

Ultimo Tango a Parigi
Le Dernièr Tango à Paris

1973   Italy-France United Artists release of a
P.E.A./Artistes Associés film
Director: Bernardo Bertolucci
Producer: Alberto Grimaldi
Screenplay: Bernardo Bertolucci and Franco Arcalli
Cinematography: Vittorio Storaro
Music: Gato Barbieri
Editor: Franco Arcalli
Running time: 129 minutes

Cast: Marlon Brando (Paul), Maria Schneider (Jeanne), Darling
Légitimus (concierge), Jean-Pierre Léaud (Tom), Maria Michi (Rose's
mother), Massimo Girotti (Marcel), Giovanni Galetti (prostitute),
Catherine Allegret (Catherine), Catherine Sola (TV script girl)

Synopsis: Jeanne is engaged to Tom, a young television documentarian. She goes alone to look at an apartment. A middle-aged,
obviously depressed man is also looking at it. After a few minutes
he picks her up, backs her against the wall, rips off her panties,
and has sex with her. They are very passionate. They never introduce themselves.

Jeanne is annoyed with Tom because he insists on doing a
cinéma verité documentary about her. He films everything she
does. Paul, the man Jeanne met in the apartment, watches a maid
wash the blood off the bathtub and surrounding walls. It was in a
hotel bathroom that his wife Rose had earlier slashed her wrists
and died.

Paul and Jeanne rendezvous in the apartment. They agree not to
reveal their names to each other and never to discuss the outside
world or to talk about their pasts. But she keeps trying to find out
who he is.

Paul meets with Rose's mother. He becomes furious with her for
wanting Rose to have absolution from a priest.

Jeanne takes Tom on a tour of her childhood house and shows
him all her antiques. She will not talk of her first love, cousin Paul.

In the apartment, Jeanne tells Paul about her cousin. He tells
Jeanne about his life as a youth in America. She is proud she got
the information from him. He hints he wasn't telling the truth.
Angry at his egotism, Jeanne masturbates.

Paul visits Marcel, who lives in the flophouse he and Rose ran.
Marcel was Rose's lover. Paul doesn't know what Rose saw in
Marcel.

Jeanne gets angrier with Tom. She comes to the apartment. Paul
sodomizes her, forcing her to renounce the holy family, the Church,
and all that broke her will as a child. It is painful for her. She
obeys.

In her wedding dress, Jeanne returns to the apartment, telling
Paul she couldn't leave him, although engaged to someone she
insists she loves. To find her true love, Paul says, she "must go up
into the ass of death." He orders her to cut the nails off two fingers
and put the fingers "up my ass." She obeys. They are both
delirious with passion.

Paul sits by Rose's coffin. He insults her terribly. He realizes that
he never knew her. He cries. He calls her sweetheart. He wishes he
knew why she killed herself, so he could do the same.

Jeanne is upset to find the apartment deserted. Paul has left her.
Tearfully she asks Tom to look at the apartment. He thinks it
smells. He insists that the two of them live somewhere else, as
adults.

On the boulevard, Paul comes up to Jeanne, who insists their
relationship is over. He won't accept her decision, and he tells her
all about himself. They spend the day getting drunk in a café where
a tango contest is being held. She alternately tells him she loves
him and that their relationship is over. She masturbates him, but
then runs off. "It's finished!" He chases her to her mother's
apartment. She tells him her name and kills him with her father's
gun.

P auline Kael was directly responsible for making *Last
Tango in Paris* ("the film that has made the strongest
impression on me in almost twenty years of review-
ing"), a national *phenomenon* in the United States
(as *Time*'s prerelease cover story called it), the subject of everyone's movie conversations—three months before
it was distributed here. Her famous 4000-word rave in *The
New Yorker* (Oct. 28, 1972), which United Artists reprinted
in its entirety as a two-page ad in *The New York Times*,
began:

> Bernardo Bertolucci's "Last Tango in Paris" was presented for
> the first time on the closing night of the New York Film
> Festival, October 14, 1972; that date should become a land-
> mark in movie history comparable to May 29, 1913—the
> night "Le Sacre du Printemps" was first performed—in music
> history. There was no riot, and no one threw anything at the
> screen, but I think it's fair to say that the audience was in a
> state of shock, because "Last Tango in Paris" has the same kind
> of hypnotic excitement as the "Sacre," the same primitive
> force, and the same thrusting, jabbing eroticism. The movie
> breakthrough has finally come. . . . This must be the most
> powerfully erotic movie ever made, and it may turn out to be
> the most liberating movie ever made, and so it's probably only
> natural that an audience, anticipating a voluptuous feast from
> the man who made "The Conformist" [1971], and confronted
> with this unexpected sexuality and the new realism it requires
> of the actors should go into shock. Bertolucci and Brando have
> altered the face of an art form. Who was prepared for that?

Such a review coming from America's most influential critic
couldn't help but convince an excited American public (and

*Paul and Jeanne spend their last delirious moments together
intruding upon a tango contest—as much of an anachronism as
Paul.*

Bertolucci, Brando, and Schneider discuss the scene in which Paul pursues Jeanne through the crowded Paris streets.

those in the critical establishment who hadn't as yet seen *Last Tango*) that Bertolucci had created a work of art. But Kael's evaluation apparently didn't have much effect on Italy's courts, whose members acted with a different kind of shock to the Italian-French production. In Bertolucci's native country, a Bologna (where the picture opened) court ordered the picture seized and banned, long-windedly charging it with:

> . . . obscene content offensive to public decency, characterized by an exasperating pansexualism for its own end, presented with obsessive self-indulgence, catering to the lowest instincts of the libido, dominated by the idea of stirring unchecked appetites for sexual pleasure, permeated by scurrilous language— with crude, repulsive, naturalistic, and even unnatural representation of carnal union, with continued and complacent scenes, descriptions and exhibitions of masturbation, libidinous acts and lewd nudity—accompanied offscreen by sounds, sighs, and shrieks of climax pleasure.

This ban lasted only about two months, until early February, when it was released in America. But in the midseventies an Italian court banned it permanently, had all prints seized and a negative burned (fortunately, Bertolucci made several negatives), condemned stars Brando and Maria Schneider, revoked Bertolucci's civil rights for five years, and gave him a four-month suspended prison sentence.

In France the picture had no problems with censors in 1972–73 and quickly became a box office sensation. But in England release was held up until the sodomy sequence was deleted. In America attendance, bolstered by Kael's review, a tremendous UA publicity campaign, and the censorship furor in Italy, boomed (despite post-Kael reviews far less laudatory than Kael's), with lines around the block and sold-out five-dollars-a-seat reserve engagements. There were several attempts at the local level to ban the picture on obscenity charges, but UA had success winning court decisions. Also ineffective was a C rating (condemned) given *Last Tango* by the United States Catholic Conference, which argued: "*Tango* is an artistic failure and therefore its much touted sex scenes and blunt language cannot be justified on esthetic grounds. . . . [*Tango*] operates in a moral vacuum and emphasizes the male lead's 'sexual binge' rather than throwing light on the human condition."

The controversy over whether *Last Tango* was erotic art or pornography was worldwide, with everyone from feminists to Alberto Moravia to Norman Mailer writing their two dollars' worth. It was a complicated issue. For instance, while some insisted that because its sexual scenes are simulated, they shouldn't be compared to the explicit sexual encounters found in hardcore pornography; others believed the very fact that the Paul-Jeanne sex is simulated makes it as mechanized/emotionless/antisensual/antisexual as the explicit sex in typical pornography. Both Kael and Moravia contended *Last Tango* blazed new cinematic frontiers because its lovers communicate through sex (sex expresses their drives), rather than having sex merely to excite an audience; others complained that the specific nature of the sex, with the man in control and the woman debased through his insulting words and acts, was consistent with the standard sadomasochistic male fantasy relationship found in the most inciteful pornography—"ignoring," as Molly Haskell pointed out in *From Reverence to Rape*, "both the empirical fact that it is largely women, rather than men, who respond to the film, and the more subtle implication that our rearguard fantasies of rape, sadism, submission, liberation, and anonymous sex are as important a key to our emancipation, our self-understanding, as our more advanced and admirable efforts at self-definition." Some were offended by the strong images and Paul's gutter language; others sensed that Bertolucci was deliberately trying to shock and embarrass overly complacent viewers and praised him for liberating the cinematic form and freeing all directors to break conventions. Many objected to Bertolucci's sexist attitude, which prevented him from using scenes he'd filmed of Brando totally nude, while Maria Schneider is undressed through much of the movie;* yet few will dispute that this is the one film in which Brando *reveals himself*, dark side and all, through scenes he wrote, through improvisation, and by letting us witness his acting technique: "The real thrill of *Last Tango*," wrote Norman Mailer, "[is] the peephole Brando offers us on Brando."

Whereas Brando played Don Corleone in *The Godfather* (1972) with feelings that began and ended in his cotton-filled mouth, he plays Paul with feelings that come from the gut, from the subconscious, from the soul. Alternately ferocious and tender, confident and confused, touching and pathetic, tense and wickedly funny, Brando is continuously dazzling, is never less than amazing. He also looks terrific—for the last time (one reason the film remains popular with women). The scene in which Paul sits by his wife's body, cruelly cursing her, crying himself into a daze, unthinkingly calling her "sweetheart" (the way he really feels for her) as he rises to leave, is Brando at his absolute best. It is a performance *all* actors should study—one might have to go back to his first film, *A Streetcar Named Desire* (1951), to find him so emotionally devastating. A fascinating aspect of Brando's performance is that there are *long* stretches (among the best in the film) where it seems like he is improvising, or searching the ceilings, floors, walls, and even Maria Schneider's bare backside for his next line.

---

* Bertolucci learned his lesson. In *1900* (1977) Robert De Niro and Gerard Depardieu are shown nude.

Maria Schneider temporarily became an international star as the result of playing Brando's sex-charged young lover.

Oddly Brando and Schneider weren't the first choices for *Last Tango*. Bertolucci and Franco Arcalli conceived the original script (vastly different from the shooting script) for Dominique Sanda and Jean-Louis Trintignant, stars of *The Conformist*. Sanda dropped out when she became pregnant. Catherine Deneuve (an interesting choice!) agreed to replace her but she too became pregnant. Bertolucci rethought the female role and selected unknown Schneider, a baby-faced actress he wanted to be "a Lolita, but more perverse." I don't know when Trintignant dropped out of the project, but Bertolucci decided he wanted Brando for the lead role while seeing an exhibition of paintings by English artist Francis Bacon; spotting one picture of "a man in great despair, who had an air of total disillusionment," he thought of Brando. Brando also looked at the painting (seen in the film's credit sequence), discussed Paul with Bertolucci, and accepted the part without reading the script—knowing he'd rewrite much of it himself. Brando has never really talked publicly about why he accepted the role at a point in his career when he was so

selective. Interestingly, Brando's good friend Jack Lemmon, whose 1973 role in *Save the Tiger* bears some resemblance to Paul, offered special insight in Walter Wanger's *You Must Remember This* (Putnam, 1975):

> He did that picture because he saw values in it that were important to him. . . . We talked at length about *Tango*. He took hold of that picture and put one hundred percent into it. He wrote most of it. It was his childhood that he was writing about. No Italian wrote that. . . . Marlon would hardly do a film because it was sensational about sex. *Tango* isn't a pornographic picture. It's about a man leaning on sex because there's nothing left for him at that terrible point in his life, that male menopause. In a way what Marlon was saying was . . . don't get too close. The character . . . was saying, "This is the one way I can exist, not to have any kind of relationship in which I'm going to get murdered emotionally."

Last Tango is not about sex *per se* but, as Lemmon says, about a broken, tortured man—who reacts to his wife's suicide with confusion ("Who the hell were you?" "I don't know why you did it"), sadness, anger, guilt that his inability to show his love might have driven her to her drastic act, and shame that she would reject him so brutally—who wants to separate sex from all else. He repudiates God, his name, his bourgeois life (the landlord becomes a tenant), and the outside world—and desperately slips into a "sexistential" world. Paul can't cope with the present and fears the future (he's forty-five, alone, and has a prostate the size of an Idaho potato). At first he thinks he wants to forget the past, but he only needs to block out his adulthood. He finds solace in his youth, peacefully recalling childhood memories for Jeanne

("You think I told you the truth, baby?"). On one level, his relationship with Jeanne is like a boy's with the naughty girl down the block; they play *childish adult games*, a sophisticated, perverse version of little kids playing house. They pretend to have no names, they make animal noises, they attempt orgasms without touching, he twirls her in the air, he shoves a dead rat in her face, they trade insults about how they'll look when they get old, she has him plug in a record player knowing he will get a shock. In his life as Paul he is also going through a childish period: he has temper tantrums, throws and breaks things, has crying fits, slams doors, bites his mother-in-law's hand, and scares everyone by turning out the lights in his flophouse. At the end Paul digresses further: he yanks down his pants and moons an elderly female tango-contest judge; dying from Jeanne's bullet, he sticks the gum from his mouth on her balcony railing; he dies in a fetal position. In Jeanne he finds the perfect companion for his kid's world. In Jeanne he also finds the child he never could have, and as dirty old father to Jeanne's promiscuous daughter (he makes the rules, punishes her, bathes her, teaches her), he is able to escape into an equally safe fantasy world.

There are several reasons Jeanne is attracted to Paul. He is the father she lost back in 1958. When Paul puts on her father's hat at the end, this realization terrifies her: her father represented a bourgeois, sexist world that was responsible for her sexual repression (which she had hoped Paul was helping her overcome). Jeanne collects old relics (her house is full of antiques, her mother's apartment is full of memories, her job is to collect assorted items from the past)—and of course, Paul is an old relic. Paul embodies the dead world they inhabit: the flophouse; its long-forgotten, dried-up residents; their apartment with its broken furniture and dead rats; the street named for a dead man (Jules Verne); the café that has seen better days; the Valentino-age tango—a surrealistic dance of cadaverous people that signifies Paul's time has come. (The film abounds with imagery—some old movie references—that reflects the past, aging, and death.) For Jeanne, Paul is preferable to Tom. A Godardian documentarian with Truffaut's

exuberance, Tom uses his camera to keep a distance between Jeanne and him; between the real Jeanne and his idealized Jeanne. He wants her in a certain way, to freeze her. She resents his intrusion on her life, that he is raping her mind. It seems that all Paul wants is to debase her and that he too tries to keep her at a distance by denying her her name and her past identity. But in fact he's trying (with her consent) to get this spoiled girl to reject *her* bourgeois shackles (which he demands she renounce in the sodomy scene) so that she will be able to freely explore herself as a sexual animal. In *Women and Their Sexuality in the New Film* (Horizon Press, 1973), Joan Mellen writes that *Last Tango* is "an indictment of the bourgeois family which dominates culture and society, suppresses feeling, and 'civilizes' the savage in us all by repressing bodily needs." Molly Haskell concurs: "There have been no films, except possibly Bertolucci's *Last Tango in Paris*, that have detailed what it is like for a specific woman to overcome the mountainous conditioning against sexual release." Both Tom ("You take advantage of me!") and Paul make Jeanne do what they want, but only Paul (whose methods, granted, are a bit harsh) is trying to liberate her.

Jeanne is most attracted to Paul because he allows her to be a *child without sexual inhibitions*. She is only twenty but fears being twenty-one: "Growing older is a crime." She is attracted to and fascinated by what repels her; therefore she is obsessed with artifacts and with Paul. Much of her fear of Tom is a result of his constant look to the future ("I must start something new," Tom says. "When something's finished, we begin again," counters the *safer* Paul) and his stubborn attitude: "We're adults. . . . We can't joke like children." Jeanne wants to remain a child, to return to her pubescent years as only Paul allows her to do. And one important game she plays with Paul is to see who of the two can remain a child longest. "Are you scared?" he asks her as they are about to embark on their *make-believe* apartment game. "No," she assures him. His rules are tough, but she manages to keep up with him; in fact, she wins. When his wife is buried and he can resume a normal life, Paul breaks off the apartment-escape relationship, tells Jeanne all about himself (which she realizes she doesn't want to know), insists, like Tom, they have an adult relationship (although he's still regressing), and declares his love for her. As the tango judge says when the drunk couple interrupts her dance: "It's a contest, where does love come in?" In the outside, real world, Jeanne sees Paul as a middle-aged, pot-bellied flophouse owner. A flop. It scares her to think they'll live together "happily ever after." She doesn't want *him* to be her lover. So in a scene that echoes the finale in *Breathless* (1959), where Jean Seberg shows little concern that she caused the death of boyfriend Jean-Paul Belmondo, Jeanne shoots the poor guy.

Like most Bertolucci films, *Last Tango* is about people who should be in psychoanalysis (as the director was). *Last Tango* is a psychodrama in which characters are pulled back into their primal recesses. A great filmmaker, Bertolucci has a lush visual style. His sets of reds, oranges, and flesh colors are doused in golden light, giving a "uterine" (as the set designer described it) look to the film. His swirling camera, and the moody jazz (sax) music that climaxes at unexpected moments creates a delirious effect, like lovers in the heat of passion. This is the ideal atmosphere for Brando and Schneider to break sexual taboos. Which is exactly what they do.

Jeanne becomes increasingly cold to fiancé Tom's touch. He never notices.

The Man Who Fell to Earth

1976 Great Britain British Lion (released by Cinema 5 in the U.S.)
Director: Nicolas Roeg
Producers: Michael Deeley and Barry Spikings
Screenplay: Paul Mayersburg
From the novel by Walter Tevis
Cinematography: Anthony Richmond
Music: John Phillips
Editor: Graeme Clifford
Running Time: 140 minutes (Cinema 5 cut the picture when it was
first distributed in America. Prints ran at 117, 120, or 125 minutes,
according to different sources. In 1980 a new regime at Cinema 5
restored the picture to its original length.)

Cast: David Bowie (Thomas Jerome Newton), Rip Torn (Nathan
Bryce), Candy Clark (Mary-Lou), Buck Henry (Oliver Farnsworth),
Bernie Casey (Peters), Jackson D. Kane (Professor Canutti), Rick
Riccardo (Trevor), Tony Mascia (Arthur), Captain James Lovell
(himself)

Synopsis: A space traveler plummets to earth, landing in a lake in
New Mexico. He drinks water and thinks of his barren planet,
where his wife and two children are dying of thirst.

Using the name Thomas Jerome Newton, he goes to New York
to speak to lawyer Oliver Farnsworth. Farnsworth is amazed that
Newton has nine basic patents. He will be able to earn $300 million
in three years. "I need more," says Newton, not explaining why.
He enlists Farnsworth's aid to build a great corporation, World
Enterprises. Even by playing fairly, World Enterprises should soon
make some other corporations obsolete.

Nathan Bryce, a divorced Chicago chemistry professor, spends
his time making love to his female students. He becomes fascinated with World Color's self-developing film, which can be bought
very inexpensively (free cameras are thrown in). He wonders who
the reclusive Newton is and starts making inquiries.

Using the alias Mr. Sussex, Newton travels to New Mexico. At
his hotel he meets Mary-Lou, a maid who helps him when he
becomes sick from a fast elevator ride. She becomes his constant
companion and lover. She brings him a television set, and influences him to drink gin. Eventually, he watches many television sets
at once and drinks incessantly. Still missing his family, he initiates
a space program with all the money he has made.

Farnsworth hires Bryce to come to New Mexico and work on the
secret project. Bryce lives in a cabin on the other side of the lake
from Newton and Mary-Lou. He secretly takes X rays of Newton
and discovers that Newton's form is totally alien. Newton, who can
see X rays, readily admits he is an alien. He says he has no intention
of causing harm to earthlings.

The project is taking too long. All Newton does is drink and
watch television. He had watched American TV for years on his
planet but never guessed that it revealed nothing about the human
condition. As he becomes more human, he feels life is futile.

His relationship with Mary-Lou deteriorates when she demands
more attention. He strips off his earthling guise, and she is terrified
by his alien form. She can't make love to him, although she does
love him. Farnsworth pays Mary-Lou off to get her away from
Newton. She doesn't want the money—she wants Tommy.

Capitalist companies pressure Farnsworth to sell World Enterprises.
He refuses. Farnsworth and his gay lover Trevor are hurled out of
their New York apartment and killed. Newton is taken
prisoner. For years he is held in a deserted suite in a hotel and
subjected to painful tests. World Enterprises goes bankrupt. Bryce
begins to work for Peters, who initiated Newton's kidnapping.
Bryce and Mary-Lou marry.

Newton escapes his prison once no one cares about him anymore. He holds no animosity toward anyone. He records an album
called *The Visitor*, which he hopes his wife, who may already have
died from thirst, will hear. Knowing he can never go back home, he
can never save his dying family, that he has failed, Newton is full of
self-pity. He will spend the rest of his life on earth, as a drunkard.

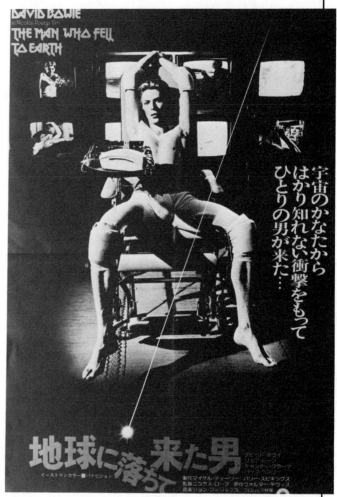

*This Japanese poster of the film that has become an international
cult favorite shows Newton strapped to a chair while
undergoing tortuous experiments from doctors.*

There is some validity to the seemingly wild notion
that *The Wizard of Oz* (1939), with its journey into
a mysterious world, fantasy elements, and homesick-
ness theme, has influenced the majority of pictures
made since. In fact, Steven Spielberg's *E.T. The Extra-
Terrestrial* (1982) is *The Wizard of Oz* in reverse: instead of
having one of us (Dorothy) travel to an alien environment
where three friendly inhabitants (the Scarecrow, the Tin
Woodman, the Cowardly Lion) facilitate a desired return
home, a peaceful alien (E.T.) visits our world and three of us
(the three children) help it find a way back home. Likewise,
in the flawed yet fascinating *The Man Who Fell to Earth*,
peaceful alien Thomas Jerome Newton becomes stranded on
our planet and three earthlings (Farnsworth, Mary-Lou, and
Bryce) try to help him accomplish his plan, which, although
they don't fully realize it, is to build a spaceship capable of
traveling to his planet. But *The Wizard of Oz* (the *film,* not
L. Frank Baum's somewhat gloomy book) and *E.T.* are *modern*

fairy tales in the sense that they provide children with the happy, consoling endings they have become accustomed to. Like Terry Gilliam's *Oz*-influenced *Time Bandits* (1981), *The Man Who Fell to Earth* is an old-fashioned fairy tale for those adults who read Jonathan Swift and believe that our world, and those who run it, can be cold, cruel, and unfair. And it's a fairy tale for those kids who still read those surprisingly morbid Grimm stories about characters who fall from grace (Newton's "fall" to earth signifies his descent into purgatory) and are punished (how Newton suffers). Unlike in the Grimm stories, he does not repent and receive salvation— Newton chooses to wallow in self-pity rather than come to terms with his own fallibility and with the other reasons his mission fails, so he dooms himself to eternal damnation. Tragically, Newton can never go home: his three friends aren't as comforting or resourceful as Dorothy's and E.T.'s, and his own homeward drive is far too weak for him to accomplish the near impossible.

Director Nicolas Roeg never spells out what Newton's mission on earth is. Always one who attempts to turn his viewers into puzzle solvers (which explains his fragmentary editing style), Roeg intentionally did away with Walter Tevis's explanation. In Tevis's novel Newton was sent from distant Anthea to build a ship that will ferry Antheans from their dying planet back to earth. Once on earth, the Antheans intend to become dominant in business (setting up many World Enterprises divisions), politics, and the military, on an international scale. Just as viewers of Raoul Walsh's bizarre satire *The Horn Blows at Midnight* (1945) somehow root for angel Jack Benny to destroy our evil earth, readers of Tevis's book desire an Anthean takeover because only then can we avoid a nuclear war: it's an interesting concept. In the film, there is no mention of a specific planet called Anthea, nor must we consider a choice between colonization and nuclear destruction. We can't even understand the purpose of Newton's space vehicle: does he want to travel back to his planet with water, transport water via an elaborate shuttle system, or return to get his family? Adding to the confusion

rather than clearing it up, Roeg has told interviewers that there is a possibility that the Newton of the film is no spaceman at all, but a reclusive Howard Hughes type who hallucinates what it would be like if he came from a waterless planet to earth. (The building of the spaceship is certainly the next step for the man who built *The Spruce Goose*, the world's largest plane. That project also failed.) True, many shots in the film, including those of Newton's thirsty family on his barren planet and that of the American pioneers who spot Newton's limo through what seems to be a time warp, could be visions of an hallucinating genius. But we can't so easily dismiss the scene in which Newton reverts to his alien form to jolt Mary-Lou into seeking a more suitable lover. (Just as civilized white teen-ager Jenny Agutter rejects aborigine David Gumpilil, who is alien to her, in Roeg's 1971 masterpiece *Walkabout*, Mary-Lou finds she can't make love to Newton when he is in his alien form.) This sequence proves to my satisfaction that Newton is not from our planet. Unfortunately, Roeg neglects its other purpose: in the book, when Newton looked at his Anthean form in the mirror, "his own body stared back at him but he could not recognize it as his own." This moment is pivotal because it is when Newton should realize, and be terrified as a result, that in his mind he has indeed become an imitation human being. (He is like those Indian tribesmen of the New World who forgot their own languages after explorers took them for lengthy visits to Europe.)

As in other Roeg films—*Walkabout, Performance* (1970), *Don't Look Now* (1973), *Bad Timing* (1980), *eureka!* (1983)— we have a character who finds himself in a completely strange environment/situation. (By casting singers like Mick Jagger, Art Garfunkel, and David Bowie, Roeg figured their discomfort from moving from the stage to the screen would transfer to their characters.) The cultural collision causes the character to grope for parts of himself that have been latent, so that he might survive. As a result, he is able to formulate a more accurate self-definition. Invariably, the character learns truths about himself that cause disillusionment and disappointment. For instance, the civilized girl in *Walkabout* becomes scared when her primitive sexual instincts are revealed; and the macho gangster Chas (James Fox) in *Performance* is unhappy to learn that he has homosexual tendencies. Like Swift's Gulliver in the land of the tiny Lilliputians, Newton, though kindly, thinks the intellectually inferior earthlings to be no more than a race of chimpanzees, or (as he states in the book) insects. He is sure that after studying them for fifteen years on television he knows all about them. But, he discovers, "the strange thing about television is that it doesn't tell you anything." As time passes he finds himself being vacuumed into this human race instead of remaining above it, and becoming one of the "frightened, self-pitying hedonists." As Tevis notes, Newton realizes that television perpetuates the "fantastic lie that America [is] a nation of God-fearing small towns, efficient cities, healthy farmers, kindly doctors, bemused housewives, philanthropic millionaires," and he discovers "an aspect of strong and comfortable and hedonistic and unthinking humanity that his fifteen years of television watching had left him unaware of." Even living in near seclusion, Newton becomes infected by the earthlings he feels superior to. Of course, one who suffers from an open wound called loneliness is not immune.

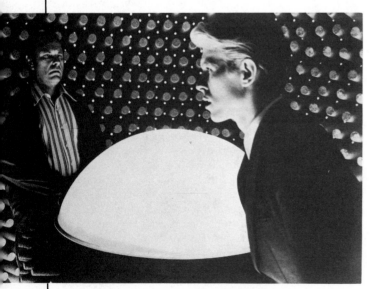

Newton assures Nathan that his secret plans will not harm anyone.

(L) Mary-Lou is always available for sex, but Newton is more intrigued by images of humans than by flesh: He constantly gazes into mirrors at his own human form and at television monitors. (Above) Destroyed by his experiences on earth, Newton becomes an alcoholic.

Farnsworth, who is a homosexual in the *film*, Bryce, who is divorced (he is a widower in the book), and Mary-Lou, who is an insignificant, unattached New Mexican hotel maid, are naturally attracted to Newton, another outsider. He gives meaning to their dreary lives. Lawyer Farnsworth ("I got a brand new life") can enjoy taking on the big boys: Polaroid, Du Pont, IBM. Teacher Bryce, who had frittered his life away making it with coeds, can now satisfy his scientific curiosity by doing applied research in exciting, unexplored areas. A one-time nurse and the type who brings home birds with broken wings, Mary-Lou, who's thrilled "to be part of a story," has found the perfect lover to mother: someone who faints, has a bloody nose, and vomits within the first minute of their acquaintance. Unfortunately, none of Newton's three friends can provide him with stimulation. While waiting for his ship to be constructed, he begins to see life as they once did, as being without meaning, without purpose. (Unlike Mary-Lou, he doesn't believe in God.) Human pressures he doesn't comprehend build up within him, and as Tevis writes, "he, the Anthean, a superior being from a superior race, was losing control, becoming a degenerate, a drunkard, a lost and foolish creature, a renegade, and, possibly, a traitor to his own." A man in exile, a man without an island, he loses himself in sex with Mary-Lou (their relationship is platonic in the novel), booze, and television (he goes from one set to six to sixteen). His addiction to gin and television ("Stay out of my mind!" he screams at his blaring sets) is obviously symptomatic of his unhappiness and self-destructive nature. In his life with Mary-Lou, which starts out as romantic as Gary Cooper's with Audrey Hepburn in *Love in the Afternoon* (1957), which they watch on TV, he becomes like the typical overburdened business executive. I believe that his domestication, as much as anything, leads to his drinking and guilty withdrawal—after all, he has a real wife and family elsewhere. In the Roeg-photographed *Petulia* (1968), Shirley Knight bakes cookies in an attempt to win back ex-husband George C. Scott and Scott hurls them through the air, signifying he doesn't want to return to a dull, stifling marriage. Similarly, when Mary-Lou makes cookies for Newton, he knocks them in the air, signifying he can't stand being the stereotypical American husband caught in a deteriorating marriage.

Another reason Newton is depressed is because he was unprepared for the ruthlessness he finds on earth. A nice guy, with no weapons, who doesn't dislike anyone—just like Billy Budd, whom he sees hanged on his TV screen—he cannot combat those powerful forces (capitalist leaders, CIA, FBI) who fear he will put the world's greatest monopolies out of business. A sense of melancholy pervades: Mary-Lou (well played by quirky Candy Clark) laments the disappearance of America's trains; we hear nostalgic songs like "Try to Remember" and "Blue Bayou" on the soundtrack; we see those enterprising American pioneers embarking on building America. The impression we get is that Newton had come to earth too late, when the desensitized people of the nuclear age have forgotten their ancestors' pioneering spirit and have settled for creature comforts like television, and have become, as a result of living in a capitalistic world, "Liars! Chauvinists! And Fools!" It is a world that the Newton of the novel fears bringing Antheans to because he worries they will be corrupted, as he has been; fittingly the American landscape Roeg shows us is at once beautiful and uninviting.

Peter O'Toole was set to be Newton at one time, but rock music idol David Bowie makes a better choice. Bowie, who would be the male lead in Tony Scott's *The Hunger* (1983), is fine playing pained, passive characters. As Newton he gives an appropriately subdued, sympathetic performance. With his orange hair, great height, and anemic look, Bowie does indeed seem like an alien. His birdlike features actually contribute to our empathy for Newton, who, unlike the muscular Atlas, must bear the weight of his world on shoulders that are brittle. We know what Newton must be feeling when on the soundtrack Eddy Arnold sings "Make the World Go Away (and Take It Off My Shoulders)": Newton feels enormous guilt that he can't carry out his mission, but his burden is too great; he doesn't have a chance because on earth it is the strong, unfortunately, who survive.

Marnie

1964 Universal
Director: Alfred Hitchcock
Producer: Albert Whitlock
Screenplay: Jay Presson Allen
From the novel by Winston Graham
Cinematography: Robert Burks
Music: Bernard Herrmann
Editor: George Tomasini
Running time: 120 minutes

Cast: Tippi Hedren (Marnie Edgar), Sean Connery (Mark Rutland), Diane Baker (Lil Mainwaring), Martin Gabel (Sidney Strutt), Louise Latham (Bernice Edgar), Bob Sweeney (Cousin Bob), Alan Napier (Mr. Rutland), S. John Launer (Sam Ward), Mariette Hartley (Susan Clabon), Bruce Dern (sailor)

Synopsis: Sidney Strutt discovers that his secretary Marion Holland has cleaned out his safe and disappeared. The case is quite similar to four other robberies. Marnie Edgar is a thief. She assumes aliases, takes jobs in rich firms, and walks off with the contents of their safes. She suffers tremendous guilt, has nightmares, and becomes frightened during thunderstorms and when she sees anything bloodred, but these feelings have less to do with her being a criminal than with an experience in her childhood that was so traumatic she blocked it out completely.

After robberies, Marnie visits her horse Florio. She detests all men, but loves Florio because he asks for nothing from her but friendship. Some of the money she steals pays for Florio's care; much of the rest she gives to her mother, Bernice, who lives in Baltimore. Bernice, a rigid, Bible-quoting, man-hating woman who is lame, believes Marnie is traveling secretary to a gentleman. Marnie loves her mother and can't understand why her mother never returns her affection.

Marnie applies for a job with a new firm. Mark Rutland, the head, has heard his client Sidney Strutt discuss the woman who robbed him. Without telling Marnie he is on to her, he gives her the job. When Marnie becomes hysterical during a thunderstorm, it becomes obvious to Mark that she has grave psychological problems. He is greatly taken with her, much preferring her to Lil, the available sister of his dead wife.

Marnie robs the firm's safe. Mark tracks her down and insists they marry or he'll turn her over to the police. After the wedding, it's clear to him that she will hate him if he forces himself on her. He agrees to leave her alone, but he goes back on his promise. She tries to drown herself. He rescues her.

Marnie and Mark return to his estate. She insists on separate rooms. When Sidney Strutt comes to a party at Mark's, the terrified Marnie assures Strutt that he's never seen her before. Mark backs Marnie up. Lil is suspicious. She learns that Marnie, who said she was an orphan, has a mother in Baltimore.

Knowing Strutt will soon figure out the truth, Mark decides to repay him and the others she stole from. But Marnie wants to sneak away.

Marnie rides Florio in a fox hunt. Florio fails to clear a wall, and lies in agony. Marnie is forced to shoot him. Marnie tries to rob Mark's personal safe. He stops her, then tells her she can have the money. She cannot bring herself to take it. He takes her gun from her. They drive to Baltimore. Bernice gets angry with Mark for insisting she tell the truth about what happened in Marnie's past. In a little girl's voice, Marnie tells him to leave her mother alone. This jars her memory to that fateful night in her childhood. Her mother was a prostitute. There was a thunderstorm. A sailor tried to comfort Marnie. Or molest her. Bernice pulled him away and hit him with a poker. He fell on her, injuring her leg. Fearing for her mother, Marnie killed him with the poker.

Marnie knows the truth: about her mother, about that night, about herself and what led her to be who she is. She goes off with Mark, agreeing to stay with him rather than go to jail.

While the lightning storm rages outside, Marnie is frightened when Mark approaches her inside his office. Because females the world over coveted Sean Connery for his James Bond image, it was very apparent how strong Marnie's fear/hatred/revulsion of men was when she reacted this way toward Mark.

Alfred Hitchcock often dialed M for murder—and for mystery. His catalog of female characters included Melanie (Tippi Hedren) in *The Birds* (1963), Marion (Janet Leigh) in *Psycho* (1960), Madeleine (Kim Novak) and Midge (Barbara Bel Geddes) in *Vertigo* (1958), Margot (Grace Kelly) in *Dial M for Murder* (1954), and even the one nonblonde of this group, Guy Haines's ill-fated wife Miriam (Laura Elliot in a supporting role) in *Strangers on a Train* (1951) in the dozen years before he adapted Winston Graham's *Marnie*. How could he not be intrigued by a beautiful heroine whose real name is Margaret, is nicknamed Marnie, and uses the aliases Mollie, Mary, and Marion?

Grace Kelly was set to make her movie comeback as Marnie, six years after becoming princess of Monaco. But a delay in the filming schedule as well as protests from her subjects forced her withdrawal. When this great star was replaced by Hitchcock discovery Tippi Hedren, the ex-model who'd impressed few critics with her debut in *The Birds* (critical response to the film and her performance in it has justifiably improved over the years), most everyone was disappointed in the picture even before it went before the cameras. It was clear that it had to be extraordinary Hitchcock for it to win approval, and that it was not. Upon release, it was blasted by American critics like no Hitchcock film since *Stage Fright* (1950). The nicest remarks came from Andrew Sarris— "*Marnie* is a failure by any standards except the most esoteric"— and Edith Oliver of *The New Yorker*—"*Marnie* is an idiotic and trashy movie with two terrible performances in the leading roles, and I had quite a good time watching it."

But Marnie proved popular with critics in France and

Hitchcock splits the screen to create a visual pun. On the left the deaf cleaning lady cleans up the boss's office, while on the right, Marnie cleans out the boss's safe. Mark is aware of Marnie's thievery, which, in fact, is what attracts him to her. Hitchcock told François Truffaut: "A man wants to go to bed with a thief because she is a thief. . . . It's not as effective as Vertigo, where James Stewart's feelings are clearly a fetishist love. To put it bluntly, we'd have had to have Sean Connery catching the girl robbing the safe and show that he felt like jumping at her and raping her on the spot."

England (Robin Wood, its most persuasive champion, called it "one of Hitchcock's richest and most fully achieved and mature masterpieces"), and several years later, when films were at last being examined in terms of sexual roles and relationships, it became popular in America as well. *Marnie* is the one Hitchcock film where his blonde with an icy veneer remains cold and sexually remote in the bedroom; it is also, as Molly Haskell believes, the film where he finally sides with his blonde, and "one of his most disturbing and, from a woman's point of view, most important films." Now joining feminist and European critics in their defense of *Marnie* are viewers who see it for the first time and are pleasantly surprised to find a finely, if stiffly, acted, intriguing film—lacking excitement perhaps, but not the simplistic "disaster" they'd always read about. Other new fans appreciate the rare opportunity in movies to be privy to the intimate sexual problems of a married couple.

Hitchcock considered *Marnie* an unusual mystery because the search is not for a criminal but for a criminal's motivations. It's possible that even he didn't realize that this *search for motivation* is *not* the key to the film, and those viewers led to believe it is will find the final scene infuriating. First and foremost, *Marnie* is about a woman with many aliases, who is involved in a desperate *search for identity*, who can only stop living a life of lies if she learns the truth about her past. Finding out *exactly* what happened on that fateful, fatal night in Marnie's childhood is not necessary: it makes no difference if little Marnie killed a client of her prostitute mother, as in the film, or if her prostitute mother went crazy and killed her illegitimate baby, as in the novel. What matters is that Marnie learns of an event, any event, that happened in *her* life just before she moved permanently into a world of make believe. (If made twenty years later, *Marnie* might be about a multiple personality like Sybil.) This bit of

history is the shaky foundation on which she can build a *real* life. Actually, the particular events that transpired on that horrible night only explain the content of Marnie's nightmares and the reason she reacts hysterically to thunderstorms and the color red; and *her mother's motivations* for denying Marnie motherly love and indoctrinating her to detest all men (thereby ruining her child's life). The revelations also serve to let viewers draw parallels between Bernice and Marnie: both have led double lives; both have prostituted themselves in that mother made love to men and took their money and Marnie worked for men and took their money. Neither the revelations in the book (where the mother dies) nor those in the film sufficiently explain why Marnie is a thief and is frigid (even supposing the sailor tried to molest Marnie); but that's fine, because we can deduce the reasons early in the film.

When the film opens, Marnie is running off with the contents of Sidney Strutt's company safe. It is significant that she is in disguise: that she spends most of her life not looking like herself is a sign of her self-hatred; it also indicates that she wishes to step out of herself so that if she is caught it is not Marnie but one of her aliases who is being thrown in jail. Strutt describes her to police as if she were a horse he'd purchased, referring to her "good teeth" and legs: "She pulled her skirt down over her knees as if they were a national treasure." Marnie is not far off when she thinks men only think of women as animals. Mark describes his kindly father: "If you smell anything like a horse you're in"; zoologist Mark agrees with Marnie's assertion that he views her "like another animal you caught." The men in Marnie's nightmarish world are filthy pigs (as the psychology books she's read imply)—it is only when Mark changes *after* he has had his way with her that she can *tolerate* him (she never says "I love you").

Marnie wonders why her mother shows her no affection.

Marnie's fascination for what's behind a man's safe door is equivalent to Strutt's (and initially Mark Rutland's) fascination for what's under her skirt. For man-hater Marnie, the penetration of his safe and the taking of his prized money is the symbolic rape of a man who'd like to rape her, who has insulted her constantly with roving eyes. She achieves an onanistic sexual release through her safecracking, but the act alone isn't satisfying because of its perverse nature and the guilt she suffers. The love she lavishes on her horse Florio, whom she rides immediately after her crimes, is, as Robin Wood suggests, "a substitute for sexual fulfillment." But even capping her symbolic rape with a fast ride on Florio is not enough. She needs a *healthy* sexual release—with a good man, *if* he exists.

The street where Marnie lived as a child in Baltimore is dreary and claustrophobic, impressing us with the notion that even as a child Marnie had the need to *escape* from her existence. That she came from poor stock tells us that she steals only from rich men because she has resentment for those monied men (women are these men's secretaries and cleaning ladies) who look down at her class. The obviously phony backdrop of the sea at the end of the street coupled with the obvious rearview projection in the riding sequences conveys that we've entered an unreal, nightmare world. (Some critics insist we are just seeing shoddy production values.) This world doesn't lie between life and death as in *Vertigo* (also moodily scored by Bernard Herrmann and photographed by Robert Burks), but lies between truth and what is perceived by Marnie's mixed-up mind.

Marnie visits her mother. Even here Marnie lies. She tells her mother that she's earned the money she's giving her by being secretary to the fictitious Mr. Pemberton. The money she gives her mother is her way of trying (unsuccessfully) to win her mother's love. That her mother takes her money but gives Marnie no affection upsets Marnie terribly because her mother insists that she accepts no money for babysitting neighbor child Jessie, to whom she openly gives her love. (In the novel, oddly enough, Bernice is very loving to Marnie.)

Marnie tries to please her mother in every way and repeatedly assures her that she will never have anything to do with men: "Decent women don't have a need for any men." So already we understand Marnie's thievery and frigidity. In these scenes with Marnie's mother, we are reminded of how Norman Bates was swallowed up by his mother in *Psycho*. Bernice, with her rigidity and her cane is filmed as if she were a witch (Bernice and Marnie seem to be the basis for the sick mother-daughter relationship in Brian De Palma's 1976 chiller *Carrie*). Back-lit while standing in Marnie's door so that we can't make out her face, she is as menacing as Norman's "mother" in *Psycho* during the shower-attack scene when we can't make out her face. Robin Wood cites a number of other moments that are reminiscent of *Psycho*; for example: "At the end of the film, when Marnie and Mark leave, lighting and make-up give Mrs. Edgar's face a corpse-like appearance—she seems almost an embalmed body, a living death." Hitchcock feared the police, but he seemed even more worried about how strange, domineering mothers affect their offspring.

Marnie meets Mark Rutland. There is a thunderstorm when she visits his office. She backs fearfully against the wall. A high camera angle shows that it is the storm (with all its implications) that she fears. But Hitchcock moves to a close shot of Mark comforting her, and we realize that she is also feeling threatened by him. To us Mark seems like an honorable man, but Marnie doesn't trust him. And *she* proves to be right. He is looking for a way to control her, to possess her. When he catches her after she robbed the safe (the film's one true suspense scene has her cleaning out a safe as a cleaning lady cleans up the office), he forces her into marriage. We trust Mark because Sean "James Bond" Connery is playing

Aboard ship on their honeymoon, Mark slides off Marnie's nightgown. This was a film about sex made before the cinema was permissive enough to permit nudity, so Hitchcock excited viewers with a subtle, creative use of the frame.

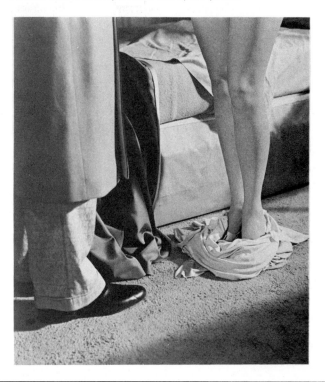

him, but we must question *his motives* for desiring Marnie. If the film were told from his point of view, it would be easy to see that Mark chooses Marnie over the available Lil precisely because he wants to have sex with a virginal, frigid woman: it is a male fantasy to sexually conquer a woman who supposedly hates *all* men. Also, and more importantly, he is sexually aroused by her thievery. Mark is one weird guy who just happens to own a book called *Sexual Aberrations of the Female Criminal.*

Marnie and Mark are married. We think back to Val Lewton's *Cat People* (1942) where bride Simone Simon is afraid to make love to groom Kent Smith and they stay in separate rooms. Mark thinks he can be as patient with Marnie as Kent was with Simone, but he breaks his promise to his bride and takes her sexually. It's an interesting scene. Sean Connery, who as James Bond is capable of seducing lesbian Pussy Galore, tenderly kisses Marnie, and for a while we're certain she is responding to his caresses. But the camera finds Marnie's eyes and we can see that she is sickened by what he's doing to her: she has not been seduced, so in effect he is raping her. Unlike some movie heroines, Marnie does not fall for the man who rapes her: she'd like to see him dead or steal from his safe to pay him back in kind. To his credit, Mark is equally repulsed by his act. It will not happen again. Now that he has satisfied his lust/curiosity by making love to this "unavailable" woman—and found the experience not gratifying—he changes his attitude toward Marnie. Again, to his credit, he doesn't cast her away or divorce her: he now decides to help her find her identity. He won't let her run away from herself and her frightening past. He won't let her commit suicide. When Marnie jumps into the ship's swimming pool from where she can be rescued, rather than jumping overboard, it becomes clear that she doesn't want to die. That she has read psychology books about women such as herself and is willing to take part in a word association game with amateur Freud, Mark, are further indications that she wants to solve her problems. When she comes out and says "Somebody help me!" we are not surprised. When it becomes apparent that Mark wants to help her now instead of continuing to sexually blackmail her, she subconsciously opens up to him as she has to no other man.

The climactic scene as far as the Marnie-Mark relationship is concerned is when Marnie shoots Florio, who has been crippled in a fall. Interestingly, in the novel, she doesn't shoot the horse (someone else does) because she is too busy rescuing Mark, who has also taken a hard fall and lies facedown in the mud. Yet in both cases Marnie's action shows us that she has switched her allegiance to Mark from Florio. She no longer has psychological need for this horse who, until Mark's appearance, has been the only living creature with whom she could reveal her real self; the one friend who liked her for herself and expected nothing in return (money/sex), her one possession which was not acquired through thievery, and her substitute child ("There . . . there now") for the baby she'd been afraid to have, for obvious reasons. She has found *a human being* who will not turn away from her no matter what she does—or refuses to do. She finds she cannot rob *his* safe. He grabs the gun (a phallic symbol) from her, implying she is giving him permission (hesitantly) to again pursue her sexually; a sign of trust.

Mark takes Marnie back to Baltimore and forces her mother

As Hitchcock's character placement implies, the sides are drawn, and Mark stands firmly by Marnie. In the party scene Sidney Strutt, his wife, and Lil (R) look accusingly at Marnie.

to reveal the incident (mother's deep, dark secret) that torments Marnie's subconscious. Once Marnie hears the story, she at last has an intimation of who she is. She understands the factors that made her into the person she detested. She is now able to analyze herself. For Mark, who fell in love with an illusion (as do many Hitchcock heroes), there is the challenge of staying in love with a *real* woman. For Marnie, there will be a long period of picking up the pieces. For now she's willing to compromise and give Mark the benefit of the doubt as he'll do with the *new* her. There is no final kiss—Hitchcock did away with the final love scene included in the treatment—just a simple "I don't want to go to jail. I'd rather stay with you." He has no complaints.

What physical pleasure Marnie receives is derived from riding Florio.

Massacre at Central High

1976 Brian Distributing release of an Evan Company production; later distributed by New Line Cinema
Director: Renee Daalder
Producer(s): Harold Sobel (and Bill Lange, uncredited)
Screenplay: Renee Daalder
Cinematography: Burt Van Munster
Music: Tommy Leonetti
Song: ''You're at the Crossroads of Your Life'' by Tommy Leonetti
Editor: Harry Keramidas
Running time: 87 minutes

Cast: Derrel Maury (David), Andrew Stevens (Mark), Robert Carradine (Spoony), Kimberly Beck (Teresa), Roy Underwood (Bruce), Steve Bond (Craig), Damon Douglas (Paul), Rainbeaux Smith (Mary), Lani O'Grady (Jane), Steve Sikes (Rodney), Dennis Court (Arthur), Jeffrey Winner (Oscar), Thomas Logan (Harvey)

Synopsis: It is David's first day at Central High. He sees three bullies named Bruce, Craig, and Paul order Spoony to wash off a swastika he painted on his locker. No forms of protest are permitted here. David meets his old friend Mark, who he once helped out of a bad jam at their previous school. Mark tells David that the school can be like a country club for him if he becomes friends with Bruce, Craig, and Paul. But the three bullies tell Mark that David seems like a troublemaker.

At Mark's insistence David tries to ignore the bullying tactics employed by Mark's friends. They mock fat Oscar and hit him with towels, they dump books on Arthur, the student librarian, and they wreck poor Rodney's jalopy. David asks Arthur if he wants help to fight the bullies. ''We lose our own battles,'' he says. David offers to fix Rodney's car. Mark worries about his friend but tells the others that he will straighten him out.

David's only new friend is Teresa, Mark's girlfriend. The bullies decide to rape Spoony's friends Mary and Jane. When Teresa catches them, they throw her into the hall. David sees this and charges into the classroom. He beats up the three before the rapes are accomplished. The bullies tell Mark he has only one more chance to talk to David.

Mark spots David and Teresa, with whom he has just quarreled, skinny-dipping in the ocean. Jealous, he tells his three friends that he tried to talk to David but he wouldn't listen. While David is trying to repair Rodney's car, the bullies drop the car on him and his leg is crushed. He can no longer jog—the one outlet for his anger. Teresa tells Mark that David had refused to make love to her that night on the beach—out of loyalty to Mark. Mark feels guilty.

David kills Bruce by breaking a cable on his hang-glider. He kills Craig by having him dive into an empty swimming pool. He kills Paul by rolling his van down a cliff. Mark discovers David is responsible for the murders. David challenges him to stop him. Mark loves David too much to fight him. David loves Teresa and agrees to let Mark live for her sake.

For a time, everyone in school is on friendly terms. But soon they all try to enlist the help of their hero David so they can obtain power. Fights and arguments break out all over school. David is disgusted and builds pipe bombs to eliminate the students. Arthur, Rodney, Oscar, Spoony, Mary, and Jane are killed.

David challenges Mark to shoot him to put an end to his murder spree. But Mark can't do it. David locks Mark and Teresa in his workshop and goes to the school, where a student-alumni dance is taking place. He has hidden a pipe bomb in the school. Mark and Teresa break free and come to the dance. David tries to get them to leave the gym before the blast. They refuse and dance. Realizing that they will not leave, that they are willing to sacrifice their lives, David rushes into the basement and retrieves the bomb. He takes it outside where it explodes, killing him. Mark and Teresa agree to tell the police that Spoony had left the bomb and David had given his life to save everyone.

The idea to make *Massacre at Central High*, the utterly beguiling underground favorite, came from Bill Lange, who served as uncredited coproducer, with his partner Harold Sobel, and released the picture through his Chicago-based Brian Distribution Company. "It was the first film made after *The Texas Chain Saw Massacre* [1974] that had the word 'Massacre' in its title," Lange told me recently. "It was to be a pure exploitation film." So how did it become a somewhat mysterious art film in which the required violence is not gratuitous—as it is in most exploitation films—but is used to illustrate *political* themes? According to Lange, director-writer Renee Daalder is responsible "for making it an intellectual film. We gave him some ideas we wanted in the plot and he wrote the script. We lucked into Daalder. He was recommended by Russ Meyer, a good friend of mine, when I was looking for a director. Daalder was a Dutch cameraman." Although Lange likes the picture Daalder gave him, he admits that the violence wasn't nearly as strong as he wanted. That, plus the intellectual nature of the film, is what he thinks was responsible for the picture's failing to make back its costs. "Cult films don't make money," he states.

Massacre at Central High was made in three weeks, with the principal photography done at a small Los Angeles college and the hang-gliding sequences filmed in Malibu. It was

Once a good guy, David carries out his plan to murder many of Central High's "finest."

made nonunion, with actors getting minimum union scale. The fine low-budget cast included Robert Carradine ("He doesn't remember the four or five days he worked on the picture," claims Lange); Andrew Stevens ("a real hot dog in those days"); Kimberly Beck ("Tommy Leonetti's step-daughter"), who gives a surprisingly effective low-key perform-ance as the pretty, sweet Teresa; sexploitation vet Rainbeaux Smith; and Lani O'Grady, who in 1977 would star in TV's *Eight is Enough*. Best of all was the lithe, hollow-cheeked star Derrel Maury ("cast by the guy who cast *The Godfather* [1972]"), yet he's the only cast member, other than Beck, who seems to have disappeared. The other significant figure on the film, though not on screen, was Tommy Leonetti, whom we remember from TV's original *Your Hit Parade*, and for giving highly-publicized testimony against the Mafia. Leonetti wrote the film's score (which, as critic Amy Taubin points out, includes "strains of *Deutschland Über Alles* as David contemplates his scene of destruction"), sang the song that runs over the opening credits, and did most of the television promotion for the picture.

Massacre opened in drive-ins in upstate New York in September of 1976, and did promising business. However, when it played in Washington in October, business was soft. It next opened in Atlanta at Thanksgiving, and attendance was low due to bad weather, a factor, also, for its poor performance in the Dallas-Houston area. Having had three successive unsuccessful runs in major markets, by Christmas *Massacre* had a bad stigma attached to it. And though it would eventually play all over America, it rarely was rented by desirable theaters for extended plays. Inconsequential reviews in daily papers contributed to its failure to become a box office hit. Lange says, "It wasn't until it played at the Thalia in New York in 1980 and Vincent Canby gave it a good review in the *Times* that people really discovered it. Then everyone was calling up to have it screened for them."

Canby's influential review began:

> Working within the very conventional frame of the teen-age exploitation picture, Miss Daalder has made a witty, surprising, very entertaining low-budget movie that doesn't easily fit into any category. *Massacre at Central High* is both a teen-age exploitation picture and its send-up. At the same time it's a morality tale that works a few intelligent variations on *Death Wish* [1974], which didn't have a thought in its head. It might even be read as a metaphor for the rise and fall of the Third Reich. . . . Any film that so efficiently juggles so many ideas deserves attention.

Soon after (December 10, 1980), Amy Taubin wrote in the *Soho News*:

> I went to see *Massacre at Central High* because the *Times* reviewer said it was a first feature by an unknown woman director. I sat through this coming-of-age-as-Revenger's Trag-edy movie trying to detect traces of a feminist vision. I found an alienated one, and that turned out to be an accurate observation: because Renee Daalder is a Dutch male director whose relation to American high schools was probably about what Brecht's was to Chicago when he wrote *The Irresistible Rise of Arturo Ui*. I'm not claiming that *Massacre* is nearly as complex or as politically focused a work as the Brecht, but there are similarities. Another descriptive comparison—a more politically oriented *Carrie* [1976].

Massacre is clearly a political allegory, but what exactly is Daalder's political message? Both Canby ("At times she seems to be saying 'Don't mess with established authority. Things can only get worse,' plus a little of 'those who live by the sword,' etc.") and Taubin ("There is a free-floating Third Reich theme that foreshadows the contradictions of punk") admit confusion trying to decipher the politics. I'll go along with them. Nevertheless, let's look at the film until we reach that point at which Daalder's intentions can only be guessed at.

Paradoxically, Central High is off-center within the frame when we first see it. Daalder has tilted his camera, shot from below, and used a wide-angle lens to give his image a distorted look. We immediately can tell there's something mighty peculiar about this school—it looks as foreboding as an insane asylum. Seeing the school's elite—Bruce, Craig, and Paul—feasting on grapes at lunch as if they were deca-dent Roman emperors, dislocates us in place and time. As do Mark and David's cloudy references to past events, which sound as if they transpired in some other age, perhaps in some other world (earth?). It's almost like we've entered a parallel world. Central is like no high school we know: students talk in subdued tones, there is a student lounge, all students own cars; nothing makes sense: the school's lone political dissident (Spoony) paints a swastika, symbol of repression, as his expression of freedom; the school's neo-Nazis order him to wash it off because they dislike protest even when it seems to support their politics. Oddest of all is the absence of adults. There are references to the school librarian, Rodney's father, the school janitor, and the principal, but we never see them or any other parents or teachers. Since none of the teen-agers have surnames we must doubt that adults exist in this world. Amy Taubin made this astute observation: "In *Massacre* repressed rage and its return in apocalyptic violence function entirely within the context of an adolescent peer group that doubles for adult society. . . . These adolescents behave just like the adults on whom they model themselves. It is not necessary to show the adults because they co-exist with the kids, inside their bodies. They, the adults, are Body Snatchers."

At the end, "adults" do appear. But they are alumni, so in effect still part of the student body. Their cadaverous appear-ances make it clear that once a teen-ager stops being a teen-ager and graduates from Central High, he or she, in essence, dies. We have entered a surreal world, where corpses dance, where in the absence of elders (as in *Lord of the Flies*) it is the young who set up a caste system and individually come to represent various ideologies. Could Central High be the dream world of some history/political science student? (Daalder's use of blackouts certainly contributes to the dream-like effect.) It's a weird notion I know, with shades of *The Cabinet of Dr. Caligari* (1919)—the dream of an asylum inmate—but it's probably the only one that gives logic to the film.

Central High is controlled by Bruce, Craig, and Paul, who rule by brute force and through fear. Perhaps they are meant to symbolize the German Nazis ("they're a little-league Gestapo," Teresa remarks) who infested Daalder's native country, but they could also represent henchmen in Czarist Russia, or fascists elsewhere in history. They are the oppressors, the rest of the students are the oppressed: fat Oscar is symbol

Mark and Teresa (Kimberley Beck, a pretty and talented unknown) try to figure out what to do to stop David.

of the persecuted; Arthur is the intellectual; Mary and Jane (as in marijuana) and Spoony represent burned-out hippies of the anti-intellectual variety, whose sixties' activism has disappeared in many whiffs of pot smoke; Rodney is the peasant-farmer (he mentions his father's chickens); Harvey is the cowardly bourgeois; the rest of the students are the masses. Mark, the conservative, and Teresa, the liberal, don't like what goes on at Central High, but they are afraid to upset the status quo. David is the outsider, the freedom fighter who helps the oppressed wherever they exist. Because he lives in his workshop, we can assume that he also represents the working people, the class that historically initiates urban revolutions (including the one in 1917 Russia).

Bruce, Craig, and Paul attempt to *crush* the rebellion by dropping a car on David. Only injured, David successfully carries on a campaign of guerrilla warfare. It results in the leaders' *fall* from power: Bruce plummets from the sky, Craig dives into an empty pool, Paul flies over the side of a cliff. For a time, it appears a classless society has replaced the authoritarian regime at school: Arthur helps Rodney with his math; students cheer Oscar's rope-climbing; Mary and Jane sense that the students are talking about real things for a change, "questioning their values a little"; students gather together. But everyone treats David as a celebrity and there can be no heroes in a classless society. Perhaps David should have held back his revolution until the students had been politically educated and until there had been established a more solid alliance among the various factions. Or perhaps he should have left the revolution up to the students, when they were ready to participate. Because in brief time everyone is out for personal gain, be it wealth or power; and everyone tries to befriend David so he will help them rule. As David tells Mark, the once oppressed have become as bad as their former oppressors. This is certainly one of Daalder's themes! Rather than allowing these people the time to get things together, David becomes a Lenin figure who won't allow the politically naïve to rule, and then a Stalin or Robespierre figure who conducts purges. He kills all those who crave power or who have become decadent (Rodney takes Bruce's car just as Russian peasants seized land after the revolution). So those

people for whom there was need of a revolution are also bad. *Now* we've reached that point at which we can only guess what's in Daalder's mind.

First, I guess that there is a minor theme: people and life are more important than ideas and politics: David is wrong to kill the students whose major "crime" was that they were unprepared to take over the school. Even David knows he is wrong. David despises himself by the end of the film but he has more wrath for a disappointing world where people take a neutral position (a centrist position reigns supreme at *Central* High) while there is oppression. He is especially appalled that Mark and Teresa, the only people in school to have both physical and intellectual attributes (leadership qualities), remain neutral when Bruce, Craig, and Paul torment their classmates, and also remain neutral while David kills the students. Which brings us to what I guess to be Daalder's major theme: one must fight oppression whether it comes from the extreme right—Nazis, the Czar, and Bruce/Craig/Paul—or the extreme left—Communists, terrorists, and David. Only at the end, when Mark and Teresa break out of their bonds of neutrality and put themselves on the line for what they know is right, does David have his faith in humanity restored. He dies, but knowing he can allow the world (the school) to exist because brave humanists are its watchguards, he dies happy. His mission to politicize Mark and Teresa, to make them activists, has been accomplished.

Central High is a blackboard jungle: Craig tries to rape Mary and Bruce holds Jane back.

As Mary (L), Jane, and Spoony look on disdainfully, Arthur is killed by an eardrum-bursting blast that shoots through his hearing aid.

1981 Paramount
Director: Frank Perry
Producer: Frank Yablans
Screenplay: Frank Yablans and Frank Perry, Tracy Hotchner,
Robert Getchell
Based on the book by Christina Crawford
Cinematography: Paul Lohmann
Music: Henry Mancini
Editor: Peter E. Berger
Running time: 129 minutes

Mommie Dearest

Christina accepts an award for her mother. Posters of Faye Dunaway as Joan Crawford fill the background.

Cast: Faye Dunaway (Joan Crawford), Diana Scarwid (Christina Crawford as an adult), Steve Forrest (Greg Savitt), Howard Da Silva (L. B. Mayer), Maria Hobel (Christina Crawford as a child), Rutanya Alda (Carol Ann), Harry Goz (Al Steele), Michael Edwards (Ted Gelber), Jocelyn Brando (Barbara Bennett), Priscilla Pointer (Mrs. Chadwick), Xander Berkeley (Christopher Crawford as an adult), James Kirkwood (master of ceremonies)

Synopsis:* It is 1939. Joan Crawford is one of Hollywood's biggest stars. But she tells boyfriend lawyer Greg Savitt that she isn't content living in her Hollywood mansion with just her devoted secretary Carol Ann and housekeeper Helga. Greg arranges for Joan to adopt a baby girl. Joan names her Christina and promises "to give her all the things I never had." But Joan is obsessed with perfection, and Christina finds it impossible to live up to her mother's standards.

As Joan's career slips badly, she begins to take out her problems on her daughter. After the girl speaks disrespectfully to her, she spanks her. After she catches Tina mimicking the way she puts on an act for her adoring public, Joan angrily cuts off her curly locks. This begins a pattern of child abuse that will never cease.

After a heated argument, Greg walks out on Joan. She takes many lovers, for whom she cares nothing, and has Christina call them "uncle." She also takes solace in her fans.

L. B. Mayer informs Joan that she is through at MGM because her pictures have been losing money. This is a terrible blow. One night Carol Ann wakes up Christina and her adopted brother Christopher. They must help their mother destroy her rose bushes. Joan's behavior becomes increasingly irrational.

Joan's Oscar-winning performance in 1945's *Mildred Pierce* is the start of a major career comeback. But her problems in dealing with Christina continue. There is a "night raid," in which Joan discovers Tina has left her dresses on wire hangers. She beats the girl with a hanger, then makes her scrub her already spotless bathroom.

Joan sends Tina away to the prestigious Chadwick Country School. Coming home for a visit, the teen-age Tina is told by her mother that she hasn't enough money now that Warners has canceled her contract. Tina will have to work to support her schooling. But Tina discovers that her mother has been spending much money on herself. Tina is caught attempting sex with a boy at school. Joan yanks her out of school but tells a visiting reporter that Tina was expelled.

Tina is sent to a convent school, where she is to be "cleansed." Several years later she comes home and meets Joan's new husband, Al Steele, chairman of the board of Pepsi Cola. The couple will move to New York and Joan will help publicize the soft drink. When Steele dies, Joan stops a move to have her ousted from the board.

Meanwhile, Tina embarks on an acting career. She gets a role in a soap opera. When she becomes ill, she learns her mother is substituting for her and is drunk when performing.

Joan Crawford dies in 1977. Carol Ann tells Christina that Joan always loved her. Christina is glad to hear this because, despite everything, she loved her mother. But both she and Christopher are cut out of the will. Christopher says, "As usual, she has the last word." Christina asks, "Does she?"

---

* It is important to stress that this is the synopsis of the film, not the book by Christina Crawford. There is a vast difference.

Mother-and-daughter feuds make for reams in print; they also make for reams of inaccuracies: . . . the greatest inaccuracy is the feud itself. It takes two to feud and I'm not one of them. I only wish the best for Tina.
—Joan Crawford,
in her autobiography
A Portrait of Joan (Doubleday, 1962)

Regardless of the above quote, which with hindsight seems ludicrous, it is quite clear that Joan Crawford didn't truly want the best for her adopted daughter, and that she was indeed a willing participant in a feud between the two that reached Hatfield-McCoy proportions. For in her will she snubbed thirty-eight-year-old Christina and her thirty-five-year-old son Christopher (also adopted), "for reasons which are well known to them." Feeling her mother's insulting rebuke had disparaged her character in the public eye, Christina decided the time had come to tell her version of the Truth, to make people realize who the real villain had been, and, yes, pick up some big money on the side. So she wrote the most blistering of the "tell-all" movie star bios, *Mommie Dearest* (Morrow, 1978), in which she revealed her hellish life as daughter to Joan Crawford, a great Hollywood star but also an alcoholic, a child beater, a tyrant. The book sold around four million copies and became the talk of the land. Even though the public regarded Christina's motives as mercenary (few believed her talk show rap about writing the book "to help even one child who suffers child abuse"), and even though her detractors (including Crawford's grown-up adopted twins Cathy and Cindy) claimed her story had as much validity as *The Amityville Horror*, and even though she was unfairly treated as a leper by Crawford fans and people in the industry who felt child beating wasn't enough reason to tarnish a glittering star's reputation, she accomplished what she desired. In one swoop, Joan Crawford's carefully nurtured image of being the ideal, loving working mother was gone with the wind; and the world had one less goddess and one more witch.

Considering all the controversy surrounding the book and the hoopla regarding the making of the movie—Anne Bancroft was replaced by Faye Dunaway after being unsatisfied with eighteeen shooting scripts (including one by Christina that no one liked)—it was virtually impossible for anyone to bypass *Mommie Dearest* once it hit the screen. What came as a surprise, however, is that the film instantly had a *repeat* audience. These weren't admirers of Crawford but cultists who loved the film's camp value, who came to the theater dressed as Joan Crawford (1981's version of Dr. Frank-N-Furter), and who, imitating Dunaway in the horrendous "night raid" sequence, screamed "No more wire hangers . . . ever!" whenever they passed the dry cleaners. Paramount was happy with the unexpected business in the face of terrible reviews and changed its straight newspaper ad to one that had "NO MORE WIRE HANGERS . . . EVER" in large bold print, followed by a drawing of a coat hanger and the catchline "The biggest mother of them all." However, they reluctantly withdrew it when producer Frank Yablans, who took his film most seriously, threatened to sue because he found that the ad was "obscene, vulgar, offensive, salacious," and that it embodied "a racial slur of the poorest taste." Nevertheless, the only people who liked Yablans's picture were those who wanted a good laugh.

Truly it's staggering how much unintentional humor can be found in *Mommie Dearest*. How about when Diana Scarwid inexplicably slips into a southern accent? Or the awful makeup applied to Rutanya Alda as her character Carol Ann ages over the years (ever see *Countess Dracula* [1972]?). And that "wire hangers" night raid scene goes on for so long (two of the book's raids were combined) and is so unrelievedly melodramatic that it borders on the ridiculous. Speaking of ridiculous, cultists always cite impossibly bad lines used by Greg as he says good-bye to Joan and she tries to win him back by using her feminine wiles. Can even the screenwriters explain the meaning of "If you're acting, you're wasting your time. If you're not, you're wasting mine"? I was even more amused when these writers couldn't think of a proper retort for Greg after an insult from Joan, so simply had him grab and shake her and ask inappropriately "Are you crazy???" But *much* worse is Christina's speech over her mother's corpse: "Oh, Mommie. I always loved you so. It's over. The pain. There's no more pain. You're free. Free. Oh, Mommie. Mommie . . . Oh, Mommie." It reminds me of the tuxedoed Steve Allen reverently reading inane lyrics from rock 'n' roll songs like "Who Put the Bomp (in the Bomp, Bomp, Bomp)" as if they were great literature.

But *Mommie Dearest* isn't so bad that it should be dismissed as camp. It is mediocre and trivial, not worthless. Although she overacts terribly at times, Faye Dunaway gives the picture a needed lift, with a gallant effort. She didn't play a villain but someone she considered "a warrior," someone who had to fight an uphill battle (notice that Crawford's torturous jogging ends with her running *up* a driveway*) against an industry that has no sympathy for overaged leading ladies. Dunaway is particularly convincing when using a snide sense of humor, when looking genuinely hurt, when excited by work (she's like an oldtime reporter on a deadline), or when feeling desperate and frustrated, as in the scene when Joan destroys her rose garden and bloodies her face. I also like the way Dunaway shifts her eyes in such a way that you can immediately recognize Joan's feelings (approval, hurt, suspicion, spite, anger, resentment, fury) toward Christina at the time.

(T) Joan holds baby Christina as if she were an Oscar, while Greg and Carol Ann (far right) look on. (B) In a ceremony held years later Al Steele and bride Joan consider each other prizes.

A king on his MGM throne, L. B. Mayer—the one man Crawford makes no attempt to emasculate—gets rid of fallen queens like Joan as heartlessly as Henry VIII.

Breathing heavily between sentences (characteristic of both Dunaway and Crawford), her eyebrows thickly painted, wearing those trademarked ankle-strap shoes and Adrian-type gowns with shoulder pads, Dunaway (whose face is remarkably made up) convinces us she is Joan Crawford. In fact, when I now see Crawford in films, for a few seconds it's hard to readjust to how she really appeared. But even so, the question arises: is Dunaway actually playing the behind-the-glitter Crawford, whom Christina knew intimately? I think not.

Director Frank Perry wanted *Mommie Dearest* to "explore the ambivalence of love and hatred that goes into the basic family relationship." No matter that Perry didn't accomplish this because no one wanted to see *that* picture anyway; but his statement is significant in that it implies he never intended to deal with the specifics of the particular relationship of Joan and Christina Crawford but wanted to generalize about all such relationships. Such a plan of attack guarantees issues being clouded over and precludes anyone's pointing an accusatory finger at Joan Crawford, because there is no way of knowing if she did *exactly* what the Crawford in the film does. What's more regrettable—and unforgivable considering that this film was supposed to replace lies with facts—is that the sheepish filmmakers, hoping to dodge negative backlash from Crawford friends, opted to add still another *fictional* chapter to the life of Joan Crawford. Not only is almost everything in Christina's book ignored, but also almost every event that takes place in the film is fabricated, major characters like Greg and Carol Ann are made up entirely or are composites while real people are eliminated (because of possible lawsuits), only two film titles are mentioned, and special care seems to have been taken not to reveal anything new or solid about Crawford. No wonder Christina Crawford has said the film bears no resemblance to reality.

The filmmakers were so keen on having viewers think Dunaway was capturing Crawford's essence that they had her play the Crawford who was familiar to viewers—the Crawford of the movies, newsreels, and personal appearances—when we should have been presented with a Joan Crawford who was totally alien to us. (The filmmakers obviously figured viewers would think Dunaway was doing a dismal job if they didn't recognize her Crawford.) Essentially, viewers are subjected to watching Dunaway play variations of some of Crawford's memorable movie scenes, which the filmmakers substituted for events in Crawford's real life. For instance, when Dunaway acts obsessively about keeping her house dirt-free and orderly, we flash back on Crawford acting similarly in *Harriet Craig* (1950) and *Queen Bee* (1955). When Dunaway wields an ax, the scene plays so well because Crawford was an ax-murderer in *Strait-Jacket* (1964). When Dunaway is judged unsuitable to adopt a child, we remember all those Crawford shopgirls of the thirties who met resistance because of their backgrounds while attempting to break through social barriers. When Dunaway confidently stands up to the all-male board of directors of Pepsi ("Don't fuck with me, fellows!"), we think of Crawford's indomitable gun-slinging saloon owner

Joan, Christina and Chris, are a happy family for a Christmas radio broadcast. Although ignored by the filmmakers, Christina's book revealed that Joan made daily calls to a New York Christian Scientist for her instructions on how to discipline her children.

in *Johnny Guitar* (1954), who forces all the men in a posse to back down. Dunaway as a business executive? Remember Crawford as the head of a trucking firm in *They All Kissed the Bride* (1942). When Dunaway has her climactic argument with Joan's ungrateful (for good reasons) teen-age daughter, we remember Crawford's climactic confrontation with ungrateful teen-age daughter Ann Blyth in *Mildred Pierce* (1945), Crawford's most famous film. When neurotic, Dunaway is reminiscent of Crawford in films like *Possessed* (1947). When pitiful, we recall invalid Crawford in *Whatever Happened to Baby Jane?* (1962). Oddly, when Dunaway is hysterical, we recall *Bette Davis* in that film. Since *Mommie Dearest* was a major, major film, there can be only one explanation for Paramount's casting journeyman Steve Forrest as Dunaway's leading man. It's another case of the filmmakers wanting to simulate Crawford's old films. Viewers who remember Crawford's post-1944 films, when she was at her peak as an *actress*, know that with rare exceptions—like John Garfield in *Humoresque* (1946) and Henry Fonda and Dana Andrews in *Daisy Kenyon* (1947)—she had weak leading men. It was calculated that with nonhero types like Dennis Morgan, Van Heflin, Jack Carson, Zachary Scott, Robert Young, David Brian, Barry Sullivan, and Wendell Corey by her side, Crawford's strong performances would seem more like tours de force, so much would she dominate the screen. So it is with Dunaway and Steve Forrest, the most forgettable of actors. (In contrast, character actor Howard da Silva, as a "respectably" vile L. B. Mayer, holds his own with Dunaway, much the same way villainous Sydney Greenstreet did with Crawford in 1949's *Flamingo Road*.)

Because the picture jumps from one Crawford-movie-type scene to the next, we get the impression that we're watching many vignettes strung together, without time reference. (It would have been a good idea to use Christina as a narrator who could fill in voids in the story and discuss her own feelings about certain incidents.) The effect is that even the least suspicious viewer is too aware that the filmmakers are using only the events *they* want to show, instead of following Crawford's life chronologically. Viewers who come to the film hoping for insight into Crawford to help them formulate opinions are restricted to being *voyeurs*, not capable of better understanding Crawford's sickness.

* An actor Crawford thought inspiring was Lon Chaney, her costar in the silent *The Unknown* (1927). She admired his willingness to torture his body offscreen in preparation for playing his deformed characters.

In truth there are a couple of moments in the film that are insightful, that capture the book's point of view. In the birthday party scene, in which little Tina insists on changing her dirty dress before pictures are taken, a look in Crawford's eye reveals she is aware that her daughter has calculatingly used her mother's cleanliness code against her, to annoy her. It is the first time Joan realizes Christina is both manipulative and mocking toward her. (Later, Joan concludes that Christina *deliberately* embarrasses her and *deliberately* defies her.) At times we see the witch of Christina's childhood: the reflection of crazed Joan that appears in the mirror while Tina mimics her; the hideous face covered with thick beauty cream during the night raid; the woman who cuts out Greg's face from all photos, causing the little girl to worry that she can make everyone (even her) disappear. And we see the mother who considers her adopted child a possession: she holds her brand-new baby as if it were an Oscar. Perhaps the scene that should be the most insightful, because it hints Crawford's troublesome professional life couldn't help but detrimentally affect her private life, is the one in which L. B. Mayer "fires" Crawford from MGM. Peculiarly, neither Joan ("Mayer didn't want me to leave, but he realized how unhappy I'd become") nor Christina wrote about a meeting that happened just this way. (Since both Crawford and Mayer are dead, the filmmakers didn't have to worry about making up the dialogue of such a conference.)

It's strange that the filmmakers decided to make up events and characters, because so much in the book they were supposedly adapting (which is by no means as exploitative as people were led to believe), would have given us insight into Crawford.* But as mentioned, the filmmakers had no desire to stir up controversy. Christina made three observations in her book that may help us understand her mother and the nature of her relationship with her daughter: "She developed a belligerence about life, an assumption that people were destined to betray her, that her life was a battle against ever-imminent defeat"; "She'd become so afraid of spontaneity, of anything she couldn't directly control"; and "She had a way of holding out the promise of great rewards in return for voluntary slavery. She held out the promise of undying love in return for total devotion; but in my experience with her it never quite happened." Why didn't the filmmakers deal with any of this?

How does Christina come off in the film? Not too good, I'm afraid. When young, she's spoiled and conniving, somewhat like a bad seed. As a teen being played by Diana Scarwid, an actress who plays *all* her characters passively, she gets on one's nerves. As Vincent Canby wrote in *The New York Times*, "The odd thing is that through what appears to be the cumulative effect of unfortunate writing, casting, directing, and acting the character of Christina eventually turns into a sanctimonious, vengeful, colorless if pathetic prig, just the sort of woman her detractors would have us believe her to be." The movie *Mommie Dearest* makes one believe Joan and Christina Crawford deserved each other.

---

* A mystery. In Christina's book, she states Joan didn't tolerate grades below A. Why then does the film include a scene where Christina gets a B and her mother thinks nothing of it? I suspect that in this scene as well as the entire film, the filmmakers are undermining Christina.

1974 Cinema 5 release of a Python (Monty) Pictures Ltd. in association with Michael White
Directors: Terry Gilliam and Terry Jones
Producer: John Goldstone
Screenplay: Graham Chapman, John Cleese, Terry Gilliam, Eric Idle, Terry Jones, and Michael Palin
Cinematography: Terry Bedford
Songs: Neil Innes
Additional music: De Wolfe
Editor: John Hackney
Running time: 90 minutes

Cast: Graham Chapman (King Arthur), John Cleese (Sir Lancelot), Terry Gilliam (Patsy), Eric Idle (Sir Robin), Terry Jones (Sir Belvedere), Michael Palin (Sir Galahad);* Connie Booth, Carol Cleveland, John Young

Synopsis: Swedish titles reveal that almost everyone was sacked during the making of this movie.

It is 932 A.D. Arthur, the self-proclaimed king of England, rides through the countryside with dignity despite having no horse. His servant Patsy claps coconut shells together to simulate the sound of hoofbeats. Looking for knights to join him in Camelot, Arthur begs entry into a castle. The guard bores him with a long discourse on swallows, but doesn't let him inside.

Arthur arrives in a poor medieval hamlet where a knight named Belvedere presides over a witch trial. Since the woman weighs more than a duck, Belvedere concludes she is a witch and agrees to her execution. This is the type of man Arthur wants to have join him in Camelot.

In time, Sir Lancelot, Sir Galahad, and the cowardly Sir Robin join Arthur. But Arthur decides not to go to Camelot. "It's a silly place."

God orders Arthur to find the Holy Grail. He and his knights arrive at a castle where insulting Frenchmen won't let them inside. They build a giant rabbit and put it in front of the castle door. The foolish Frenchmen drag it inside. Unfortunately, Arthur and his men forgot to climb inside.

A learned modern scholar tells Arthur's story. An unidentifiable knight rides by and slashes his throat. The scholar's wife is horrified. Police arrive.

Sir Robin meets a three-headed knight who wants to kill him and have tea. Robin runs away. Galahad enters the spooky castle Anthrax. There he finds many maidens who wish to tend to his every need. But before they can get around to oral sex, Lancelot "rescues" Galahad.

A cackling blindman tells Arthur and Belvedere where they must travel in search of the Grail. In a misty forest, they are stopped by some knights who order Arthur to cut down the tallest tree in the forest with a penny. The heroes escape by debilitating the knights with the words "Eki! Eki! Eki!"

In Swamp Castle, the effeminate Herbert is upset because he is about to marry. He shoots an arrow into the forest, with a note that asks for help. It kills Lancelot's servant. Lancelot charges into the castle, killing and maiming everyone in sight. He is upset that Herbert isn't a maiden in distress.

Years pass. Robin's minstrels are eaten. The knights meet an enchanter who tells them of a message in a cave. A vicious rabbit that guards the cave kills several knights but is destroyed by a Holy Grenade. On the wall of the cave is a reference to the Castle of Aargh. Patsy falls over dead.

Robin and Galahad are whisked into the Gorge of Eternal Peril when they can't answer a bridgekeeper's tricky questions. But when Arthur proves to know more about swallows than the bridgekeeper, the bridgekeeper is whisked away.

Arthur discovers that the Castle of Aargh, containing the Holy Grail, is guarded by the insulting Frenchmen. He amasses his army and orders an attack. However, the police investigating the scholar's murder break up the battle and throw Arthur, Belvedere, and Lancelot into a paddy wagon.

---

* The members of Monty Python play various roles in addition to their primary characters

Monty Python and the Holy Grail

Initially Arthur (Graham Chapman) has only his servant Patsy (Terry Gilliam) to accompany him on his travels. Soon he recruits (L-R) Sir Belvedere (Terry Jones), Sir Lancelot (John Cleese), Sir Robin (Eric Idle), and (not in photo) Sir Galahad to help in his search for the Holy Grail. They keep their hands out and skip along as if they were on horses.

By the time *Monty Python and the Holy Grail* played in America. the Monty Python troupe, consisting of Englishmen John Cleese, Graham Chapman, Eric Idle, Michael Palin, and Terry Jones, and American Terry Gilliam, already had an enormous cult following worldwide. Its celebrated television series, *Monty Python's Flying Circus,** featuring the Englishmen in an assortment of lunatic skits and Gilliam's equally wild animation, debuted on the BBC in fall 1969 and by 1974 had been sold to a dozen foreign markets, including the United States, where it played on fifty-two PBS stations. The group's move into film, spurred by boredom as well as financial considerations, was only natural since its youthful fans (ranging from sixteen to forty years of age) composed the major film audience as well. Until I was dragged to *Holy Grail* and was unexpectedly impressed by the group's collective and individual talents (as comics, as writers), I had intentionally avoided both the television series and Python's first film, *And Now for Something Completely Different (1972),* a reworking of *Flying Circus* routines, directed by Ian McNaughton. I did so because any time a Python enthusiast

---

* The group made up their name shortly before going on the air. As John Cleese told Gordon Gow, *"Monty Python* touched a communal nerve. *Monty* had connotations of people with seedy little moustaches trying to pretend that they'd had something to do with the war in the desert. And *Python* was all the treachery of a musical agent type."

described the group's material, it sounded unwatchable—after all, how often can you trust someone else's taste in *comedy?* As a Python fan myself now, I realize how difficult it is to describe anything Python does and make it sound funny. It's nearly impossible to impress people with this fact: stupid and silly (as opposed to "sophisticated") humor, *if* intelligently conceived, can fit into the contours of great comedy. It truly can be hilarious watching a bunch of distinguished looking Englishmen running around acting, talking, singing, and dressing like fools. Python skits are, as their TV catchphrase contends, "completely *different"*—most comics have done take-offs on Little Red Riding Hood, but only Python replaced Grandma with astronaut Buzz Aldrin—but what makes the Pythons so special, if not "entirely original" (as many fans insist), and their comedy so brilliant, is that before going off in their own direction, they have studied, mastered, and indeed incorporated the multifarious styles of those talents who have pioneered major comic traditions.

Among Python's obvious influences are Goons Peter Sellers, Harry Secombe, and Spike Mulligan and their shorts, including Richard Lester's *The Running, Jumping, and Standing Still Film* (1959) (slapstick, fast-pacing, high-speed razzle-dazzle camera tricks); the Marx Brothers (an anarchist style, a distinct snobbery toward snobs, outlandish Groucho Marx-like musical production numbers); film stars Alastair Sim, Ian Carmichael, Terry-Thomas—all three found in *School for*

Scoundrels (1960), the most sidesplitting English comedy—and Alec Guinness (British characters ranging from stiff-upper-lipped to zany, from aristocratic to lumpen proletariat); W. C. Fields (absurdism à la 1934's *It's a Gift*—"Open the door for Mr. Muckle!"/"Do you know Carl LaFong?"—surrealism à la 1941's *Never Give a Sucker an Even Break*); television innovator/genius Ernie Kovacs (absurdism, surrealism, parody, offbeat characterizations, satirical pieces about television—particularly quiz programs); early *Mad*, when it was a ten-cent comic and was edited by Harvey Kurtzman, later Terry Gilliam's boss (absurdism, parody, women as sex objects—Python is as unprogressive as Benny Hill in regard to women: they are either old, ugly, and shrill, as when Terry Jones plays them in drag, or are beautiful nymphomaniacs); the revue *Beyond the Fringe* (blackouts, political satire—"We're obliquely satirical," Gilliam told me in a 1981 interview. "We do more satire when there's a right-wing government in power in England"); and *Bedazzled* (1968), written by and starring *Fringe* alumni Peter Cook and Dudley Moore (irreverence).

Steve Allen might have also influenced Python, although I don't know how much the English members could have seen of him back in the fifties. For he too is an extremely intelligent, straight-looking comic genius who enjoys nothing better than being silly. Bringing up Allen permits me to illustrate what I mean when I say Python uses concepts that other comics might also think of and then takes them into the stratosphere. *One* case in point: in his heralded PBS series *The Meeting of the Minds*, Allen brought together odd contingents of historical figures for lively round-table comic discourse; when Python assembles historical figures, they play soccer.

What's clear about Python's characters is that they are extremely competitive, even combative, whether playing soccer, engaging in one-man wrestling matches (a Graham Chapman routine), participating in bizarre races (for people who think they're chickens, for people with no sense of direction, for people with weak bladders), or arguing. Make no mistake, Python characters love to argue—before John Cleese settled on his Ministry of Silly Walks he contemplated a ministry where the members are routinely angry with one another—and most of their dialogues are in fact arguments: about such things as whether the obviously dead parrot Cleese recently

Arthur's expedition is repeatedly interrupted by weird, obstinant, and obnoxious characters.

purchased is deceased or asleep, or whether an argument that is taking place is indeed an argument ("It is!"/"It isn't!"/"It is!"). In addition to their argumentative nature, Python's characters are distinguished by their stubbornness, foul manners, loquaciousness, loudness, and desire to complain ad nauseum. Most unusual is that Python characters are rarely sympathetic. They have no audience-endearing physical quirks (a big nose, a big belly, a weakling's body, bad eyesight); nor do they remain children, as do Lou Costello, Jerry Lewis, or Curly of the Three Stooges. To the contrary: they are imposing men, physically and intellectually speaking, and are always on the attack. Significantly, it is for their talent alone that the members of Python are liked. Because they each play so many characters and because they write in tandem, we *never* can figure out anything about the individual actors' personalities. In an interview with James Vernier for *Twilight Zone* magazine (May 1982), Terry Gilliam attempted to clear up some of the confusion:

> There is a difference between the Cambridge and Oxford people in Python and also in *Beyond the Fringe*. The Oxford people seem nicer. They're shorter to begin with. In *Beyond the Fringe*, the Cambridge half was Peter Cook and Jonathan Miller. Both tall and sharp. The Oxford side was Alan Bennett and Dudley Moore, both small and gentler. John Cleese, Eric Idle, and Graham Chapman were the Cambridge half of Python, much more acid and sharp. Michael Palin and Terry Jones were Oxford and I always sided with them. We're shorter, more humanistic. It's very odd. Perhaps all the short ones at Oxford don't survive.

That takes care of the writing. As for the direction, shared by Terry Jones and Terry Gilliam on both *Grail* and the much less amusing *Life of Brian*,* Gilliam told me: "My strength is visuals. Not that visuals interest me more than performances—it just comes easier to me. On *Grail*, I designed the sets and spent most of my time working with the cameraman, and Terry Jones spent most of his time with the actors. On *Life of Brian*, Terry directed and I designed everything, but it didn't work as well because I wasn't able to position the camera except in a few situations. It should have looked better."

I think *Holy Grail*, which had publicity ads that claimed it "makes *Ben-Hur* look like an epic," looks marvelous. It has all the visual elements necessary to create a "poor man's epic": mist, mud, medieval villages, colorful costumes, special effects, peasants living in squalor, a lot of men in beards, witches and magicians, and wondrous Scottish forests, lakes, landscapes, and castles. I think it's impressive that a group of novice filmmakers were ambitious enough to attempt a period piece, albeit a comedy. Yet Python counts on our laughing because someone (Python, but not Python per se) had the gall to make a historical picture with such shoddy production values that all horses are invisible and the sound of galloping steeds is made by striking coconuts together. Because the straight-faced, straitlaced actors skip along foolishly as if they were truly on horses, Python constantly reminds us that we are watching a film and that Arthur and his men are really actors—the twist being that Python knows

---

*Terry Jones directed *Monty Python's The Meaning of Life* (1983); Terry Gilliam directed the animated sequences.

there is no chance we'd ever forget this fact. What we have is a spoof of "alienation"/"audience-distancing" techniques. (The only other possibility is that we're watching a bunch of medieval insane asylum escapees who believe they're Arthur and his legion.) *Holy Grail* attempts to do many things. It pokes fun at the French, homosexuals, communists, kings, even historian Sir Kenneth Clark. It is, as Vincent Canby states, "a sendup of the Arthurian legend, courtly love, fidelity, bravery, costume movies, movie violence, and ornithology." It is a funny alternative to such delirious non-Hollywood movie interpretations of the Arthurian legend as Eric Rohmer's *Percival* (1978), Robert Bresson's *Lancelot of the Lake* (1974), and John Boorman's *Excalibur* (1981). It mocks cowardice (Sir Robin's minstrels sing of his fleeing from danger), but is harsher on senseless British gallantry and chivalry: there is no funnier scene than when the sword-wielding Lancelot blindly charges into a wedding ceremony at Swamp Castle and indiscriminately kills dancing women, children, guards, servants, the best man, and the bride's father because he wrongly believes he's rescuing a maiden in distress ("I just get carried away," he apologizes). Heeding the words of the knight in Ingmar Bergman's medieval tale *The Seventh Seal* (1956), who decides "Life is a meaningless quest," Python puts down Arthur's long, irresponsible hunt for the Holy Grail while his people starved. *Holy Grail* does all these things, but foremost it mocks a group of philistine filmmakers (again: Python, but not Python per se) who would attempt such a lavish production on a minuscule budget, with amateurs on the screen and behind the camera, and without, apparently, bothering to tell the local police that they'll be doing location shooting.

The impression is given that Python hired a lot of hammy, unreliable actors to play the parts of the characters the always serious knights meet on their journey. (Of course, Python members also played these parts.) It's as if as soon as the camera was turned on, these actors intentionally forgot their one-lines of dialogue ("Go in that direction and you'll find the Holy Grail") and started improvising so they could steal the scenes. Remember how Jack Benny tried to accomplish simple errands like buying a tie, only to be hassled by one of Mel Blanc's nervous characters or that smiling sarcastic salesman who said "Eeeyyyesss"? Python also sets up a series of human roadblocks who prevent Arthur's mission—and the film—from running smoothly. Just as the men Benny ran into (Can't you see him as Arthur?) never had respect for a king of comedy (Benny played himself), those who meet Arthur couldn't care less that he's king of England. These characters aren't impressed by social standing: Dennis, the peasant communist, tirelessly objects to being treated like an inferior; the French castle guard tells Arthur "I fart in your direction, your mother was a hamster and your father smelled of elderberries," before dumping rubbish on Arthur's head; and finally, the Scottish cops arrest all the actors just as the film's climactic battle is about to begin. What really drives Arthur crazy is that most of these characters are such know-it-alls. They exhibit unbearable conceit because they are expert about something: one guard knows about swallows; the French guard knows about Englishmen; the communist knows about the way things should be in England; Sir Robin's minstrels know about Robin's true cowardly nature ("They were forced to eat Robin's minstrels," our narrator tells us, "and there

The fair horny maidens of the Castle Anthrax are ready to give Galahad anything he desires.

was much rejoicing"); the enchanter knows about putting on a good special effects show ("What an eccentric performance," comments Arthur) and about the killer rabbit who guards a cave ("I told you so," he gloats when the rabbit attacks those knights who didn't heed his warning to be careful); and the bridgekeeper knows the answers to his tricky questions (stupid Galahad wrongly guesses his *own* favorite color and disappears into the Gorge of Eternal Peril). Making things particularly frustrating for Arthur is that none of these characters will ever admit to being wrong. For example, when Arthur informs the Black Knight that the knight's arm has been cut off in their sword fight, the Black Knight insists: "It is not." When Arthur cuts off his other arm, the knight laughs, "It's just a flesh wound." When both legs go, he compromises a bit, "All right, let's call it a draw." Anything not to lose an argument.

The Python members are at their best in *Holy Grail*, as both the knights and the weird inhabitants of medieval England. Indeed much fun comes from trying to figure out which actor is playing which character, particularly when heavy disguises are used. Python cultists always know. The picture contains so many funny characters, lines ("That rabbit has a vicious streak a mile wide"), and incidents (Arthur's religious contingent reads from *Armaments Chapter II* as they bring forward the Holy Grenade with which to battle the rabbit) that we truly become involved in the quest. Therefore the abrupt ending is somewhat unsatisfying—even if it is right, considering Python's "filmmakers-as-jerks" concept. Gilliam returned to medieval times for his *Jabberwocky* (1977), starring and cowritten by Michael Palin, so it's evident that at least some Python members feel that all medieval ground wasn't covered by *Holy Grail*. Perhaps some day fans of *Monty Python and the Holy Grail* (who aren't necessarily the same people who adore *Life of Brian*) will get to see Arthur, Lancelot, Galahad, Robin, Belvedere, and, of course, Patsy, finish their ridiculous mission.

Morgan!

Also known as *Morgan (A Suitable Case for Treatment)*

1966 Great Britain British Lion release of a Quintra production (released in the U.S. by Cinema 5)
Director: Karel Reisz
Producer: Leon Clore
Screenplay: David Mercer
From his teleplay *A Suitable Case for Treatment*
Cinematography: Larry Pizer and Gerry Turpin
Music: John Dankworth
Editor: Victor Proctor
Running time: 97 minutes

Cast: Vanessa Redgrave (Leonie), David Warner (Morgan Delt), Robert Stephens (Charles Napier), Irene Handl (Mrs. Delt), Arthur Mullard (Wally), Newton Blick (Mr. Henderson), Nan Munro (Mrs. Henderson), Bernard Bresslaw (policeman)

Synopsis: London artist Morgan Delt often daydreams about gorillas swinging freely through the jungle. If he were a gorilla he knows his life would be less complicated and happier. He loves his communist mother but she makes him feel guilty for having forsaken the revolution. And although she likes his wife Leonie, she considers him a class traitor for having married an upper-class woman. But no matter: Leonie divorces Morgan because he is hopelessly childish and withdraws from reality. Morgan loves her deeply and hopes to win her back before she marries stuffy art dealer Charles Napier. He tells her he is seeing a psychiatrist. He tells his mother that he fears that one day he'll be taken away in a straitjacket.

Leonie becomes upset that Morgan won't leave her alone and keeps sneaking into her house—once their house—and playing pranks on her. She loves him still but gets a court injunction to keep him away from her. Morgan goes to Charles's art gallery and threatens him with a gun. Charles doesn't take Morgan seriously so is surprised it has bullets. Charles tosses him out.

Morgan doesn't know how to drive but he sleeps in his and Leonie's car outside Leonie's house. Leonie is happy to see Morgan, although part of her still wants him out of her life entirely. Morgan tells her she should have children by him rather than let Napier babies grow inside her. When they were married, she had refused to have children.

Leonie and Morgan sleep together. In the morning, Morgan proposes but is rejected. His car—"It's a world of sanity"—is towed away.

Morgan tries to ruin Leonie and Charles's love life by putting a recording of an explosion under her bed. Then he puts a real explosive there. When Leonie's mother, Mrs. Henderson, who detests Morgan, sits on the bed, she is terrified but unhurt by the blast. Wally the Gorilla, Morgan's mother's wrestling friend, knocks out Charles and he and Morgan kidnap Leonie. They go to a secluded Belgian lake. Leonie is angry and won't speak to Morgan. But when she sees how frightened he is, she makes love to him. He tells her, "Nothing in this world seems to live up to my best fantasies except you." Charles drives up.

Based on Leonie's testimony, the judge sends Morgan to prison for defying the injunction. He is released on the day Leonie marries Charles. Wearing a gorilla costume, Morgan crashes the party. But his costume catches on fire and he rides a bike into the Thames. Afterward, he lies in a garbage heap and has a nervous breakdown. He imagines he's killed by a Russian army firing squad that includes Leonie, Charles, and his mother.

Pregnant Leonie visits Morgan at the asylum. He asks if the baby is his. She smiles that it is. He touches her stomach, smiles slyly, and turns back to his garden, which he has formed in the shape of a hammer and a sickle.

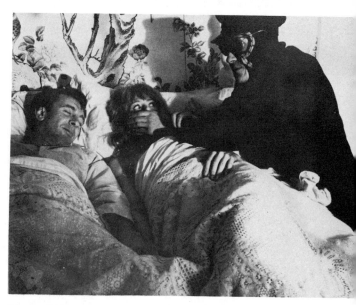

Morgan kidnaps Leonie while Charles sleeps peacefully at her side.

Moviegoers of the sixties and early seventies who experienced the civil rights, free speech, antiwar, and fledgling women's movements readily identified with screen characters who were at odds with society. Aware that this audience was rejecting the unsullied heroes and heroines of the fifties, movie makers here and abroad made pictures that were, according to Neil P. Hurley's *Toward a Film Humanism* (Delta, 1970), "introverted, highly personal statements, not infrequently an *apologia pro vita sua* for misfits, neurotics, and socially marginal types." Some pictures that gained cult status, particularly among college students, not only had nonconformist leads, as do most cult films, but were about nonconformity per se. Among old films, with out-of-the-ordinary characters who fight for their individuality, that became big favorites with students were *It's a Gift* (1934), *Modern Times* (1936), *Sylvia Scarlett* (1936), *It's a Wonderful Life* (1946), and *Rebel Without a Cause* (1955). New cult pictures with the same basic theme included *A Thousand Clowns* (1965), *Morgan!*, *King of Hearts* (1967), *The Graduate* (1967), *I Love You, Alice B. Toklas* (1968), *Five Easy Pieces* (1970), *Quackser Fortune Has a Cousin in the Bronx* (1970), *A Clockwork Orange* (1971), *Harold and Maude* (1972), *The Ruling Class* (1972), *Billy Jack* (1972), and, a bit later, *One Flew Over the Cuckoo's Nest* (1975).

Karel Reisz's *Morgan!*, one of the major pre-Midnight Movie cult films, fits into an it's-okay-to-be-crazy-in-our-insane-world subgroup. I have little appreciation for *Morgan!* and some of the other films in this category because they perpetuate the notion that a character's irresponsible actions can be condoned if he's certifiably nuts. It's irritating, for instance, that viewers of *King of Hearts* are manipulated into envying the loonies who use their benign insanity as an excuse to withdraw from a "mad" war-happy world, and into applauding Plumpnick (Alan Bates) when he chooses to join them in the asylum at film's end. The crazies should flee the asylum when they have the chance and attempt to improve the world—instead of copping out. Likewise, viewers shouldn't be so quick to cheer Morgan's devil-may-care behavior, when it is his way of shirking social responsibility. Worse, if we looked past Reisz's deceptively charming veneer, we'd see that Morgan's fantasies and wild antics are symptomatic of impending personal disaster.

Early in the film Morgan tells Leonie "I believe my mental situation is extremely illegal." We are amused by the line and don't take its content seriously. After all, writer David Mercer deceptively gives Leonie, who knows more than we do about the degree of Morgan's mental problems, a line that *she* would not say: "Everyone takes you seriously until they get to know you." (That's a line suitable for uninformed Charles Napier.) Coming from Leonie we believe it. Never do we consider Morgan other than a man who has reverted to innocent childhood, someone who isn't potentially harmful to others or himself. After all, Reisz and Mercer treat those scenes where he threatens Charles with a gun and a switchblade with humor, as they do the scene in which Morgan places an explosive under Leonie's bed. We should be concerned, but Reisz makes us laugh. When Morgan announces "I'm back!" and Leonie stifles his happiness with a cold "I don't want you!" we automatically side with the rejected man. We ignore how upset Leonie becomes when she can't get Morgan to leave her alone and admire his efforts to win her back over her futile protests—just as we forgave Errol Flynn and Fred Astaire for being obnoxious in their stubborn pursuits of Olivia de Havilland and Ginger Rogers, respectively. The physical abuse Morgan endures while chasing Leonie—he is tossed out on the sidewalk, he falls down the stairs, he is dragged by Charles's car, his gorilla costume catches fire—we simply chalk up to his odd form of gallantry. And we laugh while Leonie *and* Morgan get sadder and sadder.

What Reisz and Mercer keep us from realizing is that the most important aspect of the film is not how Morgan tries to win back the woman he loved and lost, but how Leonie deals with the often pathetic advances of a man she loves but can't be with without being destroyed. Instead they reinforce our wrong gut feelings that Leonie would be happy to be back with Morgan. Rather than having Charles Napier, Morgan's rival in love, be worthy of Leonie, he is presented as an easily exasperated upper-middle-class snob. We can only conclude that Leonie is marrying such a man to spite Morgan. We want to choose her man for her: an artist over an art dealer, one who loves beauty rather than one who loves money. But no choice should have to be made. Why must Leonie marry immediately after her divorce? Can't she live on her own, for a little time at least? Perhaps Mercer wanted to provide the film with the proverbial "time element": Morgan must win back Leonie *before* he loses her forever. That's a poor excuse.

What really makes us think Morgan and Leonie are an ideal match is that at times she acts as childishly as he does. (What we fail to take into account is that at other times she acts like an adult.) For instance, when he pounds his chest like a gorilla partaking in a love ritual, she reciprocates in kind. Like Morgan, she walks around the house singing,

humming, daydreaming. She even owns a baggy sweater, Morgan's trademark. Her ride in Charles's car reveals her Morgan side: she stands up, sings, drops her shawl on Charles's head while he drives. When they arrive at her house, Leonie is delighted to see Morgan camped outside, and admits to Charles "I sort of like him." These words are a hint to the hopeful romantics among us that Leonie still loves Morgan. And when she lets him watch her bathe and then make passionate love to her, how can we doubt it? When she still rejects him, we get angry with her for being so stubborn. But we are being unfair. If Reisz had allowed us to see the extent of Morgan's insanity, instead of camouflaging it with a consistently humorous tone, we surely would side with Leonie, a woman who must protect herself from a dangerously insane man.

Reisz might have opened the picture with Morgan in the midst of his nervous breakdown, lying in the garbage heap in his charred gorilla costume, and made the rest of the film a flashback. For in this scene those diverting fantasies of gorillas swinging through the vines are replaced by a nightmarish vision of himself being shot at and killed by everyone he knows. Placed only near the end, as it is, this nightmare sequence seems out of sync with the rest of the picture. It reminds me of *Deep End* (1971), Jerzy Skolimowski's film in which the comedy is too suddenly halted in the last scene when the love-obsessed John-Moulder Brown loses control and accidentally kills Jane Asher. If Skolimowsky had made *Morgan!*, perhaps Morgan would end up accidentally killing Leonie—it would make sense. Only in the breakdown sequence do we realize Morgan is not someone we should

Morgan feels his child's kick when the pregnant Leonie visits him in the asylum.

Marxist Mrs. Delt and wrestler Wally appear in court when Leonie gets her divorce from Morgan.

consider our hero, but is a paranoid schizophrenic who is dangerous to himself and others (even those he loves). Leonie realizes the severity of his illness during those touching moments when she sadly lays her head on her couch and looks away from him, and when she sits silently on the raft and twirls an umbrella. We may like Morgan's sweet side and sympathize with him during his battle with insanity, but we mustn't ignore his mean slyness, or force him on Leonie, or be amused by his plays for her affections. Yet we should recognize she is kind when she tells him "I don't want you back, but I'm glad I had you." And what can be more ego-boosting and reassuring to Morgan than her having his child rather than Charles's?

In David Mercer's teleplay *A Suitable Case for Treatment*, Morgan (not an innocent free spirit but a jaded adulterer who ends up with another woman) was played by veteran English actor Ian Hendry. With twenty-four-year-old David Warner, who'd only had a brief bit in *Tom Jones* (1963), replacing Hendry, Morgan conveniently fits into the long line of frustrated, alienated *young men* who have populated the British cinema since the early sixties. Morgan fills the gap between Albert Finney's angry working-class bloke in Reisz's *Saturday Night and Sunday Morning* (1960) and the likes of angry, aimless, music-crazed youth Phil Daniels in *Quadrophenia* (1979). That Morgan is a communist, whereas those other young men are apolitical, is "acceptable" because when he talks politics, or looks reverently at visages of Marx, Lenin, and Trotsky (unlike his late father, he despises Stalin), or adorns his path with hammers and sickles (on carpets, mirrors, flower gardens, and Leonie's poodle), we can rationalize that he is crazy. Mainstream filmmakers have never been comfortable with communist characters, so even when what they have to say makes perfect political sense, it is established first that they haven't all their marbles. Filmmakers fear audiences won't accept a sane communist telling them what's wrong with the world. So Morgan joins Earl Williams in *His Girl Friday* (1940), Preacher Casey in *The Grapes of Wrath* (1940), and even that delirious alien peacemonger in the ludicrous

Plan 9 From Outer Space (1956), as one of the left-wingers who are allowed to speak candidly simply because viewers will think them too wacky to listen to. (What is most admirable about *Reds* [1981] is that it presents a respectable communist.)

In fact, Morgan's insanity is shown to be partly the result of his politics. He may be alienated from society, but he is equally disillusioned with a stagnated proletarian revolution. At this point, he is more interested in a backward evolution of man to ape than in the "continuous revolution" of Lenin. He is someone who strives for individuality, no longer someone trying to bring about a classless society in which individuality is frowned upon. He is indeed a "traitor to his class," as his well-meaning communist mother moans, and his guilt is great, as is evident when he sees her as one of his executioners in his nightmare. To him, his fantasies about being a gorilla— free, strong—are just as valid as his mother's fantasies about an impending revolution. Morgan is no longer a radical but an eccentric artist along the lines of Gully Jimson in Joyce Cary's *The Horse's Mouth*. It's a shame, because he can offer Leonie no sound political reasons for living with him instead of bourgeois Charles.

Morgan! has lost much of its cult over the years because stylistically it is extremely dated. We have long overdosed on the then-novel use of freeze frames, fast-speed photography, insertions from old movies, and the juxtaposing of images signifying "illusion" and "reality." But the offbeat performances of David Warner and Vanessa Redgrave still stand out. (Robert Stephens would make his most memorable impression as the title character in Billy Wilder's underrated 1970 seriocomedy *The Private Life of Sherlock Holmes*.) Most of the picture faded from memory over the years, but the image of lanky, sad-eyed Morgan in his baggy sweater, slinking around Leonie, is indelible. Not everybody liked Warner's Morgan—his stage Hamlet in London that year was even more controversial—but that he got anybody to empathize with this character was an accomplishment. For, as we have come to see, Warner is ideal as a screen villain, rather than a hero. His coltish looks, gruff voice, and strident manner made him an odd yet inspired choice for the role.

Vanessa Redgrave had debuted in *Behind the Mask* in 1958, and was so embarrassed by her performance that she had to be coaxed into appearing in *Morgan!* She is extremely beautiful as Leonie, sexy and amusing. She also manages to convey an intelligence that is not found in Leonie's lines—thus giving the character an added dimension that would make her especially desirable to her intelligent ex-husband. Redgrave won the Best Actress award at Cannes for her portrayal, and that set her off on a long, successful, and controversial career. With the possible exception of her lead in *Agatha* (1980), none of her roles seem as difficult as Leonie, who must react throughout to a character who is not fully defined. In an interview with *Radio Times* (September 1971) she said, "David's interpretation of Morgan was so delightful and charming that I became sure that Leonie had to have a side that loved him deeply, always would love him, in spite of not really understanding him." What I find most special about Redgrave's performance is that she gives the impression that Leonie, unlike anyone else, struggles to understand Morgan. Therefore we can believe Leonie when she tells Morgan's mother, "I really tried."

Ms. 45

also known as *Angel of Vengeance*

1981 Rochelle Films release of a Navaron Film production
Director: Abel Ferrara
Executive Producer: Rochelle Weisberg
Screenplay: Nicholas St. John
Cinematography: James Momel
Music: Joe Delia
Editor: Christopher Andrews
Running time: 84 minutes

Cast: Zoë Tamerlis (Thana), Steve Singer (photographer), Jack Thibeau (man in bar), Peter Yellen (second rapist), Darlene Stuto (Laurie), Editta Sherman (landlady), Albert Sinkys (Albert), Jimmy Laine* (first rapist), Bogey (Phil)

Synopsis: Thana works as a seamstress in New York's garment district. She is friends with Laurie and two other female coworkers, but lives a lonely existence in a small apartment in Clinton Gardens. She doesn't enjoy her job because her boss Albert always is yelling at his female employees or is acting patronizingly toward her. Each day the four women must march past men who line the streets and fling obscene remarks at them. Laurie protests vehemently, but Thana must remain silent because she is a mute.

Returning from work one night, Thana is raped in an alley. She stumbles into her apartment. It is being robbed. The thief rapes her. She grabs her iron and smacks him on the head. She kills him and places him in the bathtub. The next day, she cuts his body up into little pieces, which she places in bags. She puts the bags in the refrigerator and gets rid of them one by one throughout New York. The newspapers begin reporting the discovery of parts of an unknown body. When a man retrieves one of Thana's bags and without examining the contents goes after her to return it, Thana runs away. He catches up to her in an alley. She turns and fires the gun she took off the dead rapist. The man falls dead.

Thana has trouble concentrating. At home, her nosy landlady and her yapping runt of a dog, Phil, get on her nerves. She gives Phil some of the rapist's body to eat. At work, her boss complains that she's not making her best effort. He wants her to come to the office's costume party. She tells him she'll let him know.

The four seamstresses eat lunch at a hamburger joint. A man and woman neck nearby. When the woman leaves, the cocky man tries to flirt with the four women. Laurie tells him "Fuck off!" and he backs away. But when Thana smiles, he coaxes her to come back to his beautiful studio. As soon as they enter what turns out to be a cheap studio, Thana shoots and kills him. At night, Thana dresses like a hooker and goes out. She kills a pimp who is beating a prostitute. She goes into Central Park. Gang members surround her as she wanted them to. She shoots them all down. A sheik picks her up. She kills him and his chauffeur. She meets an unhappy man. Her gun misfires. He places it against his own head and kills himself.

Thana continues to dispose of parts of the rapist's body. She gets annoyed at Phil's barking and sniffing and takes him for a walk. She ties him to a post near the East River.

Thana goes to the costume party. The landlady enters her apartment and finds a head. She calls the police. Thana wears a nun's habit, boots, and much lipstick. Albert flirts with her. When he crawls under her habit, he spots the .45 in her corset. She kills him. Thana begins to shoot all the men at the party. Laurie stops her by fatally stabbing her in the back. Thana screams, the only time anyone has heard her utter a sound. She points her gun at Laurie, who backs up in terror. But Thana does not wish to harm her.

The landlady mourns for her missing dog. But Phil is not dead. He runs up the stairs and scratches at the door.

* Actually Abel Ferraca.

Thana walks behind her fellow workers as they pass men on the street who barrage them with lewd remarks. Laurie, in front, yells back at them. Zoë Tamerlis told me: "At first Thana has admiration for Laurie, but later she feels contempt. Laurie talks a lot but she's hypocritical. Thana can't talk, she can't bullshit. Her only way to respond is through action, which is more honest."

I caught up with *Ms. 45* about a year after its release, when it had received fine reviews, and a few months after it played briefly as a Midnight Movie. It was second-billed to *Amin: The Rise and Fall* (1982) at a sleazy 42nd Street theater, not far from the garment district where Thana is employed. For the uninitiated: the legendary 42nd Street theaters, in which so many film fanatics grew up, have so deteriorated that with the exception of diehard movie buffs the only people who dare enter the darkness are pimps, pushers, alcoholics, addicts, and assorted degenerates who want to get off their feet or elude the police for a couple of hours. In the nonporno theaters, the fare of the day is bloody horror, kung fu, and sex and strong violence pictures because with such a dangerous clientele (almost exclusively men sitting alone), theater owners know better than to risk showing a dull film. (Hermann Hesse adaptations never play 42nd Street.) When not yelling at each other, the men excitedly talk back to the screen, cheering brutality (as was the case with *Amin*) and, misogynists all, directing lewd comments at every female character. Predictably, when Thana is being raped at the beginning of *Ms. 45*, an unsympathetic soul cackled: "How does it feel, baby?" I would guess that the feminists who attacked this film—some feminist critics voiced support—were angry with the male filmmakers for subjecting Thana to rape, not once but twice, and filming these scenes in such a way, with a gun in the frame, that violent men would want to identify with the rapist. But something fascinating happens. Once these men identify with the rapist, the filmmakers have Thana conk him on the head with an iron and kill him. Then she chops him up into little slabs and stores his parts in the refrigerator. Unexpectedly, the men who had whooped all through *Amin* and the obscenely gory previews of *Dr. Butcher* (1982), whimpered worrisomely "Oh, my God!" and slumped in their seats and shut up. Never has a 42nd Street theater

Thana allows a photographer to pick her up so she can kill him. Tamerlis: "Laurie told off the photographer, but he went after Thana anyway. But after Thana finishes with him, he'll not go after anyone else."

been so quiet and disciplined as when Thana went through her rounds and murdered every offensive male who crossed her path. Had the men in this audience witnessed their own possible fates if they continued to relate to women as they did? Certainly they could all identify with the foul-mouthed men Thana and her female coworkers must pass between each day in the garment district as if they were walking the gauntlet; could they also see themselves as the pimps, gang members, and pickup artists that Thana does in? The criminal element could enjoy such grotesqueries as *The Last House on the Left* (1973), in which two teen-age girls are kidnapped and tortured, and *Maniac* (1981), in which a psychopath scalps his female victims, but *Ms. 45*'s director Abel Ferrara and screenwriter Nicholas St. John didn't want to satisfy the sick men in the audience— they wanted to chastise them for being so revolting toward women and to scare them off. In an early scene, Thana starts to unbutton her blouse. Experts of exploitation films expect her to unbutton it all the way, look at her nude image in the mirror for a while, and then take a shower so men can get an eyeful. At the 42nd Street theater I could sense the anticipation. But just as Thana is about to disrobe, an imaginary hand shoots under her blouse, accompanied by a frightening blast of music, and the rapist's cadaver suddenly appears behind her. It is a shocking scene—Thana stops disrobing—and has a strange effect on the audience: the men worry that if she starts to strip again, they will end up being scared again; consequently, they'd rather have Thana keep on her clothes and do without nudity. So in a way, *Ms. 45* works as an odd form of therapy.

In a recent interview, Ferrara told me that "There was no conscious decision not to have nudity in the film. Zoë Tamerlis was willing to do it. It was just a flash decision to not have it. We were aiming at a cold sexuality, a violent tone. Roman Polanski is an influence on all my work." While Ferrara points to Polanski's *Macbeth* (1971) as the film which most influenced the tone of his first two films, *Driller Killer* (1979) and *Ms. 45*, the plot and thematic elements of *Ms. 45* seem patterned after Polanski's *Repulsion* (1965).

Catherine Deneuve is another beautiful, sexually confused young woman. While Thana works in a subordinate position as a seamstress, Deneuve is a beautician's aide. Both suffer sexual harassment going to and coming from work. Both kill men who force themselves on them sexually. While corpses rot in their apartments, both continue to go to work for a time, both lapse into a temporary shock state while at work, both begin missing work. Like most Polanski characters, Deneuve and Thana both are subjected to meddling neighbors (and their dogs) that intrude on their privacy and their thinking—in *Driller Killer*, the maniac finally goes off the deep end when a loud punk-rock group moves into his building. The two women become increasingly isolated, but they go in different directions: Deneuve becomes paranoid and kills all men who come after her in her apartment; Thana breaks free of her initial paranoia and goes out into the city after men before they have the chance to come after her. Deneuve goes crazy—but Thana, though acting "crazy," remains rational: she does not kill her lesbian friend Laurie, who has fatally stabbed her, and she does not kill her batty landlady's dog Phil, despite how much *he* annoys her. "The public had a lot of trouble with the character," says Ferrara. "Thana isn't clearly defined. At times I think her sympathetic, and at other times, fascistic. It shook up people to see an innocent person like themselves suddenly become a wanton murderer." Since many people loved the vigilante-justice character played by Charles Bronson in *Death Wish* (1974)—which professes that it's okay to kill scum—it's a relief that these exploitation filmmakers created a vigilante who, despite having sympathetic motivation for her actions, scares the living daylights out of all of us.

The mute Thana represents all the women of the world who don't speak out against the daily outrages they are subjected to from men (bosses, boyfriends, strangers): a constant barrage of come-ons, orders, insults, patronizing conversation. "I just wish they would leave me alone," she writes, but she hasn't the nerve or the capacity to tell men to "Fuck off!" like the brave Laurie. She is the passive female—her job is sewing— who kills a man with an iron, symbol of the stereotypical unliberated woman, signifying that woman's passivity is not insurmountable. She picks up the rapist's gun

Halloween party victims of Thana's shooting spree. She shoots only men. According to Saul Shiffrin, whose Rumson Films now distributes Ms. 45, *he has trouble selling it to cable because it is too intense for the average viewer.*

Two posters for Ms. 45. *On the left, Thana is seen shooting down gang members who surround her in a park. On the right is a poster similar to one used for a James Bond movie. Tamerlis: "While the picture had its run in New York, I was shot in the hip by a sniper while dressed similarly to Thana when she pursued victims. It was very suspicious. I like Thana a lot. I knew a lot about her that others didn't. That she came from a banal, religious background . . . that her handicap was psychosomatic from way back. Her dream was to be a model, but she had no hope of leaving the sweatshop. She was very innocent. She'd seen a lot but hadn't done anything. She had a conscience but not a whit of consciousness until she is raped. The film obviously is about physical rape—but it's truly, in my more elaborate view, about anyone who's been raped or screwed over in any way. The real villain is Thana's boss, who wants to keep his women for forty years in his service. He's the one person she sets out to kill."*

(obviously a phallic symbol)—she will use their weapon to destroy them. Thana, who had been the epitome of the desperate, faceless lone woman in New York, now becomes an angel of vengeance (*Angel of Vengeance* was the film's foreign title as distributed by Warner Bros.). As she methodically, savagely, and silently avenges her abuse, she becomes far more intriguing than other cinema women who have retaliated for their own rapes: Raquel Welch in *Hannie Calder* (1971) and Margaux Hemingway in *Lipstick* (1976), to name just two. Ferrara credits Tamerlis, then a seventeen-year-old with an otherworldly resemblance to Nastassia Kinski, Simone Simon, and Bianca Jagger, for "giving the character more complexity than there was in the script. Zoë herself is complex." And a fine actress, who, Ferrara says, is trying to make it in California after acting in films in Italy.* Thana

never speaks, but Tamerlis gives her remarkable presence. Considering that she was a high school student who hadn't been in films previously, she is extremely composed. I'm surprised no studio scout has taken an interest in her, because as we can see when she dresses up in a nun's habit with heavy makeup, high boots, and her .45 stuck in her garter, she has astounding sex appeal.

What really distinguishes *Ms. 45,* in addition to Tamerlis's fine performance, is the gifted direction by Abel Ferrara. Foremost, the picture is highly stylized. Witness the bizarre costume party massacre scene filmed in slow motion; it is truly surrealistic. Ferrara often uses a wide-angle lens to good effect ("I like using the wide angle when I film on location"); particularly impressive is the scene in which the guy chases Thana down the alley and runs toward the camera, which

*In fact, in 1983, twenty-year-old actress-playwright-composer-model Tamerlis (known as Tamara Tamarind in Europe) was busy finding resources to finish filming a 420-page script she wrote called *Curfew, U.S.A.,* directed by Christian Edward Saint de Laurent (which she hopes will be completed for 1985's Venice Film Festival). A three-million-dollar political thriller (preliminary filming had been done in Mexico, the Caribbean, France, Italy, and the U.S.), *Curfew* attacks American imperialism and deals specifically

with the radicalization of a liberal American actress (to be played by Tamerlis) who performs a political assassination. Tamerlis told me it is "a critique of both bourgeois feminism and America's left—which talks but doesn't act—told from a revolutionary perspective. Like Thana in *Ms. 45,* actress Una Horn develops a consciousness whereby she can *act* on her conscience. It's the most hopeful drama of America I can conceive of."

Dressed as a nun, Thana blesses the bullets she'll use to kill men. Tamerlis: "It's a paradox: she's a 'crafty Christ' dressing as she does. That's what a revolutionary person has to be."

distorts his image at the precise moment Thana's bullet smashes him in the skull and sends him reeling over backward. I also like the scene in which Thana studies herself in the mirror and keeps pretending to shoot in different directions: it is downright eerie seeing her dressed in the habit, wearing lipstick, and acting like a cowboy or Belmondo's gangster in *Breathless* (1961) (as he drives along and aims his finger and makes shooting noises) while Ferrara uses slow motion and adds a sproingy noise on the soundtrack. I'm also impressed by the way Ferrara incorporates his music. He uses horns and drums, not just a synthesizer, which is utilized in many low-budget films. Thus the music adds to the feel of the film (and the New York City locales), i.e., the pulsating, heart-beat music before Thana shoots the photographer in his heart; the sleazy music (sax riffs) when Thana dresses like a hooker to go hunting for pimps and gang members; the blazing sound as Thana does away with the sheik and his chauffeur.

Ferrara inserts much humor into his morbid storyline. I also got a kick out of all Ferrara's weird characters. Of landlady Editta Sherman, *The New York Times* wrote, "There hasn't been a screen performance so hair-raising since Frances Faye played a madam in *Pretty Baby* [1978]." (In typical exploitation film fashion, the blurb the filmmakers attributed to the *Times* about the film as a whole was "Hair-raising!") The landlady's a great movie character, who wears a hat over long stringy gray hair and keeps pictures of both her husband and dog Phil on her mantel. All the other characters are memorable as well. Since this film was made by men, it's amazing that *every* male character (including Phil) is obnoxious. Even when we only get to hear them say one or two lines, we can deduce their awful personalities: one partygoer talks about paying three hundred dollars to screw a virgin; another tells his girl he's changed his mind about having a vasectomy. Put these men together in the world's power elite with boss Albert (who's always yelling at his seamstresses or putting the make on Thana), the conceited photographer (who smooches with his girl, then flirts with Thana the moment she leaves), the gang members, the sheik, the rapists, and the rude men who line the streets, and what's a girl to do?

1946 20th Century-Fox
Director: John Ford
Producer: Samuel G. Engel
Screenplay: Samuel G. Engel and Winston Miller
From a story by Sam Hellman
From the book *Wyatt Earp, Frontier Marshal* by Stuart N. Lake
Cinematography: Joseph P. MacDonald
Music: Alfred Newman
Editor: Dorothy Spencer
Running time: 97 minutes

Cast: Henry Fonda (Wyatt Earp), Linda Darnell (Chihuahua), Victor Mature (Doctor John Holliday), Walter Brennan (Old Man Clanton), Tim Holt (Virgil Earp), Ward Bond (Morgan Earp), Cathy Downs (Clementine Carter), Alan Mowbray (Granville Thorndyke), John Ireland (Billy Clanton), Grant Withers (Ike Clanton), Mickey Simpson (Sam Clanton), Roy Roberts (the mayor), Jane Darwell (Kate Nelson), Russell Simpson (John Simpson), Francis Ford ("Dad," the old soldier), Don Garner (James Earp), Ben Hall (barber), Jack Pennick (coach driver), Fred Libby (Phin Clanton), Joe Farrell MacDonald (Mac), Mae Marsh

Synopsis: Arizona. 1882.* Wyatt, Morgan, Virgil, and James Earp are herding cattle. Old Man Clanton and his oldest son Ike come by and offer to buy the cattle at a low price. They are turned down. Wyatt mentions that he'll go into Tombstone that night. James, the youngest, stays at the camp while his brothers go into town.

Drunk Indian Charley starts shooting up the town. When the sheriff quits rather than tangle with Charley, Wyatt apprehends the culprit. The mayor offers him the job of marshal when he finds out he is the famous Wyatt Earp who cleaned up Dodge, but Wyatt declines.

The Earps find James has been murdered and their cattle rustled. Wyatt suspects the Clantons. He accepts the job of marshal and makes Morgan and Virgil his deputies. Wyatt visits James's grave. He talks of a time when kids can grow up safely.

Wyatt, who loves to play poker, gets angry when Chihuahua, the pretty entertainer at the saloon, lets a professional gambler know what cards he holds. He throws her in a water trough. Famous gunslinger Doc Holliday, who runs the town's gambling, returns to Tombstone and tosses the gambler out. He challenges Wyatt to a draw when he learns he is marshal but changes his mind when he sees Morgan and Virgil backing up the unarmed man. Instead, he and Wyatt have a drink together and become friends, much to the chagrin of Chihuahua, Holliday's girl. Wyatt is concerned about Holliday's tuberculosis, and that he won't stop drinking. He is impressed by Holliday's knowledge and sophistication.

A pretty young woman named Clementine Carter arrives from Baltimore. She was Holliday's fiancée. She informs Wyatt that Holliday had once been a physician, but had left when he got sick. Wyatt is much taken with her, but tries to get her back with Holliday. Holliday insists that she leave. She agrees to. Holliday proposes to Chihuahua. But he rides away by himself.

Wyatt discovers James's pendant around Chihuahua's neck. She says Doc gave it to her. He races after Holliday's stage to bring him back to Tombstone. They draw on each other. Holliday is shot in the arm. Holliday makes Chihuahua tell Wyatt Billy Clanton gave her the pendant. Billy is outside her window and shoots her. There are many shots but he gets away with Virgil on his trail. Virgil enters the Clanton home. Billy has died. Old Man Clanton guns down Virgil, as he'd done James. He and his sons go into town.

Holliday performs surgery on Chihuahua. He considers going back into medicine. But she dies. He decides to join Wyatt and Morgan when they battle the Clantons.

The Clantons wait at the O.K. Corral. There is a great gun battle. Doc is killed, as are Clanton's three sons. Old Man Clanton grieves. Wyatt wants to let him go so he'll suffer, but Old Man Clanton pulls a gun and Morgan kills him.

The town is peaceful. Clementine will be the new schoolmarm. Wyatt and Morgan are going home to see their father. Wyatt tells Clementine he may pass through again one day, and pay her a visit. She'd like that.

---

*In fact, this action took place in 1881.

My Darling Clementine

Henry Fonda strikes his classic pose as the patient, philosophical, and playful Wyatt Earp.

Critics have long regarded *My Darling Clementine* as a classic, but when writing about John Ford's *core* westerns they've usually set it aside and concentrated on *Stagecoach* (1939), *Fort Apache* (1948), *She Wore a Yellow Ribbon* (1949), *The Searchers* (1956), and *The Man Who Shot Liberty Valance* (1962)—all, *conveniently,* with John Wayne. Only in recent years has it emerged from the shadows of the Ford-Wayne westerns: partly because of increased interest in Henry Fonda, and partly because it appeals to many people who usually don't like westerns.

My Darling Clementine is a different kind of western. While nine people are gunned down (five Clantons, two Earps, Chihuahua, and Holliday) and there is much violence, its gentle title does not seem inappropriate; while a major theme of the film is violent retribution (as in *Hamlet,* from which Thorndyke and Holliday recite), it can be, and has been, described as "lovely," "poignant," "nostalgic," "sentimental" "tender," "sweet," and "poetic"—words rarely used to *compliment* a western. When we leave the theater after Wyatt Earp has brought peace to Tombstone, we feel peaceful. We haven't forgotten the killings, but we remember other images better. Such as Wyatt balancing himself on the back legs of his chair, and, like a little country boy, putting one foot, then, quickly before he falls, the other on the street post in front of him; Clementine climbing off the stage into the dusty, deserted street, and immediately establishing herself in Wyatt's eyes as the prettiest lady in Tombstone; Wyatt and Clementine taking a long majestic stroll to the town gathering, her hand on the crook of his arm, her skirt blowing slightly in the wind, he looking proud. (Ford filmed this from many angles and varied long, medium, and closeup shots); Wyatt and Clementine watching the other dancers and wanting to join in—but he (as she knows) is too shy to ask; Wyatt and Clementine dancing ("Make way for the marshal and his lady fair!"); the four Earps sitting around their campfire chatting about life and love, revealing a deep affection for one another; Wyatt visiting James's grave, not on Boot Hill but in a peaceful valley under a heavenly sky (we recall Fonda's Abe Lincoln kneeling by Ann Rutledge's grave in Ford's 1939 film *Young Mr. Lincoln*).

More than the violence, we remember the way people relate to each other in Ford's west. It's the director's own version of "realism." Foes speak to one another hesitantly, with clipped dialogue so they won't betray themselves. They're polite, but we sense hostility. Pronouns are dropped: "Sure is rough country"; "make you an offer"; "not interested." Characters rarely change their expressions or the levels of their voices, lest they reveal their innermost thoughts. Notice how Old Man Clanton (played by the incomparable Walter Brennan) refuses to show emotion, and even at his most demonstrative,

barely curls his lips into a snarl or semismile, or moves his big eyes. Or the way Wyatt seemingly remains calm in the face of disaster: we never know if he's scared. This stance does not only apply to the men. Clementine maintains her composure when she's with Holliday and he's being difficult, and when she's found Chihuahua. Even the usually emotional Chihuahua, sitting with her guitar, won't let herself reveal her feelings of jealousy and worry when she sees Clementine approach Holliday's dinner table. To change expressions is to show vulnerability, not the wise thing to do in this west, where bluffing is as important as a quick draw.

And we remember the music. Not Chihuahua's obnoxious cowboy songs, but Alfred Newman's lyrical score, with several variations on the title tune. Simple music: harmonicas, fiddles, guitars, and a cowboy chorus are employed at different times. Also impressive is how Ford uses *no* music in the final shootout, and the silence helps build the suspense. (How different this scene is from the finale in 1952's *High Noon,* where Tex Ritter's soulful ballad is used to provide the tension the visuals lack in themselves.) And we remember the wit, less rowdy here than in other Ford films. Wyatt's visits to the tonsorial parlor. Wyatt smelling like a desert flower after his haircut. The Shakespeare crowd at the Birdcage wanting to ride the tardy Thorndyke around town on a rail ("Be reasonable, marshal"). This conversation: "Mac, have you ever been in love?" "No, I've been a bartender all my life."

And last but not least, we remember Joe MacDonald's glorious black-and-white photography. Shot after shot, this is truly a beautiful movie. Tombstone at night, with the streets half lit by light filtering from the buildings. The saloon, with thick smoke hovering in the air. The valley, with mountains in the distance and a hazy gray, panoramic sky overhead. Back-lit shots: Indian Charley in the doorway of Kate Nelson's boarding house; Holliday (with shadows falling on him) and Clementine conversing outdoors, lit by the glowing night sky; Old Man Clanton waiting for the shootout, his dark hat set against the white sky. My favorite frame: Wyatt walking alone down the middle of the road that leads to the O.K. Corral; to the left is a row of town buildings, above is the huge sky, and straight ahead in the distance is one of the enormous rock monuments of Monument Valley.

But here's the rub. Tombstone is in southern Arizona, whereas Monument Valley is all the way to the north, mostly in Utah. The terrain around Tombstone is relatively flat. A director who could deliberately distort geography would also be willing to alter history; most people who have reservations about *My Darling Clementine* are angry with Ford because he did just that in order to perpetuate the myth of *Wyatt Earp as hero*. The real Earp was a horse thief who jumped bail in Arkansas in the mid-seventies. He was soon thereafter a pimp (no hero) in Wichita, who became a low-level policeman (no marshal) so he'd not have to pay fines levied on his girls; when he beat up a constable he was arrested. Historians dispute whether he was town marshal of Dodge or just an assistant lawman. In any case, he used his position to strong-arm cowboys, a lot he detested, knocking them unconscious (his specialty) and jailing them (at $2.50 an arrest) for crossing into the better part of town. He took graft and muscled in on the liquor and gambling trade. It was in Dodge that he met Doc Holliday, the former dentist (not physician) turned murderer, who followed Wyatt to Tombstone.

Five Earp brothers came to Tombstone, including Warren, who is not in the film. James, really older than Wyatt, was in the liquor business, making him the one Earp with a steady job. After working several confidence schemes, Wyatt ran for sheriff and Virgil for marshal—they were defeated. Wyatt and Morgan did find brief employment as Wells Fargo messengers; and at the time of the O.K. Corral gunfight were temporarily deputized by the acting city marshal: Virgil. From the start there was an ongoing feud between the Earps and Cochise County Sheriff Johnny Behan, who suspected that the Earps and Holliday were responsible for a series of Wells Fargo stage robberies. (Complicating matters: Behan's mistress Josie was sweet on married Wyatt.) On Behan's side was the *Daily Nugget* and most Tombstone residents, including the Clantons and McLaurys—families the Earps accused

Chihuahua lets Clementine know that Tombstone isn't big enough for the two of them.

Walter Brennan as the despicable Old Man Clanton.

of being cattle rustlers and horse thieves. The Earps' strongest supporter was power-hungry mayor John T. Clum, who was also editor of the *Tombstone Epitaph,* which was most responsible for spreading glorifying tales about the Earps.

Historians agree that James Earp was not murdered by the Clantons but lived long past the events depicted in the film; Old Man Clanton died several months before the O.K. Corral battle; neither Virgil Earp nor Billy Clanton was killed prior to the shootout and indeed both took part; the showdown was triggered by the Clantons and McLaurys, who spread the word that the Earps and Holliday were guilty of a stage robbery and murder; Virgil and Morgan were wounded in the shootout, Doc Holliday survived with only a scratch (he'd died in 1885 in a sanitarium), and, on the other side, Ike Clanton was wounded and Billy Clanton and Tom and Frank McLaury were killed.

After the gunfight, only the *Epitaph* claimed the Earps were heroes. The words etched into the stones of the three men buried on Boot Hill read, "Murdered on the streets of Tombstone." The Earps were tried for murder and it's likely that they were only acquitted because the judge was their friend. *The Tucson Star*: "We sincerely believe that no disinterested man can read the testimony and not come to the conclusion that Clanton and the McLaurys were shot with their hands up. . . . The whole series of killings cannot be classified as other than coldblooded assassination." Tombstone didn't forgive the Earps. A couple of months later, Virgil was crippled for life by an assassin's bullet. Three months later, Morgan was killed by an unknown assailant. The Earp clan brutally gunned down a couple of men they thought responsible (including an innocent man they mistook for Indian Charley) and fled Arizona, which for years tried to have them brought back to face new murder charges. Wyatt's deserted wife, angered that he had run off with Josie, committed suicide.

It's obvious why John Ford did not film the true story. Having the deaths of James, Virgil, and Billy Clanton be the cause of the big gunfight is certainly more compelling than a dispute between the bullying Earps and their political opposition. There is no mention of the McLaurys in the film, and I suspect that (1) Irishman Ford would never consider having Irish villains, and (2) a family feud between the Clantons and Earps would serve his themes better. On one of those "History of Man" charts in which we see our evolution from ape to civilized man, the brutal, stoop-shouldered, whip-wielding, gun-toting Clantons represent the Neanderthals, and the princely, walking, gun-toting Earps the Cro-Magnons, one step away from Homo Sapiens. The Earps as a family are meant to pave the way for civilized man, and for civilization. Earp thus becomes one more western hero who tames the west but then has no place in it. Like Ethan Edwards at the end of *The Searchers,* he must go away. (There is speculation that it was 20th's idea, and not Ford's, that Wyatt ride away at film's end.) As in most Ford films about families, family members must die or be sacrificed (i.e., James, Virgil) so that there can be a regeneration (Wyatt and Morgan will reunite with their relatives) and the family unit can assimilate into a larger "universal family," as in *The Grapes of Wrath* (1940) and *The Searchers.* Progress for mankind. Some viewers may not be happy, however, with Ford's opinion of what and who should be part of the civilized Tombstone. To Ford, the civilized town must have a church, a school (Clementine will be the new schoolmarm), a tonsorial pastor (where bearded men can become civilized with two shakes of a razor), a theater for Shakespeare readings, and law and order. It will be populated by white, religious-minded families, and French cooks; but outlaws like the Clantons and Holliday, professional gamblers, professional gunmen like Wyatt and Morgan, prostitutes like Chihuahua, Mexicans like Chihuahua (Wyatt calls her an Apache), or Indians like Indian Charley don't fit in. (In *The Searchers,* Ford changed his tune, realizing that for civilization to succeed, all races, whites and Indians in particular, must mix.)

Wyatt Earp has been portrayed many times in films, most notably by Walter Huston in *Law and Order* (1932), George O'Brien in *Frontier Marshal* (1934), Randolph Scott in *Frontier Marshal* (1939), Richard Dix in *Tombstone, the Town Too Tough to Die* (1942), one of my favorite B westerns; Joel McCrea in *Wichita* (1955), and Burt Lancaster in *Gunfight at the O.K. Corral* (1957). The only film which showed Wyatt as he really was, *Doc* (1971), in which Harris Yulin played him as a scoundrel, is the worst Earp film ever made. It figures.

The "heroic" Earp makes an ideal character for Fonda, who gives a wonderfully sincere performance. "He is the kind of lawman even a cop hater like Ford could admire," write Joseph McBride and Michael Wilmington in *John Ford* (Secker and Warburg, 1974), "cool and loose, motivated by family ties and a sense of justice, a man who influences others more by example than by force." Unlike Wayne, whose characters ended up representing his own conservative, manifest-destiny politics, Fonda played actual American characters (romanticized perhaps but real) and fictional men who embodied a liberal or progressive conscience, who are voices of reason in turbulent times. Like Tom Joad, Abe Lincoln, and Mister Roberts, Wyatt Earp in *My Darling Clementine* perfectly suited Fonda's screen persona. Brave, moral, virtuous, noble, simple, calm, and dignified. He is so steadfast in his beliefs that in some ways his character is too predictable. That's why the Doc Holliday figure is brought into play. He is the tragic figure who, unlike Wyatt, cannot accept the advent of civilization because by all rights *he* should fit in but can't although he is more intellectual, more learned, better dressed, more cultured (he drinks champagne) than Wyatt. He is also blessed with the power to cure the sick—but he makes no attempt to cure himself. Although Wyatt is not a church-going man, he believes in God; Holliday (who delivers Hamlet's "To be or not to be" soliloquy) believes in man's freedom of choice—and in his case, he meekly *chooses* to yield to the inevitable death he carries in his lungs. Because he has given up his choice, he is tormented by his own cowardice in not facing his obligation to be a doctor, not a martyr. As J. A. Place writes in *The Western Films of John Ford* (Citadel, 1974), "Doc fails where Wyatt succeeds—at coming to terms with his own sense of loss and living with his solitude. He does not have the dimensions of a hero, which would enable him to do this, but through his failure we understand Wyatt's heroic proportions."

The scenes between Holliday (well played by Victor Mature, underrated by those who consider him one of Hollywood's all-time worst) and Chihuahua (Linda Darnell miscast) seem to be out of a Henry King movie rather than one by John Ford. But their tempestuous moments are served well by their contrast with the polite "courtship" scenes between Wyatt and Clementine Carter (lovely Cathy Downs never had such a fine role again). The real Earp probably never said the film's final line, "Ma'am, I sure like that name—Clementine," but I'm inclined to believe that Fonda's Earp, after riding off toward the rock monuments (and into mythology) in the last shot, will hurry back and marry the schoolmarm.

Publicity shot of Wyatt and Doc ready to battle the Clantons at the O.K. Corral.

also known as *Curse of the Demon* (as it was retitled for American distribution)

1957 Great Britain
Director: Jacques Tourneur
Producer: Hal E. Chester
Screenplay: Charles Bennett and Hal E. Chester
From the story ''Casting the Runes'' by Montague R. James
Cinematography: Ted Scaife
Music: Clifton Parker
Editor: Michael Gordon
Running time: 95 minutes (British version), 82 minutes (American version)

Cast: Dana Andrews (Dr. John Holden), Peggy Cummins (Joanna Harrington), Niall MacGinnis (Doctor Julian Karswell), Athene Seyler (Mrs. Karswell), Maurice Denham (Professor Harrington), Ewan Roberts (Williamson), Liam Redmond (Professor Mark O'Brien), Peter Elliot (Kumar), Reginald Beckwith (Mr. Meek), Rosamund Greenwood (Mrs. Meek)

Synopsis: Professor Harrington is terrified. He tells Dr. Julian Karswell that he is willing to call off his investigation of Karswell's devil cult. It is too late. The parchment which Karswell had secretly passed to Harrington has been destroyed. Harrington drives home. An enormous fiery demon emerges from the woods and flies through the darkness. Trying to escape, Harrington backs his car into a pole and is electrocuted.

Dr. John Holden arrives in London to attend a paranormal psychology convention and help Harrington expose Karswell. He does not believe in witchcraft or the devil. Upset by Harrington's death, he vows to continue the investigation of Karswell. He befriends Harrington's pretty niece Joanna, who tries to convince him Karswell is dangerous.

Holden goes to the library to study witchcraft. Karswell introduces himself and invites him to visit his country estate. He secretly slips a parchment with runic symbols into Holden's papers.

Joanna reads to Holden from Harrington's diary. It mentions the parchment that Harrington had which flew from his hands into a fireplace as if it were alive. Harrington had believed he was under a witch's spell. But Holden shrugs this off.

Holden and Joanna visit Karswell's estate, where he and his mother are holding a Halloween party for orphans. Karswell tries to impress Holden by doing a little white witchcraft. An enormous storm kicks up. Karswell tells Holden he has three days to live.

Karswell tells his mother he does what he does out of fear. He can't stop.

Holden's parchment flies from his hand to the fireplace. The cover on the fireplace stops it. Holden admits to Joanna that he has developed some fear. When he visits some satanists to get permission to hypnotize a patient named Hobart at the asylum—who has gone insane while under Karswell's command—he begins to hallucinate. They tell him he has been chosen to be a victim.

Joanna brings Holden to a seance assembled by Mrs. Karswell. The medium, Mr. Meek, starts talking in the voice of Harrington, telling Holden that he isn't strong enough to fight Karswell. Holden breaks into Karswell's estate to steal a book on witchcraft. He is attacked by a huge cat. Karswell appears and says that the cat—now a gentle housecat—is a small demon. When Holden leaves he becomes frightened by a smoke ball that flies through the trees.

Holden hypnotizes Hobart. He learns that the only way he can save himself is to return the parchment to the one who passed it. Hobart thinks Holden is trying to pass him his parchment and jumps out a window to his death.

It is nearing ten P.M., the time Holden is supposed to die. Holden has finally been convinced of the existence of the underworld. He discovers Karswell has kidnapped Joanna and they are on a train to Southampton. Holden enters their compartment. The nervous Karswell makes sure Holden doesn't pass on the parchment. But when the police enter, Holden slips the parchment into Karswell's coat. Karswell picks it up and immediately knows he is the one in danger. The parchment blows from the train and the desperate Karswell chases after it. Far down the tracks it burns. The demon emerges from the woods at ten P.M. and tears Karswell apart. The police think he has been run over by a train and burned.

Night of the Demon

It has a British setting, a laid-back, somewhat stuffy (educated) hero, an intellectual, diabolical villain, a daffy mother and other out-of-the-ordinary characters, and a mixture of wit and suspense; the hero ventures into a den of strangers and feels paranoia, the suddenly nervous hero must solve a mystery and track down the villain before he is killed himself, the hero and heroine stop squabbling and join forces, a train becomes a setting for intrigue. That all these elements found in *Night of the Demon* were characteristic of early Alfred Hitchcock films is not unexpected. What's surprising is that critics have never seen the parallels. Charles Bennett, the original scriptwriter on *Night of the Demon,* wrote the story and/or screenplay for such Hitchcock classics as *Blackmail* (1929), *The Man Who Knew Too Much* (1934), *The 39 Steps* (1935), *The Secret Agent* (1936), *Sabotage* (1936), *Young and Innocent* (1937), and *Foreign Correspondent* (1940).

I sent Bennett a copy of the first volume of *Cult Movies,* and he wrote me a letter, from which I excerpt:

> Only one thing upsets me . . . gave me desperate nights of sleeplessness, painful days of reflection, agonies with regard to where I must have missed the boat. . . . You omitted *Night of the Demon*—renamed by Columbia idiots *Curse of the Demon* because Columbia (the great minds) feared that if they used the word *Night* the movie would be confused with the Elizabeth Taylor–Richard Burton movie *The Night of the Iguana* (1964)!!!!
>
> Actually the history of this movie was a sad one. I bought the rights to Montague James' story, "Casting the Runes," and wrote a screenplay called "The Bewitched." It engendered a great deal of excitement out here in Hollywood. Dick Powell, Robert Taylor, and others wanted to play the lead. But time rolled on . . . not as long as I might have waited. . . . and I was in England directing a TV series (ghastly) . . . On the very day that I was leaving . . . Mr. Hal E. Chester turned up and asked me to sign a little letter granting him the rights for a certain amount of money for six months, if he could set it up. Very tired and on the way to the plane, I signed the Goddam thing . . . but as soon as I arrived back in Hollywood I was informed that RKO (Bill Dozier in charge) had okayed the purchase of my script with me as my own director. Too late. Hal Chester held that wretched little piece of paper in England and I hadn't even received a penny in advance.
>
> Unable to do a damn thing, I had to sit by while Chester made the biggest balls up of a good script that I have ever seen . . . even rewriting . . . but somehow the movie, perhaps because the fundamentals of my screenplay couldn't be entirely wiped out, succeeded. To add insult to injury I frequently get letters, even now, from cult-type organizations, asking me to write something about *Night of the Demon* because it is still loved in peculiar areas.
>
> Not that any of this matters, but I am still galled by the fact that, due to my own stupidity and my desire not to miss my plane back home, I was sort of hustled into giving an okay which thereby robbed me of the big chance to direct what I

As a roaring train whizzes past, Karswell looks up and spots a demon from hell descending on him. Was the inclusion of the physically imposing demon, instead of leaving it to the viewer's imagination, a good idea? Director Tourneur and screenwriter Bennett thought not.

believe could have been the historical movie of my life. Oh, well! These things happen. And my script must have had more than something because even after Mr. Chester's mangling, it is still, in certain circles, a *Cult* movie.

Night of the Demon/Curse of the Demon certainly deserves its cult following. It is the best horror movie of the science fiction–dominated fifties, the most intriguing film ever made with a witchcraft theme, and the most intelligent, visually impressive entry to the genre since director Jacques Tourneur, followed by Mark Robson and Robert Wise, made that classic series of B horror films at RKO for producer Val Lewton in the early forties. Although producer Hal Chester (who gave himself coscreenwriter credit) insensitively rewrote Bennett's script, several times according to Tourneur, it somehow retained the grace and literate quality, as well as the sinister feel and elements of mystery and *suspense* (as opposed to *shock*) that distinguished Bennett's Hitchcock scripts. (Moreover, Chester couldn't entirely wipe out the spirit of the M. R. James source that was present in Bennett's adaptation.) If the picture falters in spots it's not so much that the dialogue lapses into triteness as because the low budget prevented reshooting awkward moments (i.e., on occasion there are jarring jump cuts). The story itself is powerful, great spooky fun, and well constructed, despite Bennett's contention that some of his scenes that fleshed out the characters and provided essential motivation for their actions were eliminated. (Also unfortunate is that the print

which most often plays in America is minus thirteen minutes of the original, including, I believe, the extremely effective scene in which Holden visits the satanist farmers and hallucinates.)

What really compensated for the excessive alteration of Bennett's screenplay is that Jacques Tourneur was hired to direct. (Of course, this was no consolation to Bennett, who yearned to direct himself.*) The material was perfectly suited for this exceptional director of Lewton's first three horror gems: *Cat People* (1942), *I Walked With a Zombie* (1942), and *The Leopard Man* (1943). Where he had once convinced viewers that ancient curses (*Cat People*), voodoo spells (*I Walked With a Zombie*), and fate/doom signs (*The Leopard Man*) shouldn't be too easily discounted, even in a Christian world, now he had them open their minds to the powers of witchcraft. Once again everyday (working) men and women are thrust into a strange environment, where things transpire that are beyond their comprehension. Again we venture into the shadowy Tourneur-Lewton world, where light and darkness, good and evil, science and magic, and fate and free will battle continuously. Here characters are controlled less by reason than by their subconscious: psychologist Holden had his predecessor in Tom Conway's psychiatrist in *Cat People*, released when psychiatry (as well as hypnotism) was taboo in

*Bennett writes me: "Tourneur was a wonderful person. I would never blame him for what happened to the film. I blame only Hal Chester. Never Jacques. He did the best he could with what he was told to shoot."

Audiences jump when two little boys in evil masks leap out at Holden during Karswell's annual magic party.

the cinema. As in the Lewton films, there is the theme of dehumanization (physical appearance/mental state). In *Cat People* Simone Simon, who everyone thinks insane, turns into a cat—because unlike "real" women she can't have sexual intercourse; in *I Walked With a Zombie*, Christina Gordan, who some think insane, becomes, in effect, one of the walking dead—her brain no longer functions; in *The Leopard Man* James Bell, who has gone insane, dons leopard skin and fangs and satisfies his bloodthirsty, sexually motivated urges. In *Night of the Demon* Karswell (menacingly played by Niall MacGinnis) doesn't actually lose his mind but rather becomes temporarily deranged. When things go awry he loses the ability to rationally determine his life's course. In Tourneur-Lewton, people become dehumanized when they lose their free will. Karswell becomes victim of his own conceit, power lust, and paranoia (a sensation all diabolists must feel). As in the Lewton films, an individual isn't just presented as insane—we are made aware of the process involved in his losing touch with reality. Karswell realizes that he is tempting fate by consorting with the devil, and tries to *retain his humanity* by doing such generous things as holding parties for orphan children and treating them to a magic show. But we see he has lost his battle—he is even mean to his mother.

Holden is skeptical during Mr. Meek's seance. Joanna (standing), Mrs. Meek and Mrs. Karswell (R) watch the man go into a bizarre trance.

At this time, Hammer Studios was initiating its series of updated horror classics. The trend was for strong violence and gore (as well as strong sex). But Tourneur went back to his forties roots, preferring to frighten his viewers through such fundamental fears as darkness, sudden sounds, and wild animals. (For Tourneur, "jazzing it up" or becoming gimmicky meant including the bizarre, unnerving séance.) No horror director has ever been able to create an atmosphere so beautiful, yet so ominous. Tourneur always loved having his imperiled hero and heroines walk alone at night through trees, shrubbery, grass: in *Cat People* Jane Randolph is followed through a park; in *I Walked With a Zombie* Frances Dee follows a moonlit island trail; in *The Leopard Man* a young girl is trapped in a cemetery. *Night of the Demon* is no exception. Following a terrifying fight with Karswell's housecat—which had turned into an enormous panther—Holden walks through the forest by Karswell's house. The forest had seemed almost comforting moments before, but now it's eerie. It's as if the limbs of the trees are about to reach out and grab Holden. The road to Karswell's estate is also eerie—it is lined with shrubs so close together that one can't help feeling trapped. The sky, too, is threatening—it seems to be looking down on Holden. The darkness is more noticeable. Footprints from some large, invisible creature form in the soil. A smoke ball flies through the sky. No wonder Holden runs. He falls, the smoke ball disappears. What a frightening scene, yet nothing has really happened. Holden will try to chalk it all up to his imagination; and viewers are left to decide if everything was indeed imagined by him.

Also visually striking and quite creepy is the windstorm scene where Karswell tries to prove to Holden that he has the ability to perform witchcraft. (A weird atmosphere has already been created by villain Karswell in clown makeup, and kids running around in scary masks.) In *The Celluloid Muse* (Angus and Robertson, 1969) Tourneur told interviewers Charles Higham and Joel Greenberg:

> I had a fight over the staging of the storm scene. We had to rent twelve aerial engines from World War I. We were on an exterior location, and these were great long trees, and if we'd had half a storm it would have been inadequate. We had truckloads and truckloads of dead leaves, and we set the radial engines whirling—cost a fortune, no one would talk to me. They said, "We'll do it with generators, electric machines," and I said, "No, it's got to be a hell of a storm, it's got to blow over the prams and the nurses in the garden, and all the chairs." So we had all these huge engines going: there was so much noise you couldn't hear anything.

It's such an amazing storm, Karswell apologizes to Holden for miscalculating his power.

Val Lewton was known for not showing brutal acts or proof of the supernatural. He left much to the viewer's imagination. When Tourneur directed *Night of the Demon,* he wanted viewers to argue over whether there truly are supernatural occurrences in the picture. When (much to both Tourneur's and Bennett's chagrin) producer Chester inserted scenes in which the gigantic, fiery demon flies out of the woods and destroys Harrington and Karswell, he of course changed the picture. There has been enormous controversy about the inclusion of the demon, with critics almost invaria-

As in many Hitchcock films, the suspense builds on a train. Holden wants to place the parchment on Karswell (who has kidnapped and hypnotized Joanna), but he knows what Holden is up to.

bly coming out against it in favor of subtlety. Bennett believes "its presence took a major movie down to the level of cheap horror crap." (Chester added the monster to bring in the kiddie crowd—the demon was the highlight of the promotion campaign—which is odd, since the picture was given an X rating in Britain, so only those sixteen and older could see it.) In the best horror movie book, *An Illustrated History of the Horror Film* (Capricorn, 1968), Carlos Clarens complains about the presence of the demon—yet it is the demon that graces the book's cover. So, I believe most critics dislike the demon for no other reason than they know it was studio-imposed. Except for a shot where the demon looks like King Kong in drag, riding an invisible bicycle, I think the demon is terrific. I am in favor of this vile creature as big as a house and ugly as sin, that rips Karswell to shreds with its claws and tosses him to the ground in disdain. Val Lewton's theory was to not show what takes place in the dark because it can never be more terrifying than what the viewer can imagine. But this demon is more terrifying than anything imaginable. It's the scariest monster in film history as far as I'm concerned (no matter that others think it ludicrous). As to the complaint that the demon's presence reveals too much, I can't buy it. This demon is but one creature from the underworld, just one small part of the world of diabolism.

Tourneur was never great with actors—pictorial quality and the poetic fluidity of his images is what he's known for—but *Night of the Demon* does contain some fine performances, particularly MacGinnis's. I'm glad that the beautiful Peggy Cummins, so outstanding in *Gun Crazy* (1949), got to be in at least one more top-grade film. *Night of the Demon* also was the last really good starring film for Dana Andrews, who gives a stalwart portrayal. Tourneur had to convince him to come to England to play the part. The pair, who worked together in *Canyon Passage* in 1946, would make another film together in 1958. *The Fearmakers* was not a horror movie, but interestingly the plot bears striking similarity to *Night of the Demon*. A returning war vet discovers that communists have infiltrated his advertising agency: it's another witch hunt story!

Night of the Demon is an exceptional, adult horror film. For that we can point to several remarkable twosomes: Bennett and Hitchcock; Tourneur and Lewton; Andrews and Cummins; and last but not least, Karswell and his controversial demon.

Nightmare Alley

1947 20th Century-Fox
Director: Edmund Goulding
Producer: George Jessel
Screenplay: Jules Furthman
From the novel by
William Lindsay Gresham

Cinematography: Lee Garmes
Music: Cyril J. Mockridge
Editor: Barbara McLean
Running time: 111 minutes

Cast: Tyrone Power (Stan Carlisle), Joan Blondell (Zeena), Coleen Gray (Molly), Helen Walker (Lilith Ritter), Taylor Holmes (Ezra Grindle), Mike Mazurki (Bruno), Ian Keith (Pete), Julia Dean (Addie Peabody), James Falvin (Hoatley), Roy Roberts (carnival owner)

Synopsis: Young, handsome Stan Carlisle loves the excitement of working in a carnival. He enjoys feeling superior to "the yokels" who pay to see the acts. He is even fascinated by the lowest act in the carnival, the geek who bites the heads off live chickens just for a bottle a day and a place to sleep. "How can anyone get so low?" he asks.

Stan passes out cards for Zeena, who does a mind-reading act. Zeena used to be in the nightclub circuit, but her partner Pete has turned into a hopeless drunk. Pretty Molly, "the Electric Girl," tells Stan that Zeena and Pete used to work a remarkable blindfold code that made them unique in the field. Stan pumps information from Pete by giving him liquor. Pete tells Stan that it's easy to hook people by giving general information that they will assume applies only to them.

Pete dies. Stan had accidentally given him wood alcohol to drink. He tells no one. Stan seduces Zeena. She teaches him the blindfold code and they start performing it at the carnival. Stan gives code words from the audience, and the blindfolded Zeena picks up his cues and answers startled people's questions. Molly watches with delight.

A sheriff comes to the carnival and threatens to close it down. Stan talks to him, making generalizations which the sheriff thinks apply only to him. The soothed sheriff goes home. Stan is proud of himself. He seduces Molly, telling her that he doesn't love Zeena but is only interested in her because of the code.

Finding out about Stan's infidelity, Zeena and Bruno, Molly's strongman friend, force Molly and Stan to get married. Molly offers to do the act with him. "The Great Stanton" soon is the headline act in an exclusive Chicago nightclub. Stan goes in cahoots with a coldhearted consulting psychologist named Lilith Ritter. She provides information on her rich clients. One client, Mrs. Peabody, is so comforted when Stan says her dead daughter is alive in the spirit world that she offers to build him a temple. Her rich friend Ezra Grindle tries to expose Stan as a hoax. But using information provided by Lilith about the lost love of his youth, Dorey, Stan convinces Grindle he is a true mystic. Grindle gives Stan $150,000 and promises to build him a tabernacle if he can make Dorey appear for him. Stan coaxes Molly into helping him pull off a hoax. She is worried about Stan. He suffers nervous, guilt-caused fits, and he is beginning to believe he has godlike qualities.

At night in his garden, Ezra waits with Stan for Dorey's appearance. When Ezra sees a woman he thinks to be Dorey at the far end of the garden, he begs for God's forgiveness and for a second chance with Dorey. Molly becomes so upset that she reveals the hoax. Stan knocks down Ezra and he and Molly flee. Stan goes to Lilith to collect $150,000. She only gives him $150 and says she will tell the police he killed Pete. Stan leaves without his money. He sadly says good-bye to Molly, realizing he loves her and she'll be better off without him. He becomes an alcoholic bum, and a fugitive.

Stan asks McGraw, a carnival owner, for a job. He becomes the geek. That night he has a drunken, crazy fit like the geek at the old carnival used to have. Molly, who has also taken a job with the carnival, soothes him. She says she'll look after him.

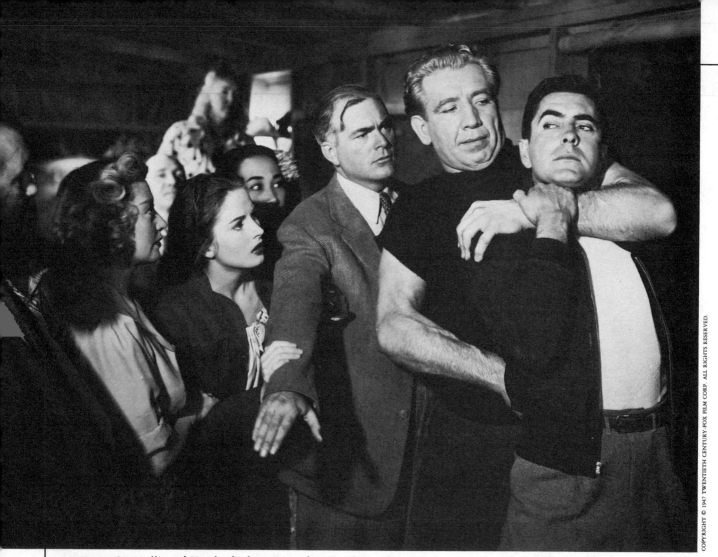

As Zeena (L), Molly, and Hoatley look on, Bruno lets Stan know that since he slept with Molly he'd better marry her.

The year 1947 was a peculiar year for movies. Particularly for lead actors. James Mason in *Odd Man Out,* Robert Mitchum in *Out of the Past,* Lawrence Tierney in *Born to Kill,* Henry Fonda in *The Fugitive,* and Gregory Peck in *Duel in the Sun* all lay dead or dying at the end of films. Charlie Chaplin, of all people, played a murderer bound for the gallows in *Monsieur Verdoux.* And romantic idol Tyrone Power played a geek.

Actually, Power's Stan Carlisle, his memorable character in *Nightmare Alley,* the grimmest of forties melodramas, is a geek for only one day, taking up but a few minutes of screen time. We never even see him perform his repugnant carnival act, in which he bites the heads off live chickens and probably performs unmentionable sidelights. But Carlisle's role in the rest of the film—he is an opportunistic, woman-using, blasphemous cad—was already enough to startle and repulse many of Power's fans. Power, arguably Hollywood's most handsome star, had become 20th's most popular actor by playing heroes not heels. In such image-making films as *The Black Swan* (1942), *The Mark of Zorro* (1940), and even *Jesse James* (1939), in which he was more a Robin Hood figure than an outlaw, he'd been the justice-seeking champion of the common people. But here he was trying to con them, take their money, and make fools of them. When Power had romanced lovely Linda Darnell in numerous films, he had been a touch brash, but he'd also been sincere, tender, and

faithful—the ideal dream lover for Power's female admirers. But as Stan Carlisle, charmer with a Cheshire grin, he seduces every woman who can help him get ahead in the world, and tosses them aside once he can no longer exploit them. The glorious swashbuckler had become a cheap, two-timing swindler. Always quite serious about his acting, Power had been disappointed in the previous roles given him at 20th, so he persuaded studio head Darryl F. Zanuck to give him the chance to play the despicable Stan Carlisle, hoping that such a role would open up new avenues for him. Unfortunately, perhaps Power's best film (it was his personal favorite) became one of his few flops at the box office.

In the 1940s, when *film noir* came into vogue and the darker frame became a haven for evil, corruptive forces, melodramas dropped the comical mix they'd had in the past and became blatantly pessimistic. But no picture of the era projected such a corrosive atmosphere as *Nightmare Alley.* Such nastiness and cynicism wouldn't appear elsewhere until Billy Wilder's *Sunset Boulevard* (1950) and *The Big Carnival* (1951). And such sleaziness wouldn't appear in another A picture for more than twenty years. For it's just as sleazy in the haunts of the successful and superrich as it is around carnival sideshows and in flea-infested hotel rooms. The miserable world we see mirrors the country's postwar malaise. The sorry people in this world are deeply depressed; lonely (Zeena lost her man, Mrs. Peabody her daughter, Ezra Grin-

dle his lover, Carlisle his dog Chip); devoid of spirit; alcoholic; so desperate for entertainment that they'll pay to see carnival freaks and mind readers; has-beens or never-will-bes; poor with no hope of getting money or rich with no good use for the money; jealous and suspicious of their neighbors; and convinced that they've gotten a rotten deal in life. They're all vulnerable to any smooth-talking Pied Piper who offers them salvation. It's a sad world, where anyone (even Carlisle) who opens up to another person will invariably be taken advantage of and deprived of whatever is meaningful to him (money, pride, love). It's an awful world, where even the person who seems to be the most insensitive (Carlisle) meets and is crushed by someone who is worse (Lilith).

In *Time* (November 3, 1947) James Agee wrote:

> *Nightmare Alley* would be unbearably brutal for general audiences if it were played for all the humor, cynicism and malign social observation that are implicit in it. It would be unbearably mawkish if it were played too solemnly. Scripter Jules Furthman and director Edmund Goulding have steered a middle course, now and then crudely but on the whole with tact, skill and power. They have seldom forgotten that the original novel they were adapting is essentially intelligent trash; and they have never forgotten that on the screen pretty exciting things can be made of trash.

Nightmare Alley has been criticized in various quarters for veering away from the most shocking (tasteless) aspects of William Lindsay Gresham's no-holds-barred novel, sweetening the story, and opting for a "Hollywood ending," in which Molly's love (her face in the last scene has a heavenly glow) saves Carlisle's soul. Seymour Peck of *PM* complained, "Censorship being what it is, Fox couldn't have projected the full terror of Gresham's book. They are even, you might say, afraid to try." But considering that *Nightmare Alley* was made way back in 1947, by a major studio, as an A picture to star its top romantic lead, it's really quite amazing how daring it is. How many other pictures of the time had geeks, dipsomaniacs, premarital sex in which the woman *doesn't* become pregnant (there's a quick scene of Carlisle dressing after making love to Molly), and discussion of God?

The powerful script by Jules Furthman mixes the rise-and-fall promise of the same year's John Garfield boxing film, *Body and Soul* (1947), and thirties gangster movies, with the still-controversial alcoholism premise of *The Lost Weekend* (1945). (Plus it delves into psychiatry, then a gimmicky, controversial film subject.) Furthman, one of Hollywood's most celebrated screenwriters, seems also to have borrowed from Josef von Sternberg's *Blonde Venus* (1932), which he scripted. In that film, Marlene Dietrich, unfairly tossed out of her home by husband Herbert Marshall, degenerates from top nightclub performer to cheapest whore. She thinks her drop into purgatory is deserved—just as Carlisle thinks he is meant to be a geek. She, like Power's character, loses everything including her dignity. *Blonde Venus* has a wonderful ("Hollywood") ending in which Marshall takes Dietrich back— just as Molly welcomes Carlisle into her arms. Significantly, Dietrich is shown to be a loving wife and a loving mother to cute Dickie Moore at the beginning of *Blonde Venus,* someone who only turns to a sinful life through an unfortunate set of circumstances. In other rise-and-fall films as well, the formula calls for the characters who will end up leading an

(T) Molly gives clues to mind reader "The Great Stanton." Shady psychologist Lilith is the cool customer with the cigarette; to her left are her clients Ezra Grindle and Addie Peabody—soon to be Stan's victims.

(B) Stan visits Lilith's office, lit in classic film noir style, and they begin an unscrupulous alliance. Stan is a louse; she is a viper.

immoral life to be shown sypathetically at the beginning. *Nightmare Alley* may compromise in some instances, but Furthman was brave in one way in particular: from the beginning Stan is a louse. That he spent his youth in an orphanage (where he was beaten black and blue) and a reform school, and that he once had a dog named Chip, does nothing to make us think kindly of him. He gives alcoholic Pete a bottle so he can pump him for information (accidentally killing him in the process); seduces Zeena so he can learn her mind-reading code and then two-times her; seduces naïve Molly with no intention of marrying her. The nicest thing he does is bring Molly a Coke. Carlisle thinks of the people who come to the carnival as "yokels," chumps he can use as stepping stones (he also sees Pete, Zeena, Molly, Mrs. Peabody, and Ezra Grindle in this way) on his rise to "the top of the world." He predates Andy Griffith's folksy hoodwinker who wins over our nation in *A Face in the Crowd* (1957)—only no one rescues Griffith from his descent into oblivion. Like Griffith, Carlisle comes to believe in his superiority and, mistakenly, his greatness (justifying in his own mind his defrauding the public); and in his immortality. Because he attempts to be a god, his fall brings him to the low point in human existence.

It is to Power's credit as an actor that when he plays the

Stan travels down the steep road to purgatory.

scene in which Carlisle proves that he truly loves Molly—his emotional good-bye to her at the train station, when he gives her all his money and kiss after heartfelt kiss—Carlisle is instantly so likable and sincere that we forgive him his past trespasses. It's important that we have this reaction or we'd not be willing to accept Carlisle's being saved from a life of geekdom a few minutes later. Power's performance is outstanding as he moves from gum-chewing, soda-drinking, T-shirted hot shot to cigarette-smoking, boozing, sharply-dressed conniver, to mad-eyed, drunken geek. It was a rare role for Power in that it is cerebral rather than physical. Gone is the boyishness that marked his early films. Instead we find a hardened cynical world-beater (paying back the world for his horrible upbringing). I can't imagine the younger Power having played such a chancy, bitter role. Or the fellow who was Zorro playing that hotel room scene in which newlyweds Carlisle and Molly worry about their future. When Molly offers to do Zeena's mind-reading code with him, Carlisle is suddenly ecstatic, and poor Molly is relieved he no longer seems sorry about their shotgun wedding. In my favorite moment in the film, Carlisle's head turns away from Molly and his eyes look into the bright future; he smiles victoriously like a used car dealer who just thought of a surefire way to sell a lemon, and says, "I'm only sorry that I didn't think of it earlier." At this moment, Power makes you shiver.

Nightmare Alley is filled with other outstanding performances, from leads Joan Blondell (always underrated), Coleen Gray (a cross between Linda Darnell and Terry Moore, and one of my favorite minor stars), and particularly Helen Walker, whose final scene is dynamic (who would have expected such a vile, cold-blooded characterization from her?), to the supporting performers Taylor Holmes, Julia Dean (the kindly, demented old lady in 1944's *Curse of the Cat People*), and Ian Keith, who does a turn that reminds us he was a Shakespearean actor. The solid acting was to be suspected considering that Edmund Goulding was at the helm. Fine performances had been the hallmark of this often-overlooked director's career, which included such films as *Grand Hotel* (1932), *Dark Victory* (1939), *The Old Maid* (1939), *The Great*

Lie (1941), *The Constant Nymph* (1943), *Claudia* (1943), and *The Razor's Edge* (1946), in which Power played a true mystic. But what is surprising about *Nightmare Alley* is how Goulding, working closely with cameraman Lee Garmes, turned the picture into an exercise in style. The noir photography is stunning, turning what is essentially a strong drama into a frightening horror film. All the sets, including the carnival and Grindle's cathedrallike garden are eerie and claustrophobic. Even Lilith's office has patterned shadows on the wall, making it just as uninviting as one of the hotel rooms where single-source lighting is employed. I was surprised to read that an enormous carnival was set up on ten acres of ground, because the way the film is shot made me suspect that all outdoor scenes were filmed on a huge soundstage. As the film's title would suggest, those scenes at the carnival have a surreal, nightmarish quality—it seems as if a character would have as much difficulty leaving the midway as he would escaping the hall of mirrors. It seems as if there are no exits—which is why I assumed the carnival tents were set up indoors. The carnival set seems even smaller, even more claustrophobic, because of the way the camera is employed. At one point, when Carlisle is following Pete around at night, the mobile camera winds its way around the curtain or side bar of a carnival platform, and twists downward around some stairs to find the actors behind the platform, as if it were a cobra slithering its way down a tree. Very little space is used. Interestingly, Goulding includes many shots of Carlisle's back. He is either sneaking away (i.e., from suspicion in Pete's death) or is in the midst of plotting some sneaky scam. We can't trust him. But these repeated shots also build up our realization that he is vulnerable. More important, they give us the impression that Carlisle (who when seated looks as if he could be praying) is, in his subconscious, suffering from guilt, self-hatred, and embarrassment. These are feelings he thinks he must hide. Carlisle would like to be tough and amoral—it would make things so much easier—but, alas, he has a conscience.

Mention should be made of how well Goulding uses music. In *Kings of the Bs* (Dutton, 1975), Clive T. Miller writes:

> Perhaps most exciting of all is Cyril Mockridge's outstanding but unobtrusive music score, full of activity and eerie discomfort, with occasional undertones of terror. The music is used sparingly, at strategic points, and then as much ironically as dramatically. Notice the adept intimations of Stan's doom (mixed with the terrifying echo of the geek's screams); the ironic romanticism [violins play] when Stan resorts to the final words for getting Molly to go along with the Grindle ruse, the attestation of his love for her and utter reliance upon her; the drama and high irony when Grindle views the apparition and proclaims his own objectiveness (and the organ, playing beneath the words, swells).

Miller calls *Nightmare Alley* the "quintessential B movie spoiled by an A production." However, I believe that its continuing popularity is due to its uneasy mixture of A production values and B plot elements. And surely, this film wasn't spoiled. It truly stands out among Hollywood melodramas. It's too bad *Nightmare Alley* didn't do better with fans; then Tyrone Power might have tried something similar to *Detour* (1946) or some other sleazy B film, instead of returning quickly to respectability after only one gallant attempt to shake his hero image.

The Parallax View

1974 Paramount
Director: Alan Pakula
Producer: Alan Pakula
Screenplay: David Giler and Lorenzo Semple, Jr.
From the novel by Loren Singer
Cinematographer: Gordon Willis
Music: Michael Small
Editor: John W. Wheeler
Running time: 102 minutes

Cast: Warren Beatty (Joseph Frady), Hume Cronyn (Rintels), Paula Prentiss (Lee Carter), William Daniels (Austin Tucker), Kelly Thorsden (L.D.), Earl Hindman (Red), Kenneth Mars (former F.B.I. agent), Walter McGinn (Parallax Corporation representative), Jim Davis (Senator Hammond), Bill Joyce (Senator Carroll), Bill McKinney (assassin), William Jordan (Tucker's aide), Stacy Keach, Sr., and Ford Rainey (commission spokesmen)

Synopsis: Senator Carroll is assassinated at a luncheon in the Seattle Space Needle. Thomas Richard Lindern, a waiter, is spotted holding a gun. He is chased, and plummets to his death. A second waiter with a gun leaves unnoticed. A commission holds months of investigations and concludes Lindern acted alone.

Three years pass. Newscaster Lee Carter visits her former boyfriend, Joe Frady, an Oregon reporter. She says that her life is in danger, that six others at the luncheon have died mysteriously. Frady thinks she's being paranoid. Soon after, Lee is dead. The autopsy says she deliberately killed herself but Frady knows differently. Although his editor Bill Rintels always complains he's trying to create news rather than reporting it, Frady decides to pursue his story.

Frady goes to a small fishing village where one of the witnesses to Carroll's assassination was drowned. A rough deputy (Red) tries to beat him up, but Frady wins the fight. The sheriff (L.D.) is much friendlier to him. He takes Frady to where dead witness Alan Bridges met his fate. A dam sluice had opened and tons of water poured into the area in which Bridges fished. The sheriff pulls a gun on Frady just as a siren announces the sluice is opening again. Frady and the sheriff struggle and are swept away by the water. The sheriff drowns. Frady searches the sheriff's apartment. He discovers test applications to the Parallax Corporation. Frady escapes from the deputy in a wild car chase.

Rintels refuses to believe Frady is on to anything. Frady takes the application test to a psychology lab. He allows a former murderer to answer the questions. Using an alias, he applies to Parallax.

Frady meets Austin Tucker, a former Carroll aide. He asks Frady if he recognizes a second waiter in a photo of Carroll's luncheon. Frady doesn't. The boat they are on explodes. Tucker and his aide are killed.

Using his alias, Frady checks into a fleabag hotel. Parallax agent Jack Younger contacts him and says his aggressiveness (as shown in his test answers) makes him valuable for certain corporations. So "Richard Parton" becomes part of the organization. In the Parallax building, Frady spots the waiter from Tucker's photo. He follows him to the airport and onto a plane. But the assassin only checked in a suitcase that contains a bomb. Frady secretly delivers a message to a stewardess. The plane, which carries a prominent senator, returns to L.A. When everyone is off, it blows up.

Rintels listens to a secret tape of Younger speaking to Frady. The deli delivery boy is Parallax's assassin. Rintels is poisoned, the tape erased. Frady spots the assassin and follows him into the hallways above a convention hall. Senator Hammond is below preparing for the night's speech. Frady believes the assassin will try to kill Hammond with a rifle that lies there. But the assassin kills Hammond with a second rifle. People look up and spot Frady, near the unused rifle. They think he did it, Frady has been trapped. He runs. The assassin guns him down. Several months later, a commission reports that Frady had blamed Hammond for killing Carroll and had sought revenge. Frady was the lone assassin.

The first time we spot Joe Frady he is almost hidden in a crowd that gathers for Senator Carroll's arrival at the base of Seattle's Space Needle. Is he trying to be inconspicuous? The senator "really looks terrific," proclaims newscaster Lee Carter, who, unable to keep her objectivity, adds "he's the ideal father, husband, and leader." How Carroll contrasts with Frady: Carroll, with his beautiful wife by his side and swooning admirers around him, is confident, well dressed, well groomed, gregarious; Frady is alone (looking as if he has no friends in the world; certainly no wife), sloppy, withdrawn. A guard stops Frady from following Carroll up the elevator because he hasn't press credentials; Lee tells the guard she doesn't know him. We realize an attempt will be made on Carroll's life. We think back to all the social misfits who have been arrested for attempts (many successful) on politicians' lives; and our first suspect for potential assassin of Carroll becomes Frady—even though he's being played by movie hero Warren Beatty. But in *The Parallax View*—a term referring to the slight difference between the image seen through the viewfinder of a nonreflex camera and the image as seen through the picture-taking lens—the point driven home is that things aren't what they seem. This makes us paranoid. In fact, Frady is not out to kill Carroll, just write a story about him. Yet Carroll is killed. While we know the armed assassin played by Bill McKinney is there to make sure the murder occurs (he is the "second gun"), we never find out if it is he or Thomas Richard Lindern, the waiter with the gun everyone notices—the film's Lee Harvey Oswald—who actually commits the act; or if Lindern was in on the crime, a fall guy among the conspirators, or an innocent man "set up" to take the rap, posthumously. And who are those men who we too quickly

Lee tells Frady that those people who saw Senator Carroll assassinated have been dropping off like flies. He tells her she is paranoid when she insists her life is in danger. Soon after, she is dead.

assume to be cops or Secret Service agents, who chase Lindern across the roof and precipitate his fatal fall? We know very little—just that the investigating commission is wrong in ruling that Carroll's death was the work of a lone assassin, Lindern. And this makes us even more nervous.

Alan Pakula's *The Parallax View* falls into that suspense-spy-horror subgenre that caters to us paranoids who are sure there are active conspiracies (in and out of government) geared to undermine the democratic political process and root out (ruin, set up, dispose of) various individuals (business competitors, political opposition, charismatic leaders, those who know too much). Other such "paranoia" films with political overtones include *Invasion of the Body Snatchers* (1956 and 1978), *The Manchurian Candidate* (1962), Costa-Gavras's *Z* (1969) and *Missing* (1982), *Executive Action* (1973), the documentary *The Second Gun* (1973), *Chinatown* (1974), *The Conversation* (1974), *Three Days of the Condor* (1975), Pakula's *All the President's Men* (1976), *Winter Kills* (1979), and *Blow Out* (1981). *Parallax* received extremely mixed reviews when it was released—some critics thought it exploited the assassination wave hysteria and Watergate climate; but through the years it has been the one film that comes up constantly during conversations in which people theorize about the John Kennedy assassination (even though *Executive Action* deals specifically with that event). No film more believably details (it all seems so simple) how a conspiratorial network can pull off political assassinations, get away scot-free, and leave a fall guy—the proverbial social misfit—to take the rap.

For those of us who steadfastly believe there was a conspiracy behind JFK's murder—who are still suspicious of alleged ties between Oswald and the CIA and Navy Intelligence, and between Jack Ruby and the FBI and Dallas police; about the Oswald lookalike who made himself visible passing out left-wing literature earlier in the month; about how Kennedy's motorcade was conveniently rerouted past the book depository where Oswald worked; about communications malfunctions between Kennedy's men in Dallas and Washington on the day in question; about how quickly the media was informed that Oswald was the lone assassin; about how Ruby was able to walk past Dallas police and, on national television, murder Oswald before he could testify; about how Ruby died before his own trial; about how blowups of photos taken of the infamous grassy knoll indicate there were men with pointed rifles; about how recordings dispute the claims of "experts" as to the number of shots fired; about how the Zapruder film clearly shows Kennedy's head being knocked forward *and* backward, as if bullets came from two directions; about how an inordinate number of witnesses "died" in subsequent years; about why there has been no reopening of the case; etc., etc.—*The Parallax View* is our blueprint for conspiratorial machinery. Nothing in the film seems farfetched. We accept that a business which has so much power that it is protected from government scrutiny and prosecution, and which has unlimited finances, manpower, and technical and psychological expertise, can accomplish (get away with) anything. We accept that such an agency would assassinate politicians of divergent political philosophies just to disrupt the country's social fabric. (After all, assassination targets have been a mixed political bag; from Malcolm X to George Lincoln Rockwell; from Martin Luther King to George Wallace.) We believe such an agency would incorporate sophisticated testing methods for recruiting purposes—as many of our corporations already do. We see that even the cleverest, most

At the site where one witness supposedly drowned, the friendly sheriff proves to be a murderer. Frady uses his fishing line to knock a gun from his hand.

Parallax agent Jack Younger (a fine low-key performance by the late William McGinn) makes himself at home in Frady's hotel room. Frady is using an alias in order to infiltrate Parallax.

resourceful *individual,* who can escape repeatedly (from the sheriff, the deputy, Tucker's booby-trapped boat, the plane with the bomb) will get it in the end if he puts up a challenge, or simply gets in the agency's way. In this world, unlike that of *All the President's Men,* the individual cannot triumph; the truth will not win out: at the end, a commission gives an erroneous report on how Frady killed Carroll, while it sits in front of a scales-of-justice "truth" symbol. *The Parallax View* is a strangely satisfying film because it agrees that our paranoia is well founded.

If you want to make a picture about "paranoia," this is the one to study. In *The Parallax View,* a character can just as easily be killed when in a crowd as when alone; in the air (a plane), on land, on the ocean; in a pastoral or urban setting; on the west or east coast (the Hammond building, I believe, is in Atlanta); by gunshot, explosion, drug overdose, drowning, or being knocked from a roof. Those who kill may offer a friendly hand (the sheriff, Jack Younger); or provide food and drink (the waiter, the sheriff who gives the appreciative Frady a sandwich before trying to kill him, the deli delivery man). Or may refuse to be seen ("I wouldn't step out that door," Younger suggests calmly). Those being killed don't even know why they're being targeted—the assassins' own better-safe-than-sorry paranoia forces them to cover up assassins with murders of harmless witnesses. Because they know nothing of consequence about the Carroll assassination (although Tucker becomes slightly suspicious of the *second* waiter in his photograph), none of the people they speak to believe they're really in danger—until it's too late. Even friends don't seem to care. Casual acquaintances are not to be trusted, strangers are enemies.

We never get a clear look at anything. Characters are filmed standing behind glass or curtains. We see their reflections in glass and water. They are filmed in long shot so we can't really make them out; or in extreme closeup so we can't really see what's going on around them. We never have the

necessary information to let us relax. Often we will just glimpse parts of bodies (backs, legs, feet, hands); sometimes we won't see anyone at all. Pakula will place his characters in darkness or cover them with shadows, or have them move back and forth between shadows and light so we have no clue for deciding whether they are good people or evil people. Interestingly, in a scene in "Richard Parton's" fleabag-hotel room, the shadow covers hero Frady and the bright light is on Younger's serene face—the reason for our chills. There is an icy sensation to the entire film created by Gordon Willis's slightly off-center camera angles, those shots of people seen through or reflected on glass, shots of empty halls and great chambers, the alien feel to some of the modern buildings, and the hollow sound of voices coming through glass or over microphones. (It's especially creepy seeing Senator Hammond's face while hearing the recording of the speech he's to deliver that night.) Pakula uses sound brilliantly; to build our tension, and jolt us: whispering voices, shouts, rushing water that "drowns out" voices; explosions, gunshots, ringing phones, buzzers, clinking ice, ticking clocks, train whistles, blasting sirens, drumbeats. The chilly music contributes greatly: the tinkling piano, harp, and flute (piccolo?); and most important, the trumpet fanfares that sound like death marches, fading out just before catastrophic events. Then there's silence, the most terrifying sound of all.

And there's always the fear of the unknown—the world Frady travels. Only his newspaper office has a homey atmosphere; the modern skyscrapers lack the warm-human feel, as they are but mammoth black slabs of glass and steel.

Lorenzo Semple, Jr., adapted *The Parallax View* from an extremely confusing, pretty dreadful book by Loren Singer, which bears slight resemblance to the film. (The book is really about the uneasy alliance and rivalry between *two* men earmarked for death.) Pakula and David Giler altered Semple's script, changing (at Warren Beatty's suggestion) the hero from a cop back to the reporter of the novel and making it

Gordon Willis's dramatic lighting patterns effectively build an atmosphere of paranoia. Here Frady, realizing he has been set up as fall guy in Senator Hammond's assassination, finds himself trapped by the real assassin.

clear that the assassination in question is not John F. Kennedy's (as Semple had implied in his version) by adding the opening Carroll assassination sequence. Rather than dealing with facts, Pakula preferred to "do a metaphor, a fictional reality"—a half realistic, half surrealistic "nightmare based on the terrors of our time." In an interview with Andrew C. Bobrow for *The Filmmakers Newsletter,* Pakula stated:

> The film was designed as myth, with archetypal people, characters, and places. In the film, which is full of alienated people wandering around in totally alienated worlds with a seeming absence of continuing relationships, the editor represents certain nineteenth century American humanist values: tradition, rootedness, responsibility, optimistic belief in the perfectability of man and that we live in the best of all possible worlds in the most enlightened society so far created by man—a kind of old-fashioned decency and optimism. In a sense he is an anachronism in the piece.

Hume Cronyn, who plays editor Bill Rintels, is one of several actors who turn in splendid performances in small roles. The always impressive Paula Prentiss (as a woman terrified because she knows she's going to be killed), Walter McGinn (debuting as the shrewd, overly polite and paternal Jack Younger), Kenneth Mars (as a cynical "non-former FBI agent" who drives a children's train in an amusement park), and Bill McKinney (so dominating in a silent role) are unforgettable. Warren Beatty is also quite good in the lead.

Unlike Mal Graham in the book, Frady is not on a hit list from the beginning for having witnessed an assassination. Unlike Graham, Frady doesn't expect to die. He is somewhat like Peter Breck's foolishly motivated reporter in Sam Fuller's *Shock Corridor* (1963), who pretends to be insane so he can investigate a story in a mental hospital. Like Breck, Frady wants to win the Pulitzer prize. Like Breck, he wrongly believes a Pulitzer prize story guarantees his immortality. Breck really goes insane, Frady is killed. A lesson learned? It's easy to see why Beatty was attracted to Frady. He could return to *Mickey One* (1965), about a comic in trouble with the organization, and again play an individual consumed by paranoia, who'll be scared "as long as I live." Beatty also could play one of his many bad-lucked heroes who dies at the end of the film.

The Parallax View has flaws—mostly as the result of Pakula's sacrificing story-clarifying scenes for pacing. I like to believe the information left out builds our paranoia and disorientation. The only thing I really dislike is the obligatory car chase. What other deficiencies it has are more than compensated for by that mesmerizing montage Parallax candidate "Richard Parton" watches—with images of mother, apple pie, the Statue of Liberty, and an accusatory Uncle Sam (Wants You) juxtaposed with images of Hitler, brutality, poverty and superheroes—and a tremendously unnerving visual metaphor: dead Senator Hammond's out-of-control golf cart knocking into tables with red, white, and blue tablecloths.

Phantom of the Paradise

1974 20th Century-Fox release of a Harbor production
Director: Brian De Palma
Producer: Edward Pressman
Screenplay: Brian De Palma
Cinematography: Larry Pizer
Music: Paul Williams
Songs: ''Goodbye, Eddie, Goodbye,'' ''Upholstery,'' and ''Somebody Super Like You'' sung by Harold Oblong, Archie Hahn, and Jeffrey Comaner; ''Faust'' by William Finley; ''Special to Me'' and ''Old Souls'' by Jessica Harper; ''Life at Last'' by Ray Kennedy; ''Faust'' (reprise) and ''The Hell of It'' by Paul Williams
Editor: Paul Hirsch
Production design: Jack Fisk
Set decoration: Sissy Spacek
Running time: 91 minutes

Cast: Paul Williams (Swan), William Finley (Winslow/the Phantom), Jessica Harper (Phoenix), George Memmoli (Philbin), Gerrit Graham (Beef), Jeffrey Comaner, Archie Hahn and Harold Oblong (singing group), Keith Allison (country and western singer)

Synopsis: Winslow Leach is backup pianist for the Juicy Fruits, the nation's number one rock group. But in his spare time he writes serious music. Looking for a new sound to open his Paradise nightclub, evil record producer Swan has his aide Philbin purchase the song he overhears Winslow singing. When Winslow goes to Philbin's studio, he is kicked out. He sneaks into Swan's mansion. There he meets Phoenix, a pretty girl who is trying out as a backup singer. She has been given Winslow's song to sing, but his name isn't on it.

Swan arranges for Winslow to be arrested for heroin possession and sent to Sing Sing. When Winslow hears that the Juicy Fruits, whom he hates, have made a hit record of his song, he breaks out of prison. He goes to destroy Swan's studio, but gets his face mangled in a disc-press machine. When he falls into the river, everyone thinks him dead.

The Paradise is about to open. Winslow sneaks into the wardrobe and puts on a cape and bird mask. He becomes the Phantom of the Paradise. When he blows up the Juicy Fruits' car, Swan realizes there is an intruder about. He tricks the Phantom into writing him a cantata of Faust to be performed at the opening of the Paradise. It will be for Phoenix, whose smashing audition has won her the star spotlight. The Phantom signs a contract in blood.

Swan tells Philbin that he resents Phoenix's perfection. He won't allow her to be his star. Not telling the Phantom, who loves Phoenix, Swan searches for a personality to symbolize his new sound. He turns a fussy gay pill popper into Beef, a Frankenstein monster who sings. His backup group is the Undead.

In a secret room, the Phantom finishes his cantata. He is able to talk and sing despite mangled vocal chords because of a voice box. When he completes his music, Swan orders him to be walled up. But the Phantom kills his guards and escapes. He tells Beef that if he sings his music, he'll be killed.

Philbin keeps Beef from fleeing in fear. The Paradise opens. Beef sings a wild song to the delight of the large, wild crowd. At song's end, the Phantom shoots an electric bolt at him. Beef is electrocuted on stage. The audience is deliriously happy. Phoenix comes on. She sings a slow song. The audience loves her. Swan has a new superstar.

The Phantom tells Phoenix to come away with him. But she has agreed to marry Swan on national television. She doesn't know that Swan has planned to have her assassinated at the ceremony—the ultimate in entertainment.

The Phantom stabs himself with a knife. But he does not die. His wound will open only when Swan dies. The Phantom looks through Swan's video tapes. He discovers that Phoenix has sold herself to Swan, and that Swan sold himself to the devil. Swan will always remain young—he can only be destroyed when the videotape is destroyed. The Phantom sets fire to all the tapes.

The televised wedding ceremony begins. The Phantom thwarts the assassination attempt. Philbin is killed by the bullet. As the crowd cheers, Swan removes his mask. He is aging by the second and dying. With his death, the knife wound on the Phantom opens up. No longer in Swan's spell, Phoenix mourns Winslow. We see the shape of a burning bird.

T wentieth Century-Fox won the studio bidding war for *Phantom,* Brian De Palma's one-of-a-kind rock-(black) comedy-horror film, by happily shelling out $2 million, a record for an independent pickup. With understandably less enthusiasm, 20th then paid an additional $350,000 to Universal Studios because *Phantom* obviously bore strong resemblance to *Phantom of the Opera,* a Universal property. De Palma lengthened his title to *Phantom of the Paradise* (for a time it may have been called *Phantom of the Fillmore*) to appease King Features, which owns the famed *Phantom* comic strip; and De Palma optically replaced all visual references to ''Swan Records'' in the film with Death Records, because it turned out Swan was a small label for Atlantic Records. Still it all seemed worth the trouble. Bolstered by *Variety*'s thumbs-up review, 20th and De Palma

The Phantom flies toward the stage of the Paradise to prevent the marriage of Swan and Phoenix and her death.

The tormented Phantom composes a contata of "Faust" for Phoenix.

predicted *Phantom of the Paradise* would gross a whopping $35 million. Instead, it was one of the year's biggest flops.

De Palma and producer Edward Pressman decided the picture fared so badly because of a poor marketing strategy, in which the target viewers were youthful rock fans. They now theorized that it was impossible to create a cinema rock "event" from scratch, that the reason *Woodstock* (1970) and *Tommy* (1970) did so well was that they were presold. (Even so they failed to take into account that *Phantom* mocks the very audience they had tried to attract, and that Paul Williams's amusing musical parodies and serious ballads were anathema to such an audience.) Consequently, Pressman designed a new campaign geared for a *movie* rather than a rock concert audience, highlighting De Palma's cinematic audacity and the beauty-and-the-beast theme. Nevertheless, *Phantom* never did find its mass audience, although as a cult film in cities like Los Angeles and New York it did find comfortable slots at revival houses and, for a time, on the Midnight Movie circuit.

I first saw *Phantom* in 1974, in a nearly empty Hollywood theater. I *loved* the picture. *I* should have been the target viewer: I cheered young, noncommercial filmmakers; I shared De Palma's obvious affection for the horror genre (and it helped that I knew he was capable of making good horror films, as *Sisters* [1973] had shown); I lamented that the upbeat rock and roll of the fifties and sixties had evolved into the mean-spirited, theatrical glitter rock of Alice Cooper, Mott the Hoople, and the Rolling Stones of the seventies. I was aware that the film is flawed—it's terribly paced, it's sloppy, and has a trite, terribly confused ending—but I was excited by the visual bravura, amazing vitality, humor (one in joke: Philbin was named after Mary Philbin, who played opposite Lon Chaney in the 1925 silent *The Phantom of the Opera*), and innovation. Remarkably, De Palma put together a simple storyline despite combining plot and theme elements from numerous sources, including Goethe, Oscar Wilde, Nathanael West, Gaston Leroux's 1911 novel *The Phantom of*

the Opera as well as the 1925, 1943, and 1962 movie adaptations; *King Kong* (1933), *Beauty and the Beast* (1946), possibly *The Hunchback of Notre Dame* (1923 and 1939 versions), and Alfred Hitchcock's *Psycho* (1960) and *The Man Who Knew Too Much* (1956), with its assassination-attempt-at-concert sequence. Stylistically, De Palma pays homage to Hitchcock (the tracking camera, the 360° camera turn around a stationary figure), old-time serials and forties B films (the wipe, the iris, the montage), Rouben Mamoulian's 1932 version of *Dr. Jekyll and Mr. Hyde* (the point-of-view shot as our hero-monster first approaches the theater), silent American films like Chaney's *Phantom of the Opera* (often the film runs at fast silent-film speed, as when Winslow breaks out of prison and into Swan's record-manufacturing building), and silent German expressionistic films like the 1919 classic *The Cabinet of Dr. Caligari* (the distorted images, the very high-key lighting, the surrealistic Jack Fisk sets that seem appropriate for an amusement park crazy house). All this De Palma juxtaposes with modern techniques (split screen), "hip" irreverent humor, and violence, the distinguishing trait of seventies' horror films.

Although I was the only one I knew back then to admit liking the Carpenters, for whom Paul Williams wrote the million-selling "We've Only Just Begun" and "Rainy Days and Mondays," I was indifferent to Williams. So I was surprised by his clever score for *Phantom*. (If you dislike his score for *Bugsy Malone* [1976], which I think even more infectious, then you should probably disregard my praise.) I particularly like the two songs by the Juicy Fruits: "Goodbye, Eddie, Goodbye," which opens the film with a nostalgic bang, seems to mix the Diamonds ("Little Darlin' "), Chuck Berry (parts of "Route 66"?), White Doo Wop groups, the Shangri-las ("Leader of the Pack"), hair-combing male singers in *Grease* (the play opened in 1972), and the splendid rock spoofs (complete with emotional chatter in the middle of songs) that the Mothers of Invention used to do at the Garrick Theater in Greenwich Village, circa 1966. Even better is "Upholstery" ("where my baby sits-a close to me"), done in the tradition of the Beach Boys ("Carburetors, man, that's what life is all about"). The one other number that stands out is "Somebody Super Like Me (the Beef Construction Song)." Strutting across the stage as Tim Curry might have played a singing Frankenstein Monster—his spit curls are full of glitter, red scars mark his face, antlers adorn his waist—sounding like a furious, egocentric David Clayton-Thomas, Beef personifies the seventies rock-star-as-god/devil concept. Ironically, this scene is central to the reason my enthusiasm for *Phantom* has diminished, because amazingly, Beef, who seemed so outrageous by 1974 standards, looks tame today. We've gone far beyond him. But how could De Palma or anyone else have imagined the depraved acts that would emerge with Punk and New Wave music—take a look as the fascinating documentary on punk music *The Decline of Western Civilization* (1981)—which insist on taking their weird, sado-masochistic fans with them on their death trips?

Looking back, it's hard to believe the hostility some critics felt toward the film. "Brian De Palma's *Phantom of the Paradise* marks the point where spoof-horror meets rock-opera and I go home," squawked the London *Observer*'s Russell Davies. *Daily News* critic Rex Reed, never De Palma's greatest

One of the film's fine production numbers: a performance by the Juicy Fruits, a vile version of the Beach Boys.

Times change: In 1974 the Undead (the group that replaces the Juicy Fruits) seemed extreme, but in our present age of punk they are almost tame.

admirer, said, "Pay a visit to Brian De Palma's new film . . . and you'll want to throw up. I can't think of anything within recent memory that I have hated more than this terrible rock and roll parody of *Phantom of the Opera*. Totally lacking in structure, style, coherence, and talent, it is one of the most disgraceful abuses of money that has been trashed upon the screen since *Candy* [1968]. It should be reviewed with a machine gun, since it seems to have been made with one." Fortunately, reviews like this were balanced by fairer assessments. Pauline Kael, who has long admired De Palma's ability to manipulate an audience, criticized the director's inability to stage intimate scenes or tell a simple story, but expressed admiration for his wit, manic theatricality, and wild love for his medium. Also she recognized back then that De Palma's amateurish streaks and erratic talents (which are still very much in evidence) are not, in his case, liabilities. His unpredictability—you can't count on him to direct or write two scenes in a row that are polished or follow cinematic conventions—is one of the reasons he's been an interesting filmmaker.

Probably the most perceptive 1974 review of *Phantom* was written by Frank Rich for *New Times*. One of the few critics who realized that the film contained a message to go with the horror and music, he wrote, in part:

Americans have grown impatient in their wait for the end of the world and have taken to acting out that frustratingly delayed climax here and now—even to the extent of turning

Swan begins to control Phoenix. A De Palma joke: Actress Jessica Harper (a striking screen debut) sits under a sign that bears her name. "I was so young then," the queen of the out-of-the-mainstream movie told me in a 1981 interview. "I didn't know what to do in front of the camera. I was out of control. I'd definitely play the part differently if I did it again. . . . I liked working with Brian. I like Phantom *too. But I don't consider it a horror film like many people do. A lot of foreigners—from Argentina or France—come up to me on the street and say they've wanted to meet me after having seen* Phantom *seven or eight times. That's so nice . . . and bizarre."*

the specter of nonsensical mass murder into a basis for entertainment. . . . Where the film pays off, and what makes me feel it is the most original American film comedy I have seen this year, is in De Palma's grotesque depictions of an America intent on killing itself—bloody visions that he has devised entirely within the context of his metaphor of record-industry-as-doomsday-machine.

In an excellent interview conducted by David Bartholomew of *Cinefantastique* (Vol. 4, No. 2, 1975), De Palma's words tell us Rich truly zeroed in on the film's theme:

The film endeavors . . . to tell us about this whole culture. That it is obsessed with death, with destroying yourself, burning yourself up, consuming yourself for entertainment and amusement. I think it is a culture looking for bigger and better highs, whether it is nostalgia or reminiscing or Armageddon. It is whatever moves them, and the intensity of what moves them is being escalated all the time. It's a very desensitized, de-emotionalized culture. They have turned themselves off with drugs and detachment and they're looking for things to make them feel alive. . . . That's what I think the rock world is all about: a world of people killing themselves, consuming themselves in front of you, and you're sitting there applauding "Jesus, do it better, do it bigger!"

When Beef is killed on the stage by a lightning bolt that literally cooks him, the rock audience cheers his demise. Swan realizes how bloodthirsty and selfish the fans are, even though they have never signed pacts with the devil. De Palma gets this part right. But when he has the same audience turn around and cheer Phoenix's slow ballad, there's something amiss. *This* audience would doubtlessly boo her off the stage no matter how good she is. De Palma could better make his point about the rock audience being a modern

lynch mob if they only responded positively to Phoenix's performance *after* Swan gave them the go-ahead. The rock audience is, after all, fickle and easily manipulated into believing that what the music industry's money men promote as being good is good.

It's appropriate that *Phantom* begins with Rod Serling-like narration. Most episodes on Serling's classic television anthology *The Twilight Zone* were about characters who lose their identity. In *Phantom,* Winslow becomes the symbol of all struggling young songwriters whose music (their identity) is stolen by big-shot record producers and musicians. Winslow, in fact, represents all young artists, filmmakers included, who are used and discarded without the world ever knowing they existed. Once one signs a contract with a record company or a movie studio, it may as well as be with the devil. One's freedom is lost—notice the sad bird image (our symbol for independence) at the end of the film—and one's personal integrity is compromised: the person that was is no more.

On *The Twilight Zone* characters often sought short cuts to happiness, riches, fame, and/or power by dealing with the devil. Through one cruel trick or another, the devil always won out. Such stories would appeal to De Palma. Even when I like his films, as I do *Phantom,* I become annoyed with the enjoyment De Palma receives at playing cruel tricks on his characters. Witness the sad fates of Winslow in *Phantom,* who gets his face squashed in a vinyl disc-pressing machine; Kennedy assassination freak Gerrit Graham in *Greetings!* (1968), who is killed by an assassin; Nancy Allen in *Blow Out* (1981), who is strangled seconds before boyfriend John Travolta can track her down; and Sissy Spacek in *Carrie* (1976), who gets a bucket of blood poured on her at the school prom (which then becomes a violent sequence reminiscent of the *Phantom* finale). Even when a De Palma character makes it through the bad times, she or he doesn't get off scot-free: for instance, draft dodger Robert De Niro ends up in Vietnam in *Greetings!* and Amy Irving, in *Carrie,* and Nancy Allen, in *Dressed to Kill* (1980), are victims of terrible nightmares. Manipulating an audience is one thing, but cruelty to your characters is another.

The cast of *Phantom* is extremely likable, starting with ex-Ace Trucking Company comic George Memmoli as Philbin ("I was the one who made her a money-grabbing whore and they call me a disgrace") and singers-improv comics Jeffrey Comaner, Archie Hahn, and Harold Oblong, assembled to play the Juicy Fruits and to do the group's choreography. I don't think William Finley, better in other De Palma films, is strong or sympathetic enough to carry *Phantom,* but at least he's inoffensive. Paul Williams is surprisingly amusing as Swan. And Gerrit Graham, another De Palma regular, is wonderfully funny as the gay, pill-popping Beef. When I first saw the film, however, I believe I was most taken with then-newcomer Jessica Harper, whom De Palma spotted off-Broadway in *Dr. Selavy's Magic Theater* and cast because of her "haunting" quality. A fine singer-songwriter, Harper had to wait until the disappointing *Shock Treatment* (1981) to be offered another musical role. If *Phantom* had done better, she might have gotten such a part sooner in De Palma's planned sequel to *Phantom,* in which Swan would have returned as a guru. Now that's a film some of *Phantom*'s many cultists might have signed a blood contract to have seen.

1975 Australia B.E.F.-South Australian Film Corporation and Australian Film Commission (distributed in the U.S. by Atlantic Releasing)
Director: Peter Weir
Executive Producer: Pat Lovell
Producers: Jim McElroy and Hal McElroy
Screenplay: Cliff Green
From a novel by Joan Lindsay
Cinematography: Russell Boyd
Music: Bruce Smeaton
Editor: Max Lemon
Running time: the U.S. print runs 110 minutes (reviews in Australian papers list it as being 115 or 120 minutes)

Cast: Rachel Roberts (Mrs. Appleyard), Dominic Guard (Michael Fitzhubert), Vivean Gray (Greta McGraw), Helen Morse (Diane de Poitiers), Anne Lambert (Miranda), Karen Robinson (Irma), Jane Vallis (Marion), John Jarrett (Albert Crundall), Margaret Nelson (Sara Waybourne), Tony-Llewelyn Jones (Tom), Jacki Weaver (Minnie), Christine Schuler (Edith Horton), Frank Gunnell (Edward Whitehead), Kay Taylor (Mrs. Bumpher), Kirsty Child (Dora Lumley), Wyn Roberts, Ingrid Mason, Jenny Lovell, Janet Murray, Bridgette Phillips, John Fegan, Gary MacDonald

Synopsis: Saturday, Saint Valentine's Day, 1900. The girls of Appleyard College prepare for a picnic. They exchange valentines, and breathlessly read the love poems enclosed. The only girl who cannot go to the picnic is Sara, a young orphan, who is being disciplined by Mrs. Appleyard. Sara loves the prettiest girl, Miranda, who tells her she should find someone else because "I won't be here much longer." The girls ride off in Mr. Hussey's wagon. They head toward Hanging Rock, a five-hundred-foot volcanic formation. Two instructors accompany them: the beautiful, popular Mlle. de Poitiers and math instructor Greta McGraw, a plain woman with "masculine intellect."

The picnic is held near the Rock. For some odd reason, everyone's timepiece gets stuck at twelve o'clock. Love always on her mind, Miranda cuts a cake in honor of Saint Valentine. She, Irma, Marion, and the childish Edith decide to explore beneath the Rock. As they cross a stream they are watched by Michael Fitzhubert, an English lad staying with the Cosgroves, his uncle and aunt, who sleep nearby. Their young chauffeur Albert also sees the girls. Michael immediately falls in love with Miranda. The girls climb into the formation.

They go higher and higher. It is like a maze. The girls rest. When Edith awakens, she sees her three companions, stockings and shoes in hand, climbing farther, as if in a trance. The picnickers below are like ants. The girls climb higher. Edith warns them not to. She screams and runs downward.

The wagon returns late at night. Mrs. Appleyard is informed that Miranda, Irma, Marion, and Miss McGraw are missing.

A search is conducted on the Rock. It continues for several days but no one is found. Michael becomes obsessed with finding Miranda. When everyone else gives up the search he gets Albert to accompany him to the Rock. The next morning Albert finds the nearly delirious Michael with a piece of cloth in his hand. He follows Michael's trail and finds Irma unharmed. Irma tells the police she remembers nothing.

Michael and Irma wander in the woods. They are miserable. Michael, who still thinks of Miranda, and Albert have nightmares. The stress also gets to Mrs. Appleyard. Her students are ostracized. Parents report they are withdrawing their girls from school. An instructor gives notice. Appleyard takes out her distress on poor Sara, threatening to send her back to the orphanage because her benefactor hasn't paid her tuition. Sara wishes she could be with her brother, separated from her long ago.

Irma visits the school. The girls attack her, demanding to know what happened on the mountain. Mlle. de Poitiers pulls them off her. Mrs. Appleyard says Sara's guardian has taken her away. But handyman Tom discovers Sara lying dead in the greenhouse. She either jumped or was pushed from the window above. Albert dreams his orphan sister came to him.

Appleyard goes off. Her body is found beneath the Rock. She jumped. No one else was ever discovered there.

Picnic at Hanging Rock

When you go to sleep, people come and steal your body.
—A belief expressed in Peter Weir's
The Last Wave (1977)

On Saturday, Saint Valentine's Day, in 1900, two instructors and eighteen of the nineteen young ladies who attended Appleyard College, an Australian finishing school located near Woodend, in the state of Victoria, spent the day beneath Hanging Rock, a formidable five-hundred-foot-high, million-year-old uncharted volcanic formation. It was supposed to be *their* picnic at Hanging Rock, but the insects lunched on the remnants of their cake, and the Rock—or was it nature itself?—devoured, that is *swallowed whole,* instructor Greta McGraw and three young ladies named Miranda, Irma, and Marion. More than a week later Irma was found on the rock by a young Englishman, Michael Fitzhubert, who had never given up hope. Irma was unharmed, "intact," but she couldn't remember what had transpired on the Rock. McGraw, Miranda, and Marion were never seen again. The scandal brought about the ruination of the college; and, following the mysterious death of the nineteenth young student, Sara Waybourne, which some attributed to stern headmistress Mrs. Appleyard, who was in an awful state of depression, Appleyard committed suicide by jumping from the Rock. Did these astounding events really happen?

In her novel *Picnic at Hanging Rock,* from which Peter Weir adapted his flim (a landmark in Australia's New Wave), Joan Lindsay manipulates us into believing her narrative is true by cleverly quoting from what are supposed to be *actual* police transcripts of interviews with witnesses at the scene, and *actual* extracts from turn-of-the-century newspapers; her introductory cast of characters concludes with "and many others who do not appear in this book." Yet her brief preface hints that she is playing a game:

> Whether *Picnic at Hanging Rock* is fact or fiction, my readers must decide for themselves. As the fateful picnic took place in the year 1900, and all the characters who appear in this book are long since dead, it hardly seems important.

Most Australian book and film critics concluded that Lindsay had based her strange tale on an actual mystery surrounding Hanging Rock. (Has it become a tourist site, like our Amityville House?) However, for her book *The Murders at Hanging Rock* (Scribe, 1980), Yvonne Rousseau did a little detective work. There was no college for young ladies established in the Woodend locality mentioned until 1919, twenty-seven years after Mrs. Appleyard supposedly migrated from

All is quiet, and time literally comes to a halt during the school picnic beneath Hanging Rock. While four young girls go off to explore the Rock, the other girls, Mlle. de Poitiers (under a parasol), and Greta McGraw (dressed in black) read poetry.

England. In Lindsay's novel, great importance is given to the fact Saint Valentine's Day coincided with a Saturday picnic—but in 1900, Saint Valentine's Day fell on a Wednesday. There were no newspaper accounts of missing or murdered persons during this period or on any day between 1897 and 1905—the extent of Rousseau's research; and, as far as she could tell, no one in Woodend has ever heard of the so-called "notorious" disappearances. Rousseau: "Hanging Rock, then, has no history so far this century, at least, of mysterious disappearances; and Appleyard College's disintegration under the rock's influence is only imagined."

My Australian film correspondent Beth Robinson tells me there was great interest in Australia in the book when it was published in 1967 because Lindsay was the first female novelist in that country to come from a well-known and esteemed aristocratic family. The book was a best seller, despite Lindsay's unwillingness to join in the debate about its content. With the release of Weir's movie, its popularity grew considerably. Although I have no way of being sure, I'd guess Lindsay's inspirations for her first book were an interesting literary conglomeration that includes Henry James (as much for his

depiction of Europeans in a barbaric world, and his depiction of upper class snobbery, as for the psychological terror and haunting atmosphere found in *The Turn of the Screw*), William Wordsworth (serious nature poems), H. H. Munro (bizarre tales), James Barrie (children's need for escape from the adult world), transcendentalists Ralph Waldo Emerson and Henry David Thoreau (the divinity of nature), and D. H. Lawrence. Especially Lawrence: not only for his books' extreme eroticism but, more important, for his belief—central to both Lindsay and Weir—that man, dehumanized by a western culture that stresses intellect at the exclusion of physical/sexual instincts, should realize that he is part of nature.

Lindsay's book is a delight. And Weir is extremely faithful to it. With minor exceptions, what Lindsay describes is up there on the screen in all its detail. Cinematographer Russell Boyd even put dyed (orange-yellow) wedding veils over his lens in order to capture the *feel* of Lindsay's outdoor scenes, to capture a "lost-summer" feeling. Characters are exactly as they are in the book (except that Sara is not as mousy). Casting is impeccable, as if Lindsay chose the actors. So why is the film so much less satisfying?

The first part of the film is absolutely spellbinding. No picture I can think of has a more sinister atmosphere. But once Michael and Albert rescue Irma and the action shifts away from the Rock, I lose interest. Compared to the fascinating occurrences on the Rock, everything, including the girls' hysterical reaction upon seeing Irma again, Sara's death, and the deterioration of Mrs. Appleyard, is anticlimatic. I get annoyed that everyone conveniently has some form of amnesia, that the police are so polite while questioning Irma even though delay could be fatal to those on the Rock, that the search doesn't intensify after Irma is found. (I get the feeling that this wasn't the best search ever conducted for missing persons.) And, although Weir is making a point (also made by Lindsay), I wish that some of the characters would come out of their guilty silence and theorize about what happened to those girls. I keep wanting Weir to take the camera back to the Rock, if only for an atmospheric "walk" through the dark. I'd even settle for the entire replay of the girls' ascent instead of the slow-moving Jamesian courtship of Michael and Irma. It's infuriating.

Those chilling scenes on the day of the picnic (made more ominous by Gheorghe Zampier's Pan Pipes), in which unknown primeval forces are at work and the rock formation seems to take on a sexual, brutal life of its own, are as suitable to Weir as Lindsay—which is why they are so impressive. Only a few directors (Nicolas Roeg in 1970's *Walkabout;* Terrence Malick) allow natural surroundings to dominate scenes; so for viewers—all who have walked into a strange natural environment (especially at night) and had the creepy sensation that the trees, bushes, rocks, soil, and sky aren't happy about being disturbed—the films of Peter Weir are special. However, once Weir starts concentrating on the aftermath of the disappearances, we feel we've seen it all before. It's one thing to read about a Victorian boarding school when the author (Lindsay) actually suffered in one (1911–1914, in the very school that eventually left Melbourne and moved to Woodend in 1919): we know that there is autobiographical basis for her observations regarding the bursting sexuality of the girls in an oppressive environment and her angry feelings toward headmistresses who were more interested in keeping up appearances than in students. But when a young male filmmaker like Weir adapts Victorian-boarding-school material, even if accurately, we can't help missing the first-person perspective. To give Weir his due, his opening—girls wash in flower-scented water, whisper amongst themselves, hold hands, blow kisses, passionately read love poems, exchange valentines, and help each other tie their corsets (love perfumes the air) all counterpointed with cold, austere shots of the unfriendly school building—effectively conveys that Appleyard College is not so much a finishing school as an institute for sexual repression for Miranda and her followers. But after the disappearances, when sexual repression is no longer the major concern, Weir has nothing original to work with. Horror movies with sadistic head-mistresses are a dime a dozen. Even Rachel Roberts's domineering presence can't make the school scenes interesting (they're just sad) when we care more about Miranda and the Rock.

In Weir films from emerging cult hit *The Cars That Ate Paris* (1974) to *The Year of Living Dangerously* (1983), aliens to any environment are in for a bad time—as a result of the

With this erotic shot of the girls tightening each other's corsets, director Weir conveys metaphorically that the sexually repressed teen-agers are bursting with sexuality.

people, as a result of hostile natural forces. As screenwriter Cliff Green points out, a theme of *Picnic,* reflecting in a way "the history of Australia," is that "Europeans who intrude into a timeless environment are . . . rejected and in some cases destroyed by subtle forces, beyond [their] comprehension." It's an interesting theme, but it's less clear in the film than the book ("Australia," writes Lindsay, "where anything can happen"). It may be my foolish oversight but I wasn't sure that Mrs. Appleyard (played by the Welsh Rachel Roberts) was supposed to be English. In any case, I can't see where her demise is determined by anything more than the financial collapse of her school; perhaps like English lad Michael (who also is in a constant state of duress), she should have had a vision or two. As for other Europeans Mlle. de Poitiers and English gardener Mr. Whitehead (spared because of his love for nature?), how does the theme apply to them?

Two other things that greatly bother me about the later scenes. That Albert and Sara are brother and sister is only hinted at in the novel, and that's how it should be. Weir concentrates too strongly on their spiritual attachment. In a film it becomes too coincidental, too predictable, and too contrived. It really doesn't matter if they're related. Their not reuniting only adds to all the other frustrations. Their story only serves to distract us further from the mystery. Finally, I'm disappointed that Weir chose to have a narrator tell us of Mrs. Appleyard's death—vividly detailed in the novel. That it takes place on the Rock could have provided us with one more visit to the intriguing locale which we feel has been abandoned by Weir and the Woodend search team. Why not go out with a bang, with nature again in control, as in *The Last Wave,* where Richard Chamberlain looks out at the ocean and sees a five-hundred-foot mountain of water heading his way?

(TL) Mlle. de Poitiers comforts the unhappy Sara, who is sure her beloved Miranda will never return. (BL) English lad Michael Fitzhubert also longs for Miranda, to whom he lost his heart at first sight. (Below) The strict Mrs. Appleyard tries to maintain her composure although her world crumbles around her.

Fiction or not, why do Miranda, Marion, and McGraw vanish? There is no theory that totally works. Because so few females disappeared, the possibility of foul play is always there—although it seems unlikely that Michael and Albert are homicidal sex maniacs as some critics contend. That the Rock would reject the lovely young Irma and accept fossilized Greta McGraw is totally confusing. Of course, that adds to the mystery. Did a UFO pass by, was there bush/nature retribution, did Michael and Miranda elope? All theories have backers. Did they pass through a time warp? Or into another dimension? Is it all a dream?

I believe that the girls' ascent through the rock formation and their subsequent disappearance represents both their rite of passage into sexual womanhood and an *escape* (they are embraced, not physically harmed or kidnapped) into another world that has no sexual repression. The time is ripe for a sexual union between nature's mysterious forces and the horny young ladies who, be they "flowers" (as Weir's visuals imply metaphorically) or "apples" (from Appleyard), are ready for picking. It's the first year of a new century, it's Saint Valentine's Day (once the day of a pagan fertility ritual), it is high noon. And it just so happens that the girls who picnic below are virgins, dressed in white frocks (perfect for sacrifices or weddings), and bursting (in tight corsets) with sexual feel-

ings (as we saw back at school). Above them looms the very interested Hanging Rock, its mighty protrusions jutting out from perfectly symmetrical boulders—distinct phallic imagery. The girls are aware that it is a volcanic structure, perhaps capable of a second eruption: "Just think, a million years," marvels one girl, "waiting just for us." Naturally it's Miranda, the embodiment of love, who cuts the cake and dedicates it to Saint Valentine, the only saint she knows or cares about. Then she heads for the Rock, three girls behind her, all looking expectant—as if they knew that someone—or rather something—was waiting for their arrival. The small stream (water as sexual symbol) they come to offers them a chance to turn back, but Miranda leads them on. Her leap, which Michael witnesses, is in slow motion. I don't think Weir did this to show his trick photography but just because her leap over the stream really takes place at the slow speed. Time stopped at twelve, we have gone further into a surreal world. Do we see a naughty look on Miranda's face, as if she were sneaking off to see her lover? The girls walk up the incline. The shots of the phallic boulders now merge with shots of narrow vaginal passageways through the rocks and womblike caves and caverns. "Metaphorically they are exploring the hidden depths of the instinctual world—a world of sensuality and passion," writes Ed Roginski in *Film Quarterly* (Summer 1979). The girls nap, and it's as if something is watching them, deciding whom to accept and whom (Edith) to reject. Miranda, Irma, and Marion—seemingly intoxicated by the air or hypnotized—climb farther, with no intention of going back. They remove their shoes and stockings so they can walk

(T) *As the four girls walk toward Hanging Rock the atmosphere becomes thick with mystery and sex. (L-R) Irma, Marion, and Miranda follow Edith. (B) The lovely Miranda leads the way up the rock formation. Does she know what awaits them?*

on the sacred ground. Looking below they notice that the picnickers are like ants—the girls have moved out of our world. With their next steps they will move into a second, sensual world.

The key to it all is Miranda. Quite simply, she is not of this world. Strictly speaking, she is not a human being. She is a flower to Sara. She is a swan to Michael. A sex object to Albert. A love object to the rest of the girls. A vision, a dream to herself. An ideal (a goddess) to Mrs. Appleyard. A (Botticelli) angel to Mlle. de Poitiers. To us she is the embodiment of sexual desire stifled, as was her namesake in Shakespeare's otherworldly *The Tempest*. Except for her reference to "human beings," Marion could be describing Miranda when she says, "A surprising number of human beings are without purpose, though it is probable that they are performing some function unknown to themselves." Miranda doesn't know what her mission is on Saint Valentine's Day. She only knows that it has something to do with love and, as Sara says emphatically, that "she wasn't coming back." I believe that it was Miranda's mission to deliver sexually repressed girls, and even virginal Greta McGraw, into a world of sexual freedom, far away from adults like Mrs. Appleyard and the uncaring parents who would entrust them to such a witch. I am reminded of a *Twilight Zone* episode in which two kids whose parents are always squabbling and ignoring them dive into their swimming pool and surface in a happy world for children, looked over by a kindly old lady who has much love to offer them. I am also reminded of *Peter Pan*: I believe Miranda has taken herself and three others into a sexual never-never land.

1978   Paramount
Director: Louis Malle
Producer: Louis Malle
Screenplay: Polly Platt
From a story by Polly Platt and Louis Malle
Based on material in *Storyville, New Orleans: Being an Authentic Account of the Notorious Redlight District* by Al Rose
Cinematography: Sven Nykvist
Music adaptation and supervision: Jerry Wexler
Solo Piano: Bob Greene
Editor: Suzanne Baron
Running Time: 109 minutes

Cast: Brooke Shields (Violet), Keith Carradine (Bellocq), Susan Sarandon (Hattie). Frances Faye (Madame Nell), Antonio Fargas (Professor), Mathew Anton (Red Top), Diana Scarwid (Frieda), Barbara Steele (Josephine), Seret Scott (Flora), Cheryle Markowitz (Gussie), Susan Manskey (Fanny), Laura Zimmerman (Odette), Gerrit Graham (Highpockets), Mae Mercer (Mama Mosebery) Don Hood (Alfred Fuller), Don K. Lutenbacher (Violet's first customer)

Synopsis: This setting is Storyville, the redlight district of New Orleans, in 1917. In Madame Nell Livingston's brothel, one of her whores, Hattie, gives birth to a little boy she names Will. It is her second child. Violet, her twelve-year-old daughter, has grown up in the house. She doesn't know who her father was. She is still a virgin but on occasion will help Hattie serve a customer. Hattie tells her clients that Violet is her sister so that she won't scare off any prospective candidates for marriage. Her dream is to leave the brothel and become respectable.

Violet is an inquisitive child, and life in the brothel is endlessly fascinating for her. Here she watches and learns the business from Hattie and the other prostitutes, Frieda, Josephine, Flora, Gussie, Fanny, and Odette. Here the black Mama Mosebery practices voodoo. Here the Professor plays jazz piano while the whores and their clients frolic each night in the parlor. Violet plays with other children in the house. Her favorite is a rapscallion named Redtop.

Photographer E. J. Bellocq pays Madame Nell to have her whores pose for him. He is particularly taken with Hattie, making Violet very jealous. The women of the house think Bellocq odd since he never has sex with the women. He just photographs them during the day when the light is perfect and watches them each night in the parlor.

The night comes for Violet's virginity to be sold. A customer pays four hundred dollars to spend time with Violet. She becomes frightened, but goes through with it. He runs out when he thinks she is unconscious. But she was just pretending, she laughs to the other prostitutes. Although Violet has been deflowered, Nell continues to sell her as a virgin.

Alfred Fuller, a customer of Hattie's, proposes to her. They go off to St. Louis with Will but leave Violet behind. It upsets the girl very much. When she tries to seduce a black boy and Nell has her spanked, Violet runs away to Bellocq's house. She moves in and they become lovers. She poses for many pictures. When her spoiled attitude interferes with his photography, he kicks her out.

Storyville is closed down. Madame Nell sits in her bed in a catatonic state, not knowing what to do with her life. The Professor goes to Chicago. When Violet walks out the front door, with no destination in mind, Bellocq is there to greet her. He proposes. They gather the other prostitutes and are married. Afterwards there is a picnic by the river. Men jump off a barge to join them. They think Bellocq is the luckiest man in the world because he has so many beautiful women around him.

Violet moves back in with Bellocq. She continues to act spoiled. She complains a great deal, and Bellocq is constantly irritated by her behavior. Hattie, Foster, and Will return. They want Violet to come live with them and to go to school. They will have her marriage to Bellocq annulled. Violet wants Bellocq to come with them. But Bellocq and the others know that is impossible. Bellocq is furious Violet is being taken from him, because he doesn't think he can live without her.

At the train station, Fuller takes a family picture with his Brownie.

Pretty Baby

I f the real E. J. Bellocq, who historians believe never had sex with the Storyville prostitutes he used as his models (or anyone else), represents the classic voyeur among photographers, then Louis Malle is the classic voyeur among filmmakers. His detached style, in which the artist stands back from his subject, can probably be traced to when he was Jacques Yves Cousteau's cameraman on the undersea documentary *The Silent World* (1956). His own pictures have been impeccably shot and quite lovely, with special feeling for locale (Paris, India, New Orleans, Atlantic City), set design (particularly the brothel interiors in *Pretty Baby*), costumes, and makeup, but unfortunately he has always thought his job complete once he has established a world within his frame. Like Keith Carradine's Bellocq in *Pretty Baby*, who is transfixed by the bar while the prostitutes and their clients engage in their evening's activities, Malle merely observes his characters going about their business within his created, or recreated, worlds, rather than becoming involved in their lives and making judgments about them.

Some critics applaud his refusal to be critical, analytical, or moralistic. They contend it makes for honesty in his work. But I see less objectivity than passivity, too much artistic

Violet and Hattie. Many Brooke Shields fanatics are fascinated by Pretty Baby *because they believe it's the one picture in which she played a character very much like herself (or more precisely like her publicity-created image): a girl whose manipulative mother had her naive, defenseless daughter sell "sex" to make money.*

pretentiousness, and, worse, the lack of necessary conflicts because Malle doesn't want to choose sides. It's infuriating that he attempts to pass off a story's premise for the story itself, as is the case with *Pretty Baby*, which is a series of vignettes rather than a straight narrative, and that he tries, as critic Frank Rich complained, "to substitute flavor for substance." It's certainly valid that a director's priority be to capture the "reality" and singular flavor of a setting or an era, especially if he is an impressionist like Malle; but why would a director consistently choose *controversial* subjects about which he has (or will express) no opinion? *The Lovers* (1959) deals with adultery, *The Fire Within* (1963) with suicide, *Murmur of the Heart* (1971) with incest between a fourteen-year-old boy and his mother, *Lacombe, Lucien* (his best film, 1974) with a Parisian teen-ager's collaboration with the Nazis during World War II, and *Pretty Baby* with child prostitution, yet his characters are kept within such strict guidelines that even when they commit acts that sound drastic or outrageous in the telling, everything's quite tame on the screen. All because Malle doesn't want to manipulate his audience in one direction or the other. He is reluctant to give characters enough hateful, endearing, or sympathetic characteristics to be seen as emphatically good or bad. Without extreme personality traits or the leeway to shock viewers his characters become dull. They are also cloying and ignorant. Ever since he gave us a thoroughly obnoxious eleven-year-old girl in *Zazie dans le Métro* (1960) he has filled his screen with unlikable people. Of his films, only *My Dinner with André* (1981), quickly overtaking *Pretty Baby* as the Malle cult favorite, works despite its unopinionated director, and that's because the two actors who play themselves and wrote the script, André Gregory and Wallace Shawn, are so opinionated themselves.

Pretty Baby, Malle's first American film, cries out for a director with a point of view. But Malle backed off: "Let me make it clear that I'm a filmmaker, not a social worker. My cinema is not rhetorical and I don't send messages." Once again he took a steamy, sensational subject and strove for artistry instead of controversy. That approach itself was controversial. The picture was released during a peak period for public outrage over child abuse, child pornography, and child prostitution, and its critics were disappointed that, considering the subject matter, it did not take a stand on such issues. Malle may have presented a world with twisted morality—a child can have sex with adults, but blacks mustn't have sex with whites—but he left it to his viewers to make up their own minds about child prostitution. He thought it dishonest to portray Violet, Brooke Shields's child prostitute, as a 100 percent victim. But while it's true that the real Violet, whose fifty-year-old memories Malle discovered in Al Rose's nonfiction work *Storyville, New Orleans* (University of Alabama Press, 1974), didn't consider herself victimized when a child, it was irresponsible on Malle's part to choose *her* as his central character when countless other ex-child prostitutes could relate tales of horror. So the argument goes. The film, banned in such places as England and Ontario, Canada, was attacked because many people felt twelve-year-old Shields had been more exploited by Malle and her notorious "stage mother" Teri Shields (talk about a bad media image) than her character is in the film. While its defenders contended that *Pretty Baby* was true "art" (Vincent Canby

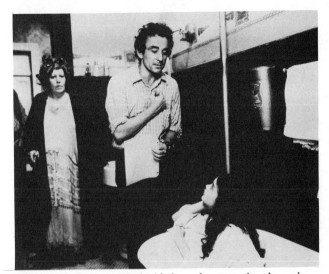

Malle tells the attentive Shields how she must play the nude bathtub sequence. Frances Faye, who plays Madame Nell, stands by.

thought it "romantic, haunting, sad, uninhibited, and wise"), its accusers worried that Shields would be traumatized for life from having posed nude for Malle, played scenes with nude adults, and had an adult lover in the film.

The sledgehammer "selling of Brooke Shields as pubescent sex symbol," which gained momentum because of *Pretty Baby,* was truly tasteless. At least, Malle didn't exploit his hot property as much as others did. He admitted concern about being accused of child pornography and contended that was why he hired a female scriptwriter, Polly Platt, who he felt could treat the touchy subject matter with sensitivity. He filmed no sexually explicit or overly erotic scenes with Shields. Most of her nude moments are those in which Violet poses for Bellocq's camera or she (Shields), in effect, poses for Malle's camera. This "modeling" Malle could handle, probably because Shields had worked as a nude model since the age of eleven months and was not embarrassed by it. But at the risk of sounding prudish, I feel uneasy when seeing the young Shields naked at other times. I don't find her being *intentionally* exploited in these scenes, but I feel embarrassed for her because of the unflattering way Malle exhibits her. She looks downright foolish when Violet is interrupted in her bath by Madame Nell and a customer, and when she stands bare-assed in front of Bellocq's locked door, banging on it to be let inside. Surely this film could do with an honest, nonexploitative scene like the one found in Jeanne Moreau's excellent *L'Adolescente* (1982), where a pretty girl of Violet's age examines her nude, changing body in a mirror. Malle obviously felt awkward dealing with a girl of Shields's age, because he makes Violet curious about *everything* but her own body. He probably figured all aspects of sex and sexuality were commonplace to Violet after having grown up in a brothel—but I don't believe this would be the case. *One thing I do like* however is that when Violet has sex for the first time, she neither regards it as an earth-shattering experience or the point in her life when she becomes a woman. *Pretty Baby* is no "rite of passage" movie.

Malle takes a polite view of all Nell's whores. They are all well paid, well fed, and healthy. None is depressed. Indeed,

Directors almost always have Susan Sarandon play scenes topless as she is known for her beautiful chest. (T) Hattie, who is proud of her breasts, is happy to exhibit them for Bellocq's camera. (B) Violet is always impatient when Bellocq performs his trade.

if a point is made in the film—other than the trite "prostitutes and their clients exploit each other"—it is that girls who grow up in brothels never do become women. Sadly, they never have experiences in the "real" world, and only learn how to do one thing to make a living. They're kids who sing "Billy Boy," play hide-and-seek, play pretend "games" with their customers, and dub men like Bellocq "Papa" because they yearn for the fathers they never knew.

Bellocq is so readily accepted by Nell's whores because he is a child himself. Witness his temper tantrums when working, or his babyish response to one of Violet's unending questions: "That's for me to know and for you to find out." At first he is attracted to Hattie. She is the one whore with adult sensibilities—she wants a husband, a home, money, security, and respectability. He makes love to her with his camera (Malle has acknowledged the concept of "filmmaker-as-rapist"), musing "I'm happy right now" when she bares her breasts for him. But he knows he can't provide her with her needs, so he turns to Violet, Hattie's mirror image but too young to be as demanding or as intimidating. He falls in love with Violet because of her beauty—certainly a consideration for an artist— and because she is as inquisitve as he. (On the other hand,

Hattie was only interested in herself.) In truth, as we see throughout the film, Violet is a voyeur too. I think the key to Bellocq can be found in a line he says to Violet: "I don't have to explain myself to a child." Violet wrongly takes this to mean that Bellocq would explain himself to her if she were older, but you can deduce the real meaning of this phrase if you simply put the word "fortunately" in front of it. Bellocq is relieved to be with a child because a woman would ask him for an explanation of himself (self-definition) that he'd find impossible to give. Bellocq is sexually and emotionally a child, and is only capable of having a relationship with another child. When he brings Violet a doll as a present, she complains, "You think of me as a child!" Actually Bellocq is making sure she *remains* a child instead of growing up too fast and passing him by. As for Violet, Malle has said that she matures in the film. But I find the girl at the end of the picture, even after having performed wifely duties, to be similar to the one at the beginning who was jumping rope and sliding down banisters.

During preproduction Malle and frequent Ingmar Bergman cinematographer Sven Nykvist spent much time studying the paintings of Renoir, Degas, and Seurat, and visually *Pretty Baby* is an impressive homage to the impressionists of the era—just as the music is a tribute to the jazz greats of the period like Jelly Roll Morton, whom the Professor is loosely based on. Each shot is beautifullly composed, and the frame becomes a mixture of muted colors, natural light, and shadows. Predictably, the strength of *Pretty Baby* is its brothel setting. It is a fascinating self-contained universe of sliding doors, wide halls, blanketless beds, cluttered closets, gilt-edged mirrors, scandalous paintings, worn carpets, love seats, and an ever-playing piano. The whores, falling out of their lacy underwear, are part of the decor. As long as Malle is concentrating on his visuals, taking a closeup of one of the heavily madeup whores or slowly zooming in on one of his characters to capture his or her innermost thoughts, things run smoothly. But when the characters speak, we are bombarded with the clichés we've heard in every bad movie set in brothels.

Characteristically, Malle avoids conflicts. A natural one would have been how the individual whores meet the challenge of the imminent shutdown of the Storyville brothels. But Malle only includes the closing of Nell's house as one of many vignettes. A greater mistake is never showing the development of the relationship between Bellocq and Violet to the point where he really would seem dependent on her ("I can't live without her"). Incompatability (he develops pictures, she cuts her toenails) cannot replace emotional conflict.

The actual E. J. Bellocq probably never so much as photographed a child prostitute, so it's odd that Malle would use him as the character who falls in love with and marries Violet. Perhaps it was convenient, since a brief biography of Bellocq also appears in Al Rose's book. Bellocq admirers must resent the liberties Malle and Platt took when writing him for the screen. The real Bellocq was about five feet tall, walked like a duck, had a thick French accent, and suffered from hydrocephaly (his head came to a point). Paramount wanted Jack Nicholson to play the part, Malle preferred Robert De Niro. I don't know how Malle settled on Keith Carradine, who neither looks nor sounds right for the role. I have liked Carradine in several films, including Robert Altman's *Thieves Like Us* (1974) and Walter Hill's *Southern Comfort*

(1981), but he can seem terribly miscast (is it his weak voice?), as in Ridley Scott's *The Duellists* (1978) and *Pretty Baby*. Carradine thinks his best work was done in this film, but I think he delivers an extremely lackluster, confused performance. Of course, it's easier to blame the character written for him to play. In any case, Carradine doesn't give the worst performance in the film. If Frances Faye, doing a horrendous Mae West imitation, mangled the word *monsieur* one more time when addressing Bellocq, I'm sure someone on Malle's set would have strangled her.

Susan Sarandon, the cinema's most adventuresome actress, in terms of the strange roles she accepts, is as usual good, not great, in a film unworthy of her talents. But she has survived worse, more forgettable films, unscathed and still in demand. At least, she got a lover—Malle, who diplomatically insisted that Hattie was the most difficult role in the film—in lieu of a meaty part. Certainly the most impressive performer in the film is Brooke Shields (who took the part rejected by Diane Lane). She is quite natural as Violet (which makes one concerned), beautiful of course, and funny. Her delivery of lines is her best, outside of *Wanda Nevada* (1979), of her thus-far undistinguished film career, and her southern accent is acceptable. She even moves well, as when she shuffles, arms swinging monkeylike, down the hall after Hattie and her client. She was a very good child actress, but I would have preferred seeing young Shields out of the brothel and in some meadow with a dog named Lassie or a horse named Velvet.

(T) Violet and her first customer. (B) Much used publicity shot of Bellocq and Nell's girls. Blonde Diana Scarwid and cult favorite Barbara Steele took minor roles in support of Sarandon (who calls herself the Helen Hayes of Cult), Keith Carradine, and Brooke Shields.

1979 Great Britain World Northal release of a Polytel film
Director: Franc Roddam
Executive Producers: Roger Daltrey, John Entwistle,
Pete Townshend, and Keith Moon (The Who)
Producers: Roy Baird and Bill Curbishley
Screenplay: Dave Humphries, Martin Stellman, and
Franc Roddam (and Pete Townshend, uncredited)
Cinematography: Brian Tufano
Musical Director: John Entwistle
Songs: "I Am the Sea," "The Real Me," "I'm the One," "5:15,"
"Love Reign O'er Me," "Bell Boy," "I've Had Enough,"
"Helpless Dancer," "Doctor Jimmy," "Get Out and Stay Out," "Four Faces,"
"Joker James," and "The Punk and the Godfather" were written
by Pete Townshend and are performed by The Who; various other
artists also perform.
Editor: Mike Taylor
Running Time: 115 minutes

Cast: Phil Daniels (Jimmy Michael Cooper), Leslie Ash (Steph),
Sting (Ace Face), Mike Wingett (Dave), Philip Davis (Chalky), Garry
Cooper (Pete), Toyah Wilcox (Monkey), Trevor Laird (Ferdy), Gary
Shail (Spider), Kate Williams (Mrs. Cooper), Michael Elphick (Mr.
Cooper), Raymond Winstone (Kevin)

Synopsis: London, 1964. The city's youth are divided into two
factions: Mods, who are sharply dressed and are obsessed with the
hard-driving music of the day, and Rockers, who wear leather
jackets and like old-style rock 'n' roll. The Mods and Rockers both
ride around on cycles, looking for excuses to rumble with each
other.

Jimmy's whole life is being a Mod. His parents think he's not
normal. And that's all right with him: "I want to be different. You
gotta be somebody or you might as well jump in the sea and
drown." Jimmy spends much time looking into the Thames.

At home, Jimmy finds peace only in his room with photos on the
wall of nude girls and rock groups, and clippings of Mod-Rocker
riots at Brighton by the sea. But he'd rather be out riding his cycle
with his Mod gang, especially his good firends Dave and Chalky.

An old friend of Jimmy's returns from the army. He is no Rocker
but dresses like a Rocker, and Jimmy won't be seen in public with
him. When the Mods pursue a Rocker after Chalky is harassed by a
Rocker gang, he turns out to be Jimmy's friend. He is beaten to a
pulp before Jimmy can say anything. Jimmy goes home disgusted.

Jimmy becomes interested in a pretty blonde named Steph who
befriends him because he has pills. He's jealous that she's with an
older guy, Pete, who takes her to Brighton over the bank holiday.
But once they arrive in Brighton she dumps Pete and comes over to
Jimmy. That night they go to a mad bash in a large dance hall.
Steph leaves Jimmy to dance with Ace Face, the coolest Mod.
When Jimmy dives off a balcony into the crowd below, to show off,
he is kicked out. He spends the night staring at the ocean.

Steph rejoins Jimmy the next day. They march together as the
Mods parade down the streets. The Mods beat up some Rockers. A
large group of Rockers retaliates on the beach, and the police break
up the combat. Mods charge through the streets, breaking shop
windows. Paddy wagons arrive. Ace Face and Jimmy and other
Mods fight the police. Steph becomes turned on. She and Jimmy
duck into an alley for a quickie. They return to the streets. Jimmy is
arrested. So is Ace Face, and the two share a cigarette in the paddy
wagon. Jimmy feels great. Steph rides back to London with Dave.

Finding pills in Jimmy's room, and learning of his arrest, Jimmy's
mother kicks him out of the house. When he returns at night, his
father chases him away. When his boss questions him about
missing work, Jimmy quits. He buys pills. But pills no longer
impress Steph, who has decided to stick with Dave. After Jimmy
and Dave fight, Jimmy realizes he no longer fits in with his Mod
friends. His world is falling apart.

He returns to empty Brighton, the scene of his greatest day. He
feels miserable. He spots Ace Face. He is now a bellboy (!) at a
hotel. Jimmy is fed up. He steals a cycle. He rides along the cliff by
the sea. The water looks inviting. He drives toward the cliff's edge.
The cycle crashes into the rocks below.

Quadrophenia

Quadrophenia, the most exciting, stirring, perceptive youth film since *Rebel Without a Cause* (1955),
was adapted from a concept album by The Who,
the British supergroup that formed in 1964 and
played in Brighton at the time of the Mod-Rocker
riots. Four years earlier, *Tommy* (1975) had been made from
another Who concept album and had done smash business,
but the group—lead singer Roger Daltrey, lead guitarist
and songwriter Pete Townshend, bass player John Entwistle,
and drummer Keith Moon (who died and was replaced by
Kenny Jones)—had been dissatisfied with the picture. Daltrey
(a fairly successful actor) had starred in *Tommy* and the
other three had appeared in it; like almost every other
film made in Great Britain in recent years, it had been
produced with lucrative international markets in mind
(the reason Ann-Margret and Jack Nicholson appeared).
Concerned that the once thriving British film industry, which
had long distinguished itself by making distinctly *British*
films for *British* consumption, was virtually dead and being
replaced by the "international film," the group insisted that
Quadrophenia make no concessions in order to do well abroad.*
So The Who do not appear. Except for Sting, of the controversial rock group Police, the members of the all-English cast
are unknown outside their native country, and the lead role
was handed to a short, scrawny bloke named Phil Daniels
(punk singer Hazel O'Connor's manager in 1980's *Breaking
Glass*), who's hardly the type to become an international
teen idol. Furthermore, the film's characters, products of
poor working-class families, speak with thick Cockney accents,
and their conversations are sprinkled with street lingo of the
'64 British-youth variety; there is much location footage that
is meaningful to British viewers but unfamiliar to most
foreigners; and there is no preface for the uninitiated defining
and contrasting the Mods and Rockers—their "civil war" is
not explained or put into historical and sociological context.†
The Who, *Quadrophenia*'s executive producers, even allowed
their extremely talented first-time director Franc Roddam
to take their well-known songs from their 1973 double album,
excerpt them, and use them in a peripheral manner to give
feeling to and comment on the visuals (which he does with
tremendous effect, especially with "Love Reign O'er Me"),
rather than forcing him to design the picture around the
lyrics. So although the $3 million film would not have been

---

*With the exceptions of *Chariots of Fire* (1982) and *Gandhi* (1982), about the
only successful English-made films of the late seventies and early eighties
that are clearly *British* pictures have been ones that deal with the music
scene, such as *That'll Be the Day* (1974), *Stardust* (1975), *Quadrophenia,
Breaking Glass* (1980), and *Rude Boy* (1980).
†It was described best in "The Blind Stomping the Blind" by Alan Platt in
New York's *Soho News* (November 8, 1979). I excerpt: "The Mod-Rocker
riots were a half-baked sub-plot in a genuine national upheaval. They were
pointless and all the more vicious for that reason. Mods were sharp dressers.
It was their way of kicking the country in the gray-flannel groin. Looking
crisp became a fetish. Rockers were dirty. Their stink was a different kind of
eloquence. Mods took pills. Rockers got drunk. Mods had jobs. Rockers
tried not to. Mods got called sissies by Rockers. Rockers got killed."

Short Jimmy, with pretty Steph by his side, is a big man when the Mods overrun Brighton, taking on both the Rockers and the police. Next to him in this formidable gathering are (L-R) ex-girlfriend Monkey, Mod king Ace Face (played wordlessly by Sting, the ex-schoolteacher who became lead singer of the controversial Police), Dave, and Chalky.

made if it hadn't been presold via the best-selling album, Roddam doesn't use The Who music to win over audiences: if you don't like the film's content, the songs (and the way they are employed) won't make you like the picture. Moreover, The Who's music is further deemphasized when Roddam includes other performers' music as well. Significantly, when Roddam has an American record on the soundtrack, it is only because the film's characters have placed the song on a turntable; since it is never used as background music (only The Who songs are used this way), it's clear that Roddam's intention wasn't to pander to the American audience but to show that American rock became integrated into the English youth culture (just as British rock of the era became a dominant force in the American youth culture).*

"England's first street film," as coproducer Roy Baird termed *Quadrophenia,* did exceptional business in its native country. This was not unpredictable considering The Who's continuing popularity there; the British movie audience was starved for a British product; and many of those who had participated in the Mod-Rocker scene were, in 1979, in their late twenties and early thirties—the prime movie audience. But The Who must have been surprised when the picture obtained cult status abroad, including the United States, for as Roger Daltrey said, "I can't see how Americans can identify with it."

I can't see how Americans can't identify with it. Young punk music fans can relate to the Mods in the film who define themselves by their musical taste, revolutionary fashions, antisocial posturing, and anarchical brand of violence. Those of us who were teen-agers or a bit older in the mid-sixties and were jolted off our unhappy path toward conformity by the same glorious music that brought about the Mod subcul-

ture in England—the Beatles, The Who, and other groups of the so-called "British invasion"—can't help sharing the nostalgia that our age group in England feels when viewing *Quadrophenia.* Even if we weren't in England during that period, so magical to all of us. One can become extremely sentimental, because Roddam's film is so authentic that it's hard to believe it wasn't filmed in 1964 with real Mods, in real Mod settings. Roddam has done a remarkable job recreating the world of the Mods and Rockers: dark, wet London streets, empty but for herds of Mods on Italian scooters or Rockers on heavy cycles thundering past in search of a rumble; dingy, sweat-filled clubs, where local bands further turn on the horny pill-popping dancers with loud, throbbing music; greasy diners; pinball joints; back alleys; dance halls; the outskirts of town where lookalike houses stand in a sorry line; Brighton, a breath of fresh air, the only sunlight. And everywhere you go there is music—driving, liberating music. And everywhere there is a sense of the utmost urgency. Most impressive is how deftly Roddam handles scenes with large crowds; especially those at Brighton, sweeping his camera forward from long shots, directly toward the front line of marchers, who move forward as if they were going to war ("We are Mods! We are Mods! We are, we are, we are Mods!!!"); then mingling among the masses during the Mod-Rocker and Mod-police battles, as if he were indeed covering a war. At times it looks like documentary footage. (How much more believable these scenes are than all those protester-police confrontation scenes we've seen in American movies.)

Roddam's realistic portrait of the Mod world is welcome. American youths felt a kinship for the English youths of the time because of their music, dress, and rebellious spirit, but, admittedly, the Mods confused us a bit. For instance, American teen-agers were unified by the music and, though we mildly argued as to who was better, the Beatles or the Dave Clark Five (guess who lost?), and then the Beatles or the Rolling Stones, we loved it all and couldn't understand how musical tastes were not only dividing England's youth

*Similarly, Péter Gothar has his early-sixties teen-agers play the music of the Beatles, Paul Anka, and Elvis Presley in his Hungarian film *Time Stands Still* (1982), not to attract an international audience but to show how music of the western *free* world contributed to the shaping of Hungary's rebellious youth culture of the period.

but causing riots, like the ones at Brighton during the bank holiday weekend we read about. (I guess back then we figured the Mods liked the groups that you could bring home to your parents, like the Beatles, the Dave Clark Five, Herman's Hermits, Peter and Gordon, and Gerry and the Pacemakers, while the Rockers opted for the more raucous groups. Well, we were wrong—as can be seen in *Quadrophenia*: the tougher groups such as the Rolling Stones, the Kinks, and The Who were also Mods—look at their sharp dress on the covers of their early albums. Apparently Rockers liked fifties rock 'n' roll, which makes it all ridiculous since fifties rock is what influenced all the Mod groups!) So it's enlightening to see a picture which finally teaches us about the Mods, and to have our suspicions confirmed that when Mods beat up Rockers as viciously as Keith Moon used to pound on his drums, the violence was pointless. In America, we could channel our frustrations and energies into the civil rights movement, and later the antiwar movement, but in England those rebellious youths who didn't have creative outlets turned against each other because they lacked a genuine foe.

No matter that Jim Stark (James Dean) wore a red jacket and mismatched clothes in *Rebel Without a Cause* while Jimmy Cooper is a fashion plate. They equally represent all volatile youths in throes of growing pains, in desperate search for their identities. There is so much about Jimmy's life American youths (and those who still remember being that age) can relate to: parents glued to the television set, only getting up to harass Jimmy; vain Sis under a sunlamp; mother's hysterical "It's not normal!" in reaction to any form of personal expression; father picking the time Jimmy's favorite group (The Who, natch) is on the television to complain loudly about the "rubbish" the young of the day listen to; parents returning home early to find an orgy going full blast; boss choosing to wash up and hold a lengthy conversation with another employee in the staff bathroom at the precise moment Jimmy is in a stall throwing up; best friend stealing Jimmy's girl; girl telling Jimmy their affair was "just a giggle"; Jimmy and his gang huddling on the dance floor, singing along to their favorite group's song as if it were the national anthem. My favorite scene is the one in which Jimmy returns to Brighton and walks up the side street where he battled police and thereby won the camaraderie of top Mod, Ace Face, and then walks up the alley where he had a quickie with Steph because she, too, had thrilled to his exploits. Who doesn't remember such a moment—the moment in your life when both the top dog in your crowd and your ideal lover saw you at your *best,* when you revealed your "true self."

Quadrophenia n: *Personality split into four separate facets.* I don't know exactly how this applies to Jimmy, but I imagine that it has something to do with his schizophrenic behavior in dealing, first, with the established order (parents, work) and, second, with his band of misfits. He doesn't fit in anywhere. That's why he's forever getting himself kicked out. He loses his job, his girl, his best friend, his family, his home. All to be different. And he is: he's always more excited, angrier, or more frustrated than anyone else; to him, every moment has great significance; no one is more devoted to the Mod "cause." That he's always breaking things reflects his self-destructive nature. He takes to heart The Who's lyrics from "My Generation": "I hope I die before I get old." He wants to be like James Dean, Buddy Holly, and Elvis, whose pictures are

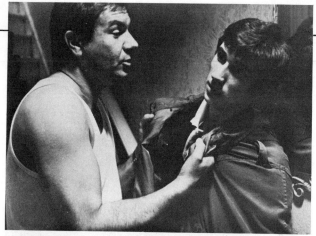

(T) At home Jimmy gets no affection or respect from his father —so he seeks it elsewhere. (B) Jimmy and Steph duck into an alley for a quickie while the rioting continues in the streets.

prominent at Alfredo's. Rather than end up like the adults he sees, he'd consider suicide: "You gotta be somebody or you might as well jump in the sea and drown." He studies the furious sea, symbol of his restlessness, solution to his misery. He "practices" being underwater (at the public baths) and diving (jumping off the balcony at the Brighton dance hall). Everything leads him to kill himself. Everyone sells out, and when Ace Face, his idol, becomes a bellboy, servant to boorish adults—it is the last straw. He steals a cycle, symbol of youthful rebellion, and rides it toward a cliff by the sea. But he gets off—disenchanted with the Mod fad—and it flies over the side, crashing into the rocks below. What the heck— today Jimmy is probably a well-respected London businessman.

In America *Quadrophenia* remains virtually undiscovered but for cultists who spread the word. I happened on it only because it was the regular feature that preceded Midnight Movie *The Rocky Horror Picture Show* (1975). It's a superb, powerful film, ambitiously directed by Roddam with great style, wit, and passion for its time and characters. Phil Daniels is so good that he may yet become a teen idol, and the other actors, including Sting, give truly believable performances. Add to all this a terrific score, made up of Who songs and numbers by Manfred Mann, the Ronettes, the Crystals, the Orlons, and other groups, and you can't help feeling that adrenaline rush we so often experienced back in the mid-sixties.

1954 Independent Productions Corporation (Simon Lazarus, President) and the International Union of Mine, Mill, and Smelter Workers

Director: Herbert Biberman
Producer: Paul Jarrico
Screenplay: Michael Wilson
Cinematography: Leonard Stark and Stanley Meredith
Music: Sol Kaplan
Editors: Ed Spiegel and Joan Laird
Running time: 94 minutes

Professional Cast: Rosaura Revueltas (Esperanza Quintero), Will Geer (sheriff), David Wolfe (Barton), Melvin Williams (Hartwell), David Sarvis (Alexander)

Nonprofessional Cast: Juan Chacón (Ramón Quintero), Henrietta Williams (Teresa Vidal), Ernest Velásquez (Charley Vidal), Angela Sánchez (Consuelo Ruíz), Joe T. Morales (Sal Ruíz), Clorinda Alderette (Luz Morales), Charles Coleman (Antonio Morales) Virginia Jencks (Ruth Barnes), Clinton Jencks (Frank Barnes), E. A. Rockwell (Vance), William Rockwell (Kimbrough), Frank Talavera (Luís), Mary Lou Castillo (Estella), Floyd Bostick (Jenkins), Victor Torres (Sebastion Prieto), E. S. Conerly (Kalinsky), Elvira Molano (Mrs. Salazar), Adolfo Barela and Albert Muñoz (miners), and the Brothers and Sisters of Local 890, International Union of Mine, Mill and Smelter Workers, Bayard, New Mexico

Synopsis: Esperanza Quintero narrates. She was pregnant with her third child. Her life was hard. She and her husband Ramón had not been getting along. Ramón's union had been contemplating a strike for the zinc miners for better wages and safer working conditions. She was angered that better sanitation in the houses—indoor plumbing and hot water—had been dropped as a union demand.

Ramón forgot it was Esperanza's Saint's Day, but his son Luis reminded him and he threw a party for his wife. For days later she forgot her misery. When a worker was injured, the men—Anglos and Chicanos—went out on strike. They picketed every day and their angry demeanor kept scabs from attempting to pass. A company representative, Hartwell, came to plan strategy. The sheriff and company foreman Anderson informed him Ramón was the ring leader. Deputies Vance and Kimbrough beat up Ramón. At that exact moment, Esperanza gave birth. They called out each other's names, although miles apart. Ramón was arrested. The day he got out, Juan was christened.

A Taft-Hartley injunction was served on the union, enjoining the men from picketing. It looked as if the strike was lost. The women at the meeting, including Esperanza, insisted that they be allowed to take over the picketing. Some men laughed, others, including Ramón, were shocked. But there was a community (not a union) vote of men and women, and the motion was approved. The women took over the picketing. Only Ramón wouldn't allow Esperanza to join in. But Esperanza disobeyed.

The women suffered much abuse. But the line held fast. The strike continued. In desperation the sheriff arrested several women, including Esperanza. She took her baby and daughter Estelle with her to jail so Ramón wouldn't have to care for them. The sheriff and his deputies were driven crazy by the women screaming for "the formula! the formula!" for Esperanza's baby. Ramón came to the jail and took the children from her. While she served her jail sentence, Ramón did the housework. Amazed by how difficult it was, he vowed to neighbor Antonio that sanitation would be included in the union demands. Esperanza returned home. She looked happy from her experience. He wanted her to stop picketing and resume her old role. She said that his telling her to stay in her place is like the racist bosses telling Mexican-Americans to stay in their place. She wants both their lives to improve, that they are strong if united.

The next morning most of the men were away getting fuel. Ramón was supposed to watch the women, but, angered, he and a few men went hunting. Esperanza's words sunk in. He told the men they must hurry back. He suspected the bosses would try something. Indeed, the sheriff and his men were evicting them, taking all the furniture from the Quintero home. Suddenly people arrived from all over. Men, women, children, workers, union men, organizers, Ramón and his men. They put everything back. Frightened, the sheriff and his men backed off. Hartwell realized he must give in on the strike. The miners and their wives had won. Ramón thanked his brothers and sisters. With their victory, they have left hope for their children, the salt of the earth.

Salt of the Earth

"I don't want to go down fighting. I want to win."

In John Sayles's *The Return of the Secaucus 7* (1981), a perceptive comedy about a group of student radicals of the late sixties and early seventies who reunite a decade later, characters remember *Salt of the Earth* as a rallying point for the political movement and the imprisoned women's "the formula! the formula!" chant as a mock battle cry for political resistance. Indeed *Salt of the Earth*, though intended for working-class people of all eras, was the one nondocumentary with which student activists of the protest years could identify. It so clearly reflected their political concerns that, catching a 16 mm print of it at some campus fundraiser for the first time, they were startled that such a film existed, especially considering it was made during the McCarthy era. They saw triumphant militant protest against a seemingly invincible authoritarian foe; characters like themselves whose political consciousness is raised (too fast perhaps) as they engage in political activity; and a film that speaks out for *solidarity* against the power elite, encompassing racial brotherhood and sexual equality. Today *Salt of the Earth* has lost none of its impact; *Norma Rae* (1979), with similar themes, may be a commendable, provocative *progressive* film, highly controversial by Hollywood standards, but by comparison to *Salt of the Earth* it is timid and gimmicky: the emphasis is on performance rather than themes; it is a celebration of an individual rather than a people; it is targeted for a liberal middle-class audience. The striking people in *Salt of the Earth* advocate reform (as did their real-life counterparts) rather than a revolutionary takeover of the mine—a bone of contention for some radicals—but for most moviegoers with political orientation no American narrative film is more inspiring and emotionally satisfying than this remarkable 1954 film.

What impresses many first-time viewers is how a film made in the early fifties should so anticipate the women's liberation movement, which didn't truly surface until the end of the sixties. "There has been no other film made for theatrical distribution in this country," writes Ruth McCormick in *Cineaste* (Vol. 5, No. 4), "that deals as basically, and as thoroughly, as does *Salt of the Earth* with the issue of women's liberation, from the politics of housework to the myth of male supremacy, the ways in which class society divides the sexes by creating false antagonism between them." *Salt of the Earth* is like an orphan in a storm. Prior to it, and for years after, no other narrative film made an issue of equality in jobs, equality in the home, and sexual equality. Perhaps the strongest female character in a progressive film,

Ramón takes the baby from Esperanza, signifying he will take care of their children and do "women's work." The sheriff is happy to see the baby go because the women in the crowded cell have been clamoring for him to get "the formula! the formula!"

Ma Joad (Jane Darwell) in *The Grapes of Wrath* (1940) represented *home*land to a homeless people and symbolized the indomitable spirit of those who struggled for human rights, but even she does not participate in political action—she leaves that to men. Except for a few World War II resistance films, most notably *Edge of Darkness* (1943)—which, safely, were set abroad—only *Salt of the Earth* dared have men and women standing side by side against the oppressors. In *Salt of the Earth* women evolve from men's subordinates to their allies and equals. Significantly, their liberation is achieved by them independently—it is not, *cannot*, be given them by men; their liberation is then, in turn, a liberating catalyst for men, who also are trapped by social convention. In her superb commentary on *Salt of the Earth* (Feminist Press, 1978), Deborah Silverton Rosenfelt writes: "Both [the women and men] learn during the course of the film that, though their needs may differ, they can best demand redress only by joining forces. The difficulty—and a major source of the film's dramatic interest—is that they learn this lesson in different ways and at different times." The liberated woman is no threat to a man; her existence will benefit him; as Esperanza assures the scared and confused Ramón: "I want to rise. And push everything up with me as I go."

The film's very existence is the result of political struggle. Director Herbert Biberman (one of the "Hollywood Ten") and producer Paul Jarrico were blacklisted in the industry, so they helped form a film company with Paul Lazarus. The Independent Production Company, financed in part by contributions, would simultaneously (1) provide film work to those denied employment in Hollywood and (2) tell "stories," as Biberman and Jarrico wrote in *The California Quarterly* (Summer 1973), "drawn from the living experiences of people long ignored in Hollywood—the working men and women of America." Its only project, as it turned out—"a crime to fit the punishment" Hollywood gave them—*Salt of the Earth* was to tell the true story of a successful thirteen-month strike at a zinc mine in New Mexico. The production would be sponsored by the International Union of Mine, Mill and Smelter Workers, which had been tossed out of the CIO for

alleged communist leanings, and have the full cooperation and participation of Local 890, the union that went on strike. Michael Wilson, who would win an Oscar as coscripter of *A Place in the Sun* (1951) but had been blacklisted in the meantime, was dispatched to New Mexico in October 1951 (three months before the strike's conclusion) to spend a month with the miners and their picketing wives. He would return twice in 1952 to discuss what he'd written with the mining community. At their insistence, Wilson eliminated scenes they feared would perpetuate negative stereotypes of the passionate Latin and the drunken Mexican: Ramón would not be unfaithful; he would only drink in moderation. "Jarrico estimates that some four hundred people had participated in reading the screenplay by production time."

With few exceptions—most notably the wonderful award-winning Mexican actress Rosaura Revueltas playing Esperanza (after Gale Sondergaard, Biberman's wife, withdrew because she is Caucasian), and Will Geer playing the sheriff—characters in the film were portrayed by those people who actually participated in the strike action. Ramón was played by Juan Chacón, the president of Local 890. (The fine, committed performances of the nonprofessionals certainly adds to the authenticity and conviction of the film.) As for the crew, the filmmakers—denied technicians by right-winger Roy Brewer's International Alliance of Theatrical and Stage Employees (IATSE)—recruited blacklisted technicians, television workers, and blacks not allowed into Brewer's segregated union.

Production began in New Mexico in January 20, 1953. Soon the establishment press began a campaign to discredit the production and to inflame its pro-McCarthy readership. Articles mentioned how "communists" were making a film near the Los Alamos testing grounds, as if the filmmakers were going to steal an atomic bomb. The *Hollywood Reporter* of February 9 contained this absurd entry:

> H'wood Reds are shooting a feature-length anti-American racial issue propaganda movie at Silver City, N. M. [Screen Actors Guild] Prexy Walter Pidgeon got the tip in a letter from a schoolteacher fan in N. M. Pidge immediately alerted FBI, State Department, House Un-American Activities Committee, and Central Intelligence Agency.

In Congress, Donald Jackson, a member of the House Un-American Activities Committee, cited a number of nonexistent scenes in the film and claimed "This picture is deliberately designed to inflame racial hatreds and to depict the United States of America as the enemy of all colored peoples. . . . I shall do everything in my power to prevent the showing of this communist-made film in the theaters of America." RKO president Howard Hughes outlined a plan of action for stopping the film from being processed and distributed.

In *The New York Times,* reporter Gladwin Hill worried: "The filming of the picture confronted the community with a microcosmic vision of the problem with which the whole nation has been grappling: what to do about suspected 'subversive' activities which nevertheless are within the law."

Fueled by such publicity, Silver City residents were, literally, up in arms. Fights broke out between vigilante groups and members of the crew. Bullets were fired into Clinton Jencks's empty car; there was a fire at the local's headquarters; store owners who serviced members of the crew were threatened.

Only intervention by Catholic clergymen and the New Mexico State Police protected the crew from being "taken out of town in pine boxes," as one vigilante group swore would happen. The day after the crew left, the house of Floyd Bostick was burned down.

To make matters worse, two weeks before shooting was concluded, Rosaura Revueltas was arrested by immigration authorities for having entered the country illegally (they hadn't stamped her passport on entry) and was detained in El Paso. Rather than risk a long trial, she volunteered to return to Mexico. Some shots of Esperanza were actually those of a double filmed from behind. Other scenes were done with Revueltas in Mexico, secretly, under the guise of being *test scenes* for future films. Her narration was also done in Mexico. Unfortunately, she would be blacklisted in her native country because of this film and never make another movie.

Eight labs in Hollywood refused to process the film. However, the filmmakers somehow managed to get it processed in a variety of sneaky ways, including passing off materials under the dummy title "Vaya con Dios." Editing took place in several secret locations, including a ladies' room in a vacant theater. Sol Kaplan got together a full orchestra to record the music. Their score is extremely good, and emotional; amazing, since the secrecy was so great that only Kaplan was allowed to see the film being scored.

Salt of the Earth had its theatrical debut in March 1954. Those critics who saw it were surprised that such concern had been voiced about this film which, basically, is pro-human rather than anti-American, which makes no pitch for revolution—just an end to exploitation and all forms of discrimination. Nevertheless, the few theaters which showed it were picketed, Roy Brewer's IATSE projectionists, who served most U.S. theaters, refused to show it, newspapers wouldn't carry ads for it, exhibitors were threatened if they showed it. As a result, only thirteen theaters in the entire country played it. (Biberman initiated a $7.5 million suit against one hundred and seven defendants he said had systematically kept the film from the public—he lost.)

Although *Salt of the Earth* did no business in America, Paul Jarrico writes me that "In France, it played for ten months, originally in a fairly small Parisian house—subtitled—and has been revived a number of times since; but a dubbed version, designed to reach a huge national audience, was not successful. In the Soviet Union, on the other hand, and in China, it had saturation bookings. And it also has played on television in a number of countries (e.g., Canada and West Germany) with, I am told, big popular approval." Even those

(T) *While hanging the laundry, Esperanza (L) and Luz Morales are visited by the more militant (L-R) Teresa Vidal, Ruth Barnes, and Consuelo Ruíz, who are intent on getting the miners to demand better sanitation in the company-owned homes. (L) After a mine mishap the angry Ramón confronts the mine operators. Charley Vidal, Frank Barnes, Sal Ruíz, and the other miners back him up. For the miners at this point, sanitation in the homes is not as important as worker safety. Later they will learn that when it comes to dignity the demands are equally important.*

The women's picket line that will bring victory in the miners' strike: better working conditions and better sanitation. "Such a film," writes Molly Haskell, "extraordinary for any time and especially in the light of the women's liberation movement . . . deserves a footnote as a rarity not only among American films, but among political ones. . . . it is the political filmmakers, brothers under the skin of oppressed minorities, who have been the most negligent in promoting the cause of women. Politics remains the most heavily— and jealously—masculine area, and the left-wing film has its own sexual mythology, preferring a vision of the peasant or laborer, in heroic silhouette, backed up—a little ways down the hill—by the patiently enduring wife."

critics who liked the picture in 1953 worried about its harming America's image(!) if shown abroad. Well, it has been shown so often abroad that Jarrico believes "it has been seen, probably, by more people than any film in history."

According to Jarrico and Biberman, *Salt of the Earth* "begged to be told without the hackneyed melodramatics which so often destroy honesty in the name of excitement. It was not the many abuses and hardships suffered by these people that loomed so significantly out of the material—it was their humanity, their courage and accomplishment." The beauty of Michael Wilson's screenplay is indeed its simplicity. We are touched by the characters because they are not epic figures—only when they stand together do they take on heroic proportions. The film is appropriately didactic (we are in fact educated), but characters do not venture into deep philosophizing or quote Marxist theoreticians; they talk and act as the characters they portray really do. The film itself is powerful and contains many emotionally charged images of people rallying to help each other; yet most of the images we react to with smiles and tears are disarmingly simple: old Mrs. Salazar joining the men's picket line; Esperanza watching her husband dance at her birthday party; the once disconsolate Esperanza returning from picketing and, later, from jail with her face aglow; Luis expressing newfound respect for his mother ("Boy! Did you see the way Mama whopped the deputy with her shoe? Knocked the gun right out . . ."), Ramón taking the baby from his imprisoned wife and accepting responsibilities, Ramón happily drinking Esperanza's coffee while he pickets. (Although the women become politicized, they never forget that they have certain talents that please men and certain talents—weapons if necessary ["the formula! the formula!"]—that can drive them crazy.)

The villain in *Salt of the Earth* is discrimination. That exercised by the white bosses on the Mexican-American workers from whom they wrangled the land. That between the workers initiated by the clever bosses who give Anglos better wages and working/living conditions than Chicanos so the two groups feel they are each other's enemies. And that exercised by male workers on their wives. A simple point or two: the Anglos and Chicanos must realize that equality with each other is irrelevant if no one is living in dignity; they must unite against the bosses, the real enemy, to assure that all their working and living standards are upgraded to a decent and safe level. Also simple: in the home, men like Ramón who want worker safety, and women like Esperanza who want sanitation (symbol of dignity) must realize that their goals are interrelated. The film details Esperanza's liberation and Ramón's reluctant acceptance of that fact, a story similar to what is going on in all the characters' homes. As Esperanza realizes, the men are *afraid* that the women will prove themselves as capable as men if given a chance. The men must give them their chance when they realize that their militant wives are the union's ace in the hole—not only have they not relied on their women enough, but the lawmakers haven't bothered putting in provisions to prevent the wives from picketing. When Ramón, in a *Life of Riley*–type scene, learns that women's housework is tough, and watches the women hold the picket line through tremendous abuse, he acknowledges his great respect for them—and, immediately, he looks as if his burden has been lightened. It is the unification of the men and women brought about by the liberation of the women that benefits the entire community and wins the strike. The women did rise, as Esperanza hoped, and they did push everything up with them.

The Seventh Seal

Sweden
1956 Svensk Filmindustri (distributed in the U.S. in 1958 by Janus Films, and in Great Britain by Contemporary Films)
Director: Ingmar Bergman
Producer: Svensk Filmindustri
Screenplay: Ingmar Bergman
Cinematography: Gunnar Fischer
Music: Erik Nordgren
Editor: Lennart Wallén
Running time: 96 minutes

Cast: Max von Sydow (the knight, Antonius Block), Gunnar Björnstrand (the squire, Jöns), Nils Poppe (Jof), Bibi Andersson (Mia), Bengt Ekerot (Death), Inga Gill (Lisa), Maud Hansson (the witch, Tyan), Inga Landgre (the knight's wife, Karin), Gunnel Lindblom (the girl), Bertil Anderberg (Raval), Erik Strandmark (Jonas Skat), Ake Fridell (the smith, Plog), Anders Ek (the monk), Gunnar Olsson (church painter)

Synopsis: It is the fourteenth century. The Swedish knight Antonius Block returns from the Crusades, and heads for his castle, where he left his wife Karin ten years before. His squire, Jöns, prays each morning, but the Knight has lost his faith. There is so much suffering in the world, especially now that the Black Plague ravages across Europe. Death comes to claim the Knight and Jöns, but the Knight convinces him to play a game of chess. If the Knight wins, Death will go on his way. Death tells him that he never loses. The game begins.

The Knight asks Death about the existence of God, but Death will not answer. Before he dies, the Knight wants knowledge. That is his only wish.

Other travelers are a troupe of actors who put on religious plays. Jof is a simple juggler who believes he sees visions of the Virgin Mary. He and his wife Mia love each other very much and hope they can give their baby, Michael, a happy life. Skat is an irresponsible oaf always on the lookout for women. During a performance Skat runs off with Lisa, the wife of Plog, the blacksmith.

Jöns comes upon Ravel, robbing the dead and attempting to rape a young woman. Ravel is the man who convinced the Knight to go on the Crusades and is now a nonbeliever. Jöns chases him away, telling him that next time he will cut his face with his knife. Jöns invites the young woman to come with him.

Jof goes into the Embarrassment Inn to drink beer. Ravel and Plog bully and threaten him. Jöns rescues Jof and, true to his word, cuts a deep gash in Ravel's face.

The Knight comes upon the actors' campsite. He shares wild strawberries with Mia and Jof and is very taken with their kindness. He almost forgets his unhappiness.

The Plague spreads. People march from town to town flagellating themselves for their sins. They believe the Plague is God's punishment. Plog, Jof, Mia, their child, and the young woman join the Knight and Jöns on their journey to the castle. They meet Skat and Lisa. Plog threatens Skat, but both men are too cowardly to actually fight. Skat pretends to kill himself and everyone goes off. Death now comes and truly takes Skat's life.

The Knight and Jöns witness a young girl being burned as a witch. They try to ameliorate her pain, but see she is too close to death to dare a rescue.

They come upon Ravel, who is dying from the Plague. They cannot help. The Knight, about to lose his chess game, knocks over the board before the final moves. The distracted Death picks up the pieces and does not see Jof and Mia ride away.

The travelers reach the castle. Karin has waited all these years for the Knight's return. She reads from Revelations. Death comes into the castle. The Knight prays to God for mercy ''because we are small and frightened and ignorant.''

It is daybreak. The sun comes out. The Plague has passed by Jof, Mia, and the baby. Jof sees Death leading the Knight, Jöns, Ravel, the young woman, Plog, and Lisa on a dance into the dark land.

I thought it would serve to remind people that they must die. . . . Why should one always make people happy? It might not be a bad idea to scare them a little once in a while.

—The Church Painter in
The Seventh Seal

From the midfifties until the early seventies, the only sure way for a guy to get a date with his dream girl was to ask her to an Ingmar Bergman movie. That impressed her with his taste and sophistication, but it was often a humbling experience; for no matter how expert the fellow was on film history, his date invariably understood Bergman better. Or at least she gave that impression through a repeated series of appreciative nods, smiles, and sighs, particularly noticeable during the film's most bewildering sequences.* Being able to give a lengthy discourse on Griffith or Hitchcock didn't matter because, she would point out, Bergman's work—so mystifying, mystical, and profound—was not based in such a popular entertainment as film. *He* came from the grand theater of Shakespeare and Strindberg (it turned out he was also part of the cinema tradition of directors Victor Sjöström and Alf Sjöberg, but who among us back then knew much about *Swedish* film history?); his words were like poetry; his images were like paintings. When it comes to Bergman, cinema dilettantes have never been intimidated by movie authorities—everyone is equally qualified to critique and interpret his pictures.

The growth of television in Sweden in the fifties cut deeply into film production. However, Bergman was already established as Sweden's lone internationally known director-screenwriter, so his studio, Svensk Filmindustri, kept producing his pictures while lesser-known filmmakers couldn't get financing. His popularity among viewers and critics became so great in his native country that eventually, *Chaplin,* Sweden's most prestigious film magazine, would only accept anti-Bergman pieces (including one written by Bergman himself under a pseudonym). In America art theater owners waited in anticipation for his pre-*Persona* (1967) pre-Liv Ullmann-Bergman masterpieces: *The Naked Night* (1956), *Smiles of a Summer Night* (1957), *The Seventh Seal* (1958), *Wild Strawberries* (1959), *The Magician* (1959), *The Virgin Spring* (1960), *Secrets of Women* (1961), *The Devil's Eye* (1961), *Through a Glass Darkly* (1962), *Winter Light* (1963), *The Silence* (1964), *All These Women* (1964).† Critics deified him, and though some viewers slept through his movies (as we see in Barry Levinson's late fifties nostalgia

---

*Women have always been Bergman's greatest supporters. This is due in part to Bergman's being considered a ''woman's director,'' one whose women characters are central, rather than subordinate, to storylines, one whose work reflects that he likes women. However, feminist critic Joan Mellen has complained about Bergman's women being ''instinctual, passive, submissive, trapped within the odors and blood of their genitals.''
†Dates are the years the films first played in America.

Although the Black Plague moves closer, Jof (L), Mia, and Skat continue to perform.

piece, *Diner,* 1982), if you wanted to prove you had culture, you went to see Bergman. "It's already possible," Hollis Alpert wrote in a 1959 issue of the *Saturday Review,* "to determine whether someone is middlebrow or upperbrow, depending on whether the word *Bergman* suggests Ingrid or Ingmar."

No Bergman film so captured the imagination of American viewers as *The Seventh Seal,* which a surprising number of today's filmmakers point to as the picture that influenced them to pursue film careers. It was a revelation to see a picture that required the audience to search for the director's meaning, just as the Knight searches for the meaning of life, in Bergman's vivid imagery and intriguing symbols, as well as his dialogue and events. And it was compelling that we didn't fully grasp Bergman's meaning at the film's conclusion or even after several viewings— after all, the Knight doesn't have his questions answered either. *"The Seventh Seal,"* wrote Andrew Sarris, "will continue to be a source of discussion for years to come—this concerns all classics of thought—the interpretations will change with the ideas and the eras of the critics." Sarris guessed correctly, for critics and viewers alike have argued over the content of *The Seventh Seal* for twenty-five years. No one has satisfactorily answered: Do the chess pieces in the game between the Knight and Death represent the individual characters in our drama? Do Jof, Mia, and their baby, who Jof believes will perform a miracle "to make one of the balls stand absolutely still in the air," represent Joseph, Mary, and the baby Jesus? What is the significance of the "wild strawberries" sequence? Where is Death leading his six captives at the end of the picture? Why is Karin, the Knight's wife, spared? (She is not one of the six we see in the distance.) Is the Knight's final prayer the act of a faithless but desperate man, or has he regained his belief in God?

Bergman based *The Seventh Seal* on a play he wrote several years earlier when he was director at the Malmo Theater in southern Sweden. Despite Bergman's stunning closeups of his actors' faces and Gunnar Fischer's marvelously composed black-and-white outdoor photography (with emphasis on gray sky, dusty land, mysterious seas), the picture remains very theatrical, its roots being Shakespeare (comedy and drama), absurdism (when drunkenly complaining about women and love, Jöns and Plog seem out of Beckett), farce (the ridiculous Plog-Lisa-Skat love triangle), and medieval morality (the Knight as Everyman) and mystery (good and evil fight over a man's soul) plays. Bergman's script itself reads as if it were a play. The only movie it reminds me of, probably because of its roving acting troupe and its members' flirtations and infidelities, is George Cukor's bizarre *Sylvia Scarlett* (1935), which itself is very theatrical, much like Shakespeare in the Park.

The Seventh Seal deals with such now familiar personal Bergman themes as Man's loss of faith, his disillusionment about life, his inability to overcome guilt and humiliation, his self-torment, fate vs. free will, good vs. evil, and conflict in marriage. All problems of the modern man. But other themes Bergman borrowed from medieval paintings that had dazzled him as a child when he accompanied his father, a Lutheran minister, through Stockholm's churches: the strolling players, the flagellants, Death playing chess, the burning of "witches," the Crusades. So *The Seventh Seal* is an allegory of our time in the form of medieval spectacle. Today we have the nuclear bomb, a terrifying reality, which is beyond the common man's comprehension but, nevertheless, may destroy us all. When we created the Bomb, we became our own God; we are responsible for mankind's destiny. *The Seventh Seal* takes place in an earlier apocalyptic age, the fourteenth century, when the Black Plague raged out of control throughout Europe. Back then, the helpless, confused common man succumbed to fate. If God wanted to destroy mankind, man would put up no resistance.

The Knight travels through a prototypical chaotic world where, the only things that can be taken for granted are Death naturally, and the presence of artists (painters, musicians, actors, and other fools), merchants, men like Jöns who are cynical about everything but God, religious fanatics, and the persecuted and victimized. All around him he witnesses dying, despair, hysteria, pestilence, and abominable acts of cruelty. He senses that if there were a God, He would not permit such misery; he reasons that if God does indeed exist and allows such atrocities, then He is a cruel God and not worthy of man's obedience and love. But something inside prevents the Knight from concluding that there is no God or that He is without mercy; and his internal struggle is intense: "Why should He hide himself in the midst of half-spoken promises and unseen miracles? Why can't I kill God within me? Why does He live on in this painful and humiliating way even though I curse Him and want to tear Him out of my heart?"

Despite the awful state of the world, everyone else firmly maintains his or her belief. The church painter tells Jöns that the Slaves of Sin are "flagellating themselves and others all for the glory of God." Jöns says that those who participated in the Crusades "let the snakes bite us, flies sting us, wild animals eat us, heathens butcher us, the wine poison us, the women give us lice, the lice devour us, the fever rot us, all for the glory of God." Everywhere the Knight looks, people are cruel to themselves and others "all for the glory of God." What Bergman finds most perverse is the way people rationalize what is transpiring as being their fault, so that God can be let off the hook. The church painter speaks of the flagellants: "The remarkable thing is that the poor creatures think the pestilence is the Lord's punishment"; another of God's apologists, the Monk, echoes these sentiments: "God has sentenced us to punishment." Jöns concurs: "Our life was too good and we were too satisfied with ourselves. The Lord wanted to punish us for our complacency." Annoyed that the people are enjoying their suffering and relishing their martyrdom, Mia muses, "I often wonder why people torture themselves as often as they can."

The Knight concludes that "the quest for life is meaningless." But he comes to realize that life itself is not, even if it does end in meaningless death. He went off on the Crusades and left his wife behind so that he could find a higher purpose in life than marriage—he now knows that the real purpose in life is to marry and have children. Jöns thinks love is as bad as the plague, but the Knight regrets he so easily dismissed it ten years past. He envies Jof and Mia, a happy, peaceful, loving couple with a child whose potential is unbounded. Sharing their wild strawberries and milk, he comes to understand that those who lead simple lives, who don't take things too seriously, who are satisfied to have faith instead of knowledge, are the happy ones. His faith in God is not necessarily restored, although his final prayer hints that it has been, but we know that he has regained his faith in humanity. I'm sure he believes he is the one who saved Jof, Mia, and their baby by distracting Death at the chessboard, and that if he had left their futures up to God, they would have been killed with the rest of the unfortunates.

Ironically, we, the viewers, see that the world has survived when the Angel of Death passes over Jof's family, so our faith in a divine being can be restored. Throughout, we believe that Death chooses his victims indiscriminately, without con-

The Knight prays to God, although he is skeptical of His existence, when Death enters his castle. (L-R) Lisa, Plog, Karin, the girl, and Jöns, face Death.

The image that appears to Jof: Death leads the Knight, Jöns, Ravel, the girl, Plog, and Lisa on a dance into the dark land. Interestingly, Karin (according to Bergman's script) is spared.

sultation with God. The ending, however, in which certain people are spared, makes us suspect that God has intervened on behalf of the survivors. There was a code of morality used in choosing who will live and who will die. Faith in God wasn't enough to guarantee one's survival—of those who die, only Ravel, the Knight, and probably Skat were short on faith. The common element among those who die is that they have all committed sins against God or humanity or both. Those who survive, Jof, Mia, their baby, and the scripture-reading Karin, as loyal to her husband as Penelope was to Odysseus, were sinless, never wavering in their faith in God, the ones they love, or humanity, always remaining optimistic

There are few more memorable cinema confrontations than the chess game between Death and the Knight in The Seventh Seal.

about the future because God will watch over them. Consequently, they are still around as the morning sun appears on the horizon for the first time in the picture, and Death dances off with his six captives to the dark land. Of this classic scene, Bergman commented in *Bergman on Bergman* (Norstedtand Förlag, 1970):

> You know that scene where they dance along the horizon? We'd packed up for the evening and were just about to go off home. It was raining. Suddenly I saw a cloud; and Fischer swung his camera up. Several of the actors had already gone home, so at a moment's notice some of the grips had to stand in, get some costumes and dance along up there. The whole take was improvised in ten minutes flat.

It goes without saying that *The Seventh Seal* is beautifully acted by Bergman regulars Max von Sydow, who gives a very subtle, subdued performance, Gunnar Björnstrand, and the luminous Bibi Andersson. Nils Poppe, who plays the simple juggler (why does he juggle with only two balls?), was Sweden's top comedian when he made his dramatic debut.

His wife, Inga Landgre, played the Knight's wife, and seems more suitable for such a serious undertaking. Bengt Ekerot, one of Sweden's most formidable theatrical actors, is so striking as Death that if he had been an American actor he might have become typecast and spent the rest of his acting life in a black robe and hood. This exceptional cast moves smoothly from morbid drama, to silly comedy, to black comedy. Although the picture itself is dated, there are many scenes in the film so memorable that they are remembered two and a half decades later. Perhaps no image is as indelible as the young girl being burned as a witch, with the Knight and Jöns standing nearby; they feel her pain but are unable to help. The scene is done quietly—in great contrast to the feverish witch burnings in Ken Russell's *The Devils* (1970)—and how devastating is the impact. It is the director's way of showing that man's confusion about God throughout history has caused him to commit great sins against man in God's name. *The Seventh Seal* is a pessimistic film by a frustrated modern man, who realizes that since we will never have absolute knowledge about the existence or nonexistence of God, life can only be satisfying and safe for those simple people who have faith, no questions asked.

1959 United Artists release of an Ashton production
Director: Billy Wilder
Producer: Billy Wilder
Screenplay: Billy Wilder and I.A.L. Diamond
Suggested by a story by R. Thoeren and M. Logan
Cinematography: Charles Lang, Jr.
Music: Adolph Deutsch
Songs supervised by Matty Malneck
"Running Wild," "I Wanna Be Loved By You," and "I'm Through With Love" sung by Marilyn Monroe
Editor: Arthur Schmidt
Running time: 120 minutes

Some Like It Hot

Cast: Marilyn Monroe (Sugar Kane/Kovalchick), Tony Curtis (Joe/Josephine), Jack Lemmon (Jerry/Daphne), George Raft (Spats Columbo), Pat O'Brien (Mulligan), Joe E. Brown (Osgood Fielding III), Nehemiah Persoff (Little Bonaparte), Joan Shawlee (Sue), Billy Gray (Poliakoff), George E. Stone (Toothpick Charlie), Dave Barry (Beinstock), Mike Mazurki (henchman), Harry Wilson (henchman), Beverly Wills (Dolores), Barbara Drew (Nellie), Edward G. Robinson, Jr. (Johnny Paradise)

Synopsis: Chicago, 1929. When Spats Columbo's speakeasy is raided on a tip from Toothpick Charlie, bass player Jerry and saxophonist Joe are out of work. Womanizer Joe gets talent agent secretary Nellie to loan him her car to play at a dance. They go to the garage just as Spats and his henchmen drive in and massacre (it's Saint Valentine's Day) Toothpick and his gang. Jerry and Joe escape. They decide they must get out of town. They dress up as women and join Sweet Sue and her Society Syncopaters, an all-girl jazz band heading for Miami. Joe chooses the name Josephine; Jerry picks Daphne.

Both Joe and Jerry are attracted to the sweet singer–ukulele player Sugar Kane. She drinks because she's unhappy that she's always falling in love with saxophone players and being dumped. During rehearsal her whiskey flask falls to the floor and Sue threatens to fire her. Daphne says it's her flask. That night Sugar climbs into Daphne's berth to thank her. Then all the other girls climb in. Sugar and Josephine become friends. Sugar says she has always been crazy about saxophone players who treated her badly. She wants to find a millionaire in Miami. One with a yacht and glasses.

The band arrives at the Seminole-Ritz. Millionaire Osgood Fielding III immediately falls for Daphne. Joe dresses up like a millionaire, with glasses and a Cary Grant accent. He meets Sugar on the beach. He talks of his yacht. She pretends to be sophisticated to impress him.

Osgood invites Daphne to his yacht. But on orders from Joe, Daphne takes Osgood dancing. Meanwhile Joe, as the millionaire, takes Sugar on board the yacht. She is impressed. He tells her that he is incapable of being excited by a woman—that if he finds one who excites him he'll marry her. Sugar asks if he'll allow her to kiss him. He agrees. She kisses passionately. He admits feeling something. When Joe sneaks back into the hotel, he finds Daphne deliriously happy because Osgood has proposed marriage and given her an expensive bracelet. Joe has to remind Daphne/Jerry that because he is a man they can't marry.

The opera convention at the hotel turns out to be a gangster convention. Spats and his henchmen attend. Jerry and Joe know they must escape. Joe the millionaire calls Sugar and says he's going away forever. Jerry and Joe try to flee. Spats spots them and there is a big chase. They hide under a table where the gangsters gather. On orders from Little Bonaparte, a friend of the late Toothpick, Spats and his men are gunned down. Now Jerry and Joe are witness to a second massacre and again flee. Joe watches as Sugar sings "I'm Through With Love." He kisses her on the mouth, saying "None of that, Sugar. No man is worth it." Sugar realizes that Josephine is no woman, and she chases after the man she loves.

Daphne and Joe climb into the boat with Osgood. Sugar jumps in too before they speed away. She and Joe kiss. It doesn't matter to her if he's not a millionaire or that he's a dreaded sax player. Jerry takes off his wig and tells Osgood they can't marry because he's a man. Osgood is unflustered: "Nobody's perfect."

We think Dana Andrews's detective in *Laura* (1944) a sick necrophiliac because he falls madly in love with a supposedly dead woman simply by staring at her alluring portrait (which causes him to fantasize about being with her and to romanticize her not so innocent life). But we are not so quick to condemn ourselves for reacting to Marilyn Monroe in essentially the same way. Fueled by our staring, with misty eyes, weak knees, and throbbing hearts, at her stunning photos and film images, our love/fanaticism for Marilyn has grown with each passing year since her mysterious death-by-drug-overdose in 1962. The impact of the photos and films cannot be overemphasized, because many of Marilyn's staunchest admirers were not born until after her death. Billy Wilder called her "the meanest woman he ever met in Hollywood," and Tony Curtis claimed "kissing her was like kissing Hitler," but that's not what we see when we stare at her irresistible image. We feel toward her a strange mixture of familial warmth; pity; lust; envy; absolute awe at her incomparable glamour, beauty, eroticism and magic (Wilder termed it "flesh impact"—you sense you can reach out and touch her); disturbing wonder about what really was and what could have been; and guilt. We don't want to hear that she was an iron butterfly, a shrewd manipulator and businesswoman, because we adore the image up there on the screen of the innocent, vulnerable, sexually generous woman. For the "true" Marilyn Monroe we flash back on the young girl, born illegitimately, whose mother spent much of her life in asylums; who was shuffled back and forth between orphanages and twelve foster homes; who lived for a time with two fanatical Christian Scientist aunts; who was raped at age nine; who stammered badly as a child; who was forced into marriage at age fourteen rather than going back to the orphanage. We think of broken marriages, miscarriages, illnesses, and breakdowns. We think of the studio executives who exploited her and of gossip columnists who slandered her. We think of all the people who tried to mold her, to educate her, to win her, to make her a great actress, to make her the consummate professional—and how she consciously and subconsciously resisted them all. We think of the brave sad woman who, through it all, stood alone. Too late, we rally behind her.

As Molly Haskell points out in *From Reverence to Rape,* women in the fifties felt jealousy and contempt for the beautiful blond child-woman with the hushed baby voice, wide eyes, moist ruby lips in the shape of an "O," a two-hour-glass figure, and a wiggly walk that makes her seem, as Jerry notes bafflingly in *Some Like It Hot,* "like Jell-O on springs." Haskell contends that while women have come to love her as much as men, "canonizing her as a martyr to male chauvinism,"

(R) Classic still shows Sugar singing "Running Wild" while the all-girl band plays "hot" music behind her. (Below) Sugar sings in the hotel nightclub.

they are now overlooking an important negative aspect of her screen persona: "women [of the fifties] hated Marilyn for catering so shamelessly to a false, regressive, childish, and detached idea of sexuality." The typical role for Marilyn Monroe was, according to Pauline Kael, "charming and embarrassing." Monroe had such remarkable screen presence that if her screen persona was, when studied in regard to sexuality, objectionable (like most "dizzy blondes," she chased after or was available to men much like the husbands of women in the movie audience), it's not surprising this has been either overlooked or forgiven. But it should be noted that some feminist critics think highly of Marilyn's sexual personality. In "Actress Archetypes in the 1950s," contained in the anthology *Women and the Cinema* (Dutton, 1977), Janice Welsch makes a strong case for the positive aspects of her persona:

> Because of their innocence and amorality, the Monroe heroines are able to dissociate sex from guilt, not only for themselves but for the men with whom they came into contact. It is Monroe's comedic talent that also makes it possible for her characters to approach their sexuality and its impact lightly, even humorously. . . . Men are attracted to them erotically at first, but soon recognize other qualities of the heroines: sensitivity, vulnerability, generosity, openness, and honesty.

The last sentence of Welsch's assessment certainly applies to *Some Like It Hot,* Marilyn Monroe's most successful and finest film.

Billy Wilder wanted to make *Some Like It Hot* (also his finest comedy) several years before it came to fruition, with Danny Kaye and Bob Hope in the male leads. Its inspiration was a German silent film called *Fanfares of Love,* coauthored by R. Thoeren, a friend of Wilder's back in pre-Hitler Berlin

who had migrated to Hollywood. Wilder bought the rights to the property, although the only thing he and script collaborator I.A.L. Diamond kept from the original was the premise: two male musicians hook up with an all-girl band. Tony Curtis, who in *Sweet Smell of Success* (1957) had proved he was more than a hank of greasy hair, and Jack Lemmon (chosen over Frank Sinatra) who was about to become Hollywood's top comic actor, were hired to play Joe and Jerry. Although her role was to be smaller than the men's parts, Marilyn Monroe came out of a two-year retirement—she had walked out on her contract at 20th because of salary and script demands—to play Sugar Kane, turning down 20th's remake of *The Blue Angel* (1959) in the process.

Marilyn brought an entourage with her for support, including husband Arthur Miller ("Men who wear glasses are so much more gentle, sweet, and helpless," states Sugar) and acting coach Paula Strasberg. Marilyn had gotten along fairly well with Wilder when they'd made *The Seven Year Itch* (1955) but this go-round she felt he was her enemy. When he suggested how she should play a scene, it so unnerved her that frequently forty takes were needed before she could deliver even the simplest dialogue correctly. Wilder resorted to pasting her lines on furniture, but even that didn't help. On painkillers because of bursitis in his arms and a back ailment that forced him to sleep in a chair, Wilder had trouble remaining patient—even though Miller informed him Marilyn was pregnant. More and more Marilyn fled to Paula Strasberg when a scene troubled her; often she would refuse to emerge from her dressing room until late in the afternoon. Her antics were causing the production to go hundreds of thousands of dollars over budget, and there was consideration about replacing her with Mitzi Gaynor. Fortunately that idea was abandoned. Wilder was disgusted with Marilyn but knew that her Sugar Kane was truly special and worth all the hassles he was enduring; as he would say years later when he felt less antagonistic toward her: "Anyone can remember lines, but it takes a real artist to come on the set and not know her lines and give the performance she did."

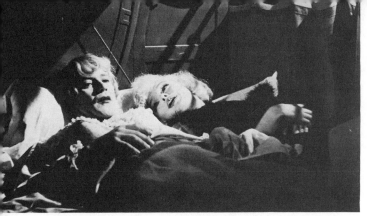

(Above) Twenty-three years before female impersonator Dustin Hoffman bedded down with an unsuspecting Jessica Lange in Tootsie (1982), Lemmon and Monroe played a similar scene. (R) Joe won't take advantage of Sugar while he's Josephine, but he's willing to do so when he pretends to be a male millionaire.

Lemmon got along with Marilyn, but Curtis greatly resented her—partly because he had to eat about forty chicken legs in one scene because of her foul-ups. He told James Brady of New York (August 6, 1973):

> She was a mean little seven-year-old, to quote Billy Wilder. Egotistical—she felt anyone else in a movie with her was a bit player. . . . Jack Lemmon and I had to be ready at 9 A.M. We dressed as girls and we'd have to get into these steel jocks and go through hours on our hair and makeup and she'd show up at noon . . . or even later. She was that erratic. Jack and I had to get it perfect every take because Wilder told us privately that whenever she was right in a take, he was going to go with that one, even if one of us was scratching himself.

In Marilyn's defense: Wilder made the film in black and white over Marilyn's objections because he didn't want the make-up on Curtis and Lemmon to make *them* look silly. This despite her having a ten percent interest in the film.

The film was completed, there was a rap party (Marilyn wasn't invited), and the picture was released to a waiting public that would make it the all-time top-grossing comedy up until that point. Attendance boomed as a result of an "MM's *bosom* buddies" newspaper ad and publicity surrounding the film's being banned in Kansas until parts of the scintillating Monroe-Curtis love scene on the yacht had been excised. Also there was a great deal of word of mouth regarding Marilyn's dynamic performance: she's plumper here than in any of her starring vehicles, but she's never been sexier as she is in her Oscar-winning diaphanous gowns (they all look like negligees), with Wilder's lighting effects directing our eyes toward her barely concealed breasts; and she's never seemed so effervescent—it's as if she truly loves all those she's working with, including Curtis!

Billy Wilder has made many films that have walked the line of bad taste. With its references to homosexuality, lesbianism, sadomasochism, oral sex ("The fuzzy/sweet end of the lollipop"), transvestism, impotence, and sex change, with MM scandalously dressed, and with its numerous double entendres, it was bound to offend some critics. But most critical reaction was in favor of *Some Like It Hot*. That's because, quite simply, it is one of the truly great Hollywood comedies. It is endlessly clever, briskly paced, deliciously acted, daring.

Like most great farces, *Some Like It Hot* deals with decep-tion and masquerade. Nothing is what it seems: a funeral car transports illegal alcohol; a funeral parlor is a front for a speakeasy; an opera convention is a gangster get-together. Everyone pretends to be someone they're not: gangsters pass as gentlemen (stupid thugs as Harvard lawyers), inspector Mulligan as a speakeasy customer, timid Jerry as an aggressive female, virile Joe as both a prim female (Eve Arden with no sense of humor) and an impotent millionaire (a Cary Grant parody), Sugar as a cultured lady. At the heart of *Some Like It Hot,* what makes it especially interesting in this era of *Outrageous!* (1977)–*La Cage aux Folles* (1979)–*Tootsie* (1982), is that it subverts traditional sexual stereotyping. Like *Sylvia Scarlett* (1935), in which Katharine Hepburn dresses as a young boy so she can have a chance in a male-dominated world, its theme is that when a person lives as the other sex, he or she has the opportunity to explore previously latent aspects of the personality, to reveal his or her real self. Daphne and Josephine are not the alter egos of Jerry and Joe, respectively: they are *more* (extensions) of the two men. *Some Like It Hot* "is not about transsexuality," alleges Brandon French in *On the Verge of Revolt* (Ungar, 1978). "It's about androgyny, the state of being both male and female."

In Wilder's screen world people are identified by what they wear, carry, or own: badges, spats, toothpicks, guns, glasses, earrings, saxophones, basses, ukuleles, whiskey flasks, admiral's caps, yachts, money, high heels, skirts, bathing suits, brassieres, bracelets, lipstick, nightgowns (Sugar, who has been around, is the only girl whose nightie isn't white and buttoned at the neck), and gowns. By film's end, that will change: characters will be indentified by who they are. The male world is characterized by Chicago 1929 (Wilder parodies gangster movies): guns, booze, murder and death, vulgarity. That's what Jerry and Joe happily escape from when they don women's clothing. Interestingly, when they become women they don't assume traditionally (for movies) silly women's poses (although Jerry refers to Josephine's carrying on with Sugar "whispering and giggling and borrowing each other's lipstick"). They become two tough, smart, fun-to-be-with broads, who will take guff from no man and are loyal friends to other women. Like Sweet Sue, they ain't sweet.

At first they take advantage of their female dress to spy on unsuspecting females who undress for bed—living out a male fantasy to sneak into a girls' slumber party. But their female side (their consciences, their sense of what's right) constantly keeps them from taking full advantage of any woman. They develop a female perspective: "We wouldn't be caught dead with men. Rough hairy beasts! Eight hands!" When Jerry and Joe first speak of men as "they" ("They all just want one thing from a girl") it's because Sue and her all-girl band are standing there; but later when the two use "they" in reference to men ("They don't care—just so long as you're wearing a skirt"), the men are by themselves. In the Jerry-Joe relationship, Jerry (who plays a curvaceous bass) is the "female" always being taken advantage of by Joe (who plays a phallic saxophone, the movie's symbol for an aggressive male "heel"); Jerry is also Joe's feminine conscience, who tells him to treat women with more respect. It is not surprising that Jerry takes to being a "female" quite easily. He enjoys the chance, as is evident when he inspiringly chooses the name "Daphne" and when he dumps all the luggage on Oswald, the first man she sees (symbolically, Brandon French points out, "divesting himself of all male burdens"). Sugar is Jerry's role model: both have blond hair, they wear identical swimsuits, they walk with wiggles, they chase millionaires. Jerry initially wishes he were dead because as a female he can't make a play for any of the women in the band; he ends up wishing he were dead because he wrongly thinks that being a male he can't marry Osgood. Enjoying the good female life, he refers to himself as female (Jerry: "I'm engaged." Joe: "Who's the lucky girl?" Jerry: "I am") and refuses to steal from Osgood and be the proverbial female "tramp taking jewelry from a man under false pretenses." Brandon French: "While it's possible to argue that Jerry is simply gay and that his relationship with Osgood is homosexual, it is equally valid to see Jerry's feminization as the expression of a 'normal' male longing for passivity and dependence, which even the more virile Joe adopts in his portrayal of the millionaire."

The male Joe dumped on women; as Josephine he becomes a bona fide friend to Sugar. He develops a sisterly affection toward her. Sugar relates to him when he's in female garb more openly than any female ever has. Only as Josephine can he see the real, wonderful Sugar, because she puts on acts for men (millionaire Joe). He learns how she would like to be treated by men, and from his female experiences has come to respect her feelings. It's significant that he kisses her full on the mouth while in full drag (a startling scene!) because it shows that even when they become a heterosexual couple he wants them to retain their special *female* bond (friendship and truthfulness). Jerry and Joe change dramatically: unlike Spats, who considers "getting soft" a sign of weakness in a man, they accept their transitions. Once a victim, Sugar changes too, taking on male characteristics: aggressiveness in love (she is on top of Joe in the yacht), chasing after a man who left her. It's an odd lot that rides off in Osgood's boat, full of sexual identity problems to sort out. But they are improving all the time; besides, as Osgood says when Jerry confesses he's a man—a line that is truly brave (no copout here!)—"Nobody's perfect."

(L) Daphne and Osgood begin the date of their lives. (R) Publicity photo of Tony Curtis.

Sullivan's Travels

1941 Paramount
Director: Preston Sturges
Associate Producer: Paul Jones
Screenplay: Preston Sturges
Cinematography: John F. Seitz
Music: Leo Shuken and Charles Bradshaw
Editor: Stuart Gilmore
Running time: 91 minutes

Cast: Joel McCrea (John L. Sullivan), Veronica Lake (the girl), Robert Warwick (Mr. LeBrand), William Demarest (Mr. Jones), Franklin Pangborn (Mr. Casalsis), Porter Hall (Mr. Hadrian), Byron Foulger (Mr. Valdelle), Robert Greig (butler), Eric Blore (valet), Margaret Hayes (secretary), Torben Meyer (doctor), Al Bridge (Mr. Carson), Esther Howard (Miz Zeffie), Almira Sessions (Ursula), Jimmy Conlin (Trusty), Frank Moran (chauffeur), J. Farrell MacDonald (desk sergeant)

Synopsis: John L. Sullivan, famous director of such films as *So Long, Sarong* informs studio execs LeBrand and Hadrian that he is going to make a film about human suffering. Knowing that message films die at the box office, they try to discourage him by telling him he knows nothing of human suffering. But Sullivan decides to dress up in hobo clothes, with only ten cents in his pocket, and do some firsthand investigation. The studio decides to turn it into a publicity stunt. They hire an entourage to follow him around in a land yacht. Sullivan's valet and butler tell Sullivan that he should call off his mission, that the poor want their privacy.

Sullivan hitches a ride with a thirteen-year-old speed demon. Everyone in the land yacht is bounced around, so they agree to meet Sullivan later in Las Vegas. Sullivan goes on alone. He chops wood for two elderly sisters. When it's obvious they want to hold on to him, he sneaks out at night and falls in a barrel of water. Freezing, he hitches a ride and ends up back in L.A., discouraged. At a diner, a beautiful young girl, who has given up trying to make it in Hollywood, buys him breakfast. He is touched and tells her he'll give her an introduction to Lubitsch. Seeing how he's dressed, she just wants a ride home. He leaves and comes back in a limousine. She thinks he stole it. He says he used to be a director. The police arrest him, as he forgot to leave a note for his valet and butler that he was borrowing the car. They come to the station to identify him. The girl finds out that he truly is a director. She insists on accompanying him on his mission.

So Sullivan and the girl, who is dressed as a boy, hop trains, sleep in flop houses, eat at missions, mingle with the poor. Sullivan's boots are stolen and replaced with an inferior pair. When there is no one to get food from, he and the girl eat from garbage cans. It's time to go home.

Sullivan can't get a divorce but tells the girl to stick around and he'll give her an introduction to Lubitsch.

That night, Sullivan walks among the poor passing out five-dollar bills. The same hobo who stole his boots knocks him out and throws him into a boxcar heading south. The hobo is struck by a train. The body is unrecognizable but the boots he wears containing Sullivan's I.D. convinces everyone that Sullivan is dead.

Meanwhile, Sullivan, suffering temporary amnesia, hits a railroad guard who bullies him. He's sentenced to a chain gang for six years. He and the other prisoners have a miserable existence. Sullivan's friend Trusty gets Sullivan permission to attend the picture show at the local Negro church. A Mickey Mouse cartoon comes on and all the prisoners laugh hysterically—including Sullivan.

Thinking of a way to get attention, Sullivan admits to the murder of John L. Sullivan. His picture is in the paper and everyone recognizes him. He is freed. Since his wife is now remarried, she has to give him a divorce. He will marry the girl, and will make comedies. He realizes how important laughter is to people who have nothing else.

Publicity shot of Sullivan and the girl entering a flophouse.

In the early forties Preston Sturges and Orson Welles were undoubtedly the two most exciting directors to emerge in Hollywood. They each possessed an audacious creative drive (Sturges was an inventor, Welles the son of one), a tremendous intellect, and a fondness for *words* and their delivery (apart from dialogue per se) that separated them from their contemporaries. Unlike most thirties and forties directors, who had been involved in filmmaking from the moment they dropped or flunked out of school, both Sturges and Welles had been well educated and, as children, had been taken on several cultural-indoctrination tours of Europe. Sturges, who evidently enjoyed these trips less than Welles, would have an anticultural bias in his films; Welles's mission would be to elevate the cultural level of film. Both men broke into show business in New York theater, Sturges as a playwright and Welles as an actor and director. Sturges moved to Hollywood in the late twenties and became one of the top screenwriters of the following decade; Welles, seventeen years his junior, made a big name for himself with his Mercury Theatre radio productions. In 1940 he too moved to Hollywood when offered a directorial contract by RKO—it was the same year Sturges convinced Paramount to let him direct his first film. The excited Welles compared making movies to playing with an electric train—an interesting analogy considering Sturges (who actually invented the first kissproof lipstick while helping out at his mother's cosmetics firm) spent much of his free time building electric trains—one of which was used in a special effects scene in *Sullivan's Travels*. Welles's first film, *Citizen Kane* (1941), was (and is) hailed as a true original. In structure (a dead millionaire's story is told in a nonchronological series of flashbacks) it resembles *The Power and the Glory* (1933), which had been scripted by Sturges. Although Welles would direct a number of masterpieces in years to come, his three-film Hollywood halcyon period lasted little more than two years. Sturges's peak period lasted only a year longer, and though his 1948 comedy *Unfaithfully Yours* has admirers, his career took an even more precipitous and inexplicable decline—after 1944 there would be no more masterpieces.

But between 1940 and 1944 *The Great McGinty* (1940), *Christmas in July* (1940), *The Lady Eve, Sullivan's Travels,* (1941), *The Palm Beach Story* (1942), *The Miracle of Morgan's Creek* (1944), *Hail the Conquering Hero* (1944), and to a lesser degree *The Great Moment* (1944)—a truly remarkable body of work—established Preston Sturges as a great comedy director. On a par with Lubitsch, Hawks, and Capra, superior to La Cava, McCarey, and Stevens. Where he had it over all other comedy directors of Hollywood's golden years was that he also wrote his films. A tremendous influence on future directors Frank Tashlin, Blake Edwards, Woody Allen, and Paul Mazursky, Sturges was, along with Chaplin, Capra, and Lubitsch, a wicked satirist. His targets were everyone and everything, including politics, society, royalty, patriotism, advertising, well-meaning liberals (like John L. Sullivan), reactionaries, management and unions (hobo Sullivan is hired to promote Moe's Pants, about which he knows nothing, and his hobo companion—the girl—is hired by the union to picket the company, about which she too knows nothing), small-town innocence, motherly love, heroism, Horatio Alger's rags-to-riches myth, and last but not least, Hollywood, which he lampoons in his scripts for both *The Good Fairy* (1935) and *Sullivan's Travels*.

In Sturges everyone has a chance to achieve the American Dream. A trackman becomes a railroad magnate in *The Power and the Glory,* a salesman a multimillionaire in the Sturges-scripted *Diamond Jim* (1935); penniless women get the opportunity to marry millionaires in *The Good Fairy, The Lady Eve, Sullivan's Travels, The Palm Beach Story,* and Sturges's script for *Easy Living* (1937); a nobody becomes mayor in *Hail the Conquering Hero,* a bum becomes governor in *The Great McGinty.* The perverse twist in Sturges is that no Horatio Alger work ethic is necessary. People can get what they want simply by passing themselves off as something they're not (a traditional element of farce): Sylvia Sidney pretends to be royalty in *Thirty Day Princess* (1933); crooked Brian Donlevy pretends to be an honest politician in *The Great McGinty;* swindler Barbara Stanwyck feigns honesty to hoodwink naïve millionaire Henry Fonda in *The Lady Eve;* 4-F Eddie Bracken passes himself off as a war hero in *Hail the Conquering Hero;* though penniless, Edward Arnold in *Diamond Jim* and Jean Arthur in *Easy Living* dress in fancy clothes to get entry into high places—similarly and ironically, in *Sullivan's Travels* John L. Sullivan trades in his rich clothes for rags to gain entry into the world of the poor. And luck plays a bigger part than honest work: a mink falls out of a window and lands on Jean Arthur in *Easy Living;* Dick

Underrated leading man Joel McCrea is surrounded by four of Hollywood's finest character actors: (L-R) Robert Warwick, William Demarest, Franklin Pangborn, and Porter Hall.

Powell wins a slogan contest in *Christmas in July;* the citizens of Eddie Bracken's hometown get the facts mixed up in *Conquering Hero;* the bum whom the Hollywood hopeful helps out in *Sullivan's Travels* just happens to be a millionaire Hollywood director. Characters in need are often helped out by kindly benefactors. In *Diamond Jim,* Diamond Jim sponsors Lillian Russell's career just as Sullivan does the girl's. Also, in *Sullivan's Travels* Sullivan walks around giving five-dollar bills to destitute strangers. When a generous lunch wagon owner gives free coffee and doughnuts to the broke Sullivan and the girl, he is rewarded with a hundred dollars. He asks why. "It's Christmas!" In Sturges, it's always Christmas. Miracles—like the birth of sextuplets to Betty Hutton, perhaps still a virgin, in Morgan's Creek—are common occurrences in Sturges films. Sturges may be cynical about the world during the Depression and war years, but he has his fingers crossed for the individual.

If *Sullivan's Travels* were indeed a film set at Christmas time, it would have a good chance to become a seasonal cult film along the lines of Frank Capra's *It's a Wonderful Life (1946).* As it is, it seems to be getting more popular every year—as people discover it on television or at Sturges retrospectives. (A remake directed by Peter Hyams went into preproduction in 1982.) Although it is not a sentimental picture, as Sturges's approach was always different from Capra's and McCarey's, it is the director's most caring, most kind-hearted film. Sullivan may conclude that filmmakers have an obligation to make comedies because all some people have is laughter, but Sturges shows us in *Sullivan's Travels* that a good Hollywood film can mix the most outrageous comedy with a social message. We laugh at the hysterical dialogue, at the farcical situations (W. C. Fields could have played the scenes with the sisters), at the satirical barbs against *irrelevant* targets (i.e., Hollywood), and at the slapstick: Keystone Kops–like chases, pratfalls (Veronica Lake trips repeatedly), characters getting food dumped on them, characters ripping the seats of their pants, characters falling into water barrels, characters getting lamps broken on their heads. But we also pay attention to the parade of poverty's victims that cross the screen. We experience the suffering, the desperation, the lack of dignity. Comedies with a social conscience have never dominated the Hollywood scene. *Sullivan's Travels* may be the best of its kind; today, its images of the destitute and the lost and forgotten are particularly relevant—especially

(Below) In the back of his chauffeured limo Sullivan proves to the girl (Veronica Lake with her peekaboo bang) that he's richer than his torn clothes indicate. (R) Sullivan's worried butler and valet wish Sullivan and the girl luck as they embark on their excursion.

since once again (as it was during Sturges's heyday) filmmakers are only giving us *escapist* films. I don't think Sturges was mocking contemporary filmmakers who wanted to make message films, especially since with rare exceptions—*I Am a Fugitive From a Chain Gang* (1932), Warners' gangster pictures, *Hallelujah I'm a Bum* (1933), *The Grapes of Wrath* (1940), and moments in Capra—no one was making such films. It's likely that Sturges wanted to relieve his guilt for not making them, so he made one under the guise of a comedy—just as Woody Allen would do less successfully with *Stardust Memories* (1981). Joel McCrea told me, "Preston always said 'We have no right to invite people into a theater and bore them for forty-five minutes.' *Sullivan's Travels* is my favorite film because it manages to blend comedy and drama so well." I imagine McCrea also likes the film because it proved once and for all that he was an excellent actor, besides being a handsome, likable screen personality. ("Sturges once said that I was one of the most underrated actors in Hollywood," McCrea writes in *Close-Ups* [Workman, 1979], "and that has always meant a lot to me.") The screen relationship between McCrea, who is well over six feet tall, and Veronica Lake, five foot two and ninety pounds, is absolutely wonderful. Sullivan and the girl have sweet feelings toward each other throughout the film, never partake in any "obligatory" bickering after she pushes him in the pool, and are always protective of one another. She's spunky and funny, he's enthusiastic and humble. Both are generous and sentimental. An ideal couple. Sturges, going along with Sullivan's "a little sex" dictum for *all* pictures, presents them both in ways to appeal to viewers of the opposite sex. McCrea is bare-chested at times; Lake, although eight months pregnant when filming was completed, does a leggy, cheesecake pose by the pool and later takes *two* sexy showers. I suppose Sturges was forced by Paramount to give Hollywood's

newest sex siren those few moments to titillate her audience, especially since through most of the film her famous peekaboo locks are covered by a cap, her hollow cheeks are covered by dirt, and her large bosom is covered by an unflattering oversized man's coat. Lake had her best opportunity to act, and she is terrific. (McCrea and Lake were reunited in a fine 1947 western, *Ramrod,* directed by André De Toth, then Lake's husband. Lake played a villainess.)

"Preston Sturges was a genius," says McCrea. "Especially at writing dialogue." According to a 1954 article by Manny Farber and W. S. Poster, "Sturges's free-wheeling dialogue is his most original contribution to films and accomplishes, among other things, the destruction of the common image of Americans as tight-lipped Hemingwayan creatures who converse in grating monosyllables and chopped sentences." What you notice during the delightful dialogues in *Sullivan's Travels* is the humor, of course, and the rhythm. It's not like in Hawks's films, where words from the various speakers overlap. Instead it's like a relay race with words as batons. The second one character finishes his sentence, another starts his. Several characters join in; there are no gaps, and the pace becomes frenetic. You won't think "That's just how people talk," as you may with Hawks, but you'll find yourself thinking "That's what great *movie* dialogue sounds like!" What adds to the effect is that Sturges often holds his camera on his actors through long stretches of dialogue. The brilliant early conversation between Sullivan, LeBrand, and Hadrian runs for 390 feet without a cutaway; the boxcar scene with Sullivan and the girl runs seven script pages without a break. What's also special about Sturges's dialogues is how he lets everyone speak. *Sullivan's Travels* is filled with splendid character actors, most of whom were part of Sturges's stock company, and Sturges democratically gives all of them important and wise things to say. In fact, the butler's speech about poverty (how only the morbid rich glamorize it) is the most significant in the film. Everyone in Sturges's cockeyed-caravan world has a voice.

Sullivan's Travels. A Swiftian journey through parts of America many American moviegoers don't want to see. In my opinion, it's the best Sturges film, the only one that doesn't lose momentum after a hilarious beginning, the one that has the most to say—to people then and to people now.

Taxi Driver

1976 Columbia
Director: Martin Scorsese
Producers: Michael Phillips and Julia Phillips
Story and screenplay: Paul Schrader
Cinematography: Michael Chapman
Music: Bernard Herrmann
Supervising editor: Marcia Lucas
Editors: Tom Rolf and Melvin Shapiro
Running time: 112 minutes

Cast: Robert De Niro (Travis Bickle), Cybill Shepherd (Betsy), Peter Boyle (Wizard), Jodie Foster (Iris), Harvey Keitel (Sport), Leonard Harris (Charles Palantine), Albert Brooks (Tom), Martin Scorsese (taxi passenger), Steven Prince (gun salesman), Joe Spinell (personnel officer)

Synopsis: Ex-marine Travis Bickle, twenty-six, takes a job as a New York City cabbie. Unable to sleep, and suffering from terrible headaches and stomach pains, he works long shifts and goes into all parts of the city for fares. He spends his coffee breaks listening to Wizard, who has an incomprehensible philosophy of life, and to other cabbies, who relate their fantasies and spout racial slurs. But he has no friends and spends his time off alone: in his cell-like room, watching soap operas or writing in his diary, or sitting in rundown porno houses.

Travis gets a crush on Betsy, a beautiful blonde who works in the presidential campaign of Charles Palantine. He gets up enough nerve to ask her to lunch. Intrigued, Betsy accepts, despite the warnings of Tom, her fellow worker. She admits being attracted to him, and agrees to go to a movie with him at night. However, when he takes her to a porno theater, she becomes angry and storms off. Realizing he's a bit unbalanced she refuses to date Travis again or to return his messages. Frustrated, Travis goes to her office and tells her she's like all the other women he's known: cold and distant. As Betsy's coworkers drag him from the office, he screams at her "You'll die in hell!"

Travis picks up a weird fare who tells him that he wants to shoot his wife with a .44 magnum for sleeping with a black. Travis's headaches get worse and his hatred for the city increases. He admits to Wizard that he's starting to get bad ideas. He buys a .44 magnum and several other guns.

Travis decides that he must get a twelve-year-old blond prostitute named Iris away from her pimp, Sport, and send her back to her parents in New Jersey. At one of their two meetings she tells him that she likes being with Sport. No matter, Travis begins his plan. He puts aside some money for Iris.

He goes into vigorous physical training. He shaves his head except for a strip down the middle. He stands in front of a mirror and challenges make-believe adversaries. He attaches several weapons to himself. He has become a dead shot at a firing range, and has even shot a would-be holdup man.

Travis decides to assassinate Palantine at a rally. But when he is chased by a Secret Service man, his plans change. Instead he kills Sport and several men who work in the building where Iris is a prostitute. He is shot several times in the bloodbath. The newspapers write of his brave deeds. Iris's parents write to thank him for sending their girl home.

Recovered from his wounds, Travis is at peace with himself and the city. One night Betsy gets in his cab. She hints that she would like to get together with him now that he's a hero. But he isn't interested. He doesn't charge her for the fare, drops her off, and rides off into the night.

Something backfired. Neither director Martin Scorsese nor screenwriter Paul Schrader wanted Travis Bickle to be another of those irresponsibly drawn Charles Bronson–*Death Wish* (1974)–type vigilantes who viewers cheer on during their one-man murder sprees. They didn't intend for anyone to identify with Travis after he goes off the deep end. By including such bits as Travis venting his twisted biblical fury on Betsy ("You'll die in hell!"), and replacing his friendly bangs with a grotesque Mohawk hairstyle, they expected viewers to be jolted into instant alienation. By having him become, figuratively, an extension of his taxi (as if he had mastered the art of Zen cabdriving) and later the weapons and metal gadgets he attaches to himself, they attempted to stress he is no longer a human being, much less a working-class hero.

But when filmmakers created a lead character who is as wrongheaded as Travis—always a racist and misogynist, ultimately a wacko—they must diligently state *in the film* that she or he is no hero to be emulated. Especially if the character is played by as likable an actor as Robert De Niro and performs brave deeds during which villains are killed and which could be misconstrued as heroic. Surely filmmakers can be less subtle in such cases without compromising their artistic integrity. Because we have learned from the history of the skillfully crafted yet decidedly unpleasant *Taxi Driver* that filmmakers must be responsible. For after seeing the picture fifteen times, John W. Hinckley, a loner whose contempt for society was as great as his obsessive love for actress Jodie Foster, chose to imitate Travis, not reject him. Travis attempted to assassinate presidential candidate Charles Palantine; Hinckley tried to gun down President Reagan, and came much closer than Travis in succeeding. Travis wanted to rescue young Iris, played by Jodie Foster, from her life as a prostitute; Hinckley "wanted to rescue" (his words) Jodie Foster, whom he courted relentlessly, from . . . Yale? Surely *Newsday* critic Joseph Gelmis was prophetic, when he reviewed the film upon its release: "*Taxi Driver* . . . is definitely not suitable for the squeamish, the impressionable, the very young, or the emotionally disturbed." (Hinckley may be the extreme case, but he is not alone: when I last saw the film, there were cheers at Travis's first appearance in his Mohawk cut and at the memorable glaring-in-the-mirror scene when, like a punk gunslinger, he threateningly challenges his fantasized opponent, "You talkin' to me???")

It's reasonable to assume that Schrader based his social outcast, at least in part, on Arthur Bremmer, who, ironically, decided to assassinate presidential candidate George Wallace after seeing *A Clockwork Orange* (1971). Like Travis, Bremmer was a loony loner who kept a bizarre diary, stuck photos of his projected target on his wall, was rejected by a blonde, and once shaved his head. It's possible that Schrader was also inspired by Bobby Thompson (Tim O'Kelly), Peter Bogdanovich's mass murderer in *Targets* (1968), although Schrader's singularly cold approach (he likes movies, not people) has always been at odds with Bogdanovich's humanistic style. Both Travis and Bobby are obsessed with guns (although in Travis's case this doesn't manifest itself until later). Both live in a cultural void: Bobby plays loud A.M. rock; Travis watches soap operas and porno loops. Both reveal immaturity: Bobby munches on Baby Ruths, Travis on Chuckles and Jujubes; each flees danger (real and fabricated) like a kid

(Above) Martin Scorsese plays one of Travis's "sicko" fares. (L) Travis becomes a frightening figure when he attaches guns to himself, as if he were preparing for guerrilla warfare.

being caught with stolen comics under his shirt. And they both know that they are losing control but can't articulate their problems: "I'm getting funny ideas," says Bobby; "I'm getting some bad ideas in my head," echoes Travis. They resort to violent acts with guns because subconsciously they are trying to overcome their stifled sexual, psychological, emotional, and intellectual developments.

Schrader has acknowledged that Travis was influenced by the protagonist in *Pickpocket* (1959), directed by his idol, France's Robert Bresson. There are similarities, but Travis is scarier and much more aggressive than Bresson's victimized thief. Maybe this is simply because De Niro has the rare ability (shared only by Marlon Brando and Bruce Dern) to portray a man smiling on the outside and exploding on the inside; never has he been more menacing than in the mirror sequence. Surprisingly, Schrader claims Travis was based mostly on himself when he was living through a particularly hellish period. "I had drawn back from the world," he told columnist Marilyn Beck. "I had retreated from friends, lived in my own private world, and escaped with drink until I finally landed in the hospital. When the pain subsided and my stomach healed, it hit me there was a perfect metaphor: someone living a life like a taxi driver, drifting through a sewer in an iron coffin, surrounded by people, but alone."

The cab-as-coffin metaphor is appropriate, for what Travis experiences as he drives silently through a civilization that has undergone a moral apocalypse is not so much a nightmare as a deathdream. The surreal has become the real. Off-speed, garish photography, camera pans that (by directorial design) seem to go in the wrong direction, and mesmerizing shots of the taxi gliding over the wet streets (recalling images from Victor Sjöström's 1920 Swedish classic *The Phantom Carriage*), through madly flashing, multicolored lights, and past shadowy figures that emerge from the darkness, establish that Travis is out of sync with the world around him. These haunting rides—the most compelling segments in the film— are brilliant mood pieces. No director has better captured the peculiarly wretched *feel* and *odor,* as well as the look, of the underbelly of New York. (How different is Scorsese's stylized, romantic city of the post–World War II era in *New York, New York* [1977].) It's a terrifying, subjective vision of the city after dark when, as Travis states, "all the animals come out." Turn on your light and the cockroaches will scatter. Pimps, drug fiends, hookers, drunks, crazies, and the lonely and lost mill about in the filth, under brightly lit porno theater marquees. The air is thick with paranoia, despair, hopelessness, hatred, black-white hostility. The accompanying music of Bernard Herrmann—completed the day he died—was the jazziest of his long career: lower-class music with seductive sax riffs and occasional trumpet leads, like that played in cynical forties detective movies when *noir* directors (rich white men) wanted to signify that the atmosphere itself was corrupt and evil. The New York we see should "be flushed down the fuckin' toilet," as Travis suggests to Palantine, but curiously, it obsesses Travis, who drives throught the worst areas of town *by choice* and spends

At Palantine's headquarters Tom (played by comedian-director Albert Brooks, who has a cult of his own) tells Betsy that she should stay away from Travis.

Travis meets child prostitute Iris. He soon becomes obsessed with returning her to "respectability."

his free time in grimy porno houses. Are Scorsese and Schrader intimating that those hypocrites who speak loudest against porno districts are the ones who make them flourish? Or, more likely, are the Catholic director and Calvinist-trained screenwriter showing us a guilt-ridden man punishing himself by immersing himself in this degrading environment? Can he cleanse his soul only by emerging from purgatory?

Like the Schrader-scripted-and-directed *Hardcore* (1979), in which self-righteous Calvinist George C. Scott tracks his missing daughter through the porno world, *Taxi Driver* borrows many elements from John Ford's seminal western, *The Searchers* (1956). Again we have a war veteran, a social misfit, an outcast, who is obsessed with rescuing a young girl (after failing to rescue a young woman) from her long-haired lover (Scar/Sport), although she is happy where she is. In order to purify his *own* soul (on the pretext of purifying the girl's). In *The Searchers*, when Scar is killed, Ethan Edwards (John Wayne) is at peace with himself and the world around him; the same thing happens to Travis upon the deaths of Sport and his cohorts. All that's missing is for Travis to point his gun at Iris, like Ethan does with Debbie (Natalie Wood), and then realize he no longer has a need to kill her.

It's important to note that both Ethan, a rebel in the Civil War, and Travis, a marine in Vietnam, were on nonvictorious sides in what they believed were wars of liberation. Then we can better understand their fanatical desires to *liberate* the young girls from foreign camps. Just as Debbie is under the spell of the evil Scar, Betsy (underrated Cybill Shepherd is perfect as the tempting WASP beauty of Travis's fantasies) and Iris (Jodie Foster hasn't enough screen time to show her remarkable depth), have fallen for the smooth lines fed them by political bull artist Palantine and pimp/conman Sport (whose one long, sharp, red fingernail indicates he does indeed cast spells on little girls). Travis's fanatical training prior to his rescue attempts is, in effect, much like the training of a soldier preparing for a mission. The military drumbeat on the soundtrack emphasizes the connection in Travis's mind between war and the task he is about to undertake. His painful, ritualistic exercises and the shaving of his head hint that he is like a flagellating monk, hurting himself to purify himself.

Taxi Driver won the Golden Palm at Cannes in 1976, took

the New York Critics' awards for Best Director and Best Actor, and continues to be an enormous favorite of fans and critics impressed by its gritty realism, orgiastic violence, standout performances, and overwhelming cynicism. But an equal number resent *Taxi Driver*, mostly because of its bleak resolution, culminating in Travis's apotheosis. Travis is pacified by his violent spree, which frees Iris. Apparently a *planned* murder that is carried out is what the shrink ordered for giving Travis salvation. (His *random* murder of the black holdup man didn't do the trick.) Now this man, whom we had considered a hopeless mental case, is a calm, sane person; someone who no longer needs to cruise 42nd and Broadway or Harlem, but picks up fares on Fifth Avenue. Unlike Ethan Edwards, Travis becomes part of the civilized world. Sure, some people commit violent acts to let the world know they are alive and, in their sick minds, to spiritually rise above the muck. But do they stop suffering after one such act, as we sense has happened to Travis? It's hard to believe a maniac

Travis talks to Sport about Iris. It is a brilliant, sparring exchange between friends De Niro and Keitel.

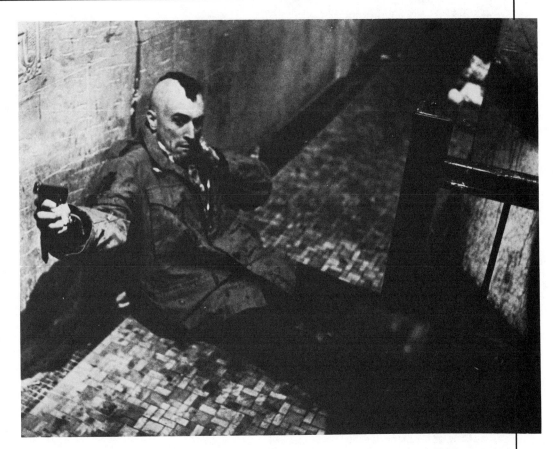

Determined to "rescue" Iris, Travis, in a Mohawk cut, charges into the grungy hotel in which she works and proceeds to shoot everyone who blocks his path. At this point he is badly injured himself.

can get rid of inner demons and become "a person" (Travis's goal in life) by committing, or attempting to commit, cold-blooded murder.

Taxi Driver is filled with other ironies that also seem wrongly conceived. That this fellow who would have angered an entire country if he had killed Palantine becomes a hero for instead killing disreputable characters (to save a young girl) seems logical—except that he'd been spotted at the Palantine rally and was certainly the object of a widespread police search. His headline-grabbing exploits should have landed him in prison. That Betsy would change her feelings toward Travis after he becomes a hero is absurd—she has seen how unhinged he is and would never become turned on to someone who once screamed she should die in hell. Moreover, Travis, a 16 mm porno addict, wouldn't think a *big date* means taking a woman to a 35 mm porno theater: he may be ignorant, but as his writing in his diary indicates, he is not *stupid*. That Travis can put on the Secret Service agent (saying his name's Henry Kinkle) prior to a Palantine rally gives De Niro a chance to be humorous, but most psychiatrists would agree that when nearing the time of an assassination attempt, the first thing to go in a potential assassin's distorted mind would be his sense of humor.

De Niro has never been better than in *Taxi Driver*. His verbal sparring with friend Harvey Keitel, in particular, is great, and we can see simultaneously many aspects of his character and the actor who plays him. The problem is that too often Scorsese has his favorite actor do a standard "De Niro bit," rather than be Travis, and in this character piece that is confusing. As in the scene with the Secret Service man. Or in those pickup scenes with the candy counter girl

and Betsy. It's the De Niro we see trying to pick up Liza Minnelli in *New York, New York* in the ballroom (only there De Niro, playing an ex-soldier who was victorious in war, exudes a bit more confidence). Part-polite, part-presumptuous, part-cocky, part-shy; half-smiling, half-crying from rejection. And when Travis's slurring machine-gun patter includes repeated phrases and questions (to give one the impression the actor is improvising) we are reminded that De Niro plays characters who have trouble articulating in all his Scorsese films, except *King of Comedy* (1983). Travis is a study in contradictions, "partly truth and partly fiction," but his schizophrenia should be represented by two sides of Travis, not one side of Travis and one side of De Niro.

Martin Scorsese is one of our most talented and important directors. When many directors have sold out, he continues to make character films instead of action films in which heroes drive speeding cars into poor people's food carts; adult films instead of kiddie fare. But he is at his best when he has compassion for his male characters: David Carradine in *Boxcar Bertha* (1972); Keitel and De Niro in *Mean Streets* (1973); Kris Kristofferson in *Alice Doesn't Live Here Anymore* (1975); De Niro in growing cult favorite *New York, New York;* and the Band in his cult rock film *The Last Waltz* (1978). It's commendable he takes chances making films with characters who aren't all that appealing, but unfortunately pictures like *Taxi Driver,* where Travis is repulsive, suffer because he feels so coldly toward his characters. Maybe he should look for projects written by screenwriters who like people, and stay away from material written by Paul Schrader, whose films— except *Blue Collar* (1978)—are populated with men you don't want to spend two hours watching.

1942 United Artists release of an
Alexander Korda-Ernst Lubitsch production
Director: Ernst Lubitsch
Producer: Ernst Lubitsch
Screenplay: Edwin Justus Mayer
From a story by Ernst Lubitsch and Melchior Lengyel
Cinematography: Rudolph Maté
Music: Werner Hayman
Editor: Dorothy Spencer
Running time: 99 minutes

To Be or Not to Be

Cast: Carole Lombard (Maria Tura), Jack Benny (Joseph Tura), Robert Stack (Lieutenant Stanislav Sobinski), Felix Bressart (Greenberg), Lionel Atwill (Rawitch), Stanley Ridges (Professor Siletsky), Sig Ruman (Colonel Ehrhardt), Tom Dugan (Bronski), Charles Halton (Dobosh), George Lynn (actor-adjutant), Armand Wright (makeup man), Henry Victor (stage manager), Holliwell Hobbes (General Armstrong), Miles Mander (Major Cunningham), Leslie Dennison (captain), Frank Reicher (Polish officer), Helmut Dantine (copilot)

Synopsis: The setting is Poland, 1939. An acting troupe headed by the egocentric Joseph Tura and Maria Tura rehearse a satirical play called *Gestapo* in which Bronski impersonates Hitler. The play is called off by authorities, so the troupe goes back to doing *Hamlet.* Each time Joseph delivers the line "To be or not to be" a soldier in the second row, named Sobinski, gets up and leaves, causing great damage to Joseph's ego. Joseph doesn't know that his line is a signal for Sobinski to meet with Maria, with whom he is carrying on an innocent (thus far) flirtation. War intervenes and Sobinski goes to England, where he joins a Polish squadron of the RAF. Poland is occupied by the Nazis under Gestapo leader Colonel Ehrhardt, but a resistance arises, giving new hope to the country.

When the Polish squadron finds out that Professor Siletsky, who has delivered broadcasts condemning the Nazis, is flying back to Poland, they give him mail to deliver to their relatives, many of whom are in the underground. When Sobinski tells Siletsky to deliver a message ("To be or not to be") to Maria Tura, he discovers Siletsky never heard of her. He becomes suspicious and informs the English brass who realize that Siletsky is going to deliver the names of the soldiers' relatives to the Gestapo. Sobinski flies to Warsaw to try to head him off. He enlists the help of Maria and Joseph. But plans go awry. Maria is summoned to Siletsky's hotel room and can't get out even after Siletsky leaves for a meeting with Ehrhardt.

Siletsky has never met Ehrhardt and he is fooled by Joseph, wearing Nazi garb. But he figures out the trickery and almost escapes. Sobinski kills him. Disguised as Siletsky, Joseph goes to the hotel to rescue Maria. While there, he is ordered to Gestapo headquarters as Siletsky. Maria tells Joseph she loves only him and that he's as great an actor as he thinks he is.

Joseph fools the foolish Ehrhardt. He gives the names of two underground leaders whom he knows Ehrhardt has already executed. Ehrhardt promises him a plane to Sweden where he'll take his "mistress" Maria Tura. But the body of Siletsky is found. Figuring Joseph is an imposter, Ehrhardt puts him in the room with the corpse, expecting Joseph to crack. But Joseph shaves off Siletsky's real beard and substitutes a fake beard. When Ehrhardt pulls it off, he thinks the dead man was the imposter and apologizes to Joseph.

The actors decide to take advantage of Hitler's visit to Warsaw to plan an escape attempt. Dressed as Nazis, they march into the amphitheater Hitler is attending. Greenberg gets the real Nazis' attention in the hallway by delivering a speech by Shylock. Because of the commotion, Bronski, as Hitler, leaves the arena with the fake Nazis and the supposedly arrested Greenberg. They go to pick up Maria. But Ehrhardt arrives and decides to wait for her secret lover. Bronski enters dressed as Hitler. After they leave, Ehrhardt tries to shoot himself.

The troupe escapes in Hitler's plane. They perform *Hamlet* in England. Sobinski watches from the second row. Joseph says "To be or not to be." A soldier in the third row gets up and walks out.

P aramount designed an upbeat publicity campaign for Ernst Lubitsch's *To Be or Not to Be,* which it expected to be a huge hit, but it was dumped when star Carole Lombard was killed in a plane crash during a war bonds–selling tour, two months prior to the picture's release. It was impossible to promote. When the film failed at the box office, Paramount execs alibied it was because audiences were too torn up by the tragic death of Hollywood's most beloved comedienne to see her so soon in another picture, particularly a comedy. It seemed like a better explanation than "Lubitsch has lost his 'touch,' " but just as suspect. It's more accurate that the majority of moviegoers stayed away because they considered a comedy set in Nazi-occupied Poland to be itself untimely. (Some insisted that it could *never* be funny, even if the Nazis were pushed out of Poland.) Cult films are often born in controversy, and few have caused such a rift among moviegoers as *To Be or Not to Be* did upon its release, three years after Germany invaded Poland, three months after the United States entered World War II. Naturally, film critics were at the forefront of the

Inspired casting allowed Jack Benny, as Joseph Tura, to play Hamlet.

heated debate. The most influential, Bosley Crowther of *The New York Times,* was one who seethed:

> Frankly, this corner is unable even remotely to comprehend the humor. . . . What is the element of mirth in the remark which a German colonel makes regarding [Joseph Tura's] acting: "What he did to Shakespeare we are doing now to Poland"? Even if one were able to forget the present horror which this implies, the butchery of a people would hardly be matter for jest. Yet all the way through this picture runs a strange imperception of feeling. You might almost think Mr. Lubitsch had the attitude "anything for a laugh."

To Be or Not to Be's reputation improved with each passing year, coinciding with the public's growing acceptance of World War II comedies: from wartime Warner Bros. cartoons in which Bugs Bunny, Porky Pig, and even the cowardly Daffy Duck battled Hitler; to such nonsense as *The Devil With Hitler* (1942) and *That Natzy Nuisance* (1943); to Bob Hope's popular *My Favorite Blonde* (1942); to those countless comedies made after the war ended in which stupid American heroes get the best of Nazi buffoons; to television's insipid *Hogan's Heroes,* a series set in a German POW camp. By 1965, when *Hogan's Heroes* debuted, *To Be or Not to Be* had come to be regarded as one of the cinema's great films—a staple in college film courses and at revival theaters (in France and England, as well as the United States), where it frequently doubles with Charlie Chaplin's earlier controversial Nazi spoof *The Great Dictator* (1940). It would be presumptuous to infer that critics like Crowther—who, it should be pointed out, raved about Chaplin's black comedy *Monsieur Verdoux* (1947), when most others attacked Chaplin for attempting humor against a background of murder and human suffering—and those viewers who agreed with them, were overly sensitive when watching the Lubitsch film. I'm sure that most of us would find it difficult to laugh at a comedy about the Vietnamese boat people or set in a Cambodian refugee camp. And would this generation be able to laugh at a comedy set inside a German concentration camp? I doubt it, no matter how hard we laugh each time Joseph Tura's Ehrhardt-imposter or the real Ehrhardt gloats, "So they call me Concentration Camp Ehrhardt!" But it's interesting to note that critics were lenient to those World War II comedies that made no attempt to impress upon viewers the grim realities of Nazi aggression and occupation in Europe, while they jumped on Lubitsch's film for daring to be both a comedy and topical. The opposite should have been the case. Remove the jokes and the exaggeration from *To Be or Not to Be,* and we still have a clever, exciting, relevant story.

If you want to defend *To Be or Not to Be,* begin by pointing out a disturbing reality: prior to its release, only a pitiful few American-made films—of which almost half were directed by men born in Europe—had dealt in any way with the Nazi menace, here or in a war-ravaged Europe. Among them: Anatole Litvak's *Confessions of a Nazi Spy* (1939), *The Mortal Storm* (1940), *Escape* (1940), John Brahm's *Escape to Glory* (1940), *Four Sons* (1940), Alfred Hitchcock's *Foreign Correspondent* (1940), *Underground* (1941), Fritz Lang's *Man Hunt* (1941); and comedies, Chaplin's *The Great Dictator, All Through the Night* (1942), which has elements of melodrama, and *World Premiere* (1941). So *To Be or Not to Be,* directed by a man who left Germany in the late twenties, was one of the

The acting troupe prepares an anti-Hitler play. Tura (on the table) is to play a Gestapo leader, and Rawitch (to his right) a general; Bronski is made up as Hitler, and Greenberg (to his left) will play a minor role as usual.

first films that debunked the Nazi myth, and that it was in production before the United States declared war makes it all the more impressive.

In fact, *To Be or Not to Be* is just as effective as propaganda as it is as farce. The picture opens with Bronski walking through the streets of Warsaw. Friendly people gather around, including happy children, and in the background we see stores named for the families who own them. It's an ideal community. Later, when Warsaw is reduced to rubble, we return to this setting. Unhappy, starving people wander through the debris of the stores we saw earlier. We get angry. When the Nazis are shown marching into Warsaw, we get angrier. But our spirits rise when the dramatic narrator, who could very well be brother of the one in Capra's later "Why We Fight" documentary-propaganda series, enthusiastically reports that there is a new spirit among Poles: "Down with the Nazis! Down with Hitler!" At this point Lubitsch includes a montage of the Polish underground arising, breaking windows, putting up anti-Hitler graffiti. This is followed by the Polish squadron in the RAF singing a patriotic song. As do most films that take place in World War II Europe, there is considerable emphasis on the bravery, resourcefulness, and indomitable spirit of the beleaguered people. America would be reluctant to help a country that has given up. When the underground blows up the railroad toward the end of the picture, we are encouraged to help them. The Poles are putting themselves on the line to thwart the Nazis' war effort, but they can't do it alone. . . .

All kinds of people are in the movement, from humble bookstore owners to hammy actors. And even among the acting troupe, all levels of people participate equally, from spear carrier Greenberg to the Polish Lunt and Fontanne, Joseph and Maria Tura—she, the queen of the theater and, as Sobinski states, an institution in Poland. If Bob Hope had played Joseph Tura, the emphasis would have been on the character's cowardice and would have overshadowed his egotism; Lubitsch wisely wrote Tura with Jack Benny in mind, because Benny (at that point in his career at least) could play a character so prideful that fear doesn't enter the picture. He is ideal as this actor who defines his wife (with whom he has an

(L) Maria pretends to be charmed by Siletsky. (R) Joseph wonders why the soldier who always walked out on his performances (Sobinski) has turned up in his bed.

acting rivalry) in this way: "Her husband is that great, great Polish actor . . ." In *Casablanca* (1942) the point made is that self-despising men like Bogart's Rick Blaine should stop being self-centered and join the war effort; in *To Be or Not to Be* the point made is that the most conceited man around should stop being self-centered until the war is won. Like Rick Blaine, Joseph must forget his jealousy ("I'll decide with whom my wife's going to have dinner and whom she's going to kill") and save Poland ("If I don't come back I forgive you. . . . If I do it's a different matter"). For the film's title refers to the existence of Poland.

Throughout, Lubitsch attacks two targets simultaneously. When the Nazis (the Gestapo, the occupation soldiers) are made to look stupid, it always reflects back on their leader, who has made them subservient, paranoid, power-hungry, tactlessly arrogant, and confused; when Bronski ("Heil me") or Joseph (who even questions Hitler's health fanaticism) mocks the leader, it reflects on the Nazis who follow him on his insane path.

Critics of the day complained that Lubitsch portrayed the Nazis as ninnies, or, better, Keystone Kops. But certainly Professor Siletsky is as shrewd and evil a Nazi as Conrad Veidt ever played. When Maria pretends to fall for his flirtations and Joseph tries to pass himself off as Ehrhardt, we worry even as we laugh because we realize just how dangerous Siletsky is. Ehrhardt is far less intelligent—it's understood that Germans follow Hitler like sheep because of his charisma, but foreigners become Nazis because they adhere to Nazi philosophy expounded by Hitler. He is the perfect comic foil for Joseph. Yet while we laugh at him, we know that he is as dangerous as Siletsky: this dimwit has the power to have Poles executed with a motion of his pen, and has made that motion so often, and so indiscriminately, that he doesn't even remember the names of those he's had killed. We never forget that he is ruthless.

Critics protested Lubitsch having a group of ham actors outwit Nazis. But if we look closely, we realize that in all of Poland, even with its resistance, *only* this acting troupe could accomplish the desperate mission required, to stop Siletsky from delivering names of underground members to the Gestapo and then to escape via Hitler's plane. Only these hammy actors, amateurs joining the war effort, have the

tremendous egos that can compete with those of the Nazis; only they have the talent for deceit and disguise that can put them on equal footing with spy Siletsky. Even so, it is made clear that for these actors to have a chance at succeeding they must *perform* as never before: Maria, who had insisted on wearing a satin gown in a concentration camp scene in a play, humbles herself by playing up to Siletsky; before attempting to deceive Siletsky, Joseph knows "I'm going to have to do the impossible. I'm going to have to surpass myself"; Bronski, who had found it impossible trying to convince the Polish that he looks like Hitler when in disguise, fools the Germans with his portrayal; and Greenberg, always a spear carrier in stage productions, becomes elevated to star when the actors need someone to attract the German soldiers' attention. Regardless of how successful the acting troupe is at the end, we are aware that they made one blunder after another and are *lucky* to get away.* (Importantly, Siletsky is smart enough a Nazi to see through Joseph's act, and would escape and reach Ehrhardt if it weren't for Sobinski, the *professional* soldier.) They realize that the Germans will soon figure out their chicanery. And we know that, once caught, they will be shot. We do *not* take these Nazis lightly!

Lubitsch is known for his comedies of manners, where even the penniless vagabond can win a princess through a combination of charm and civility, plus a little old-fashioned underhandedness. *To Be or Not to Be* is a film in which everyone tries to *impress* everyone else by being who they're not. But here it's with ruthlessness, tasteless wit, and much old-fashioned underhandedness. If one character can win over another, it is not only a personal victory (as it is in other Lubitsch comedies) but, as they are playing for higher stakes, one with greater ramifications. The continuous deception and disguises are staples of French farce, as is the bedroom intrigue, and are typical Lubitsch. So are the moments of screwball comedy (the infighting between Joseph and Maria is reminiscent of that between stage actors John Barrymore and Lombard in Howard Hawks's 1934 classic *Twentieth Century*), the sexual innuendo (Maria's eyes light up when she

---

*I have always thought that *To Be or Not to Be* would make an ideal television series. A hammy acting troupe working underground in Europe during World War II would be a terrific premise.

learns Sobinski can drop quite a load of dynamite in very little time) and downright naughtiness, and the flights into burlesque, slapstick, and exaggerated spoof. Lubitsch had flirted with satire before, usually attacking social mores but on occasion taking a political swat, as in *Ninotchka* (1939). Most impressive is how Lubitsch and Edwin Justus Mayer, whose script is brimming with clever twists and sparkling dialogue, incorporated scenes that made best use of Jack Benny's particular talents. Listen to the lines exchanged between Benny and Stanley Ridges (Siletsky) and Benny and the screen's greatest comic Nazi, Sig Ruman (hilarious as Ehrhardt), particularly the beginnings of sentences ("So they call me . . ." "Tell me . . ."): they sound exactly as if they were dialogues written for Benny's classic radio program. Those moments when Joseph stops his *Hamlet* soliloquy and, being too amazed and insulted to talk, silently watches Sobinski rise in the audience and walk out, are unforgettable. Similar things would happen on Benny's later television show during his monologues, such as a baby penguin emerging from the wings and crossing the stage on roller skates.

Directors often use their camera to make love to their leading ladies, and this was definitely the case in *To Be or Not to Be*. Never had Carole Lombard looked lovelier than in her final picture, never more glamorous, never sexier, whether seen in medium shot in her slinky white satin gown or in extreme closeup, when she has an ethereal presence. What a great dramatic actress this former Mack Sennett comedienne had become: her Maria is dazzlingly comical, then deadly serious as she becomes involved in the plot to stop Siletsky; she is half in a daze (almost whispering her lines) when meeting Siletsky and being offered the role of Nazi spy, moves into an icy calm when she can't get out of the Nazi-controlled hotel, and shows amazing intensity as the plan becomes increasingly dangerous. Lombard's reactions are stunning: her face responds to a character in one way (usually deceptively) while her eyes tell us viewers what Maria is really thinking and feeling. Lombard considered *To Be or Not to Be* her greatest film and her performance the greatest of her brilliant career. She was right.

Ehrhardt is upset he insisted on sticking around until Maria's secret lover turned up. He mistakes Bronski for Hitler.

Vanishing Point

1971 20th Century-Fox release of a Cupid production
Director: Richard C. Sarafian
Producer: Norman Spencer
Screenplay: Guillermo Cain
From a story outline by Malcolm Hart
Cinematography: John A. Alonzo
Music producer and supervisor: Jimmy Bowen
Songs: By various artists
Editor: Stefan Arnsten
Running time: 99 minutes

Cast: Barry Newman (Kowalski), Cleavon Little (Super Soul), Dean Jagger (prospector), Victoria Medlin (Vera), Paul Koslo (young cop), Bob Donner (older cop), Timothy Scott (Angel), Gilda Texter (nude rider), Anthony James (first male hitchhiker), Arthur Malet (second male hitchhiker), Karl Swenson (clerk), Severn Darden (J. Hovah), Delaney & Bonnie & Friends, including Rita Coolidge (J. Hovah's singers), John Amos

Synopsis: Two bulldozers move together to form a police roadblock. Kowalski speeds his white Dodge Challenger down the road. When he sees the roadblock he does a 180° turn and heads back. He passes a black car going in the opposite direction. We are in California. It is Sunday morning. The cars speed onward—the Challenger vanishes.

Two days earlier, at night, Kowalski returned a car to Sandy in Denver. Kowalski would take drive-away cars from Denver to San Francisco and back. Sandy told him to deliver the Challenger to San Francisco. Against Sandy's objections Kowalski insisted on leaving immediately, without sleep, to drive to San Francisco in fifteen hours. Along the way, Kowalski picked up some speed from his friend Jake.

Kowalski sped through Colorado. Cops gave chase, but he soon left them in the dust. He became an affront to all patrolmen in the state. They were determined to catch him. Kowalski listened to KOW's deejay Super Soul, a black, blind, hyperactive philosopher who gave Kowalski advice on how to elude the police. Super Soul listened in on secret police radio reports.

Kowalski drove faster and faster and his fame in the state grew. A cocky guy in a Jaguar tried to run him off the road. The Jaguar ended up in a creek. Kowalski, as usual, made sure no one was hurt before continuing.

Kowalski had flashbacks. To when he was a professional race car driver. He wasn't very good because he didn't care about the money. To when he was a cop and he stopped a fellow officer from molesting a pretty young dope suspect. He was thrown off the force for that. To his free-spirited girlfriend Vera. She had died in a surfing accident.

Kowalski went off into the desert. He was saved from a rattlesnake by an old prospector who took him to a faithhealing music ceremony in the desert being conducted by cult lord J. Hovah. Hovah gave the prospector gasoline for Kowalski.

Kowalski drove faster and faster. Into Nevada. State police pursued him in vain. Into California. The police didn't try to shoot him because he'd only committed misdemeanors. They learned he was a decorated war hero. Kowalski picked up two gay hitchhikers. They tried to rob him. He knocked them from his car.

Rednecks entered the KOW station. They beat up Super Soul. They forced him to provide Kowalski with wrong information about police roadblocks. Kowalski figured out that something was wrong. With the help of a hippie couple, Angel and his nude girlfriend, Kowalski eluded the police.

Sunday morning. Super Soul resumed broadcasting. "Speed means freedom of the soul," he stated. "The question is not when he's going to stop, but who's going to stop him."

The bulldozers move into place. Kowalski does not do a 180° turn. He smiles weakly and drives into the roadblock. His car explodes with him inside. Super Soul sits in his station, looking as if he has lost his best friend.

Publicity photo shows a cop on a motorcycle blocking Kowalski's Challenger.

We return to those thrilling days of yesteryear—not way back to the days of the Lone Ranger, when Grant was president and the nation was rebuilding after the Civil War, but to an equally distinct era that came one hundred years later. Of course, we remember them as the Dick Nixon and Delaney & Bonnie (married then) & Friends years, when the country itself was split asunder by an aloof president and an unpopular war, and the dropout counterculture was united by drugs, music, an antiestablishment bias, and abstract antimaterialistic philosophies. It's then that another lone stranger rides defiantly through the West, not on a white charger but a white Challenger (Dodge). The lawmen of the territory do not trust him ("Maybe he killed somebody") because quite frankly he gives every indication of being an outlaw; for instance, he moves so fast it's clear that he doesn't want anyone to see his face. Who is this mystery man who always leaves in a cloud of dust—just like the Lone Ranger used to do? They don't know that he used to be a cop, too—just as the Long Ranger didn't let on he had been a Texas Ranger. The Lone Ranger gave up his John Reid identity and his past when he donned his mask; the lone stranger considers Kowalski, the man he was—an ex-cop, ex-war hero, ex-professional race car driver—to be dead, and his past irrelevant. True, there is no faithful Indian named Tonto by his side, but he is aided in his adventures by people who are as excluded from mainstream society as Tonto was: black, drug-dealer Jake; black, blind disk jockey Super Soul; an old, slightly balmy prospector (the Lone Ranger's most frequent disguise); snake worshiper, faith healer J. Hovah, a white "medicine man," who provides Kowalski with gasoline;

and hippies Angel (who scouts on his cycle as well as Tonto did on his horse Scout) and his willing-to-please nude girlfriend. Yes, Kowalski would be a contemporary Lone Ranger but for one thing. He forgets to do anything heroic. Perhaps, caught in his own deathtrip, he figures that he can best serve his fellow misfits in this repressive country by dying a martyr's death and making the police, the establishment's watchdogs, seem like murderers. The trouble for us as viewers, however, is that no matter how noble his self-sacrificial gesture seems (and it seems like a stupid, defeatest, self-gratifying act to me), we can't help feeling that this pill-popping, self-destructive speed demon (whom we see in a flashback crash on a race track) is a menace to all of us on the road. For everybody's safety, we should hope that he'll be arrested. This is a time we really get annoyed a filmmaker has made all his cops be inept jerks. (Kowalski could have been a legitimate hero, despite having done nothing worthy, if the police had just been portrayed as *intelligent* fascists.)

Because the high-speed car chase in *Bullitt* (1968) had such an impact on the public (it is still unsurpassed for excitement) and on filmmakers who saw a good way to fill twenty minutes of screen time in their own dreary films, almost every action film of the following years included an obligatory car chase. This was *Vanishing Point*'s starting point. "It must have seemed like a sure-fire idea," wrote critic Roger Greenspun. "So many dumb movies have been saved by an exciting automobile chase in the last few minutes—why not make a dumb movie that is nothing but an automobile chase?" But director Richard Sarafian was more clever than Greenspun realized. He was looking for the perfect movie formula, just as surfers look for the perfect wave. He noticed that there was also a proliferation of "personal," low-budget existential films that used *the road* as a metaphor for lives that have no meaning, no direction, no beginning, and no end. So he decided to mix the car chase, hallmark of the action film, into an existential road film. He threw in some gorgeous Colorado-Nevada-California scenery (everyone was getting into nature in those days), a bit of nudity (a girl on a motorcycle in the desert???), some acoustic and psychedelic rock music* (perfectly attuned to the era), and stereotypes from the counterculture. And the youthcult ate it up. Never mind that the picture makes little sense (Who knows what the title means, for instance?) because these were the years when stoned and tripping moviegoers were so thankful for any cinematic puzzle/"head" trip that they were willing to give the filmmaker the benefit of the doubt and believe he really had something to say. "While pretending to deal with Everything, *Vanishing Point* is about nothing," complained critic Jon Carroll in *Take One*. "Burn this film."

What I find most dishonest about the film is the way Sarafian and screenwriter Guillermo Cain manipulate the youth audience into regarding Kowalski as its hero. First they make him an ex–war *hero* (not just a simple soldier) who, for the viewer's sake, is against war. (Big deal. So is everyone else. The important question is: what were his feelings about the *Vietnam* war?) Second they make him an ex-cop, but instead of showing him busting a lot of unlucky people they *only* show the time he stops a fellow cop from molesting a pretty drug suspect. Thus he becomes champion of those who can't fight back—and as Tom Laughlin realized when making *Billy Jack* (1971), even the pacifists in the movie audience love to believe that a brave violence-prone man is around to defend them and be on their side. Third, and most significant, they have "cool" characters, whom viewers would like to have for friends, befriend Kowalski. If Vera, Super Soul—who thinks of Kowalski as "the last American hero," the symbol of our dying freedom ("speed means freedom of the soul")—Jake, the old prospector, Angel, and his nude girlfriend think well of Kowalski then he must be all right. However, I seriously doubt that in the real world any of these people except the prospector would care for Kowalski. His fans would more likely be the Evel Knievel daredevil crowd. But of course, those people aren't such avid moviegoers.

There is much in *Vanishing Point* to dislike. Dramatically the film suffers because Kowalski commits only misdemeanors; as a result, the police play fairly, neither shooting their guns nor chasing him past state lines. The actors all look and act dog-tired in the desert heat, except for spry Dean Jagger. Barry Newman, who is not a bad actor (his deep voice and tough beard make him ideal for "macho" Noxema shaving cream commercials), is used so badly that he appears to be a stick figure; Cleavon Little, as a combination of Stevie Wonder, Joe Cocker doing his spastic act, and the worst deejays on radio, is simply ludicrous. Charlotte Rampling, who might have given the film a spark as a hitchhiker Kowalski sleeps with, was eliminated after previews. The dialogue is stupid ("I love your scar," says Vera) and trite, particularly the simplistic, pretentious aphorisms ("Only if you make war on

Charlotte Rampling filmed scenes with Barry Newman that were deleted from the film.

war will you overcome it"; "The best way to get away is to root right where you are"). All the women are portrayed as love objects, willing to hop into the sack with any lonely stranger (the myth of the counterculture female is perpetuated). The only misfits who don't help Kowalski are homosexuals (even youth films in those days made homosexuals into comical deviants). The ending in which Kowalski kills himself makes little sense—from his early conversations with Sandy and Jake there is reason to believe he fully intends to complete his trip to San Francisco.

There is much in *Vanishing Point* that is confusing. Did Kowalski's surfing girlfriend Vera accidentally drown or did she commit suicide because of his despondency? Are the rednecks who beat up Super Soul racist townspeople, young conservatives who resent his helping rebel Kowalski, or po-

Superanimated disc jockey Super Soul becomes Kowalski's cheerleader.

---

*Unknown Kim Carnes composed one song and sang another.

Gay hitchhikers attempt to rob Kowalski.

licemen in plain clothes, as a studio synopsis states? How can Super Soul's tiny radio station be heard clearly over three states? Why does the already tired Kowalski insist he can drive from Denver to San Francisco in fifteen hours? ("Existential reasons," insisted Jon Carroll, "which means that the director does not have the wit to invent a credible, real-world explanation.") Are all past events we see, which make up almost all of the film, supposed to be what passes through Kowalski's mind as he prepares to crash into the roadblock? And what is the meaning of Kowalski driving past himself (white car passes black car), as if he were going back in time, and his white Challenger vanishing? Is this *vanishing point* the point where Kowalski ceases to be of flesh and blood and becomes part spirit and part myth? I can't figure it out. Anitra Earle of the *San Francisco Chronicle* wrote that this scene signifies that Kowalski is "a vanishing man: the indomitable individualist whom society cannot catch without destroying, and this it gladly does." Could be.

After all this, let me admit that I half enjoy *Vanishing Point.* I've grown weary of car chases in films as has almost everyone else, but the stuntwork here (I believe by people who worked on *Bullitt*) is truly spectacular. Considering that stunts make up the major portion of the film, they had to be good. I'm also grateful that there are few actual car crashes (seeing new cars destroyed on screen is as infuriating to me as seeing rock stars smash their expensive guitars on stage for the "sake of art"), and no scenes in which our hero drives over peasants' vegetable carts, into a new restaurant, or through a large pane of glass. Kowalski drives like a tourist guide who missed the last reststop, but the scenery we glimpse is indeed breathtaking, and the camerawork from fast-moving vehicles and helicopters is stunning. What I like best about the film is its depiction of a coast-to-coast network of weirdos, dropouts, and misfits ready to help wayfaring strangers. The characters Sarafian gives us aren't real (Angel comes closest), but there really was such a network back then: you could travel cross-country and in most places find such people who'd freely offer you food, drink, drugs if you wanted them, a place to crash, and the addresses of their friends in towns along your route. To me, *Vanishing Point* is a document of its times: it is itself the prototype of the youthcult films made back then, and it also shows a finer aspect of the sixties-seventies counterculture, for which I have nostalgic feelings.

White Heat

1949 Warner Bros.
Director: Raoul Walsh
Producer: Louis F. Edelman
Screenplay: Ivan Goff and Ben Roberts

From a story by Virginia Kellogg
Cinematography: Sid Hickox
Music: Max Steiner
Editor: Owen Marks
Running time: 114 minutes

Cast: James Cagney (Cody Jarrett), Virginia Mayo (Verna Jarrett), Edmond O'Brien (Hank Fallon/Vic Pardo), Margaret Wycherly (Ma Jarrett), Steve Cochran (Big Ed Somers), John Archer (Philip Evans), Wally Cassell (Cotton Valetti), Mickey Knox (Het Kohler), Ian Mac-Donald (Bo Creel), Fred Clark (The Trader), G. Pat Collins (The Reader), Paul Guilfoyle (Roy Parker), Fred Coby (Happy Taylor), Ford Rainey (Zuckie Hommell), Robert Osterloh (Tommy Ryley)

Synopsis: Cody Jarrett's gang robs a train on the California state line and kills four railroad men. They hide out in a mountain cabin. Cody realizes that Big Ed would like to take over the gang. Big Ed and the others realize that Cody is insane. Even Verna, Cody's pretty but not so smart wife, would trade in her husband for Ed. Only Ma Jarrett backs Cody. She is the only one not afraid of him.

The gang splits up, leaving the injured Zuckie behind. His frozen body is discovered. A pack of cigarettes in his pocket bear Cotton's fingerprints, so Philip Evans of the Treasury Department realizes it was Cody's gang who pulled off the train heist. They track Cody to Los Angeles and to the motel where Cody, Verna, and Ma are staying. Cody shoots Evans and the three escape. Realizing that there is too much heat on him, Cody decides to turn himself in for a hotel robbery committed in Springfield, Illinois, at the same time as the train robbery. Evans knows Cody didn't rob the hotel, but tells Springfield authorities to go along with Cody's plan so they can trap him. Evans assigns undercoverman Hank Fallon to become Cody's cellmate, Vic Pardo, and win his trust. Evans wants to know who the fence is for Cody's money.

Ed tells his lover Verna he has arranged for Cody to be killed in prison. Roy Parker tries to drop a steel beam on Cody. Vic pulls Cody to safety. Now Cody trusts him. Ma visits Cody and tells him Ed and Verna have run out on him. She promises to take care of Big Ed.

Cody and Pardo plan an escape. But Cody learns that his Ma has been murdered and goes crazy in the prison cafeteria, causing the hospital doctors to recommend commitment in a mental institution.

Cody improvises an escape with Pardo, Tommy Ryley, and hard-of-hearing Herbert. He kidnaps Parker. When she learns that Cody has escaped, Verna tries to run. She is afraid Cody will kill her, especially if he finds out she shot Ma. But Cody stops her in the garage. Before he can strangle her, she tells him Ed shot Ma. He lets her go. He goes into Ed's house and shoots Ed. He then kills Parker.

Verna is terrified of Cody but pretends to love him again. Cody makes Vic, his one friend, his partner. Vic meets Cody's fence, The Trader (Daniel Winston). Cody and The Trader plot to rob a chemical plant. Cody and his men crawl into an empty gas truck that is to be driven into the plant by an ex-con who works there. Vic places an electrical device on the bottom of the truck so Evans and the police can follow them.

During the holdup, the men are surrounded by police. The ex-con spots Vic and recognizes him as an undercover cop. The police fire a smoke bomb. Cody tries to kill Vic but kills one of his own men. Vic escapes. He tells Evans about The Trader. Verna is arrested. She wants to bargain with Evans; she'll coax Cody out of hiding. He turns her down.

All Cody's men are killed. Cody goes crazy. Laughing, he climbs high among the petrol tanks. Vic shoots at him, plugging him several times and penetrating a tank. There are great explosions. Before he's blown into smithereens, Cody smiles. He's made it to the top of the world.

"James Cagney Is Red Hot In *White Heat*!" proclaimed the newspaper ads. "Pick up the pieces, folks, Jimmy's in action again!" There was reason for excitement. After seven shaky years (four nonhits) as independent producer of his own films, James Cagney had come home to Warner Bros. His last film at the studio had been the joyful *Yankee Doodle Dandy* (1942), and as George M. Cohan he'd sung and danced off with a much-deserved Best Actor award, and Warners reaped financial dividends; during the preceding decade he'd been Warners' top star of contemporary action films, making a particularly strong impression in its classic gangster cycle. *White Heat* was an ideal "comeback" vehicle for Cagney because in many ways it was a throwback to those gangster films that suited him so well. While the cops' methods for tracking down criminals is more sophisticated than in Cagney's earlier films, there are numerous old-time ingredients: tough dialogue, rapid editing, racing cars, well-planned heists, lots of gunfire, an unfaithful moll, snitches, a gang member trying to usurp power while our gangster hero is temporarily in jail, our gangster hero avenging himself on the coward, the gang members being trapped and massacred by police; our gangster hero dying a spectacular death. *White Heat* even reunited Cagney with Raoul Walsh, director of one of Cagney's best gangster films, *The Roaring Twenties* (1939). In that one, Cagney died in memorable fashion: his body riddled with bullets, he tries to run up a long flight of steps that lead to a building, but after shuffling up only a half-dozen steps, he does a semicircle, and weakly runs back down, collapsing in a bloody heap on the snow-covered steps.

What distinguishes *White Heat* from Cagney's earlier films is his character. Cody Jarrett resembles his previous criminals in that he's more cunning, energetic, humorous, violent, suicidal, more *everything* than any of his gang members; although cynical about the world, he is optimistic about his own future: death doesn't frighten him because he believes in his own immortality. But Cagney's thirties characters became tough, bitter killers because they grew up in a cruel world, in poverty, in broken homes, in the slums where, even for teen-agers, fighting and stealing becomes a way of life; and they became men during the Depression, when there were no honest jobs available. The gangster films Warners made in the thirties are notable because they consistently had a social consciousness: because it is the social environment that turns potentially fine citizens into criminals, we must sympathize with all of the early Cagney gangsters. We needn't sympathize with Cody because society did him wrong. Cody has another problem: he is insane. It's not his fault. His criminal father died in an institution. And his shrewd Ma would surely have trouble passing a lunacy test. Brilliantly played by Margaret Wycherly, Ma is nothing like those sweet mothers in the thirties films who were the only good influences on their wayward sons. Cody trusts no one but Ma, who's the real power behind his throne—not even his wife Verna, whom he treats like a kid (sending her to her comics, giving her a piggyback ride). In fact, his mother fixation is so weird—he even sits in her lap—that I'm sure the film would have run into trouble with censors if Cody didn't have a wife, too.

Everyone respects Cagney. Fans and critics love him. I can't remember a bad performance. His portrayal of maniac

Cody is not too happy when Bo (R) informs him that Vic, who has pretended to be his friend, is a cop.

Cody is something to behold. He is older and paunchier than we think of Cagney as a gangster, but his performance is still intense, his eyes fiery, his energy ferocious. How terrifying Cody is when, with wild eyes, he half-strangles Verna, who he thinks has betrayed him, and when he realizes Hank-Vic has double-crossed him. How pathetic he is during his headache bouts (self-induced as a child to get Ma's attention and now real), staggering across the floor like a wounded animal, mewing and moaning, driving his hurting head into the bed cushion ("it feels like a red-hot buzzsaw in my head"), waiting for Ma to massage him back to health. How terrifying, pathetic, *and* sympathetic he is in the classic scene in the prison cafeteria when he learns that Ma is dead: he can't believe it at first; he stands and says weakly, "Dead?!?"; he smashes his steel coffee cup on the table; he starts screaming; he must get away, so he starts crawling quickly across the long table, swimming through all the prisoners' food and drinks; crying, screaming incoherently, he makes it to the end of the table, stumbles to the floor and staggers forward; he interrupts his squealing only long enough to hit several guards who try to subdue him; finally held down by several guards, he screams, "I gotta get out of here!"; he is carried away, his screams stunning the other inmates into absolute silence. What a marvelous scene! David Thomson writes in *A Biographical Dictionary of Film* (Morrow, 1975): "No one could move so arbitrarily from tranquillity to dementedness, because Cagney was a dancer responding to a melody that he alone heard. Like a spirit or goblin he seemed to be in touch with an occult source of vitality. What a Bilbo Baggins he would have made; or imagine his Hyde to Fred Astaire's Jekyll."

Costar Virginia Mayo also had praise for Cagney when I interviewed her for *Focus on Film* (March 1981): "Jimmy Cagney was the most dynamic man who ever appeared on the screen. I can't say enough about him. He should have won five Oscars he was so fabulous. He stimulated me to such an

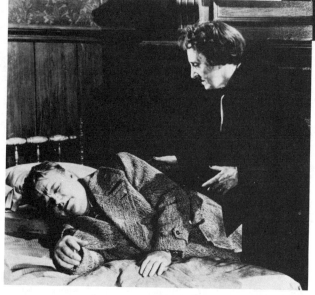

(TL) Cody strong-arms Verna until she lies that it was Big Ed who shot Ma in the back. (BL) When Cody has a debilitating headache, only Ma can nurse him. Until Vic turns up, she is the only one he trusts. (TR) With the petrol tanks about to explode, Cody yells gleefully, "Made it, Ma. Top of the world!"

extent. I must say that I didn't have to act very much; I just had to react to him because he was so powerful. You could feel him radiating all these wonderful sensations. He made a lot of suggestions to Walsh as to what he wanted to do with his part, and he was always 100 percent correct. He could have been a great director if he had wanted to be."

Mayo, generally regarded as merely a beautiful actress with a creamy complexion, could be something special when given tough-girl parts. Few people remember that this demure, delicate actress was the favorite of one of Hollywood's toughest directors, Raoul Walsh. In *White Heat,* as in Walsh's *Colorado Territory* (1949), *Along the Great Divide* (1951) and *Captain Horatio Hornblower* (1951), and a few other films in which she got away from her soft image, such as *The Best Years of Our Lives* (1946) and *The Iron Mistress* (1952), she is truly memorable. She's also brave: how many other beautiful actresses would agree to have her first shot in a picture show her asleep and *snoring,* as is the case in *White Heat?* "When you're at a studio like Warner Bros., you are usually assigned

roles by the higher-ups. But Raoul Walsh always asked for *me.* Therefore I had a great rapport with him. He loved my work as much as I loved his. Without doubt he was my favorite director. He liked me to try gutsy things and that was a great breakthrough for me. I learned to be more dramatic, more exciting, and more interpretive. I performed at my peak." Standing on a chair and admiring herself in the mirror in her mink (worn directly over her slip), flirting with everyone from Cody to policeman Evans, forcefully kissing Big Ed, weeping crocodile tears, drinking herself into childish ecstasy, fighting to control her hysteria, not listening to Ed's words when she realizes Cody will soon return with revenge on his mind, getting our sympathy for one second by recoiling from Cody's hand near her face: Mayo is always beautiful, always interesting.

White Heat is supercharged with excitement. For that we can thank Raoul Walsh, one of the best action/adventure directors in cinema history. Mayo realizes the key to Walsh's brilliance (when at his peak): "Raoul, with his hard-hitting approach, couldn't stand a movie that lacked pacing. His films *move*—that's why they were so popular." If you want to see a film *move,* take a look at the thrilling opening to *White Heat.* A master, who knows how to utilize sights *and sounds,* is at work. A speeding train comes barreling around the bend, its WHISTLE BLOWING. Max Steiner's adventure MUSIC PLAYS on the soundtrack. Above, a SCREECHING car speeds around dangerous mountain curves. Men jump from the car, its MOTOR RUNNING. One tries to shift the switch near the tracks. He must SHOOT the chain off. Inside the train, Big Ed kills one train employee. When the conductor refuses to stop the train, Big Ed SHOOTS him. Meanwhile, Cody jumps from an overpass and lands on top of the train. It still moves as he runs along, jumping from car to car until he makes his way into the engineer's booth. The train stops, as Big Ed has pulled a wire. Men on the outside SHATTER GLASS. Then there is an EXPLOSION. Next Cody SHOOTS two engineers. One falls on a switch and STEAM WHOOSHES into Zuckie's face. He is scalded. He SCREAMS in agony. End scene.

The picture continues at a remarkable pace, only slowing down when the police must explain their electronic tracking device—an obligatory scene much like the reading of voting procedures on Academy Award telecasts. Any film with characters named Cody, Big Ed, Cotton, Het, Bo, The Trader, Happy, Scratch, and Zuckie is bound to be different, and *White Heat* is certainly that. It's full of great touches—Ma never blinks her wise, alert eyes; Big Ed and, later, Verna spit out their gum before kissing; Cody eats chicken while he casually shoots Roy Parker, who is locked in the car trunk; the wind blows constantly; hard-of-hearing Herbert reads lips. Also: the "Trojan Horse" entry through the petrol company's gate; the way the prisoners whisper back and forth, up and down a line, that Cody's Ma is dead—finally whispering the news to Cody; the growing insanity of Cody: after talking to his dead mother in the woods, he concedes, "Maybe I am nuts."

Most unusual is how Walsh treats the Hank Fallon–Vic Pardo character. Typically, we would side with him. But our loyalty is with Cody. At least Cody is honest where his friends are concerned. If Cody's cold-blooded, it's because he knows those around him can't be trusted: "If I turn my back long enough for Big Ed to put a hole in it, there'd be a hole in it." Hank-Vic is no better than a filthy spy in our eyes. The cocky type, who puts his feet up on a desk when we first see him, he loses all our sympathy by double-crossing Cody. We don't like the way he gets Cody to trust him or how he smiles to himself after Cody shakes his hand. The guy's a worm, part of a whole network of government spies. It would have been simple for Walsh and his screenwriters to have made Hank-Vic into our hero. One line of dialogue in the scene in which Evans hires him would have been sufficient: "I'd like to get a crack at Cody for personal reasons—a while back he killed my (*friend, brother, father, priest, wife, homosexual lover, dog*)." But Walsh didn't want us to like someone who makes his living by betraying people. (Cody's sick and needs *help*, not treachery!) It's good to see Cody laugh and laugh as Hank-Vic fills him with bullets. And it's good to see Hank-Vic and all the other cops scamper like rats for safety when it's apparent that his gunfire has hit a petrol tank. Although they have Cody outnumbered one hundred to one and have him trapped, Hank-Vic still shoots at him, and no doubt causes this petrol plant to lose millions of dollars because of his careless aim. You have to be happy for Cody at the end, dying as he goes up in the enormous explosions, being blown into space, his ashes scattered in the air we breathe. Unlike Cagney's other gangsters who died unheroically—they had rise-and-*fall* careers in crime—Cody actually achieves immortality: "Made it, Ma," he smiles. "Top of the world!"

The Wicker Man

1973 Great Britain British Lion (in the United States it was first released in 1974 by Warner Bros., a Brut presentation)
Director: Robin Hardy
Producer: Peter Snell
Screenplay: Anthony Shaffer
Cinematography: Harry Waxman
Music: Paul Giovanni
"Cornrigs" sung by Paul Giovanni
Editor: Eric Boyd-Perkins
Running time: 102 minutes; original release print runs 87 minutes

Cast: Edward Woodward (Sergeant Neil Howie), Christopher Lee (Lord Summerisle), Diane Cilento (Miss Rose), Britt Ekland (Willow), Ingrid Pitt (librarian-clerk), Lindsay Kemp (Alder MacGregor), Russell Waters (harbor master), Aubrey Morris (old gardener–gravedigger), Irene Sunters (May Morrison), Walter Carr (schoolmaster), Roy Boyd (Broome), Ian Campbell (Oak), Leslie Mackie (Daisy), Geraldine Cowper (Rowan Morrison), Kevin Collins (old fisherman), Donald Eccles (T. H. Lennox), Jennifer Martin (Myrtle)

Synopsis: The filmmakers thank Lord Summerisle and the inhabitants of Summerisle, a small Scottish island, for being allowed the privilege to film their religious practices.

Sergeant Howie is a middle-aged policeman on the Scottish mainland. He is a deeply religious man, who serves as a lay preacher. Howie is sent a picture from an anonymous person on Summerisle, in his jurisdiction. The picture is of a teen-age girl named Rowan Morrison, who is supposedly missing without a trace.

Howie flies his small plane to the island. He is treated with suspicion by all the villagers. He thinks them strange, too. No one there has ever heard of Rowan Morrison, not even May Morrison, the woman Howie thinks is her mother. May has a young daughter named Myrtle who tells Howie she is drawing a picture of Rowan. It turns out to be a picture of a hare.

Howie stays at the Green Man pub, run by Alder MacGregor and his beautiful, sexy daughter Willow. Singing goes on all the time by men at the pub, and Howie is disturbed to hear their bawdy songs. Howie orders some food and is surprised that it all comes out of cans, since the island is known for its fine produce. Howie takes a stroll at night and sees many naked couples copulating in the cemetery. He returns to his room and is disturbed by the bawdy song downstairs directed at Willow's room. Lord Summerisle has brought her a young boy to initiate into sexual practices.

The next day, Howie visits the school where Miss Rose is teaching the girls about phallic symbolism and the boys are outside participating in a phallic maypole ceremony. He is appalled. Those at the school say they've never heard of Rowan Morrison but he finds her name on the school register. Miss Rose admits that she is dead, but says she has returned in some other form.

Howie finds Rowan's tombstone. He asks permission of Lord Summerisle to dig up the coffin. He suspects she was murdered. Outside the mansion, Miss Rose leads nude young girls in a fertility ceremony. Lord Summerisle is extremely polite to Howie, but Howie is repulsed that he and all the villagers who follow him are paganists.

Howie unearths the coffin and discovers a hare instead of Rowan's body inside. He figures that she has been kidnapped and will be sacrificed in the upcoming May Day ceremony because this year's crops have failed. Before the May Day procession, Howie knocks out Alder MacGregor and puts on his fool's outfit. He joins the parade that leads to the shore. Everyone on Summerisle is there singing and dancing. Rowan is led forward to be sacrificed, or so Howie believes. He tries to rescue her. It turns out that he is the one who is to be sacrificed. The picture of Rowan was sent to him to lure him, a good Christian, to the island for sacrifice, to appease the gods.

The villagers sing a rousing song as Howie is placed in a giant wicker man. It is set afire and burns down as the sun sets.

Lord Summerisle stands in front of the giant Wicker Man, in which Howie is to be sacrificed.

Nothing is more frustrating for a movie fan than to know that a picture about which he or she has heard or read interesting reports has been shelved by its distributor or has been yanked out of the director's hands and drastically edited by studio hatchetmen before being put into circulation. There is an undeniable mystique surrounding films that, for one reason or another, are unavailable in their directors' versions. It's as if those original versions, locked away in studio safes, *must* be undiscovered masterpieces; and as odd as it sounds, the cults that have formed around some of these largely unseen films consist mostly of people who know them only by reputation. Such is the case with *The Wicker Man,* which many people are desperate to see. "The *Citizen Kane* of horror films" according to the influential *Cinefantastique,* "a cross between *King Kong* and Gilbert and Sullivan" according to a Boston critic, the Grand Prize winner at the 1973 Festival of Fantastic Films in Paris, this British occult film has been nearly impossible to see since it first played here in 1974; especially in the long 102-minute version that was not available at all until the late seventies. The reasons for its inaccessibility has much to do with its fascination.

The strange story of *The Wicker Man** began in early 1972 when mystery writer Anthony Shaffer and Robin Hardy, his partner in a television packaging and production company, decided to make a film about paganism. It would star Christopher Lee, eager to shake his Dracula image, and be produced by Peter Snell, managing director of British Lion films. Hardy, who had once stumbled upon a secret pagan ceremony in a Cornwall village, researched the subject. Then Shaffer wrote his first original screenplay, *The Wicker Man.* British Lion agreed to finance it, hoping it would be the picture to revive the last of the great British studios. Filming proceeded

remarkably well, considering that twenty-five spread-out locations were needed for Summerisle and Lord Summerisle's mansion; filming took place in the dead of winter for a movie set in the spring; and pregnant Britt Ekland, required to take lessons for her nude dance, constantly argued with first-time director Hardy.

But the real problems began during postproduction, when British Lion was unexpectedly sold to EMI. Michael Deeley was placed in charge of film operations and Peter Snell was giving his notice. Deeley assigned aide Barry Spikings to supervise the editing, and the result was a 102-minute print that Hardy found lacking but satisfactory. Christopher Lee was also satisfied, though disappointed that as much as twenty minutes of what he considered the finest role of his career had been excised. Ingrid Pitt, another favorite of Hammer horror fans, also saw her part brutally reduced. But Deeley was not through cutting. When he tried to interest Roger Corman in buying the picture's American and Canadian distribution rights, Corman turned him down but suggested fifteen minutes of additional trimming to make it more commercial. Without informing the filmmakers, Deeley did away with the introductory Scottish mainland sequence in which Sergeant Howie is seen as a lay preacher, the "Gentle Johnny" number during which Willow initiates a young boy into sexual practices offscreen while Lord Summerisle delivers an eloquent Walt Whitman-like poem to a pair of copulating snails, and other bits; the result is that Howie's two-night stay on Summerisle appears to be just one night. So it was that an 87-minute version was released in England in late 1973 and was sold to an American tax-shelter group, Beechwood Properties, which didn't care whether the picture made money or not.

Beechwood found a distributor in National General Pictures, but when NGP ran into financial difficulties, *The Wicker Man* was transferred to Warner Bros. All Warners did was fill Beechwood's tax-shelter requirements for bookings by test-

*The story is documented by Stuart Byron in *Film Comment* (Nov–Dec. 1977) and David Batholomew in *Cinefantastique* (Vol. 6, No. 3, 1977)

marketing it in Atlanta and San Diego. Strictly speaking, *The Wicker Man* is an occult film with music, but Warners promoted it as a straight horror film. Not surprisingly, it did poor business—it was unable to deliver the shocks and gore ticketbuyers expected. At this time, *Variety* gave it an excellent review and a bright financial outlook. But Warners put it on its shelf.

Two years later the distribution rights were purchased by Abraxas Film Corporation, a small New Orleans company run by film lovers John Alan Simon, a reporter, and Stirling Smith, host of a popular regional movie-talk show. Soon thereafter, Hardy, who had moved to the United States to help salvage a career he thought irreparably damaged as a result of an unsuccessful debut film, informed Abraxas that possibly there was a 102-minute negative in existence. Calls to Deeley in the United States, from Abraxas, Hardy, Shaffer, Snell, and Lee, were initially unrewarding, then went unanswered. Calls to Spikings in England resulted in an obviously concocted story: the three hundred and sixty cans of negative film had accidentally been burned. When that story wasn't believed, another replaced it; the negative had been used as highway filler. Everyone had given up on finding the negative and was trying to locate an existing 102-minute commercial print when, amazingly, a complete print turned up in the offices of Corman's New World Pictures. Although Corman had an obligation to return it to EMI, he (or an employee devoted to film preservation) shipped it to Abraxas. In the absence of a negative, Abraxas made a dupe negative from this complete original. So the full director's version was restored!

Because *The Wicker Man* plays so rarely, I am not sure which versions of the film are available and where they play. However, I believe the 87-minute version is still in circulation, I know there is an even shorter version that plays on television, and I believe the 102-minute version is available in certain parts of the United States (though I doubt if it plays in England). At the very least, there is a long version available on video cassette, which is how I and, I'm sure, many others were finally able to see it. As it turned out, I found the film somewhat overrated, and much less profound philosophically than I had been led to believe. But it is beautifully photographed, witty, and is such an unusual entry to the genre—particularly because of Paul Giovanni's extensive and clever use of music (bawdy ballads are sung, acoustic instruments are played throughout)—that I can understand why it would impress many viewers. It's certainly worth a look, and I'm glad so much effort has been made to make the full version accessible.

The Wicker Man reminds me of a combination of the cult British TV series *The Avengers* (which twice had Christopher Lee as guest villain) and two British horror films, *Horror Hotel* (1963), in which Lee played the head of a satanic cult, and *Doomwatch* (1972). Summerisle is exactly the type of locale in which *The Avengers* superdetectives John Steed (Patrick MacNee) and Emma Peel (Diana Rigg) often found themselves: full of offbeat characters, with a mannerly megalomaniac dictator, with a deep, dark secret that borders on the supernatural. As in *The Avengers,* the humor greatly tempers the morbidity that pervades the scenario. The major difference, of course, is that Steed and Peel always solved their mysteries and escaped with their lives, while Sergeant Howie solves his

Arriving on Summerisle, Howie questions the pleasant townspeople about the disappearance of Rowan Morrison.

mystery and is killed for his efforts, surprising to all us viewers fooled by the picture's *Avengers*-like tone.

Doomwatch is about a London doctor (Ian Ballen) who comes alone to a secluded island to investigate the effects of pollution in surrounding fishing areas. Like Howie, the doctor is treated like an outsider by the island's populace who, too, are hiding a deep, dark secret (that some islanders are turning into deformed, insane creatures). The difference: in *Doomwatch* the people seem cruel when actually they're just scared; in *The Wicker Man* the islanders seem to be friendly and pretend to help Howie while actually leading him into a trap.

Horror Hotel, which is most similar to *The Wicker Man* in terms of its premise, shows what might have happened to the doctor in *Doomwatch* if the islanders weren't really decent people beneath their hostile façades. A young student (Betta St. John) is lured to a small Massachusetts town to investigate witchcraft. It turns out that she is meant to be sacrificed in a satanic rite—presided over by Christopher Lee, naturally. Like Howie she does not escape. (This picture, one of the first in England to deal with witchcraft because of its long-standing ban on the subject, has often been compared to *Psycho* [1960] because its heroine is killed off early.) *Horror Hotel* is also similar to *The Wicker Man* in its dramatic use of imagery. The satanic *Horror Hotel* has the Raven's Inn, the ritualistic Candlemas Eve and Witches' Sabbath ceremonies, a sprig of woodbine, the shadow of a cross, a dead bird with an arrow through it, and blood sacrifice; the paganistic *The Wicker Man* has its Green Man Inn, May Day ceremony, plant imagery, sunshine, hare references, and blood sacrifices.

Horror Hotel, filmed in black and white, is very dark, shadowy, and misty. By design, *The Wicker Man* is brightly photographed by Harry Waxman (a stunning job), because on the surface paganism is a joyous celebration of nature—its crueler aspects are hidden under a shroud of joviality. The songs Howie hears are bawdy, to be sure, but we welcome them because they *sound* lovely and are quite spirited. Even when Miss Rose philosophizes, we are not turned off by her beliefs: "We believe that after the human life is over, the soul lives on—in trees, in animals, in fire, in water . . ." Fair enough. The film, which opens with the filmmakers' thank you to (the fictitious) Lord Summerisle and his flock for

(R) The inhabitants of Summerisle sing, dance, and dress in colorful and bizarre costumes during a pagan celebration that culminates in Howie's sacrifice. (Above) Not knowing what to expect, Howie joins the parade. In his clown outfit he marches in front of the three blondes, played by Ingrid Pitt, Diane Cilento, and Britt Ekland.

letting them film on the island, is full of mirth. It contains songs, dancing, happy children, beautiful sexually liberated blond women, parades, a pageantry of colors, comic touches, flowers (individually pasted on trees by the set designer), and sunshine. Lord Summerisle himself seems like a benevolent leader, even if we think he's pulling off a sham by convincing his followers it is the worship of the sun and the god of the orchards that is responsible for their successful livelihood as apple growers. This liberal fellow compares favorably to the prudish, puritanical, predictable Howie. It is only when Lord Summerisle actually carries through on the terrible execution, burning Howie and animals in a gigantic wicker man, in order to appease the gods, that we side with Howie. In fact, we identify with Howie: we realize that it could just as easily be us, whether we are steadfastly religious (as is Howie) or agnostics (as is Shaffer), whom these crazed paganists are sacrificing.

Most horror films are about the triumph of Christianity over Evil. Vampire films are a good example, as we see Evil retreat in the presence of a cross. Some recent films—*The Omen* (1976) is a prime example—have shown Evil to be victorious in our decadent world, but these are in the minority. A few films, like Val Lewton and Jacques Tourneur's *I Walked With a Zombie* (1943), show both Christianity and a belief in other gods (voodooism, paganism) as having validity. *The Wicker Man* is the one film in which both Christianity and paganism are shown to be impotent. We neither believe Howie's contention that he will be resurrected nor Lord Summerisle's that Howie will be reincarnated. We neither believe that the blood sacrifice will bring about a successful crop the following year nor that Lord Summerisle will be punished for committing such a sin (except possibly by the villagers if the crops fail again). "*The Wicker Man*," said Christopher Lee in *Cinefantastique*, "is not an attack on contemporary religion but a comment on it, its strengths as well as its weaknesses, its fallibility. [It points out] that it can be puritanical and [still not] always come out on top."

Howie, stolidly characterized by British TV actor Edward Woodward, is a queer bird. He's a man who has an unquestioning belief in God, in fact is a lay preacher, yet works at a profession that relies on logic and science. It's people he doesn't understand; so he can't see that the villagers are obviously laying a trap for him. A virgin although middle-aged, he almost succumbs to temptation when Willow sings an erotic song in the adjoining room and slithers around sexual bedroom props while in the nude. His moment of weakness, considering sex with Willow outside of marriage, is balanced by rival Lord Summerisle's own moment of weakness in his own beliefs: his worried look when he considers the possibility that Howie's sacrifice won't prevent a second crop failure. Howie is presented as a Christ figure, a stranger in a strange land run by a fake lord. What I find fault with is not that he is killed, but that the constant mockery of Howie by the villagers (he ends up dressed as a fool) and Lord Summerisle (who's amused that Howie has a chance to be a Christian martyr) is presented in such a way that I get the impression it is Anthony Shaffer who is mocking Howie (and not just questioning his beliefs). It's as if Shaffer is trying to teach a true believer a lesson.

Because every episode that takes place along the way as Howie solves the mystery of the missing Rowan Morrison (a pure man's quest for the missing Grail) is presented with tongue seemingly in cheek, there is not a frightening moment before the horrifying sacrifice. Yet there is an accumulative effect whereby we become increasingly unnerved. By the end, during the parade in which everyone wears silly costumes and sings a cheery song (while Howie is being burned), we have stopped our smiling. And with hindsight, what we laughed about earlier is no longer amusing. We realize that as weird as these people are, their real-life counterparts may indeed exist. Interviewed for *Cinefantastique,* Robin Hardy observed:

> Maybe it's not too big a connection to make between the final scene of *The Wicker Man* and the Nuremberg rallies in Germany. It was no accident that Hitler brought back all those pagan feasts in his rise to power. . . . The idea that it is necessary to sacrifice people for the good of other people is never too far from the human consciousness at any one time. You can't simply say that it was something people did all those years ago and has nothing to do with us today.

1971 Paramount Pictures release of a David L. Wolper production
Director: Mel Stuart
Producers: David L. Wolper and Stan Margulies
Screenplay: Roald Dahl
From the novel *Charlie and the Chocolate Factory* by Roald Dahl
Cinematography: Arthur Ibbetson
Musical supervision and scoring: Walter Scharf
Songs: Leslie Bricusse and Anthony Newley
Editor: David Saxon
Running time: 98 minutes

Cast: Gene Wilder (Willy Wonka), Jack Albertson (Grandpa Joe), Peter Ostrum (Charlie Bucket), Michael Bollner (Augustus Gloop), Ursula Reit (Mrs. Gloop), Denise Nickerson (Violet Beauregarde), Leonard Stone (Mr. Beauregarde), Julie Dawn Cole (Veruca Salt), Roy Kinnear (Mr. Salt), Paris Themmen (Mike Teevee), Dodo Denny (Mrs. Teevee), Diana Sowle (Mrs. Bucket), Aubrey Wood (Mr. Bill), David Battley (Mr. Turkentine), Gunter Meissner (Otto Slugworth)

Synopsis: The announcement is greeted with great excitement around the world. Mr. Willy Wonka, the world's most famous confectioner, has hidden golden tickets inside five of his candy bars, entitling five young finders to a trip through Wonka's factory and enough candy to last them their lifetimes. In the town where Wonka's factory is located, Charlie Bucket lives with his impoverished mother and four feeble grandparents. Charlie dreams of winning one of the tickets.

Soon tickets are discovered. The first winner is Augustus Gloop, a fat German boy; the second is Violet Beauregarde, daughter of an American used car salesman; Varuca Salt, the spoiled daughter of a British peanut tycoon, is the third winner; the fourth is Mike Teevee, whose only interest is watching television.

Charlie's faint hopes are shattered when news comes from South America that someone has found the last golden ticket. Days later, however, the fifth winner is declared a fake. Tearing open a chocolate bar he has just bought, Charlie discovers the last golden ticket! He is the final winner. On the way home Charlie encounters an evil-looking man who says he is Otto Slugworth, Wonka's chief competitor. Slugworth offers Charlie a bribe to steal one of Wonka's Everlasting Gobstoppers during Charlie's tour of the factory. He has offered all the other children the same bribe.

The kids are allowed to bring along one adult to the factory: Charlie chooses Grandpa Joe, who leaves his bed for the first time in twenty years. Charlie and Grandpa Joe are joined by Augustus, Violet, Veruca, and Mike, who are with parents. Willy Wonka appears. He warns the children not to touch anything. He has them sign a contract. He acts coldly to them.

Wonka shows a dazzling array of wonders to his guests: the Chocolate Room, where everything is edible; the S.S. Wonkatania, which travels on a river of chocolate; the Inventing Room, where each child receives his prized Everlasting Gobstopper—an all-day sucker that lasts forever; and the Oompa-Loompas, green-haired midgets that run Wonka's factory.

One by one the children disobey Wonka's orders and get into trouble and are forced to leave. When they do something wrong, his punishment is severe and they are disqualified.

Only Charlie remains. But Wonka angrily orders Charlie and Grandpa Joe out of the factory for trying the Fizzy-Lifting Drink and bouncing off Wonka's spotless ceiling. He claims the contract is null and void—Charlie will get no lifetime supply of chocolate. Grandpa Joe is furious and suggests to Charlie that they give Slugworth the secret Gobstopper sample. But honest Charlie takes the candy from his pocket and hands it to Wonka. A smile spreads over Wonka's face. He has found the one good child he has been searching for. Slugworth appears. He is actually a Wonka secret agent engaged to test the children's honesty. Only Charlie passed the test.

Wonka takes Charlie and Grandpa Joe for a flight in his Great Glass Wonkavator. They look down on Charlie's town and the chocolate factory from high in the air. Wonka tells Charlie he has chosen him as his heir. Charlie and his family are to move into the factory. One day Charlie will succeed Willy Wonka as the world's most famous chocolate maker.

Willy Wonka and the Chocolate Factory

Essay by Henry Blinder

"So shines a good deed in a weary world."

Quaker Oats' one brief venture into moviemaking—inexplicably dumped into neighborhood theaters for one-week showcase runs—did so poorly at the box office that the giant cereal company retreated to the safety of Saturday morning TV, forever. Their series of movie-inspired candy bars, including a Willy Wonka's Super Skrunch Bar, went stale on the shelf. But in the wake of this financial debacle a wonderful, odd film remains and, in fact, endures—*Willy Wonka and the Chocolate Factory*.

With the possible exception of *The 5000 Fingers of Dr. T.* (1953), Stanley Kramer's bizarre, live-action production of Dr. Seuss's story, *Willy Wonka* stands as the strangest "children's" film ever made. It's really in a category all its own, neither a children's film nor an adult film. Its adult characters, for the most part, are scary or foolish. Its children characters, except for Charlie, are brats. When they inevitably do something wrong (selfish) they are treated viciously. Even the most benign transgression, such as Violet Beauregarde's excessive gum chewing, is punished with inordinate violence—she blows up like a blueberry and is taken away to be juiced. This peculiar treatment originated with Roald Dahl, master of macabre stories with "twist" endings, who authored both the book *Charlie and the Chocolate Factory* and the screenplay. Though the book is a children's classic, which may account for the zeal with which Quaker Oats plunged a great deal of money into the project, Dahl's screenplay is in many ways an improvement. In the book, Charlie has a father who works in a toothpaste factory, screwing the caps on the tubes. His meager salary keeps the family and relatives at a starvation-level existence. He is a vague and undeveloped character who has no real thematic function. Charlie has no father in the screenplay, only a mother—his father's absence goes unexplained. This simple

Wonka poses with the children who will be touring his factory and their parents. To the left are Charlie and Grandpa Joe.

he overacts and all but winks at you, and everybody in the world except for the girl he's talking to knows he's lying. I want to do the opposite. To *really* lie, and fool the audience. . . . I wanted people to wonder if Willy Wonka was telling the truth so that you wouldn't really know until the end of the picture what Willy's motivations were." In this regard, Wilder succeeds completely. His Willy Wonka is mysterious, aloof, unpredictable, and frightening. We have seen flashes of this character in other Wilder films but never has he been given such free rein. Wilder's totally original character is so disorienting that he makes the trip through the chocolate factory a very uncomfortable, off-balance experience for the audience as well as for the children. We don't trust him, and feel that no one, not even our hero Charlie, is safe. Gene Wilder as Willy Wonka embodies the film's wonderful and strange quality, its uneasy edge that makes it somewhat inaccessible and yet still so intriguing after repeated viewings. And only on repeated viewings, knowing that all ends well, can Wilder's performance be appreciated and *enjoyed*. His performance is undoubtedly the best thing about the film—it is inconceivable to imagine anyone else in the role.

Peter Ostrum's Charlie is a most appealing child performance. Infinitely better, for example, than Mark Lester's whimpering, vacant Oliver in the 1968 musical. Ostrum's sincere Charlie serves as a pleasing counterpoint to Wilder's aloof Wonka. Ostrum is a real boy—made more so by the caricatured children around him—with a selfish side and a good side. He's not a heroic character, he's just a boy—which makes his returning the Everlasting Gobstopper to Wonka at the end all the more impressive. How many of us would have

device, a fatherless boy, makes Charlie's connection to Willy Wonka much more dramatic. The story becomes a boy's search for his father's—surrogate Willy Wonka's—approval. Throughout the film, we and Charlie are constantly trying to break through the barrier that separates a boy from the most important man in his life. A second logical change follows the first—the inclusion of the Everlasting Gobstopper "test." All the children are offered bribes by a Wonka competitor, actually a Wonka secret agent, to steal an Everlasting Gobstopper while touring the factory. The other children are willing to double-cross Wonka. But not Charlie. Only at the point where Charlie returns the Everlasting Gobstopper to Wonka, rather than stealing it, does the parental veil of mystery drop, transforming Wonka into a warm human being, a loving father ready to give adopted son Charlie the moon and his factory. It is the supreme moment in the film: oddly this motif of a "father" testing a child's loyalty, to find a "son," never appears in the book.

Yet it is disorienting to witness Wonka, who we thought was mean, instantly become so kind. Even as the closing titles are running we can't quite believe the swift transformation (though we know we are supposed to)—not after the ordeal Wonka has put us through. "We all grew up on movies with scenes where the actor is lying," said Gene Wilder in an early seventies interview, "and you know he's lying, but he wants to make *sure* you know it's a lie, and so

Augustus Gloop plummets into a river of chocolate.

passed that test? We feel Charlie succeeds in drawing out a father's warmth (from Wonka) in the end by virtue of his goodness. Charlie's goodness is partly inherent and partly because of a proper upbringing by his mother and grandfather; the other spoiled children on the tour reflect the overindulgent influence of their parents.

The engaging direction is surprising because Mel Stuart's only prior credits were insipid comedies, *If It's Tuesday, This Must Be Belgium* (1969) and *I Love My Wife* (1970), and various documentary productions for David L. Wolper, the producer of *Willy Wonka*. In *Willy Wonka* Stuart shows an early–Richard Lester–type of comic sensibility. For the first half of the film, before we enter the chocolate factory, we crosscut between Charlie's relentlessly gloomy world to a series of hilarious incidents involving the worldwide search for the golden ticket. Many of these scenes are peppered with asides, background action, and comic throwaways reminiscent of Lester films. Stuart even cast Roy Kinnear, a Richard Lester favorite, as Varuca Salt's doting father. Once inside the chocolate factory Stuart had the sense to let Wilder take his character to outrageous places. Then he augments the wild Wilder with visuals to match his style. Witness the terrifying ride the kids take on the Wonka-captained S. S. Wonkatania. This is perhaps the most unsettling sequence in the film. As Wilder recites a chant, taken directly from the book, he becomes increasingly manic.

> There's no earthly way of knowing
> Which direction they are going!
> There's no knowing where they're rowing,
> Or which way the river's flowing!
> Not a speck of light is showing,
> So the danger must be growing,
> For the rowers keep on rowing,
> And they're certainly not showing
> Any signs that they are slowing . . .

Meanwhile, on the walls of the tunnel through which the boat travels, Stuart throws up a bizarre series of almost Daliesque images, including a worm slithering across the lips of a man, and a chicken being beheaded. The sequence epitomizes the discomforting quality of the film.

Another factor which adds to the disorienting feeling is that this lavish Hollywood-type production was filmed entirely in Munich, Germany. The locations have an inhospitably foreign look. And the film seems to take place in several centuries simultaneously. Adding to the otherworldly nature, American and British actors mingle freely in the foreground, while those in the background have a Teutonic appearance. Though the reasons for the location were budgetary, the production notes cheerfully proclaim that Munich was selected because it is the "Storybook Capital of Germany."

Quaker Oats executives might have had visions of a modern-day *The Wizard of Oz* (1939) dancing in their heads. There are definite parallels between the two films. But *Willy Wonka* is an odd variation on *Wizard*. Charlie's life in the tenement is as bleak as Dorothy's on her Kansas farm, yet down the yellowing brick road in the chocolate factory (Oz), life is really not much better. There is a claustrophobic feeling to the factory settings—no matter how fantastic the sights are, we can always see the dingy brick walls and

The Oompa-Loompas were expected to be a sensation and the object of sidelines by toy manufacturers. But they were a major reason the movie flopped.

antitheft, wire-impregnated windows that make the building like a prison. This striking mixture of fantasy and reality was labeled depressing by some critics, but it works very well in reinforcing the unsettling quality of the film. The moral isn't that there's no place like home—rather that there's no place like the chocolate factory.

The Munchkins in this story are the pietistic, overbearing, definitely-not-cute, Oompa-Loompas. Arguably the worst thing in the film, they run the chocolate factory and spout preachy songs about the bad habits of children. The songs are actually toned-down versions of vicious chants Dahl created for the Oompa-Loompas in his book. In the film, however, the Oompa-Loompas' chants are ruined by ineptly conceived bouncing words that fill the screen, obviously influenced by the success of *Sesame Street* on TV. The overall effect is tacky and wholly inappropriate in an otherwise intelligent film.

Many critics found fault with the songs and musical numbers. On first viewing they do indeed grind the film to a halt. When they come on, children in the audience inevitably take the opportunity to run up and down the aisles. Although the songs aren't memorable or conducive to singalongs, and although you won't feel the need to buy the soundtrack, several of the Anthony Newley–Leslie Bricusse numbers really are charming and hold up surprisingly well. Gene Wilder singing "Pure Imagination," with a faraway look in his eyes, is one of the film's best moments. And Diana Sowle, as Charlie's washerwoman mother, offers a touching "Cheer up, Charlie" as the boy valiantly copes with his family's abject poverty.

Willy Wonka and the Chocolate Factory is now a TV perennial. Its popularity is growing, although it will never be as beloved as *The Wizard of Oz*. This film is definitely an acquired taste: too unsettling at first, but given a chance through subsequent viewings, it grows on you. *Willy Wonka* is everything that family movies usually claim to be but aren't: witty, frightening, exciting, and best of all, truly imaginative.

1939 United Artists
Director: William Wyler
Producer: Samuel Goldwyn
Screenplay: Ben Hecht and Charles MacArthur
From the novel by Emily Brontë
Cinematography: Gregg Toland
Music: Alfred Newman
Editor: Daniel Mandell
Running time: 103 minutes

Cast: Merle Oberon (Cathy), Laurence Olivier (Heathcliff), David Niven (Edgar Linton), Flora Robson (Ellen Dean), Donald Crisp (Dr. Kenneth), Hugh Williams (Hindley Earnshaw), Geraldine Fitzgerald (Isabella), Leo G. Carroll (Joseph), Cecil Humphreys (Judge Linton), Miles Mander (Lockwood), Romaine Callendar (Robert), Cecil Kellaway (Earnshaw), Rex Downing (Heathcliff as a child), Sarita Wooton (Cathy as a child), Douglas Scott (Hindley as a child)

Synopsis: It is 1841. Mr. Lockwood, the new tenant of Thrushcross Grange, is caught in a snowstorm and must spend the night at Wuthering Heights, the home of Mr. Heathcliff, his landlord. The house is bleak and desolate; Heathcliff and his wife Isabella are unfriendly, as is handyman Joseph. Only housekeeper Ellen Dean is pleasant. In his dusty room, Lockwood hears a female voice call "Heathcliff!" from outside. He reaches out his window and feels the icy hand of an apparition. He informs Heathcliff of his experience. The brute runs out into the storm. Ellen tells Lockwood that it was Cathy who called. She tells Lockwood the history of Wuthering Heights.

Forty years before, Wuthering Heights was a happy manor. One day, Mr. Earnshaw returned from Liverpool to his young daughter Cathy and young son Hindley. He brought with him a dirty gypsy boy he'd found on the streets. He named him Heathcliff. Hindley didn't like Heathcliff and bullied him all the time. But Cathy and Heathcliff loved each other. They would go to Peniston Crag, where they had a make-believe castle, and their unhappiness would fade away. He was king, she was queen.

Mr. Earnshaw died. Hindley became lord of the manor. He kicked Heathcliff out of the house and made him stable boy. Years passed, and the children grew into adulthood. Hindley became a slovenly drunk. He often beat Heathcliff. Heathcliff and Cathy still found happiness at their castle.

But Cathy wanted to live in society, like the neighboring Lintons of Thrushcross Grange. Edgar Linton began paying her visits. Heathcliff was angry at Cathy for seeing Linton, but Cathy couldn't help herself. Although she had told Heathcliff she would love only him, she accepted Linton's attentions. When Heathcliff misunderstood some things Cathy was telling Ellen about him, he rode off in a storm. Cathy knew he wouldn't come back. She fell into deep depression.

Cathy married Linton. Heathcliff returned. During his absence he had become exceedingly wealthy. He bought up all of Hindley's gambling debts and took over Wuthering Heights. He let Hindley live in the house so he could torment him. Cathy tried to be polite to him, but he was coldhearted and conniving. Linton's sister, Isabella, fell in love with Heathcliff, and though he detested her, he married her to hurt Cathy, which he succeeded in doing. Linton realized that Cathy still loved Heathcliff.

Heathcliff made Isabella's life miserable. She wished Cathy would die so she could start living. And her wish was coming true. Cathy had willed herself near death. Heathcliff stole into Cathy's bedroom at Thrushcross Grange. They expressed their undying love for each other. She said that she was his and had never been anyone else's. He carried her to the window to look at Peniston Crag for the last time. She said she'd wait for him there. She died. He told her that she must haunt him for the rest of his life, even if it drove him mad.

Ellen finishes her story. Dr. Kenneth arrives. He had seen Heathcliff walking with a woman in the storm. He had followed them and found Heathcliff dead on Cathy's grave. Ellen says that the woman Heathcliff had been with was Cathy. "They've just begun to live." Heathcliff and Cathy walk toward their castle.

Wuthering Heights

Spanish director Luis Buñuel wanted to adapt Emily Brontë's harsh, haunting love story in 1930, at the time he made his surrealist classic *L'Age d'Or*. Like others in the surrealist movement, he considered *Wuthering Heights* "a key work because it elevates 'l'amour fou' [mad love] above everything." Unfortunately, Buñuel was not able to find backers for his project then, and wouldn't make the film, *Abismos de Pasión* (1954), until twenty-four years after he'd written the script. In 1937, with period pieces and adaptations of classic novels the Hollywood rage, Ben Hecht and Charles MacArthur, America's foremost and most expensive writing team, spent a month holed up in Alexander Woollcott's Vermont home, turning out a *Wuthering Heights* screenplay for William Wyler. It was intended for Charles Boyer and Sylvia Sidney, star of Wyler's *Dead End* (1937).

It took Wyler more than a year to convince Sam Goldwyn to film the Hecht-MacArthur script. By this time it had been decided that Boyer and Sidney wouldn't play the leads. In fact, Goldwyn was interested in doing the film only because it seemed like a strong vehicle for Merle Oberon, whom he'd borrowed from English producer Alexander Korda and was trying to make into a major Hollywood star. Wyler had no objections to letting Oberon play Cathy Earnshaw Linton: she was one of the few actresses who could project Cathy's "unearthly beauty"; and she'd been effective, if, as usual, slightly dull, in Wyler's *These Three* (1936). For Heathcliff, Wyler, Hecht, and MacArthur wanted Laurence Olivier, Oberon's costar in the English comedy *The Divorce of Lady X* (1938), although he'd yet to make an impression on the movie audience, particularly in America. Hecht remembered him from when he had apparently won the male lead opposite Greta Garbo in 1934's *Queen Christina* (on which Hecht was an uncredited writer), only to see it handed to Garbo's ex-lover John Gilbert; and according to MacArthur's wife, Helen Hayes, all three men had become interested in Olivier from seeing him lounging around the Hollywood tennis club they attended. Goldwyn was skeptical about using a relative unknown in such a big part but ultimately decided Olivier was the perfect choice. But Olivier, back in England, balked at the idea. He was willing to play the part despite his hostile feelings toward Hollywood over the *Queen Christina* insult, but he didn't want to be separated from Vivien Leigh. He would agree to take the part only if Leigh could play Cathy. Not realizing that with Leigh in the role *Wuthering Heights* would probably have become the all-time most popular romance picture (surpassing the same year's *Gone With the Wind*, which would have been Leigh-less if she'd made

True love endures. Cathy and Heathcliff are only themselves when walking through the heather near Peniston Crag. It was there as children that they swore they'd always love one another—that he'd be king and she queen.

Wuthering Heights instead)* Goldwyn wouldn't consider replacing Oberon with Leigh. He did offer Leigh the role of Isabella, but she didn't want to take a supporting role after four successive leads in English films; besides, she identified with Cathy. Olivier took the part of Heathcliff when Leigh found stage work that would keep her busy while he was in Hollywood. (Soon after, Leigh came to America herself, to play Scarlett O'Hara.) The part of Isabella went to Geraldine Fitzgerald, a unique, terrific actress who never got much recognition in Hollywood, even after deservedly getting an Oscar nomination for this film. David Niven warily accepted the role of Edgar Linton, the part he considers the worst ever written for an actor, because Wyler assured him he was no longer the directorial tyrant Niven had worked for earlier. When Niven was ordered to do forty takes of his scenes, without any instruction on how to improve what he was doing, he was not convinced that Wyler had been telling the truth. Olivier, too, was annoyed by Wyler's endless retakes and complained bitterly to the press that film was a director's medium and actors were just their puppets.

But though Wyler was director on *Wuthering Heights* and was chiefly responsible for the film's intense performances, Goldwyn rightly claimed it was *his* picture, and emphasized that point by putting his name last in the opening credits. The elegance of the film (with its lush music, its vast two-room sets lit by candles or fireplaces, its lovely costuming, stunning cinematography, romantic dialogue, handsome actors, and beautiful actresses) can be directly attributed to Goldwyn. His bold production, which took two releases before it made

back its high cost, might have been less expensive if it had been filmed in England, but that wouldn't have allowed the master showman the chance to show off. He imported an all-English cast (Oberon was actually from Tasmania,† but had moved to England), and hired a dialect instructor to make sure that actors' accents didn't vary. He reconstructed the Yorkshire moors by landscaping four hundred and fifty acres of the Conejo Hills in California and transplanting one thousand four- and five-foot-high heather plants. An entire manor was built on the grounds. But he wasn't applauded for capturing the authenticity of the novel: he shifted the story from the Regency period to Georgian simply because it allowed Oberon the opportunity to wear fancier dresses.

In 1939—the greatest single year in film history—*Wuthering Heights* won the New York Film Critics Best Picture award over such formidable opposition as *Gone With the Wind; Mr. Smith Goes to Washington; Goodbye, Mr. Chips; Stagecoach,* and *The Wizard of Oz.* It was beaten out by *Gone With the Wind* for Best Picture at the Academy Awards, but Gregg Toland won for Best Cinematography of a black-and-white film, and several others involved with *Wuthering Heights* (Wyler, Olivier, Fitzgerald, and Hecht-MacArthur) received Oscar nominations. *Wuthering Heights* immediately took its place as one of Hollywood's masterworks, and its reputation has not diminished although there has been continuous controversy surrounding the drastic differences between novel and script. Critic Judith Crist reflects the opinion of most contemporary viewers who have made *Wuthering Heights* a much-requested revival house film: "For here is a classic, William Wyler at his directorial best, a work of art in its fidelity to the wild

---

* Olivier and Leigh starred in two films together, both British-made: *Fire Over England* (1937) and *The Lady Hamilton* (1941). The latter, made at the peak of the stars' popularity, is itself a cult favorite, whose admirers have included everyone from Winston Churchill to Andrew Sarris.

---

†According to biographer Charles Higham, Oberon was actually born in India but her nationality was kept secret from the British public.

Hindley makes Heathcliff work as much out of spite for him as because chores need to be done. Ellen Dean, the storyteller, also follows his orders.

Both Heathcliff and his rival, Edgar Linton, tend to Cathy when she is attacked by dogs at Thrushcross Grange.

haunted mood of the moors, a larger-than-life romantic drama of tormented souls, souls bared in the darkness of Olivier, the depths of Oberon's eyes, the agony of longing in Geraldine Fitzgerald's quivering voice, the resigned anguish of David Niven."

There is much in *Wuthering Heights* that makes it superior viewing. Gregg Toland's photography is outstanding. His closeups, diffused with soft candlelighting effects, reveal the difference between *stars* and us common folk. As usual, Toland used deep focus—Wyler keeps doors between rooms open so sets have epic proportions. Together Wyler and Toland properly turn the manor at Wuthering Heights into a haunted house, bleak, brooding, oppressive, dark with anger and hatred. Heathcliff, with those mastiffs by his feet and the ghost of his dead love dancing in his delirious brain, could very well be played by Vincent Price in one of those Roger Corman Edgar Allan Poe films of the sixties. The tumultuous atmosphere—with electrical storms, heavy rains, and driving snowstorms—perfectly defines the term "wuthery"; but too often the atmosphere conveys characters' emotions that wouldn't otherwise be evident from their acting alone. For instance, if some of the particularly heavy scenes had been played on well-lit sets instead of on shadowy, spooky ones, they would not have worked. This is unfortunate, because in the novel the characters themselves are *forces of nature*, perhaps even more than they are human beings. Olivier and Oberon are a wonderfully romantic couple, and their scene in their make-believe castle on Peniston Crag—in which Cathy and Heathcliff express their love for one another, Cathy says that *inside* she will never change, and they embrace—is one of the most romantic bits in cinema history. Significantly, it was original to Hecht and MacArthur. Oberon is surprisingly good in the film, and Olivier is better: his lines often make no sense, but his delivery has such strength that we tend to overlook this fact.

The trouble is that if you love the novel, the characters Oberon and Olivier play may disappoint you. You may agree with Paul Trent that "the film version is merely an overblown lover's quarrel between moody, headstrong Heathcliff and his willful, selfish sweetheart . . . who sulk, battle, seek revenge." Wyler admitted that the casting made him alter Emily Brontë's conception of the characters:

> Cathy, the character in the story, was a wild explosively passionate person. Merle is not. And to have tried to force her to it would have required that she overact. . . . The same thing was true with Larry. He is naturally more cultivated, perhaps more sensitive, than the fictional character of Heathcliff.

I like *Wuthering Heights* very much. Yet I am disturbed by how much Hecht and MacArthur changed the novel. They not only altered the plot but, worse, ignored major Brontë themes. As is well known, the film covers only about half of the book. It ignores the second half, in which new Lintons and Earnshaws replace those who are dead and buried, and devil Heathcliff choreographs their lives so that they duplicate those of their once-tormented parents. People in Brontë's novel die like flies, just as in the Brontës' own lives (Emily and her five siblings died before reaching their late thirties). It is central to Brontë that characters are born when others die: Heathcliff is named after Earnshaw's dead son; Hindley's son is born when his wife dies; Cathy dies as she gives birth; Isabella dies before her son by Heathcliff reaches thirteen. To Hecht and MacArthur Heathcliff's anger is directed toward Cathy alone and all that he *intentionally* does wrong is because he spitefully wants to hurt her for marrying Linton. In Brontë, Heathcliff's fight is with all those who are civilized: it is the savage, instinctual being against the corruptive civilizing influence that degrades and oppresses those like him, and attracts those like Cathy.

Most of the Hecht-MacArthur changes were obviously made to make Cathy and Heathcliff into more sympathetic characters than they are in the book. Witness the scene when young Hindley takes innocent young Heathcliff's horse because his own is lame: in the book, it is Heathcliff who takes Hindley's horse by threatening to rat on Hindley to Mr. Earnshaw. When they are children, and are both savages and glad of it, Cathy matches Heathcliff's every misdeed and selfish act. Cathy and Heathcliff are of one soul only in the novel; she is Heathcliff, and Heathcliff is Cathy: they don't belong on earth, they are too demonic for heaven and too pitiable (from brutal upbringings) to be condemned to hell.

What Hecht and MacArthur set up, as George Bluestone points out in *Novels into Film* (University of California Press, 1968), is the typical story of the stable boy and the lady: Heathcliff is degraded to servant as Cathy is upgraded to civilized lady. All his actions in the film are to spite her for forgetting her roots, and becoming a haughty woman who only wants to dance and sing in a pretty world, who resents being touched by his dirty hands. In the film, Cathy chooses civilization over savagery: Linton, whom she doesn't love, over Heathcliff, whom she loves desperately and passionately. But this is completely the opposite of what Emily Brontë wrote, and makes Cathy into the story's villain instead of Heathcliff. In the men's screenplay, Cathy is directly responsible for all the tragedy that follows—even that which Heathcliff causes. In the novel, Cathy loves both Linton and Heathcliff. She doesn't choose Linton over Heathcliff (or vice versa): "Every Linton on the face of the earth might melt into nothing, before I could consent to forsake Heathcliff." In fact, her desire to marry Linton is as much out of love for Linton as it is for Heathcliff: "If I marry him, I can aid Heathcliff to rise, and place him out of my brother's hands."

Oberon and Olivier—unforgettable screen lovers.

In the film, when Heathcliff returns after being away for years, Cathy is truly upset because she finds it impossible to hide her love for him; significantly, in the book Cathy is openly ecstatic ("I'm afraid the joy is too great to be real!") and invites Heathcliff to visit her repeatedly—much to Linton's chagrin. Her feelings for Heathcliff have not changed, yet his reappearance has not affected her feelings of love toward Linton. She has no jealousy toward Isabella when her sister-in-law admits she loves Heathcliff. She honestly warns Isabella that Heathcliff will destroy her; Cathy tells Heathcliff, "If you like Isabella, you shall marry her." Cathy's point of view was very daring for her times: she does not believe that her open love for one man precludes her from openly loving the other. As literary critic Albert J. Guerard writes: "The oddity is that Cathy expects to 'have them both,' finds this expectation entirely 'natural,' and is enraged because neither Heathcliff nor Edgar will consent to such a ménage à trois."

Cathy cannot understand why Edgar and Heathcliff refuse to share her, or why, in this godforsaken, cursed land, men enjoy fighting over women, meting out punishment, revenging themselves, tormenting each other. Cathy sees no reason to take part in the foolish behavior of the two men and complains bitterly: "After constant indulgence of one's [Edgar's] weak nature and the other's [Heathcliff's] bad one, I earn for thanks two samples of blind ingratitude, stupid to absurdity." Cathy wills herself to die, not because she can't be with one man she loves but because she can't be with both men she loves. The film has a polished veneer but the issues are far more complex in the novel, as are the characters—and they are far more interesting.

Cathy warns Isabella that Heathcliff is only pretending that he loves her.

Zardoz

1974 20th Century-Fox
Director: John Boorman
Producer: John Boorman
Screenplay: John Boorman
Cinematography:
Geoffrey Unsworth

Special effects: Jerry Johnston
Music: David Munrow
Editor: John Merritt
Running time: 105 minutes

Cast: Sean Connery (Zed), Charlotte Rampling (Consuella), Sara Kestleman (May), John Alderton (Friend), Sally Anne Newton (Avalow), Niall Buggy (Arthur Frayn), Bosco Hogan (George Saden), Christopher Casson (old scientist), Reginald Jarman (Death), Barbara Dowling (Star), Jessica Swift (an apathetic)

Synopsis: It is the year 2293. A giant, fearful stone head flies over the barren wasteland. Below, the Brutals bow to their god. The Exterminators, the top breed of Brutals, pick up the guns that spew from their god's mouth. Zardoz speaks to the chosen: ''The gun is good. The penis is evil.''

Time has passed. Zed, an Exterminator, has sneaked into the mouth of Zardoz. He sees a man in a robe walk past. Arthur Frayn is the aviator, and it is he who has pretended to be a god. The flustered Zed shoots him and he falls from the head.

The Zardoz head flies above the invisible shield that separates the Outlands, where the Brutals live, from the Vortex, which Zardoz always told them was heaven. Zed discovers that it is not heaven but is inhabited by people called Eternals. Three hundred years earlier, a scientist had created a Tabernacle, a supercomputer, and as a result, the Eternals would live for eternity within the confines of their protective shield. Every external wears a crystal in the forehead and wears a crystal ring. The crystals give them the power of common thought and contact with the Tabernacle, which supplies them with all the knowledge of the world. In locking the Brutals out of their paradise years before, they had had to harden their hearts to human suffering on the outside.

Zed is taken prisoner by the Externals. May, who found him, wants him to breed with the women of the Vortex to give new, needed blood to the race. (The men of the Vortex are impotent.) But Consuella wants the ''monster'' killed, although she feels primitive sexual urges when she looks at him. He is excited by her as well. The Eternals look into Zed's past. He used to kill the unchosen Brutals to please Zardoz. Then he became slavemaster, making the Brutals' harvest wheat which Zardoz carried back to the Vortex. When some Eternals became Apathetics and others became Renegades and were turned old and senile, the Eternals could no longer harvest enough food to feed everyone. They turned to the Brutals for food. Zed learns from Friend, a disenchanted Eternal, that the Apathetics and Renegades crave death rather than living for eternity. Friend is turned into a Renegade.

Zed confesses to May that he decided to come to the Vortex to seek the truth after he learned that Zardoz was a fake. In a library he found *The Wizard of Oz*, about a man like Arthur Frayn who frightened people by hiding behind a mask. But May believes it is for revenge. Consuella discovers Zed and May making love. She psychically blinds him. But the pure Avalow cures him. Consuella and other Eternals search for Zed to kill him before he destroys them all by learning the secret of the Tabernacle. Friend and other Renegades disguise him as a bride. May and the others teach him everything they know through osmosis. They have an orgy. Consuella suddenly falls in love with Zed.

Zed enters the Tabernacle after finding a flaw in the crystal. He destroys it. Time goes back slightly. The invisible shield disappears. The Exterminators come into the Vortex and kill everyone they see. Most Eternals come forward happily to meet their deaths. Zed says farewell to May and other women he impregnated. They ride off to begin a new life elsewhere. Zed and Consuella take up residence in a cave. Zed permanently hangs up his gun. They have a son. They grow old and die.

The enormous stone head of Zardoz that the Exterminators worship.

In some of our more exciting terrifying dreams we may find ourselves thrust into an alien, hostile environment where we are at the mercy of strangers from another culture who want to kill us for reasons we can't comprehend. No film has better captured the essence of this particular nightmare than John Boorman's *Deliverance* (1972). Boorman—who explored a surreal, hallucinatory world in *The Exorcist II: The Heretic* (1977) and a mythical-fantasy world in *Excalibur* (1981)—simulated a dream world for a second time when he made *Zardoz*. Unfortunately, not all our dreams are worth remembering. Some are like *Zardoz:* the premises are exciting but the dreams don't carry through; they don't make sense, not so bad in itself, but they don't seem worth unscrambling until they do.

For starters, a good dream-film, like a good dream, must have a character with whom you can identify. In *Deliverance* Jon Voight, Burt Reynolds, Ned Beatty, and Ronny Cox are immediately recognizable. Importantly, we know what they are like before their scary journey downriver so we can (1) predict how they will react to certain events, and (2) be able to discern how the events effect or change them. But in *Zardoz,* Boorman makes the mistake of not immediately defining Zed. We *never* know what to expect of him. We must stand back, uninvolved, while he explores the Vortex. We may be confused by the same things that confuse him, but he confuses us more. Who is this fellow who, with a gunbelt crisscrossing his bare chest and a racy loincloth, looks like Pancho Villa in a red diaper? Are we to identify with this primitive Brutal or the superrace of Eternals he encounters, people whom Boorman fears man will evolve into? Because we are trying to learn about an alien environment and its people (the Eternals) through a character who is also alien to us (a Brutal), it's like doing a science experiment using *two* variables. It takes forever to draw conclusions, and even then they are suspect. Clearly Boorman should have shown Zed living his daily life in the Outlands, as an Exterminator of the Brutals and then a slavemaster, and as a worshiper of the god Zardoz, *before* having him enter the Vortex. I think it even would have been a good idea to have had the scene in which Zed discovers Zardoz is a fake god, where he comes upon the book *The Wizard of Oz*, come prior to the Vortex scenes.

The obvious reason Boorman didn't structure his film more linearly—other than because he hoped viewers would mistake incoherence for profundity—is that he wanted to save the *Wizard of Oz* punchline for late in the film. It's a monumental moment in Zed's life—it's like discovering that the Bible was written by Clifford Irving—but coming where it does in the film, it hasn't much impact on us other than causing us to snicker. By this time the increasingly bewildering storyline is getting out of control, and Boorman has introduced so many new themes that it has almost become irrelevant why Zed chose to enter the Vortex in the first place. We have become too involved in plot elements: Zed's exploration of the Vortex; the Eternals' treatment of their "inferior" (an animal to be caged, a "monster") prisoner, Zed (similar to the treatment of Charlton Heston by his simian captors in 1968's *Planet of the Apes*); and the dispute over his fate between Consuella, who wants to kill him, and May, who wants him to breed with Eternal women. Likewise, we're too busy mulling over ideas Boorman sets forth in the Vortex sequences: too much technology will cause our senses to dissipate; the obsolescence of sex and childbirth will emancipate women (they will become our leaders) and make men ineffectual; turbulent change is preferable to stagnation; death is preferable to immortality (the film's major theme); and the fear of death is what stimulates accomplishment. Unfortunately, this is so much to take in and sort out that when Outlands sequences (including the book-discovery scene) are inserted, they only disrupt our concentration and add to our infuriating confusion. (It's not that Boorman's themes are revolutionary or difficult, it's just that they're hard to recognize because he is not a gifted storyteller.)

It's too bad, because the Outlands sequences are important to Boorman. In fact, he believes the reason for the Eternals' downfall is not so much that they forced a false god on the Brutals and got Zed mad as that they turned the Brutals into a work force. "Once people become dependent on a slave labor force, they are doomed," Boorman said in an interview with Philip Strick for *Sight and Sound* (Spring 1974), "because decadence inevitably sets in." Because the Eternals don't have to worry about an afterlife, as they will never die, there is no need for them to believe in God or heaven. But they realize that the best way to subjugate a primitive people is to instill the fear of a god (Zardoz) in them. For Boorman, religion is an opiate for an enslaved people. It scares people into obedience by promising an afterlife in heaven (the Vortex) only to those who are obedient. It pacifies a beleaguered people. It also "justifies" the heinous actions taken by one human being, who is told he is doing God's bidding, upon another. Telling one group of natives in a colonized land that they are preferred by God over another group of natives is one way the Exterminators (the "chosen") can keep the masses under control. This prevents all the Brutals from turning on their real enemy, the Eternals.

May wants to know if Zed has come into the Vortex to

Publicity still of Zed and Consuella, who wears a see-through top.

seek the truth (she too is a truth seeker) or to avenge himself on those who exploited him in the Outlands by using a false god. But again, his reasons for coming into the Vortex are less important than his being there. The Apathetics regard him as a life force, someone who can shake them from their melancholy and their lethargy and inspire them to start sampling physical pleasures. The old, senile Renegades see him as a liberator, someone who will bring about the deaths they crave. He represents freedom for the rest of the Eternals: only he can break the Tabernacle, bring them death if they want it, or provide safe passage out of the Vortex. Once a murderer, an avenging angel, and a truth seeker (perhaps), Zed now puts down his pistol and becomes a liberator ("a slave who could free his masters"), a Spartacus, a Christ figure (is he the true God's messenger?), a Frankenstein monster that turns on the human creators who messed with the natural order, an Adam to Consuella's Eve, and even a god, once he takes a "crash course" in knowledge and replaces the Tabernacle, which had godlike traits.

Throughout British director John Boorman's checkered career, he has been accused of being a self-indulgent, pretentious director, whose films are not so much "personal" (a critic's compliment) as they are "ego trips." Yet despite pointing out his gratuitous excesses, critics have always admired Boorman because he has never taken on easy, unchallenging projects. We always look forward to his next film. When he flops we feel badly for *him* because we know how much effort he puts into each project; we don't reject him as we would a Ken Russell. Even if we don't like *Zardoz* (and most critics found it incomprehensible and ludicrous), we must at least commend him for venturing into Kubrick territory and trying to wrest away the dope-smoking intellectuals, science fiction buffs, and futurist fanatics from *2001* (1968). And it must be noted that his film has been a cult favorite—playing at revival houses, on college campuses, and on the Midnight Movie circuit for several years. What does it matter if to the rest of us *Zardoz* (which William Gallo termed "an artistic success but a cosmic failure") makes one

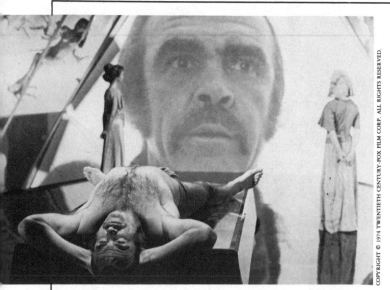

(L) Consuella and May question Zed about his past, and his memories appear on a giant screen. (Above) The direction of extras is so abysmal that this scene, in which the Exterminators receive guns from Zardoz, looks as if it were from a Monty Python film.

think of the musical remake of *Lost Horizon* (1973) rather than *2001*.

It's really too bad that Boorman took his film so seriously. Watching Sean Connery do double takes to some of the weird goings-on makes one think—hope—that he realized he was stuck in an embarrassment. I wish Boorman could have pretended before the film's release that the picture was a spoof of all big-budget, overblown epics. (In fact, a worried 20th had him add a prologue with Arthur Frayn which sort of manipulates viewers into not expecting it to be all that serious.) Made for under $2 million, this picture had everything that those awful *Lost Horizon*-type epics had with astronomical budgets. Some accomplishment! There are horrible costumes (especially those worn by the Brutals, the men in the Vortex, and Connery), hairstyles (the men in the Vortex), makeup (the Renegades, the Brutals). The props look cheap, the futuristic sets are surprisingly uninteresting, and even the diffusive photography of Geoffrey Unsworth (of *2001* fame) is unimpressive after the early shots of the giant Zardoz head flying through the sky. As in most bad spectacles, the direction of extras and minor characters is abysmal. I automatically hate any scene in which a group of characters move forward with arms extended and hands grasping, mouths slobbering and mewing, and acting like Dracula's brides. I particularly hate it when it is old people doing this and the director uses their aged features to frighten us. *Zardoz* is one of those pictures that has crowd scenes in which everyone does exactly what the next person is doing. Worse, Boorman often has a phrase of dialogue on the soundtrack that is supposed to be coming from one of the extras—only there's no one on the screen with moving lips. Perhaps no one wanted to be accused of saying some of the dialogue in this film. Why is it that in bad epics characters aren't capable of saying a normal line? Even the dumbest person around will speak as if reading from a poetry book or a pamphlet of aphorisms. Consuella (all too quickly for me) falls in love with Zed because "In hunting you I have become you"; for Zed there is no such word as shore or beach, it is "where the sea meets the land." When Boorman starts tossing in quotes from T. S. Eliot and Nietzsche, it really becomes nauseating. A definite problem is that everyone in the film is unlikable. (Consuella reminds me of a prudish PTA member. Another

bad role for Charlotte Rampling, a sexy and good actress.) I particularly dislike the Renegades and Apathetics, always seen in those awful group scenes. It's not so important to me whether they live or die as it is just getting them off the screen. Of course, some people might want to question Boorman's unpleasant massacre scene, which is like Hell's Angels getting mad at flower children. Wouldn't many of the Eternals choose to finish their lives out rather than be shot, because in a sense they would be "living" for the first time? Other questions: Why do the Exterminators wear their Zardoz masks even after realizing he's no longer their god? Why do some of the Eternals chasing Zed spend time smashing priceless statues? Why did Arthur Frayn take nude bodies with him when he flew in the Zardoz head? Etc., etc., etc.

In his interview in *Sight and Sound,* Boorman said that he "wanted to make a film about the problem for us hurtling at such a rate into the future that our emotions are lagging behind, the growing gap between our technological development and where we are emotionally." While doing research, he spent time at several American communes, which he thought quite sterile. "I became increasingly intrigued about where the commune idea might lead, supposing our society collapsed and the communes were all that survived." At this point he decided to shift the story from five years in the future to the year 2293. "The film is about today, about contemporary society, and all the characters are aspects of the human condition—they're all tendencies that are in each of us, taken to extreme forms."

Of course, we all agree with Boorman's theme that death is preferable to immortality. But he is playing with a stacked deck. Why shove us into a commune situation? Why not Disneyland? Immortality is a big bore if one has to spend one's entire life in this Vortex. These people are virtually prisoners. Boorman is their strict father, who has taken away all their privileges. All they do is sit around a circle eating fruit, baking green bread and—what a terrible scene—entering second-level meditation. Boorman's commune of the future is like a monastery without even religion to keep anyone busy. There is no lovemaking, no reading, no dancing, no playing pool, no singing camp songs, no baseball, no partying, no nothing for entertainment or intellectual stimulation. Can you blame them for wanting to die if they can't even see a movie, for heaven's sake? Even *Zardoz* would be a treat.

Cult Movies Vol. 1 contains:

Aguirre, the Wrath of God
All About Eve
Andy Warhol's Bad
Badlands
Beauty and the Beast
Bedtime for Bonzo
Behind the Green Door
Beyond the Valley of the Dolls
Billy Jack
Black Sunday
The Brood
Burn!
Caged Heat
Casablanca
Citizen Kane
The Conqueror Worm
Dance, Girl, Dance
Deep End
Detour
Duck Soup
El Topo
Emmanuelle
Enter the Dragon
Eraserhead
Fantasia
Forbidden Planet
Force of Evil
42nd Street
Freaks
The Girl Can't Help It
Greetings
Gun Crazy
Halloween
A Hard Day's Night
The Harder They Come
Harold and Maude
The Honeymoon Killers
House of Wax
I Married a Monster from Outer Space
I Walked with a Zombie
Invasion of the Body Snatchers
It's a Gift
It's a Wonderful Life
Jason and the Argonauts
Johnny Guitar
The Killing
King Kong
King of Hearts
Kiss Me, Deadly
La Cage aux Folles

Land of the Pharaohs
Laura
The Little Shop of Horrors
Lola Montès
The Long Goodbye
Mad Max
The Maltese Falcon
Man of the West
Night of the Living Dead
The Nutty Professor
Once upon a Time in the West
Out of the Past
Outrageous!
Pandora's Box
Peeping Tom
Performance
Petulia
Pink Flamingos
Plan 9 from Outer Space
Pretty Poison
The Producers
The Rain People
Rebel Without a Cause
The Red Shoes
Reefer Madness
Rio Bravo
Rock 'n' Roll High School
The Rocky Horror Picture Show
The Scarlet Empress
The Searchers
Shock Corridor
The Shooting
Singin' in the Rain
Sunset Boulevard
Sylvia Scarlett
The Tall T
Targets
Tarzan and His Mate
The Texas Chain Saw Massacre
Top Hat
Trash
Two for the Road
Two-Lane Blacktop
2001: A Space Odyssey
Up in Smoke
Vertigo
The Warriors
Where's Poppa?
The Wild Bunch
The Wizard of Oz

Index

Danny Peary has an M.A. in Cinema from the University of Southern California. He writes frequently for *TV Guide* (Canada) and has written film criticism for *Focus on Film, Bijou, The Velvet Light Trap, Newsday, Films and Filming,* the *Philadelphia Bulletin,* the *Soho News,* and other publications. He edited the anthology *Close-Ups: The Movie Star Book* and was co-editor of *The American Animated Cartoon.*